Theatre Culture in America, 1825-1860

Theatre Culture in America, 1825–1860 examines how Americans staged their cultures in the decades before the Civil War, and advances the idea that cultures are performances that take place both inside and outside of playhouses. Americans imaginatively expanded conventional ideas of performance as an activity restricted to theatres in order to take up the staging of culture in other venues: in issues of class, race, and gender, in parades and the visits of dignitaries, in rioting and the denomination of prostitutes, and in views of the town, the city, and the frontier. Joining up-to-date historical research with a firm and clear-headed grasp of contemporary critical theory, *Theatre Culture in America* offers a wholly original approach to the complex intersections of American theatre and culture.

CAMBRIDGE STUDIES IN AMERICAN THEATRE AND DRAMA

General Editor

Don B. Wilmeth, *Brown University*

Advisory Board

C. W. E. Bigsby, *University of East Anglia*
Errol Hill, *Dartmouth College*
C. Lee Jenner, *Independent Critic and Dramaturge, New York City*
Bruce A. McConachie, *College of William and Mary*
Brenda Murphy, *University of Connecticut*
Laurence Senelick, *Tufts University*

The American theatre and its literature are attracting, after long neglect, the crucial attention of historians, theoreticians, and critics of the arts. Long a field for isolated research, yet too frequently marginalized in the academy, the American theatre has always been a sensitive gauge of social pressures and public issues. Investigations into its myriad shapes and manifestations are relevant to students of drama, theatre, literature, cultural experience, and political development.

The primary aim of this series is to set up a forum for important and original scholarship in and criticism of American theatre and drama in a cultural and social context. Inclusive by design, the series accommodates leading work in areas ranging from the study of drama as literature to theatre histories, theoretical explorations, production histories, and readings of more popular or paratheatrical forms. While maintaining a specific emphasis on theatre in the United States, the series welcomes work grounded in cultural studies and narratives with interdisciplinary reach. *Studies in American Theatre and Drama* thus provides a crossroads where historical, theoretical, literary, and biographical approaches meet and combine, promoting imaginative research in theatre and drama from a variety of new perspectives.

BOOKS IN THE SERIES:

8. Dale Cockrell, *Demons of Disorder: Early Blackface Minstrels and Their World*
7. Rosemarie K. Bank, *Theatre Culture in America, 1825–1860*
6. Mark Fearnow, *The American Stage and the Great Depression*
5. Susan Harris Smith, *American Drama: The Bastard Art*
4. Jared Brown, *The Theatre in America during the Revolution*
3. Amy Green, *The Revisionist Stage: American Directors Reinvent the Classics*
2. Marc Robinson, *The Other American Drama*
1. Samuel Hay, *African American Theatre*

Theatre Culture in America, 1825–1860

ROSEMARIE K. BANK

Kent State University

CAMBRIDGE
UNIVERSITY PRESS

PUBLISHED BY THE PRESS SYNDICATE OF THE UNIVERSITY OF CAMBRIDGE
The Pitt Building, Trumpington Street, Cambridge CB2 1RP, United Kingdom

CAMBRIDGE UNIVERSITY PRESS
The Edinburgh Building, Cambridge CB2 1RU, United Kingdom
40 West 20th Street, New York, NY 10011-4211, USA
10 Stamford Road, Oakleigh, Melbourne 3166, Australia

First published 1997

Printed in the United States of America

Typeset in Ehrhardt

Library of Congress Cataloging-in-Publication Data
Theatre culture in America, 1825–1860 / Rosemarie K. Bank.
p.   cm. – (Cambridge studies in American theatre and drama)
Includes bibliographical references.
ISBN 0-521-56387-9 (hardback)
1. Theater – United States – History – 19th century.
2. Theater and society – United States – History – 19th century.
I. Title.   II. Series
PN2248.B36   1997
792′.0973′09034–dc20   96-15178
CIP

A catalog record for this book is available from the British Library

ISBN 0 521 56387 9 hardback

To my father, Julius Bank,
who sought his hope in the West and never went back;
to my mother, Anna Damm Bank,
who gave the dream a home; and
to my sister, Barbara Julianne Bank,
who keeps faith with the hope and the dream.

Contents

List of Illustrations   *page* viii
Acknowledgments   ix

Prologue: Universal Spaces   1
    The Return of Lafayette   9
    The Opening of the Erie Canal   23

1   Spaces of Representation   27
    The Town   29
    The City   42
    The Frontier   59

2   Liminal Spaces   75
    Work   77
    Class   99

3   Spaces of Legitimation   120
    Bodying Forth   122
    Sensation Scenes   138
    Displaced Play   151

Epilogue: Simultaneous Spaces   167

Notes   191
Bibliography   259
Index   281

List of Illustrations

1. A silk handkerchief commemorating Lafayette's 1824 visit to Philadelphia   15
2. Illustration from "Massa Georgee Washington and General LaFayette"   17
3. "Illumination of the City Hall upon Completion of the Erie Canal"   26
4. "Sunshine and Shadow in New York"   45
5. "Map of the City of New York in 1808"   47
6. "Box at the Theatre," by Auguste Hervieu   49
7. The interior of the Chatham Garden Theatre in 1825   53
8. James H. Hackett as Nimrod Wildfire in *The Lion of the West*   71
9. Joseph Proctor in Louisa Medina's *Nick of the Woods*   73
10. Edwin Forrest as Metamora   74
11. "Trades and Occupations: Tailor," by Louis Prang, 1874   79
12. Interior of Charles Oakford's hat store c. 1855   79
13. Intersection of Cross, Anthony, and Orange Streets, 1827   83
14. "The Soaplocks," by Nicolino Calyo   85
15. Francis S. Chanfrau as Mose   87
16. "Dancing for Eels at Catharine Market, N.Y.," from *New York as It Is*   89
17. Mary Taylor and Francis S. Chanfrau in *A Glance at New York*   91
18. *New York by Gas-Light*, "Hooking a Victim," c. 1850   127
19. "A 'Bowery' on a Lark"   131
20. "Harry Hill's 'Free and Easy'"   137
21. The Lafayette Theatre, New York, in 1827   161
22. Exterior view of the London Crystal Palace   171
23. "Agriculturalists at the Exhibition"   173
24. "The Pound and the Shilling"   175
25. The United States section of the Great Exhibition   178
26. Broadside, Catlin's Indian Gallery and *tableaux vivants*, London, 1840–1   179
27. "The New York Crystal Palace"   185

Acknowledgments

ACKNOWLEDGMENT IS AN ACT both of naming and letting go, on one hand a gesture of possession and claiming, on the other a recognition that "the words I have found . . . no longer belong to me." I am grateful to many people and organizations for sustaining me through the tediums, terrors, and triumphs of preparing this book and hold none of them responsible for its shortcomings.[1]

I want to thank the University Research Council of Kent State and the immediate past Vice Provost and Dean for Research, Eugene P. Wenninger, for Summer Research Appointments in 1985, 1988, and 1992 and for travel-to-collections grants supporting research for this book, the majority of which was first prepared during a sabbatical leave made possible by my scholarly colleagues in the School of Theatre, for which I thank them. The staffs of the Interlibrary Loan and Periodicals office at Kent State have labored against long odds to help my work move forward and I am grateful for their assistance. Thanks are also due to Media Services at the University for help and advice concerning illustrations.

In the wider world, I am grateful to Charles S. Langley and Alice Kane, curators of microtexts and newspapers at the Boston Public Library; to Kenneth Cramer, Archivist at Dartmouth College Library; to George W. Thompson, Jr., of the Bobst Library at New York University, for generously shared research; to Stuart Thayer for information concerning Indians in circuses before the Civil War, and to David Carlyon, who led me

to him; to Robert Pepper for information about eighteenth-century entertainments featuring Indians; to Bruce McConachie for sharing *Melodramatic Formations* when it was still in manuscript; to Leo Hershkowitz and
Timothy Gilfoyle for helpful suggestions concerning nineteenth-century
prostitution; to the present and past staffs of the Harvard Theatre Collection and the New York Public Library for the Performing Arts (especially
Dorothy Swerdlove and Richard M. Buck for able assistance and many
personal kindnesses); and to Melissa Miller of the Harry Ransom Humani-
ties Center (University of Texas–Austin) and Amanda Bowen of the Hilyer Art Library (Smith College) for assistance with difficult-to-retrieve illustrations.

The long process of researching and writing has bridged many changes
in my life. For her support and council, especially in moments of despair,
I shall always be grateful for the strength and wisdom of my colleague
Marya Bednerik. Through hard times, students often lightened the way
with laughter, labor, and support. In thanking those named here, I also
mean to thank all those I've taught who have helped me along: Paula Anderson, Mark Andreyko, Kristin Caruso, Patrick Dukeman, Russ Dusek,
Kathy Gray, Lynn Heberling, Jim Lile, Ian Maclennan (with special gratitude for airport trips and for taking on the tedious jobs of proofreading
footnotes and assembling the bibliography), Hedy Pufeles, Jeff Richmond,
Mary Sabetto, Bil Sheldon, Maria Silvaggi, Mark Ulrich, Alan Wilder,
and Leigh Clemons for computer lessons, Star Trek, volunteering Patrick,
good talk and much laughter, and for a next generation. To all those who
boldly go – Moscow Jenny, Manon, and especially Donnalee for walkin'
and talkin' – thanks for making my past part of your future.

In addition to those three to whom this book is inscribed – who laid the
tracks of inquiry, work, and courage early and deep – it is only a just acknowledgment of career-long debts to thank those whose support sustained
the notion that I could and would write a book. To the "Americanists" in
theatre studies – Steve Archer, Helen Chinoy, Julia Curtis, Weldon Durham, Ron Engle, Errol Hill, Cynthia Jenner, Margaret Knapp, Felicia
Londré, Bruce McConachie, Brooks McNamara, Kim Marra, Geri Mas-
cio, Jeff Mason, Walter Meserve, Tice Miller, Kent Neely, David Rinear,
Vera Roberts, Laurence Senelick, Ron Wainscott, Dan Watermeier, Don
B. Wilmeth, Barry Witham, and Alan Woods – thanks for your insights,
your scholarship, your example, and your patience, for holding the door

open even when we disagreed, for good talk, timely phone calls, and cheering letters. I am grateful also to the historian-historiographers – Bruce (again), John Gronbeck-Tedesco, Joe Roach (especially for Foucault), Tom Postlewait, Michal Kobialka (*dalej już nic*), and Frank Peeters – for giving me much to think about and new ways to think it. To Sue-Ellen Case, Liz Swain, Jill Dolan, Kate Davy, Vicki Petraka, and Janelle Reinelt my respect and thanks for good work, for battles fought, and for your company, wisdom, and laughter along the way.

To Margaret Knapp and Michal Kobialka, who read the first, truly dreadful draft of this book and still encouraged me to move forward, whose letters and calls gave me faith when I wavered, and whose personal support and integrity have sustained and inspired me throughout, I owe a debt that is beyond repayment, but I hope not beyond acknowledgment and thanks. Bless you both. Additionally, my good fortune in professional friends and colleagues has extended to my Cambridge editors, T. Susan Chang and Anne Sanow at the Press and series editor Don B. Wilmeth, who championed this book and encouraged me to keep going. To Don especially, who has supported my work and been an exemplar and friend throughout the years, I hope the world will think this book a credit to his series. Certainly his work has been an inspiration to mine. Finally, my luck in this process continued in the assignment as production editor of Michael Gnat, whose extraordinary skill, generosity, and intellect helped me bring this project to a happy conclusion.

I have sometimes thought the long process of writing a book-length manuscript most aptly described by the old saw about war: long passages of tedium punctuated by periods of extreme terror. I write these acknowledgments at a time of reflections, of claiming and letting go the long, arduous, and horrible military and personal sufferings left in the wake of the Second World War. It is a history that has profoundly shaped the historical consciousness of the generation of scholars forged by the decades since 1945 and who now face the end of this century and a new millenium. There is no aspect of the historical project that has not been changed in these decades, from a deep cynicism regarding the humanist project as mirrored in the fires of Auschwitz, Dresden, and Hiroshima, to an abiding faith in human ability, given the will, to build a better world from the ashes and lessons of the past. Without the latter, the victims of the former will have suffered in vain. The antebellumites of the nineteenth centu-

ry endured their own holocausts, fiery trials, and despairs but also generated a culture constituting the very hopes and differences of all America's
peoples. In the certain knowledge that nothing dies that is remembered
and that dreamers move mountains, I dedicate the hard work of this book
to their remembered struggle, to their hope, and to the difference their
difference has made.

Prologue
Universal Spaces

"The preface is ruled out, but it must be written."
— Jacques Derrida, "Outwork, prefacing" (1981)

"She said: 'What is history?' And he said: 'History is an angel being blown backwards into the future.' He said: 'History is a pile of debris, and the angel wants to go back and fix things, to repair the things that have been broken. But there is a storm blowing from Paradise, and the storm keeps blowing the angel backwards into the future. And this storm, this storm is called Progress.'"
— Laurie Anderson, "The Dream Before (for Walter Benjamin)," from *Strange Angels* (1989)

"I am Odysseus. I have returned from Troy."
— Tadeusz Kantor, *The Return of Odysseus* (1944)

IN "THE GARDEN OF FORKING PATHS," Jorge Luis Borges eloquently describes "an incomplete, but not false, image of the universe" conceived (in contrast to Newton) without belief in a uniform, absolute time. Instead, there are "infinite series of times, in a growing, dizzying net of divergent, convergent and parallel times," embracing every possibility. We live and die, he writes, unaware of most of these coexisting universes, inhabit some but not others, utter words in one and silently haunt another, while in some worlds we do not exist. Borges's elegant evocation of simultaneous universes resonates with physics' recent explorations of parallel universes and at the same time echoes a vastly older Native American view: that what has happened in a place is always happening. In this study of antebellum America, two sets of terms – spatial history and theatre culture – attempt to operationalize these senses of history.[1]

Borges's elastic universes of time and quantum physics' anisotropic space have much in common with the quest in American historiography for ways to escape an evolutionary and totalized view of the past, usually called "positivist." Focusing upon history as spaces collected in but not wholly governed by time facilitates writing in the peoples and experiences American historical writing has too often written out. One way to work against the grain of positivist historiography is to allow subjects to circulate, to view them as relationships rather than things. By foregrounding these relationships, a subject can be seen as simultaneously occupying multiple spaces. Operationalized in the present study, gender, to take one example, features in Chapter 1's discussion of the city and fashion, Chapter 2's consideration of work and class, and Chapter 3's recontextualization of prostitutes in antebellum theatres.[2]

Spatial history takes time to locate and describe. Accordingly, the chapters that follow discuss many things in addition to theatre. There are two dispositions that influence the structure of this book and its winding road to and from the playhouse. One seeks theatre in a larger social context, to make historical connections (as theatre scholars have ably done in recent work) between *Uncle Tom's Cabin* and abolitionist sentiment, for example, or *The Drunkard* and the temperance movement. This larger context also takes in more indirect relationships of interest to me: how knowledge circulates, for example, or locating investments in and redistributions of culture. The second disposition influencing the structure of this book grew from a restlessness with the view of cultures primarily as reflections of (and so always behind or in front of) the societies producing them. Theatre, within this view, functions as a subject or mirroring of something either before history or outside itself. This book attempts to evade examining theatre as antehistorical or as solely reflective by working the concept "theatre culture," the notion that the peoples in a culture stage themselves and perform multiple roles. In this larger sense of performance, of theatre outside of playhouses as well as within them, culture is not only or even exclusively metaphoric, a figure standing for something else, but is itself taken as constitutive of the relationships that we find circulating in and among the many universes of antebellum America. Operationalized in the present study, the performance of, say, gender promotes considering how, in antebellum America, women's volunteer associations, the Bowery G'hal, the call to regulate prostitutes in playhouses, or the publication of etiquette manuals are productive of each other.[3]

The meditations in Borges's garden of forking paths yield many reflections that are important to a spatial history of theatre culture. Like Borges's author, cultural historiography has accepted incompleteness, viewing culture, as Joseph Roach recently put it, as "not general and universal but local," neither neutral nor transcendent, but partisan, material, and historical. This incompleteness, like Borges's garden, is a far move from the Eden of facts, rules of causality, chains of being, modes of distributing evidence, certainties, accumulations of knowledge, "scientific" hypotheses and pristine methods that were once the stuff of (theatre) historical theory and practice. A nostalgia for completeness is the perhaps inescapable legacy of a subject as evanescent as performance, for while, as Roach observes, "few contemporary historians succumb to vulgar positivism" (of the sort set opposite Borges's garden in the preceding sentence), "some remain more alert than others to its more subtle reappearances – such as in the masking of ideologies as impartial conclusions or the passing off of contested events as historical facts." What constitutes a "fact" about antebellum America is further complicated by what Joyce Flynn identifies as a "complex causality of neglect" that has left American theatre history of the nineteenth century without such "traditional" studies as economic histories (allowing, for example, systematic comparisons of wages between antebellum theatre workers and others or of ticket prices to audience income), daybooks of theatrical activities in all of America's major antebellum cities chronicling who did what when; considerations of touring circuits in these decades clarifying where they were, who traveled them, when, and how often; or even publication of scholarly histories of antebellum star actors and managers.[4]

The legacy of incomplete images bequeathed to the present study by an understaffed and fragmented theatre research archive will be evident in every universe it explores. As a result, attention is skewed in the direction of the northeastern quadrant of the United States and, among urban centers, favors New York over the other large cities of that era. Antebellum cultural studies have also posited a world of largely male and white northeasterners. In all these, theatre participates in the general state of studies of American literature before the Civil War, as a 1992 assessment of its scholarly history by MLAA makes clear. Still (lest this rehearsal of inadequacies legitimate a nostalgia of its own), just as recent work in gender history challenges the hegemony of the white male subject, so recent theatre studies have reclaimed a host of subjects – little-known antebellum house playwrights, for example, circus, magic and medicine shows, popular performers, and the tastes and behaviors of worker audiences. The campaigns of the 1960s and 1970s to pluralize subjects have not been unsuccessful, though they remain short of their goals. Taken together with the postpositivist historiographies of the 1980s and 1990s, these theatre studies both yield cultural histories of subjects once considered beyond the pale of theatre history and theorize them in ways that satisfy the cognitive needs of theatre scholars on the threshold of the twenty-first century.[5]

Theatre culture, as developed here, is constitutive of multiple, simultaneous relationships. Chantal Mouffe has cast this interaction against a larger canvas, arguing that

each social agent is inscribed in a multiplicity of social relations – not only social relations of production but also the social relations, among others, of sex, race, nationality, and vicinity. All these social relations determine positionalities or subject positions, and every social agent is therefore the locus of many subject positions and cannot be reduced to only one.

In this view, as Janelle Reinelt has observed, "individuals and social groups are constantly involved in competing and often contradictory positions." These multiplicities and inconsistencies not only frustrate the great historical narratives and their underpining "myths" (as Jeff Mason characterizes these [hi]stories) but also problematize the location of hegemonies, structures, and formations. For American cultural history, as Homi Bhabha has put it,

The grand narratives of nineteenth-century historicism on which its claims to universalism were founded – evolutionism, utilitarianism, evangelism – were also, in another textual and territorial time space, the technonogies of colonial and imperialist governance. It is the "rationalism" of these ideologies of progress that increasingly comes to be eroded in the encounter with the contingency of cultural difference.

Given the building up and wearing down of these contingencies, a number of antebellum subjects in this study – class, gender, work, and race, for example – are positioned so as to respond to Roach's sense of "contested events" rather than "historical facts," a locating that risks a number of indeterminacies.[6]

The exploration of antebellum America's stagings of culture begins with two events in 1825 that stand as prologue to the chapters that follow. These events – General Lafayette's triumphal return to the United States as "the nation's guest" and the opening of the Erie Canal – collect antebellum political, cultural, and cognitive significations. They do so, importantly, in a context of economic surplus in which the excess necessary to celebrate is itself celebrated. In Lafayette's case, that celebration is reified and appropriated city by city as he makes what amounts to a royal progress around the America that lay between the Atlantic and Caribbean Oceans, the Mississippi and Ohio Rivers, and the Great Lakes. In the waning days of his visit, Lafayette traveled the Erie Canal, whose grand opening would be held less than a month after the general's departure for France. The look backward in Lafayette's return and the projection forward in the opening of the Erie Canal offered many opportunities for earlier nineteenth-century American culture – with all its exclusions, resistances, commodifications, and displacements – to stage itself. These stagings yield a topography, a spatial history of what were considered universal American values, the cultural oxymoron identifying the one ("universal" = Euro-American Enlightenment values) and the many ("American" = democratic "refinements" of these).

The two celebratory events (the general and the canal), which serve as a preliminary discourse to the cultural performances that follow, reify the ferment of these decades and its production of mutually constitutive yet conflicting cultures. Chapter 1 engages the locution (movement, mobility) of the oxymoron "universal American" in three antebellum "spaces of representation": the village, the city, and the frontier. These spaces constitute what T. J. Clark describes as "a battlefield of representations." The colonization of scholarship by myths – of individuality, transcendentalism, of America as an empty paradise, and the like – has the effect, Cecelia Tichi has argued, of voiding a sense of America as developing through historical, contextualized change. At the same time, while these "stable stories," around which a sense of American cultural history (and an academic year) could be organized, no longer lure contemporary historians as they once did, they have also – as the story of "manifest destiny," for example, makes painfully clear – been constitutive of history. In such contested spaces, Foucault observed, authority is bestowed and provisional; hence what con-

stitutes "culture" shifts, changes, and coexists with its opposites, replacements, and heirs. The "frontier," for example, yields a classical protagonist in the doomed but noble savage of antebellum Indian removal at the
same time Indian delegates stage scalping ceremonies at the nation's capital or the staged Indian appears in urban theatres. City and town battle for
cultural control at the same time the former appropriates national cultural
icons from the local representations of the latter. None of these spaces
is truer or more real than another; they are all stagings of theatre culture,
representations represented in specific antebellum locales.[7]

The cultural tensions evident in spaces of representation yield readily
to the liminal spaces of Chapter 2, which is divided between work and
"class." The word "liminal" foregrounds the shifting, transitional nature
of these spaces. An antebellum worker might, for example, "pass through"
poverty (due to unexpected or seasonal unemployment) or be caught there
for a lifetime. Similarly, "class," a term nearly as complex as the word
"culture" itself, often appears in quotation marks in this study so as to
emphasize its provisional nature – reflective, as Mary P. Ryan has suggested, of continually changing and contested relationships among, for
example, income, ethnicity, youth or age, gender, race, voluntary associations, location, taste, occupation, and the like. Given provisionality, class
and culture are not viewed as formed or fixed (a "formation" defined as a
state of being, to follow a recent positioning by Simon Frith), still less as
hegemonic formations that control what they seek to colonize. Rather,
class and culture are considered as practices or acts and their constituents.
In such a view, class does not contain culture, nor culture class; they produce each other across the unstable boundaries of desire. People in liminal spaces create and are created by alternative cultures in the threshold
areas they occupy. In the Bowery B'hoy and G'hal, to take one instance,
liminality becomes a declaration of place, a betweenness that takes definition from what it is not, as does the self-selection of its seeming opposite
"gentility." The vitality of liminal spaces confounds the view of an antebellum "authorized culture" as hegemonic (highbrow, bourgeois, white,
gendered) except as a representative space manifesting a historically lo-
catable desire to dominate.[8]

Antebellum control agenda are the focus of Chapter 3's "spaces of legitimation," perhaps more accurately written as "[de]legitimation" (to tease
the injunction of Marx and Engels against "all this theoretical nonsense
which seeks refuge in bad etymology"). The chapter considers three reg-

ulating arenas: those of the body (health, gender, and prostitutes), of sensation (temperance, abolition, and heroes), and of play (associations, riots,
and the staged disorder of American minstrelsy). The antebellum decades
witness the creation of professionals (police and firemen) and institutions
(asylums, museums, orchestras), the development of movements (diet,
temperance, abolition, sex), the discovery of poverty and of the mob, and
the advent of the popularly priced newspaper as a creator both of news
and of history. Previously private concerns – charity, consumption, gender – become subjects for staging, changing the nature of heroes, heroines,
and the challenges they face. In the regulating spaces of amusements and
improvement, forces compete for the control of culture and for ownership of its staging, while sensation deregulates such goals in its pursuit of
pleasure as release, redirection, or as an end in itself. Legitimation like
liminality, then, is treated as a contested interaction (in Joseph Roach's
sense) and as culturally constitutive both in attempts at control and in defiance of them.[9]

The Epilogue returns to the cultural oxymoron in its "simultaneous
spaces." It takes up two events, the Crystal Palace exposition of 1851 in
London and the New York Crystal Palace of 1853, that demonstrate simultaneity in the ways cultures are staged – that is, that commodifications
of material and of entertainments, in hand with ideas and values of nationality and race, undermine the possibility both of universality and of
binarized diversity. On the one hand, diversity by its presence challenges
ideas asserting hegemonies of, for example, "civilized" over "savage" or
"patrician" distinct from "plebeian." On the other hand, diversity is itself
appropriated, transformed, and redistributed by its interactions with other
cultural "universes." A number of concepts affect and are affected by these
redistributions and, in turn, suggest useful historiographical approaches
to investigating past theatre cultures.[10]

Theatre culture as a creator of historical readings is a hoarding of many
values. Antebellum America readily illustrates the difficulty of telling cultural history in terms of single values and norms. Hardly an aspect of life
in those decades has failed to produce controversy, over matters as seemingly simple as how close workers lived to their work to issues as complex
as what the words "middle class" signify. As striking as these distinctions,
however, is the struggle for authenticity that the antebellum decades themselves manifest and their inescapable projections of history as a construct.
If this book has an objective in seeing theatre as culture and culture as the-

atre, it is to highlight the created nature of these performances of past and
present, to suggest that performances are deceptive as well as authentic
and always (already) occur in contested and contradictory terrain. Further,
although as L. P. Hartley put it, "The past is a foreign country; they do
things differently there," there is also a sense in which, as Robert Louis
Stevenson observed, "There is no foreign land; it is the traveller only that
is foreign, and now and again, by a flash of recollection, lights up the contrasts of the earth." The trick in staging the past, as Brecht knew, is how
to realize the critical alienation that makes the familiar seem strange and
the strange familiar. "Similarity" and "difference," "one" and "many"
haunt American cultural history and bedevil its study – what is included,
what left out, what is developed, what suggested, and over all the twin
specters of journeying either to the already discovered country, to a familiar, same, and safe place, or, like Walter Benjamin's storm-blown angel, to the land of history as wreckage in need of a fix. Theatre culture
displays historical spaces of production, consumption, change, and appropriation, but also insists upon class as a performance, ideology a creation,
and the "authentic" as the most compelling deception of all. A number
of these "universal spaces" are framed in the two national celebrations to
which we now give place. In them we meet many of the agents in dramas
taken up in the chapters that follow.[11]

* * * * *

IN 1825, TWO EVENTS TOOK PLACE that set agenda for antebellum
America and its definitions of culture. One event looked back to the Revolutionary War and the separation of the thirteen colonies from Europe;
the other anticipated the economic and political joining of western lands
to the government of the United States. These events offered a cultural
performance of "American" intended for both foreign and domestic consumption in which the past and the future became subjects to be staged.
The theatre for these stagings was the nation itself. It offered performances
on city streets, within playhouses, by churches and legislatures, in backwoods settings and town halls, at the shrines and on the battlefields
deemed sacred to American liberty, in foundries, print shops, and glass-
works; on the water, in the air, beneath the ground, on foot, on horseback,
in carriages, on wagons and floats, by steamship and barge; with music,
bells, cannon, tears, and huzzahs, acres of food and rivers of alcohol; per-

formed by all the nation's races, genders, trades, ages, and political groups, with full hearts and at enormous expense.

From the vantage of nearly two centuries filled with acts promoting a deep cynicism about the claims of democracy, it would be easy to rehearse these events as counterfeits of liberty, justice, and plenty, often depicted in these celebrations via icons of women, Indians, and laboring blacks and whites, the very persons paid in the false coin of a promised but denied future. To center on that rehearsal, however, is to overlook the displacement and appropriation of texts like liberty and justice by parading unions, Indian tribes, African-American Revolutionary War veterans, women's societies, and the like. These performances suggest in a small way what succeeding chapters seek to write in larger terms: that antebellum American cultures do not act themselves out in imitation of an "authentic" against which reproductions can or ought to be judged true or false (though there are protocols, customs, and traditions, and though given actors may have an "ideal real" in mind). Rather, these performances, in their diversity and often in conflict with each other, constitute cultures. The celebrations of individual and communal selves staged for Lafayette's return and for the opening of the Erie Canal would not be surpassed in America, even in a nation given to self-celebrations, until after the Civil War had contested the very idea of universal American spaces.

The Return of Lafayette

When, pursuant to an invitation by Congress to visit the United States as "the nation's guest," General Marie-Joseph-Paul-Yves-Roch-Gilbert du Motier, the Marquis de Lafayette, and his party anchored at Staten Island on 15 August 1824 after a month's voyage from France, there were twenty-four states in the union and three territories. The northeastern (Maine) and northwestern (subsequently Montana, Idaho, and Washington State) boundaries with present-day Canada were in dispute, but exploration and trading routes had already established what mapping expeditions subsequently made visible: that Euro- and African-American encroachment upon indigenous peoples extended throughout the eastern portions of the continent from north to south and had crossed into the trans-Mississippi West. As one of many European travelers to the continent during the antebellum decades, Lafayette had ample opportunity to witness the changes

wrought upon the land since he had first seen it in 1777. Less than a month
after the nation's guest took ship for France, New York City staged a fit-
ting afterpiece to the general's visit, culminating a plan afoot since 1792,
the tricentenary of European appropriation of the Americas. On 4 November 1825, at the Long Island Sound entrepôt with the Hudson River, the
waters of the Great Lakes – recently opened to navigation by the completion of the Erie Canal – were, with maximum ceremony, poured into the
Atlantic Ocean. The celebrants were careful to reserve (in a container
made for the purpose by Duncan Phyfe) a portion of Erie water to send
to General Lafayette.[12]

Lafayette's 1824–5 travels in America – with his son, George Washington Lafayette; his secretary (and the chronicler of the journey), Auguste
Levasseur; and Lafayette's valet, Bastien – began in New York City with
festivities both national and local. Pressure by Sabbatarians persuaded the
New York organizers to delay Lafayette's reception until Monday, 16 August 1824, when he was escorted to the Battery in Manhattan by what Levasseur describes as a fleet of "floating palaces." The order of events in
New York set a pattern for subsequent receptions throughout the nation.
Ceremonies began with an official reception at the landing site or arrival
point, amid discharge of cannon and ringing church bells, followed by a
short march through a line of troops leading to a waiting carriage, usually drawn by white horses. Accompanied by music, the carriage moved *en
parade* to City Hall, where Lafayette would be welcomed by the mayor
and other dignitaries, express his thanks for the city's hospitality, review
a large contingent of troops and parading citizens (usually including a wagon or float of aged Revolutionary War veterans), and retire indoors to receive formally the inhabitants whose guest he was. In New York, as elsewhere in America, emotion was freely displayed: Seasoned politicians were
overcome in welcoming him, his comrades broke down when they saw
him, parents begged him to bless their children, orators fell dumb in his
presence, people waited in rain, snow, and dead of night only to catch a
glimpse of his passing – and everywhere hands reached out, mute witnesses in after years to touching Lafayette.[13]

If the love affair with Lafayette was both genuine and reciprocated, the
general's adoptive home was nonetheless faithful to the edict of the Continental Congress in 1774 that nothing should interfere with "the manufactures of this country." Accordingly, the occasion of Lafayette's visit
produced a plethora of both American- and English-manufactured me-

mentos: There were souvenir snuffboxes, commemorative plates, Lafayette platters, Lafayette flasks, Lafayette portrait jugs, a commemorative drum, and Lafayette ribbons. Excluded from most of the male-only banquets, ladies at balls showed their esteem by sporting Lafayette gloves, carrying Lafayette handkerchiefs, and wearing white dresses in Lafayette's honor. Printers were busied with biographies of Lafayette's life and with poems describing his imprisonment during the French Revolution. Painters depicted and apotheosized him. Lafayette was the man of the hour, the hero of the age, and big business.[14]

If commerce was the bill of fare, entertainment was the order of the day. During Lafayette's initial visits to New York and Boston from August to September 1824, for example, parades, balls, receptions, and theatre evenings in his honor went in hand with such sober activities as tours of hospitals, almshouses, schools and public works, church services and oratorio, university commencements, visits to former presidents, and calls upon the widows and families of deceased revolutionary leaders. In an age in which New York City sported only two theatres, there was no dearth of rooms, halls, and buildings to house concerts, circuses, Papyrotomia (paper cutouts of famous people and scenes), a Panharmonicom (a machine capable, its operators assured the public, of sounding like 206 musical instruments), lectures, "anomalies" and natural history exhibits, fine-arts collections, or a Spectaculum (home to wax figures and mechanical scenes), all readily adaptable to Lafayette-connected updating. "Illuminations" were staged in his honor at the American Museum in New York (5 September) and at the newly christened Lafayette Museum (13 September), and fireworks and a balloon ascension were presented at Castle Garden (22 September) on the eve of Lafayette's departure for Philadelphia and Washington. These entertainments were interspersed with and proceeded or followed by dinners of Herculean dimension, providing ample opportunities for speeches, toasts, and the drinking of healths. The general's appeal as entertainment was still evident years after his departure. In 1830, for example, Auguste Hervieu painted a panorama for Mrs. Trollope's Bazaar (see Chapter 2) – a combination shopping mall and entertainment center in antebellum Cincinnati – entitled *The Landing of Lafayette*, which depicted his reception by the Ohio River city's prominent citizens.[15]

America's theatres also adapted to the moment, varying specially created pieces with standard fare. The Chatham Garden Theatre in New York, for example, offered a gala performance of *Twelfth Night* (17 August 1824).

The Park Theatre presented topical pieces celebrating events in Lafayette's life – *The Siege of Yorktown* and *La Fayette; or, the Castle of Olmutz* (8 and 9 September), a dramatization of Lafayette's imprisonment at Olmutz in Austria during the French Revolution – as well as Sheridan's *The School for Scandal* (20 September), "the play always chosen by General Washington." Other theatres in America's cities followed suit. There were performances of *The School for Scandal* and *She Stoops to Conquer* for the general in Baltimore and Washington, for example, and presentation of such serviceable stage pieces as *The Soldier's Daughter* and *The Honeymoon*. New Orleans supplemented these offerings with opera, a play in French, and a local vaudeville. Everywhere, Lafayette witnessed his own heroics as the prisoner of Olmutz. Samuel Woodworth's new patriotic piece *Bunker Hill Monument* was mounted by the Park Theatre when the nation's guest returned to Manhattan in 1825 near the end of his travels in the United States. At that time, the general also took in transparencies, aerial voyages, and fireworks at Castle Garden, and witnessed (11 July 1825) equestrian performances augmented with farce, musical pieces, and melodrama, at the Lafayette Amphitheatre, named in his honor.[16]

Visiting theatres in order to display oneself to the public, to receive acclamations, or to address the people was a common use of these places of assembly in the nineteenth century. Given the celebratory din that accompanied Lafayette's visits, the plays could usually not be heard, and neither Lafayette nor Levasseur, in his 1829 account of the general's "voyage to the United States," volunteered an opinion of the performances. "Some persons of taste" in New York City, however, opined to the secretary that the English stock pieces were "but poorly selected" and the companies of actors "usually feeble." When Levasseur ventured to observe that the Park and Chatham theatres in New York were nonetheless "evidently too small" for the numerous population interested in attending them and that "their construction [did] not correspond either to the beauty or wealth of the city," the worthies harumphed that they hoped visitors were more impressed with beautiful public works than elegant theatres.[17]

Neither a materialist indifference toward theatre nor a residual resistance to it among the very religious managed to suppress its production; indeed, Lafayette's visit came at the beginning of a growth spurt in entertainments. The evening fête and reception staged at Castle Garden in Lafayette's honor on 14 September 1824 suggests the diversity and display that could mark cultural performances in antebellum America. Even the sangfroid of the normally imperturbable Levasseur was warmed by this extravaganza. He describes the Castle Garden as a circular fort, originally built to defend the city, and situated on a mole in front of the Battery in Manhattan. The three-hundred-foot-long bridge that gave access to the "castle" was for this occasion carpeted, bordered with trees on both sides, and illuminated. A sixty-five-foot pyramid was erected in the middle of the bridge, lit with colored lamps, and surmounted by an illuminated star with "Lafayette" emblazoned on it. Once across the bridge, the fort was entered by passing under a floral arch created for the occasion and mounted upon commemorative cannon, above which towered a "colossal" statue of George Washington and, at the arch's center, the "genius of America" with a shield in her hand welcoming "the nation's guest."[18]

Inside, the six-hundred-foot circular hall of the castle was decorated with an arch made of national flags and with thirteen columns bearing the arms of the original states. Thousands of torches illuminated the six thousand people filling the surrounding amphitheatre, and, Levasseur reports, upon Lafayette's entrance, to appropriate music (often specially created for his visits), "the cloths which surrounded and enclosed the hall were as rapidly raised as a theatrical scene, and the interior became visible to the eyes of the crowd, who had collected in boats about the battery, waiting for this moment." As soon as Lafayette was seated

under the rich pavilion that had been prepared for him, a grand transparency was suddenly uncovered in front of him, and presented an exact picture of his residence at Lagrange, with its large ditches and fine gothic towers, having the following inscription below it: "Here is his home."

Ceremonies and exhibits over, the guests danced to waltzes honoring Lafayette and to a set of cotillions composed for the occasion. Dancing continued until 2 A.M., when Lafayette and a large group of partygoers boarded a steamboat taking him away from Gotham. Content in a job well done, the architects of this splendor – one of whom (Reinagle) designed sets for the Chatham Garden and later the Bowery Theatre – offered their celebratory work to the paying public until it was destroyed two days later by an untimely gale.[19]

The combination of material display and sacramental patriotism in the Castle Garden celebration of Lafayette quickly commodified throughout the United States into a celebration of American prosperity and development since the Revolutionary War. Much of the valorization of the past focused upon American aristocracy; visits to the homes and clubs of America's wealthy and prominent citizens and their leadership of public receptions typified the majority of Lafayette's activities as the nation's guest. The visions of America embedded in its development are those of the town, city, and frontier examined in Chapter 1. However, the celebration of Lafayette (and so the nation's past) was also a populist tribute to workers, farmers, and to the ordinary soldiers paraded in wagons of Revolutionary War veterans before the nation's guest. These values and their contest, examined in Chapter 2, were especially visible in the triumphal reception of Lafayette staged in Philadelphia on 28 September 1824.

The trajectory for Lafayette's journey emerged as invitations for visits reached him. Pledged to return to Boston for the dedication of the Bunker Hill monument in June 1825, Lafayette made his way to Philadelphia, where a number of parade rituals were on display. Although a decorative arch had been prominently featured in the Castle Garden fête in New York, Philadelphia appears to have inaugurated the vogue for triumphal arches (Fig. 1). Theirs was copied from the arch to Septimus Severus at Rome, and was forty-five feet wide, twelve feet deep, and twenty-four feet high (thirty to the entablature). It was designed by William Strickland and erected under the direction of Mssrs. Warren, Darley, and Jefferson of the Chestnut Street Theatre, where, a few days later, the refitted playhouse accommodated a civic ball in Lafayette's honor. The line of march on 28 September 1824 led from the outskirts of the city to the arch, which had been erected in front of the State House (now Independence Hall). There, a cannonade and welcoming speeches heralded Lafayette's arrival. The arch was decorated on each side with figures of Fame in bas relief. There were statues representing Victory, Independence, and Plenty on the wings of the arch and surmounting figures of Liberty and Justice, with the arms of the city between them. In addition to a military escort, totaling over four thousand of cavalry, infantry, artillery, and riflemen, with a cart for 150 veterans, the procession featured mounted citizens, marching bands, a workshop display of a sailing ship, a car of printers and their equipment printing an ode to Lafayette as they paraded, typographers carrying a banner honoring "Lafayette, Defender of the Rights of the Press," decorated carts, floats, and marching delegations of cordwinders (200), ropemakers (150), weavers (300), shipbuilders (100), working coopers (150), butchers (150), mechanics (700), cartmen (200–300), and farmers (300).[20]

As Susan G. Davis observes, Washington and Lafayette were often used as icons in parading. They were the simulacra of bravery, honesty,

Fig. 1. A silk handkerchief printed in Germantown, Pennsylvania, to commemorate the visit of Lafayette to Philadelphia in 1824 (reprinted from Octavia Roberts, *With Lafayette in America* [New York: Houghton Mifflin, 1919]).

and military genius and remained on view in parades when more radical or reformist personages did not. The Lafayette reception in Philadelphia in 1824, for all the general's evident links to aristocracy and privilege, celebrated republican virtue and Lafayette's service to labor interests. The parade had been organized democratically, with places chosen by lot. Most trades dressed plainly and used banners to identify themselves, though some adopted Uncle Sam suits, with a revolutionary cockade and Lafayette badge. Similarly, owner (rather than workshop) displays were often brightly colored, even exotic shows of economic strength and importance. Significantly, some workers marched separately from masters as "apprentices" or "the young men" of the trade. Division was foregrounded ten years later in the funeral parade staged in Philadelphia in 1834 upon Lafayette's death (funeral parades featured a riderless horse, empty coffin, and procession to a church for a memorial service). At this time, workmen fiercely contested the line of march and their place in it, and charged the parade committee with purposeful exclusion of workers from parade planning. Those workers who did participate marched separately in a division emblematic of the ongoing battle then raging between management and labor over the ten-hour day. The appropriation of a foreign nobleman to the service of American labor suggests some of the value the past, as represented by the Revolutionary War, had achieved by 1825. As staged by the celebrations marking Lafayette's return, the Revolution had erased "British" divisions in rank. In the past created by this view of the Revolutionary War, aristocrats (Washington, Lafayette) were democrats and republican laborers equaled masters. Antebellum economics would foreclose this vision while widening the gap between workers and owners.[21]

Lafayette's return also evoked readings of the past unexpressed by the myth of an American artisan system that capitalist rhetoric paraded in Philadelphia in 1824. Those delegitimated by these and other processes are considered in Chapter 3. Lafayette engaged a number of elisions and contradictions during his triumphal progress through America because, in addition to his values as patriot, democrat, and icon of American material achievement, he embodied liberty and justice on the national stage. Those in need of an actor to perform these values in their stead were not slow to seek him out. In New York, on the occasion of his arrival in the United States, "Men of color reminded [Lafayette] with tenderness," Levasseur reports, "of his philanthropical efforts at various periods, to place them in the rank which horrid prejudices still deny them." New York City had passed gradual manumission laws in 1799 and 1804, and Lafayette was known to be an opponent of slavery although a proponent both of gradualism and colonization. Lafayette's value as an icon of liberty and justice was troped in a blackface song entitled "Massa Georgee Washington and General Lafayette," performed at the Chatham Garden Theatre by James Roberts in September 1824 (Fig. 2). The joining of "Massa George," a known slaveholder, General Lafayette, a known abolitionist, African-American market and tavern performers (see Chapter 2), and an 1824 blackface act – Roberts also did "at homes," songs, dances, and related material in his own

Fig. 2. Illustration from sheet music cover for Micah Hawkins's "Massa Georgee Washington and General LaFayette" (courtesy of the Museums at Stony Brook, Museums Collection).

face – suggests a dizzying degree of appropriation and conflict that Lafayette's visit threw into ever higher relief as his voyage through America progressed.[22]

"The nation's guest" made his way from Philadelphia to Washington, in whose vicinity he spent the winter of 1824–5. In the northern states, Lafayette had received delegations of black veterans and abolitionists; perhaps in response, when Fredericksburg, Virginia, received the general, a local newspaper "respectfully solicited" owners "to keep their slaves within their lots," and warned "all colored people . . . that they are not to appear on any of the streets through which the procession will pass." Elsewhere in the South, Lafayette's presence was less incendiary, and free blacks received him in their homes and met him in public places to claim their own roles in America's past.[23]

Lafayette was also sought out by Native Americans. In the nation's capital in late November, two Choctaw and Chickasaw leaders Lafayette had recently met at Monticello made known to him their needs and grievances. Lafayette's journey from Washington in February of 1825 led through North and South Carolina, in heavy spring rains and over mired roads, to Charleston. Journey by ship and steamer to Savannah and Augusta, Georgia, brought Lafayette to the home ground of those Indian tribes who, like the Choctaw and Chickasaw, were threatened with "removal." The succession of Monroe's Secretary of State John Quincy Adams to the pres-

idency in 1825 boded ill for Indian appeals for justice (see Chapter 1). Lafayette advanced, over roads little more than wilderness tracks, to Macon,
then a newly established frontier village. The Creek Indian territory Lafayette's party crossed beyond Macon led to an Indian agency where "the
treaty was formed by which the tribes inhabiting the left bank of the Mississippi consented to retire to the right bank." This evacuation, to take
place in 1827, was widely contested among Indians. Both sides of the controversy were deliberately staged for Lafayette's party and those escorting it across Georgia into Alabama. Indian homes were visited, food and
drink shared; on one occasion Levasseur demonstrated French dances
and an Indian Creek ones. The state of the Indian nations was discussed
by them with Lafayette at length. Clearly, the evidence of permanent Indian homes and settlements, farming and animal reserves, culture, and
education mocked the removal rhetoric (which Levasseur's account often
reprises unsympathetically) characterizing Indians as primitive and savage wanderers. The presence in Indian territory of fugitive slaves repay-
ing refuge with labor fueled removal sentiment among local whites,
whose press "passed lightly over this part of the journey."[24]

When Lafayette's party forded the Chattahoochee River and entered
Alabama, they crossed the western boundary of the thirteen original states.
Levasseur, who dominates white accounts of this portion of the general's
travels, emphasizes a tradition of Indian esteem for Lafayette handed down
from Revolutionary times. Lafayette's reception by the Creek leader Chilly
McIntosh and his people is recorded as being staged as a royal progress.
Lafayette is cheered ashore; his carriage is borne palanquin-like from the
Chattahoochee into the Creek village. There, he is hailed by the Creek
leader (in English, that stilted version of Indian speech that often characterizes white-authored works) as "one who, in his affection for the inhabitants of America, had never made a distinction of blood or colour" and
called "the honoured father of all the races of men then dwelling on that
continent." Lafayette is escorted to homes and the agency school, and entertained with "a Ball Play" lasting about an hour: a two-team combat in
paint and athletic dress involving rugged competition with rackets for control of a ball. Throughout this part of Levasseur's journal, Lafayette's majesty is paralleled by the young McIntosh's skill as a veritable William Tell,
an athlete (his gymnastic ability wins the ballgame), and as the mournful
leader of a declining people. In Levasseur's characterization, Indians are
apathetic, laconic, and uncivilized, and simultaneously adaptive, industri-

ous, and brave. The American government is praised for taking Indian lands by treaty rather than "by extermination or war" [*sic*], yet Levasseur/ Lafayette mourns "those prejudices which induce civilized man to endeavor to impose his mode of life on all those nations who still adhere to primitive habits and to consider the invasion of districts in which this pretended barbarity still exists as noble and legitimate conquest."[25]

Chilly McIntosh joined the white Alabamans escorting Lafayette from Augusta, Georgia, through the Indian territory in Alabama to Montgomery. His presence and the Indian reception at the Chattahoochee River are scrupulously omitted from press accounts of the Alabama delegation that met Lafayette at the state line. Levasseur described the Indian presence in detail, refuting accounts of Indian women as abused and subservient chattel and commending the courtesy of Indian men in assisting Lafayette's party over flooded roads and bridges. McIntosh, who interpreted for the Indians they met along the way, explained the Creek identification of Lafayette with freedom from English tyranny and so their own identification with the Revolutionary past that their forebears had supported. Levasseur's account condemns exploitation of Indians by territory whites, whose behavior in many instances, he observes, excelled "in cruelty and want of faith." His journal, however, carefully differentiates between these whites and the American government, and extends Lafayette's council to the Creeks to live in harmony with their American "friends and brothers," as Levasseur characterizes the federal government:

The conduct of the American government is of an entirely different character, as regards the Indian tribes. It not only protects them against individual persecution, and sees that the treaties made with them by the neighbouring states are not disadvantageous to them, and are faithfully adhered to, but it also provides for their wants with a paternal solicitude. It is not a rare circumstance for Congress to vote money and supplies to those tribes, whom a deficient harvest or unforseen calamity have exposed to famine.

Levasseur's fatherly democratic government stands in sharp contrast both to the federal government's history with respect to Native Americans by 1825 and to the conditions under which the Indians Lafayette encountered during his travels were actually living. Both that history and those conditions would degrade significantly in the antebellum decades.[26]

Lafayette's arrival outside New Orleans on Sunday, 10 April 1825, extended the texts of material display, sacramental patriotism, republican rhetoric, and the performance of diversity that the nation's guest embodied into the first chiefly trans-Mississippi state to have entered the Union (1812). Successive home to Spanish, French, and American governments – and still, in 1825, half French in descent and language – Louisiana welcomed the hero of the Brandywine and Yorktown on the ground of its own testament against the foreign, the site of the 1815 Battle of New Orleans. (The nationally celebrated victory here of Andrew Jackson would help carry this presidential candidate to the White House in 1828.) General Lafayette's presence on this battlefield provided the happy occasion for staging past triumphs and future greatness in a doubly historic present time, shrewdly evoked by Lafayette in uniting French and American republicanism against "European" despotism and aristocracy in his speech of thanks to the governor of Louisiana.[27]

The parade conveying Lafayette into New Orleans had little of the populist about it and much of aristocracy, American style. It consisted largely of politicians and functionaries of the state and city, port and harbor officials, judges, bankers, military escorts, bands, and the inevitable carriages of Revolutionary War veterans. The parade route through the city led to a triumphal arch erected in the Place d'Armes (presently Jackson Square), which lay between the river and City Hall (the Cabildo), where Lafayette would be housed. The arch, Levasseur reports,

was sixty feet in height, forty of which were below the springing of the arch, by fifty-eight in breadth; the arcade was twenty feet wide and twenty-five feet long; it rested on a socle imitating Sera-Veza marble; the base, forming a pedestal of green Italian marble, was decorated with colossal statues of Justice and Liberty.

The arch itself sported keystones of the twenty-four states strung on a fillet spelling the word "Constitution." Above it two figures of Fame, with trumpets, carried banners naming Washington and Lafayette; below them a scroll proclaimed, in English and French, "A grateful republic dedicates this monument to Lafayette." Above Fame, the figure of Wisdom held a bust of Benjamin Franklin. The names of the signers of the Declaration of Independence active in the Revolutionary War were inscribed on the arch, amid decorations representing national trophies. Three days later (13 April), the arch and surrounding buildings were illuminated, and crowds again acclaimed the nation's guest.[28]

After the usual welcoming speeches, the dignitaries left the sodden precincts of the Place d'Armes (Lafayette arrived in New Orleans during a torrential rainstorm) and repaired to the Cabildo. City departments had been moved and the Cabildo, formerly a rundown office building (which Levasseur inaccurately describes as "the hotel of the municipality"), had metamorphosed into the elegantly appointed "house of Lafayette." Troop review from the balcony followed, including "ninety Choctau [*sic*] warriors, our late allies in the Seminole war, who arrived here from their native village three weeks ago, to join their tribute of indigenous homage to the general expression of public joy." It gratified Lafayette, Levasseur tells us, "that his name was familiar to the warriors of the most distant nations, and that [the Louisiana riflemen with whom the Chocktaw were parading] had admitted among their troops these brave Indians."[29]

The balance of Lafayette's five-day stay in New Orleans centered around dinners, a ball in a remodeled theatre, illuminations, private visits, and numerous receptions – of citizens of Spanish descent, of lawyers, of parties of women, of physicians, and by masons at a banquet. The general also went to the theatres, on 11 April 1825 visiting both the American (Caldwell's) Theatre for a playing of (inevitably) *La Fayette; or, the Castle of Olmutz* and then the French-language Orleans Theatre for a showstopping ovation, the last act of the comedy *L'École des Vieillards,* and a cantata. Lafayette was again escorted to both theatres, as well as to a ballroom, on Wednesday, 13 April; and on the evening before his departure for the north, the nation's guest visited the opera, where he was acclaimed, and witnessed *Lafayette in New Orleans,* a vaudeville "written by a Creole." On the last day of his stay, Lafayette received a deputation representing "the free blacks who in 1815, courageously assisted in the defense of the city." The interview was given full play in the bilingual *Courier* of 19 April 1825. Officers of the Corps of Men of Colour thanked Lafayette for receiving them and emphasized their fellowship with him in the cause of democracy. Lafayette returned their thanks and commended their valor. In what may have been a diplomatic negotiation of proslavery and racist sentiment, the newspapers stressed Lafayette's thanks to local officials and the governor of Louisiana for the chance to meet the black veterans.[30]

Levasseur's depiction of Lafayette invests heavily in the general's popularity with and significance to all of America's peoples, and certainly the secretary's own interest in Native Americans (Levasseur never missed a chance to tour Indian villages, mounds, or encampments) and slavery influenced his portrait of "the nation's guest." At the same time, Lafayette himself sought chances to interact with Indians and blacks, both slave and free during his travels (as the New Orleans examples suggest), and disenfranchised veterans reprised Lafayette's history in North America on the sites sacred to the Revolution and the War of 1812. The general continued on his way, leaving New Orleans 15 April 1825, heading up the Mississippi River to St. Louis, over the Ohio River into Tennessee, Illinois, Indiana, Kentucky, Ohio, and West Virginia, overland through Pennsylvania to Pittsburgh and Buffalo, via the almost completed Erie Canal to Rochester, and by horse and carriage to Boston, where he arrived 15 June 1825 – four months and five thousand miles since leaving Washington the previous winter – to keep his promise to appear at the dedication of the Bunker Hill monument. Throughout the journey, Lafayette continued to join the remembered past to the celebrated present.[31]

At Kaskaskia, Illinois, Lafayette entered a "free state" for the first time in his journey from Washington, D.C. He was not expected in the frontier village, then in the midst of a late spring encampment of fur traders. There, he met the daughter of a Six Nations leader named Panisciowa; she and her family, in the aftermath of the Revolutionary War, had been displaced from the Great Lakes to the territory of the Kickapoo along the Illinois River. She carried with her a June 1778 letter from Lafayette thanking Panisciowa "for the courageous manner in which he had served the American cause" as a member of the general's command. This veteran's heirs would reprise Panisciowa's fate in the years following the Black Hawk War of 1832 (see Chapter 1), which would remove Indians of the Illinois tribal confederacy, as well as of the southeastern tribes Lafayette had encountered in Georgia and Alabama, to the trans-Mississippi West.

At Buffalo, which had been captured and destroyed by British, Canadian, and Indian forces in December 1813, Lafayette met the Seneca leader Red Jacket (see Chapter 1), whom he had first encountered at a council at Fort Schuyler, New York, in September of 1784. Red Jacket, whose party had sided with the British in the Revolutionary War, now appeared to Levasseur "much broken by time and intemperance." In "obstinately adhering to his native language" and customs, as Levasseur states it, Red Jacket testified to a history that had, in the forty years separating the Revolutionary War from Lafayette's return, located the Senecas outside the national past of which Lafayette was the living emblem.[32]

As a simulacrum of American diversity, the foreign Lafayette was a focusing lens for American dreams of "universal" liberty and justice and their unchallenged elisions. In slave Louisiana, one dignitary said of the general, "Never was there seen, nor will there perhaps ever again be seen a whole nation of freemen rising spontaneously in one mass, to present to an individual unclothed with power the noble and pure homage of their gratitude and affection." This vision of "Lafayette-as-America-wanted-to-see-itself" required the erasure of differences as extensive as those affecting race, customs, language, equality before the law, and always (already) differences of gender – all accounts of Lafayette's visit include but trivialize the official and unofficial presence of women into ceremony, decoration, or icon. A wishful "universal American" was constructed on the historical site of the unthought. Lafayette's return, like that of Odysseus, evoked its own dream of Troy: the *treu Traum* (true dream) of confederation victorious over a strong enemy, but also the nightmare homecoming in Ithaca, with its legacy of violations and its memories – of promise, counterclaims, and future strife.[33]

The Opening of the Erie Canal

If the return of Lafayette focuses a particular remembered past and valorized present that is hard to credit in these times of delegitimized celebrity, heroics, and totalizing rhetoric, the opening of the Erie Canal foregrounds texts of commodification, material display, and national development. Here, the "universal American" gazed from a present "opening" of the West for economic expansion to the future antebellum text of manifest destiny (see "The Frontier" in Chapter 1). The canal was a plank in the Monroe Doctrine, calling Europe to recognize republican greatness. The theme was evoked by New York Governor De Witt Clinton when he predicted the canal would influence agriculture, manufactures, and commerce on a national level, indeed, "the holy cause of Republican Government" itself. The waterway, whose piecemeal construction had begun in 1793 (though the official groundbreaking was 4 July 1817), was operational along most of its route for two years before completion, generating enough revenue by the time of its grand opening 5 November 1825 to promise to offset its seven-million-dollar construction cost. With a labor force of eight thousand men moving goods along its course, the canal was a major employer for and developer of the state of New York. By 1850, tonnage from states west of Buffalo exceeded that of New York, and the movement of immigrants bound for the old Northwest Territories contributed to the incorporation of northern states into the Union: Michigan (1837), Wisconsin (1848), and, beyond the territories, Minnesota (1858).[34]

Erie Canal historian Ronald Shaw describes "one of the most striking aspects of the literature of the Erie Canal" as "its constant identification of local with national interest." To be sure, the state of New York had concerns of its own at stake (chiefly the desires for Federal aid and an increase in its own importance and wealth), but canal builders also saw "Clinton's ditch" as a bond of union preventing the detachment George Washington had feared between East and West along the Appalachian Mountains. The Erie Canal was also viewed as a buffer against Canadian expansion, whose British power New York no less than New Orleans had felt in the War of 1812. National interest was a text specifically evoked when some of the guns used by Admiral Perry's fleet at the Battle of Lake Erie in 1814 were fired along the length of the canal to herald the entrance of the *Seneca Chief* into the waterway near Buffalo on 26 October 1825, the start of its journey to Manhattan. The canal boat's name ironically evoked Red Jacket's people, whose confederation lands embraced the headwaters of the Mohawk River, the waterways bearing their names (Seneca Lake, Lake Oneida), and the lands to the south of Lake Ontario. Their reserves in western New York were deeply implicated in "the triumph of American institutions" over European ones that the Erie Canal represented to its supporters.[35]

The completion of the Erie Canal was proclaimed in each town and city along its 363 miles from Lake Erie in the West to Albany in the East, then south along the Hudson River to the Atlantic Ocean. Celebration usually began with the arrival of the *Seneca Chief* and its cargo of dignitaries, produce, and artifacts gathered and shipped from the West: cedar and maple logs, whitefish, potash, a canoe from the shores of Lake Superior, and two kegs of Lake Erie water. The cabin of the *Seneca Chief* was decorated with a portrait of De Witt Clinton in a Roman toga (painted by George Catlin, the American artist who would shortly gain fame as a portraitist of Indians). Celebrations similar to those greeting Lafayette's arrival – balls, songs, decorative arches over the canal, banners, speeches, militia escorts, bands, illuminations, fireworks, transparencies, artillery salutes – continued after the *Seneca Chief* moved on to its next destination. The lead vessel was soon followed by the *Noah's Ark* (from Ararat on the Niagara River) with its cargo of birds, fish, insects, bears, and two young Seneca boys. Behind her the *Superior* transported two fawns, while the *Niagara of Black*

Rock carried more dignitaries, and the *Young Lion of the West* native produce and more "western" animals. The flotilla eventually included canal commissioners and engineers, eight steamboats, and numerous private craft.[36]

The procession entered New York Harbor on 4 November 1825. A "Grand Aquatic Display" was staged opposite the Battery involving forty-six lavishly bedecked vessels (federal, state, and local), their arrival heralded by cross-cannonading from Brooklyn Navy Yard and the Battery. The vessels moved to the Long Island entrepôt with the Atlantic Ocean, where numerous speeches were made and Lake Erie waters – a portion reserved for General Lafayette, returned to France after his final travels from the Bunker Hill dedication to Washington – solemnly poured into the sea. On the Battery awaiting the return of the "Grand Aquatic Display" was a "Grand Procession" of five thousand marchers, representing fifty-nine units, lined up behind the standard of their profession, trade, or society and led by mounted trumpeters and a marching band. The parade route extended from the Battery to City Hall. As with celebrations of Lafayette, printers struck off an ode composed for the occasion (here by Samuel Woodworth), butchers rode in their aprons, firemen struck tableaux on their machines, the coopers assembled large casks, and tailors, tanners, cordwainers, hatters, bankers, cobblers, the professions, and numerous societies paraded with politicians and officials in celebration of republican achievement.[37]

There followed the by-now familiar gatherings, speeches, banquets, bell ringing, illuminations, transparencies, and fireworks (Fig. 3). Souvenir badges, sketches, handkerchiefs, glassware, pennants, and turbans were purchased, some worn to the Grand Canal Ball, "in honor of Lafayette," held at the Lafayette Amphitheatre. There, three thousand people danced around a maple sugar canal boat made in Utica, which floated in water from Lake Erie. At Castle Garden, where the previous year Lafayette had walked through his first commemorative arch, the *Noah's Ark* treated patrons to a cargo of "western" animals, birds, fish, and Seneca Indians. Celebrations over, the *Seneca Chief* made its slow way back to Buffalo carrying a keg of Atlantic water to be ceremoniously mixed with the waters of Lake Erie.[38]

* * * * *

Fig. 3. "Illumination of the City Hall upon Completion of the Erie Canal"
(from Wilson, ed., *Memorial History of the City of New-York*, vol. 3).

LIKE LAFAYETTE'S RETURN, the opening of the Erie Canal looked
backward even as it looked ahead: back to the Revolution and War of 1812
that secured lands from "foreign" encroachment; back to Indian cultures
nostalgized, coveted, and imitated, even as they were compromised, deni-
grated, and rent asunder; back to a patrician culture proclaiming democracy but characterized by slavery and privilege; back to a valorized artisan
patriot whose claim to past glory would secure little future ease, for himself or for those he excluded from the workplace; back to an iconized, sen-
timentalized womanhood that would be changed forever by dispossession,
slavery, and by developments like the Erie Canal and its demand for markets and workers. In the same antebellum spaces marked by these returns,
however, the men and women who participated in, were segregated from,
were beguiled by, or who appropriated Lafayette's visit and the opening
of the Erie Canal also created and performed other definitions of the native, staging diversity in the very words and deeds that formulated American cultural spaces.

I

Spaces of Representation

America is the best means of prophesying, if I may say so, what the world will next be, and what we will next do.
  – Anthony Trollope, *North America* (1862)

America is the country of the Future. From Washington . . . through all its cities, states, and territories, it is a country of beginnings, of projects, of vast designs, and expectations. It has no past; all has an onward and prospective look.
  – Ralph Waldo Emerson, "The Young American" (1844)

The wilderness masters the colonist. It finds him a European in dress, industries, tools, modes of travel, and thought. It takes him from the railroad car and puts him in the birch canoe. It strips off the garments of civilization and arrays him in the hunting shirt and moccasin. It puts him in the log cabin of the Cherokee and Iroquois and runs an Indian palisade around him.
  – Frederick Jackson Turner, *The Frontier in American History* (1893)

I N THE BEGINNING," John Locke observed, "all the world was America." In his plangent and often appropriated phrase, Locke captured the hope and fear of European history: that paradise might be found again – and again be lost. The America of this imagining was Rousseau's tabula rasa, the pristine forest primeval whose wonders would soothe then wipe away the failures of civilization and open a scene of limitless possibility. It was a vision positing an empty space, a willed denial of the two-hundred-year history already written and writing within the landscape of

27

this imagining by the time Lafayette became the nation's guest and the Erie Canal focused attention on trade with the western states. The projection of a "paradise America" had also something desperate and last-ditch about it, a holding action by Europeans against time and a refusal by their descendents to engage the changes of sensibility that "the American experience" had already exerted upon peoples, red, white, brown, and black, female and male.[1]

European travel books about America, destined to reach epidemic proportions in the antebellum decades, often betray the absence of a perceptual scheme capable of encompassing the extent to which the new world and the old differed. British travelers in particular sought England in America and were usually disappointed. Their books often project an oppressive and threatening wilderness wherein the sublime elements of the forest primeval (the Hudson River Valley, Niagara Falls, the great rivers) are sublime less as manifestations of the wild than as mirrors of the tamer beauties of art, a sublimity that found expression in the great American landscape paintings of the antebellum decades. Despite an uncivilized terrain and populace, or perhaps because of them, America was envisioned by European visitors as the great laboratory of democracy, the Europe of the future, as Anthony Trollope suggests in one of the phrases framing this chapter. The relationship to the old and the new, suggested in the Prologue, the perception of a historic mission in (as the phrase from Emerson declares) a nation without a history, reflects an ambivalence repeatedly encountered in European assessments of the United States in the antebellum decades, whether the traveler took America seriously, as did Tocqueville, or longed only for the gardens of home, as did Mrs. Trollope. If America was paradise, to these tourists' eyes it had been claimed by unproven and hardly divine inhabitants.[2]

Home-grown responses to the native landscape were likewise ambivalent. The word "American" in eighteenth-century British usage was applied almost exclusively to Amerindians, until issues of taxation in the 1760s and 1770s prompted Samuel Johnson and others to apply the word to the rebellious descendents of Europeans. Like "American," "Indian" was also an invention. The living embodiments of this construct figured prominently in the early history of "paradise"; hence for the descendents of European immigrants to claim "American" as their nationality was strangely to sit on both sides of the Thanksgiving feast, to be at once the native space receiving the foreign invader and the explorer penetrating the unknown. Was the real America, then, America "out there," the land across the Mississippi beyond whose bourn, prior to midcentury, few white travelers, foreign or domestic, had yet ventured? Or was America "in here" in the antebellum decades, in the eastern towns and cities where "paradise" had longest been contemplated? What perceptual scheme could the sons and daughters of the new white Eden offer if Locke's beginning had begun?[3]

Many disciplines explore the tremors occasioned by these attempts at national definition – of America as paradise, of the native and the foreign, of the landscape, of the old and the new, of the laboratory of democracy, of the past and of the future. This chapter takes up these stagings as they are particularized in the town, city, and frontier, not to reauthorize the "stable stories" around which, even when opposing them, cultures have been presumed by scholars to organize themselves, but to explore the currency of those ideas. Overwhelmingly, antebellum myths of origin and mission were white-generated, sexist and racist in standing aloof from equitable application, even when insisting upon the "universality" of the story and quest. Even so, myths of national definition could appeal to women and nonwhites as expressions of their own quests for freedom and self-realization. Within the sites of town, city, and frontier, philosophical, aesthetic, and cultural views developed productive of such constructs as the idyllic village and the staged Yankee, the demonized antebellum city and its fashions in urban lives and cultures, and a dramatized frontier seen both as heaven and as hell. These winding roads of myth and practice leading to and from the playhouse traverse a minefield of contesting perceptions. The mappings of America that emerge, both from contemporaneous and subsequent participants, emphasize diverse, interactive, and simultaneous cultural universes. This chapter explores these worlds as cultural sites.[4]

The Town

In capturing the imaginations of Europeans and their descendents, the land that was and would become the United States after 1825 escaped containment merely as geography. The idea that the native space was a state of mind, of transcendence, is a construction of the American landscape as a town, a society of New England hamlets and villages of the sort often home to the men and women who generated and disseminated the diverse ideas captured under the rubric "transcendentalism." Most of those called transcendentalists did not like the term and claimed not to know what it meant; yet at the same time they insisted upon and utilized the individual and group identity it bestowed. A commerce in American intellectual as well as business speculation would have surprised Alexis de Tocqueville, writing in 1835–40 of his 1831–2 inspection of the new Eden, who observed "that in no country in the civilized world is less attention paid to philosophy than in the United States." Mistaken in this as in many of his speculations about America, the young French aristocrat would have found Romantic philosophy widely referenced, pro and con, among the growing number of American magazines published between 1830 and the Civil War. He might have been even more surprised to think that the ideas American transcendentalism generated would have anything to do with an also burgeoning American theatre.[5]

A wide scholarship about American transcendentalism acknowledges its debts to European Romanticism – particularly to Kant, Fichte, Schelling, Victor Cousin, Coleridge, and Carlyle – to ancient philosophy, and to the Orient. Despite these debts to the old and the borrowed, the need to fix precisely the onset of intellectual "America on the move" to a 19 September 1836 meeting in the home of the Rev. George Ripley in Boston betrays a self-conscious desire to locate the utter historical moment of birth, of separation from the past. Indeed, this "birth" was announced in Emerson's *Nature*, which appeared just two weeks before the historic gathering in Ripley's study. The Transcendental Club, as they were known – and it was very much in the grain of the era that like-minded townspeople created formal associations such as clubs – met four or five times a year for about four years. The longevity of transcendentalism extends well beyond these formal meetings, however, into Thoreau's *Walden* (1854), Whitman's *Leaves of Grass* (1855), and into American culture before the Civil War. Twentieth-century scholarship has often looked to transcendentalism as the source of American individuality and found appealing its vision of intellectuals as central and powerful in society. Similarly, the force of the myth of what Alexander Saxton calls "the white Republic," the self-created political, intellectual, and cultural history of the new Eden, haunts many antebellum stagings of the town. The specter, as recent scholarship often notes, is the tension between the individual and the communal.[6]

A recognition of gains and losses in its New England (often Puritan) legacy colored transcendental inquiry, and, despite Emerson's denial of history, that legacy lent a genealogy to those inquiries. Central to the club's cognitive charter was a dissatisfaction with Unitarian theology's base in the rationalism of Locke, a philosophy that Ripley's group believed impugned the mind's capacity to transcend sense experience and tap directly into truths. Naturally, the Unitarians opposed this line of thinking and scorned its roots in Cousin and Coleridge. Less effective philosophically in rebutting transcendentalism than in demeaning it socially, establishment critiques delighted in depicting transcendentalists as fanciful dreamers. As Dickens put it, "On inquiring . . . I was given to understand that whatever was unintelligible would be certainly transcendental." Even the antebellum author and essayist Lydia Maria Child, who troubled to inform herself, described transcendentalist writing as mystical, obscure, and prime matter for jesters.[7]

The intricacies and varieties of transcendental philosophy lie beyond this study, but two of its aspects bear directly upon theatre culture. The first (and most obvious) connection is that between nature and such concepts as genius and beauty. Truth, transcendentalist essays and lectures suggested, was directly revealed to individuals, either through contemplation or in communion with nature, via flashes of internal illumination or insight. These flashes alternated with foggy periods of shadow. In moments of vision, nature (the projection of the Universal Spirit and the source of the creative flow) made true manifestation of itself in individuals. Coleridge's perception of Kean's acting as "reading Shakespeare by flashes of lightning" exactly captures such moments, just as reviews of antebellum American art (novel, painting, and theatre) frequently employ a light-centered, painterly vocabulary to discuss the beauties and limitations of the imagined. Such illuminations (in the visually electric sense of the theatrical illuminations of the period) were, to the transcendentalists, ethical as well as epistemological moments. In them, the conflicts between light and dark, vision and the lack of it, between solitude and social pressure, allow individuals to define what they value and who they are.[8]

The loss (via declared independence) of a lineage through (Lockean) rationalism freed the transcendentalists to consider a different inheritance – one indebted, to be sure, to Romanticism, but a genealogy rooted in their adaptations to the American scene of Lockean political liberalism. This second aspect of transcendental philosophy is reified in theatre culture in appropriations that are in their own ways as ambitious as Locke without Locke: for example, in the creation of iconic figures – Yankee, Indian, frontiersman – that embody admired yet equivocal national traits, racist figures both in the local sense and in the planetary sense of genetics. That both transcendentalism and antebellum American theatre had a politics reads against a frivolous (excessively abstract) transcendentalism as well as against a frivolous (material-minded) theatre, both critiques of the time. As constituent rather than only reflective of political philosophy, theatre recouples with social life in a significant way; but before we explore, here and in subsequent chapters, some examples of that joining, it is useful to forge a few more links with aspects of transcendental philosophy.[9]

Scholars of transcendental thought note its apprehension both about antebellum America's mindless materialism and its invocation of "progress" as a justification for slavery, the exploitation of labor, massacres and removals of Indians, the rape of the land, and wars of imperialism and racism. Transcendental advocacy of a common source for, and hence the fellowship of, humankind (i.e., the Universal Being/God/Over-Soul) offered a conceptualization of America as a sequence of interrelated parts. The opposition of the state to individual morality, however, led transcendentalism to its celebrated civil disobedience against government policies and practices. This posture, of interrelation but separation, as recent criticism notes, opened a gap between the individual and the state requiring mediation. Utopian communities such as Brook Farm and Fruitlands offered one solution; reform by education or by personal example offered others; and a reassessment of the Constitution in light of American political experience offered transcendentalism's most trenchant mediation of all.[10]

Emerson argued the state had no philosophy, history, or tradition, since these were meanings and values the individual generated; hence the state's moral authority was bogus. The optimism underscoring the idea that the state could or would wither away, yet civilized life proceed – the self-reliance of "You think me the child of my circumstances; I make my circumstances" – would have mystified European (especially German) Romantics, for whom government could never be dismissed. European intellectuals, oppressed equally by state and bourgeois society, were not men and women of the American town. In New England communities, on the other hand, transcendentalists were the bourgeoisie, white men and women of property and standing whom the state would not presume, as it did in parts of Europe, to impede in traveling where and publishing what they pleased. Such towns were likely to be tolerant of the eccentricities of their home-grown, educated white men (if not women) of good family.

In its opposition to a host of moral ills and their own complicity in them, transcendentalist civil disobedience was no less sincere for the benignities that underscore rather than obviate its reconciliation with the state, and that state's complex, racist politics.[11]

The tensions that had developed in the years between the Constitution and his own meditations suggested to transcendentalist Orestes Brownson a distinction between civil order (laws) and civil society (the aggregate of people whose existence forces the dialectic between natural and social rights). It is with civil society, he argued, that principles/history/tradition/authority rest. Insofar as the U.S. Constitution indeed mediated morality and policy, there would be a civil order defining the spheres of the individual, of society, and of the state. Brownson recognized that American society was already constitutive and mediating, that individual morality and state policy were transcended by civil society, requiring continuing redefinition of the individual constituted by statute. Emerson notwithstanding, the national tablet was far from blank, in Brownson's view; laws were engraved upon it, history inscribed upon paradise.[12]

Applied social experiments, such as Brook Farm (1841–7), underscored fundamental tensions in transcendental democracy between individuals and communities. Although all members of that collective were to do humble work, for example (indeed, the human mission, according to Emerson – who was not a resident – was to produce, not just to be), not all participants were class equal. Mechanic members, who did much of the community's necessary work, were to be culturally "leveled up" to bourgeois values and decorum in a way German Romantic intellectuals would have found incomprehensible. Those workers responded with resentment against Brook Farm's "aristocrats." Coincident with this classism was an open education policy at the Farm that prepared children of humble backgrounds even for college. Bourgeois parents favoring class segregation opposed educating the Irish cook's daughter, just as Bronson Alcott found Bostonians opposed to the admission of a black girl to his school. Ultimately unsuccessful in addressing its social inequities, even after its 1844 reconstitution as a Fourierist phalanx, Brook Farm, like many aspects of transcendentalism, privileged a staging of individual development for which no social organization could substitute. At the same time, the communal context shaped that development much in the way a transcendent town is a site for liberty but also repression. The tensions among class-licensed rebellion, interrelated yet contesting social parts, civil disobedience, and mediation are, not surprisingly, signaled by the theatrical work Brook Farm produced.[13]

Performance formed a regular part of colony life at Brook Farm. A large upper room was set aside as a theatre, and a smaller carpenter shop was occasionally pressed into use for Amusement Series works. A natural amphitheatre (near the phalanstery built after the shift to Fourierism) serviced elaborate outdoor pageants on at least two occasions: an Elizabethan one with music and dance, and a production the following year of scenes from *A Midsummer Night's Dream*. A complete index of the Farm's theatrical repertory does not appear to have survived, but their large theatre gave life to at least three melodramas: *The Corsair, The Rent Day*, and *Pizarro in Peru; or, the Death of Rolla. The Corsair*, a dramatization by Glover Drew of Byron's often dramatized poem, served as a curtain raiser for *Pizarro*, Sheridan's version of a late-eighteenth-century spectacle of conquest by the German "father of melodrama," August von Kotzebue. *Pizarro* was in preparation for a week and was the Farmers' most ambitious dramatic effort, featuring a chorus of sun maidens that had been coached by John S. Dwight (subsequently a prominent American music critic) through one of Mozart's masses. *The Rent Day*, Englishman Douglas Jerrold's 1832 melodrama of agrarian life based upon Sir David Wilkie's painting of that name, reflects the Farmers' interest in *tableaux vivants*. These, dances with dialogue, readings from favored authors like Scott and Shakespeare, discussions of drama, and musical evenings of part singing, "with all the characters and choruses," of sections from popular operas like *Zampa, Norma*, and *The Caliph of Bagdad*, inventory some of Brook Farm's stagings of culture. Significantly, when the community retrenched and reorganized in 1844, the Amusement Series was not dropped. Indeed, one scholar argues, performance was an essential part of Fourier's philosophy of integrated individual–social life, as Brook Farm interpreted it.[14]

Whether performances at Brook Farm were intended only to develop transcendentalist–Fourierist individual–social integration among the Farmers or also to proffer a statement of social philosophy to those who walked from nearby towns to see the performances, or who experienced them while visiting the community from Boston, is not wholly clear. Certainly, *Pizarro*, with its courageous, self-sacrificing, and doomed noble savage is a jarring choice for an anti-Indian-removal sect, though consonant with *The Corsair*'s rebel crushed by civil power, an intersection of individual and political also visible in *The Rent Day*. These tensions at Brook Farm await more contained study elsewhere, but the interrelationship between performance inside and outside theatres suggests itself not only among utopian transcendentalists, but among those who lived "in the world." There, the letters and diaries of transcendentalists indicate fairly general theatre attendance, social interaction with actors, and regular reading of and reference to plays. The many short-lived but influential transcendentalist journals refer to the benefits of play reading and contain reviews of productions. In addition, transcendentalist journals ran reflective pieces such as Margaret Fuller's analyses of audience taste, arguing for standards above mere popularity and against moral condemnations of theatre as a form. In reviews of books for and against the theatre, transcendentalists recognized that influential people of their class, speaking in support of amusements, as Henry Ward Beecher did in an 1848 Boston lecture, did much to end lingering religious prejudice against theatre. Even Emerson – who could be enchanted by Fanny Ellsler's dancing but was more likely to express dismay at the gap between his vision and the stage's – visited the theatre all of his adult life (as did other members of his circle) and lent his voice to the argument that theatre attendance should be a matter of taste, not morality.[15]

Transcendentalism's views of nature and the communitarian, within Brook Farm and outside it – taken with its playmaking, advocacy of theatre as an art form, and social interaction with theatre people – provided a medium through which the individual, social, and political can be combined. That medium, from the perspective of theatre culture, is its vision of the town (and by extension of the nation) as a benign, aspiring community, both cultivating its garden and getting on with its business. Art historians link the visionary aspects of transcendentalism to antebellum American luminist painting; indeed, they see the optimism of transcendentalism reflected in a variety of American art, luminist and not, where "the commonplace becomes heroic, and the insignificant monumental." (Ripley at Brook Farm speculates upon transcendentalism, he writes, as the result of milking a cow.) The town is alternately present and absent in antebellum paintings: In some cases it is depicted on the canvas (as in John Mix Stanley's 1850–2 *Oregon City on the Willamette River*), whereas in others it waits patiently in the wings to receive the laboring artist, the returning sailor, or the struggling farmer (e.g., Washington Allston's 1835 *American Scenery. Time: Afternoon with a Southwest Haze;* Fitz Hugh Lane's c. 1850 *Ships in Ice off Ten Pound Island, Gloucester;* or Thomas

Cole's 1846 *Home in the Woods*). The aura of the town embraces the resting laborer in William Sidney Mount's 1836 *Farmers Nooning* and George Caleb Bingham's 1847 *Raftsmen Playing Cards;* indeed, even when the scene is one of the "forest primeval," the men of the town are already there to tell us what of paradise they have seen (e.g., Asher Durand's 1849 *Kindred Spirits,* portraying the departed artist Cole and Cole's friend William Cullen Bryant conversing in a rugged American landscape).[16]

The depiction of civilized life that this town-based art represents often painted paradise in retrospect – the studio contemplation of on-site sketches of the embracing forest, the opening meadow, or the verging ocean – nonetheless sublime for being already bordered by impinging civil society. Indeed, the men of the town referenced themselves repeatedly, through portraits and by drawing themes for painting from literature – Durand from Bryant's poems, Quidor from Irving's works, Cole from Cooper or from lives larger than fiction (e.g., *Daniel Boone and His Cabin at Great Osage Lake,* 1826). Conversely, literature referenced painting, not just in descriptive scenes and a critical language appropriating painterly rhetoric (foreground and background, light and shade, outline and filling, literalness, coloration), but also in theatrical renderings, such as William Dunlap's staging of James Fenimore Cooper's *The Spy* in 1824 or Louisa Medina's adaptation of Robert Montgomery Bird's novel *Nick of the Woods* (1836–8). The "Nature" of artworks arches over the town, an idealized nature, to be sure, but a nature inextricably interwoven with the transcendental reading of morality forged through conflict.[17]

Samuel Woodworth's *The Forest Rose; or, American Farmers* (1825), offers an example of how theatre consitutes some of the ideas one can locate in transcendentalism and plays them back to a larger theatre culture. Described as "a pastoral opera" (though it played for most of its extensive career in American repertories as a straight Yankee play, rather than as a musical), *The Forest Rose* is a celebration of the American town, about the depiction of which its stage instructions are firm:

The overture expresses the various sounds which are heard at early dawn, in the country, commencing at that hour of silence when even the ticking of the village clock is supposed to be heard. It strikes four, and a gentle bustle suceeds, indicating the first movements of the villagers. A confused murmur gradually swells on the ear, in which can be distinguished the singing of birds, the shepherd's pipe, the hunter's horn, etc., etc., etc., until the united strength of the band represents the whole village engaged in their rustic employments. Distant view of a village spire, on which the dial plate of a clock indicates the hour; the stage represents a farmyard, separated from a field by a pale fence with a gate. On the right of the actor is a cottage, and on the opposite side a rustic arbor of a grapevine.

To this scene, enter the farmer-hero and two "milk maids" to sing the glories of autumnal nature, concluding, "What are city joys to these?" It is a scene right out of Asher Durand (see *The Babbling Brook* [1851] with its cows), and the play's unmatched record of forty years on the boards in all the major U.S. cities and London has led theatre historians to offer *The Forest Rose* as the most successful American play of the first half of the nineteenth century.[18]

The drama that unfolds in this bucolic paradise has many analogues in the plays of the antebellum decades. Here, Lydia, scorned for humble birth yet scorning secret marriage to her city sweetheart Blandford, is paired with Harriet, who longs for the glimpses of urban life offered her by the English traveler Bellamy. Repeatedly, interludes (usually musical) still the action of the play and clarify the value of nature, an out-of-doors whose calm purity could only produce virtuous characters. Accordingly, at no point in the play is there even a remote chance the female characters – the Squire's daughter, Harriet; Lydia Roseville, the wealthy farmer's daughter; poor Deacon Forest's daughter, Sally; or his black servant, Rose – will lose their grips on the moral core of the town overarched by nature. The libertine foreigner Bellamy remains wholly outside this paradise, where "every native rural charm" adorns the family farm. Even the urban hero loses his way in the forests of home until set upon the true path, literally and figuratively, by the staged Yankee (Jonathan Ploughboy). In the transcendent town, class consciousness has no place and is reduced to a remnant of the dead (and foreign) past: the city man's deceased "high-minded father. . . . He was an Englishman, you know, and that will account for his only foible, which was family pride." Alexander Saxton characterizes this past as a politics of (class) deference typical of earlier Republican society and its drama. In the world of the town where moral centers remain intact, the roses of the "forest" escape corruption, if not calumny from outside. (The displaced Bellamy promises to "quit the country of savages . . . but I will not fail to notice you all when I publish my *Three Months in America*.")[19]

Though the Yankee piece primarily plays the rural setting in a lighter vein – as in *The Green Mountain Boy* (1833), *The People's Lawyer* (1839),

and *The Vermont Wool Dealer* (1840) – it was not the only approach to
the town. Sometimes the intersection of real and ideal in the dramatized
village eventuated in shadow rather than clarity; yet even a tragic ending
never obscures the town as a model of civil society as it ought to be. That
model in *The Forest Rose,* Saxton reminds us, is relative to class and race,
normalizing the vernacular Jonathan while isolating the black Rose – an
example, Saxton concludes, of the hardening racism of Jacksonianism. In
its universalist aspects, the beauty of the village in conflict with the ugli-
ness of vice forces the consideration of political power: Who will rule paradise and who will be its leader/heroes? Despite its depiction as Eden, the
village offers up a host of social problems: *The Drunkard* (1844) and the
enslaved community of *Uncle Tom's Cabin* (1852), for example, as well as
the local embezzlers and imported roués of *The Forest Rose.* Antebellum
plays set in towns share the moral problems of those set in cities; indeed,
many, if not most, of the villains of melodrama are homegrown, like its
heroes and heroines – men of the town and/or American. The morality of
civil society was an ubiquitous issue in these decades, and while the transcendental response can be identified as that of the town, neither did it
arrogate virtue exclusively to the village. A redemptive nature was accessible to all, even when legal and social equity were not.[20]

An American-generated drama, in quantity and quality, can be identified by 1830, though American periodicals continued to call one into existence. Here (as has been suggested by others in the context of fiction),
what was actually solicited was a certain *kind* of American drama. Walter
Meserve estimates that 90 percent of the plays written between 1829 and
1849 were by actors or journeymen playwrights. Though the transcendentalists were not unique in associating with actors and stage authors, it was
one thing to be a welcome boon companion in one of the nation's many
clubs and another to be heralded in prestigious journals as a native Shakespeare or Garrick.[21]

What the transcendent town offered, in addition to a construing of
communal morality, was the earliest American "type" character, a staged
Yankee, and with him an opportunity for the "genius" of American actors
and playwrights to express itself in roles and settings not also traditional
in foreign (specifically English) repertories. As with the type characters
that would follow him (and her – a female staged Yankee also emerged in
these decades), the Yankee of theatre culture offered up a combination of
those particular elements taken to differ from culture to culture interwo-

ven with characteristics accepted as "universal" to life and art. Rather than reconciling the particular and the universal, however, the staged Yankee exacerbated the formal tension between the real and the ideal, between local color and "Nature to advantage dressed," between regional dialect and the language of Emerson's "Over-Soul."[22]

The staged Yankee is a phenomenon of the antebellum decades, rising with James H. Hackett's imitations and stories in the mid-1820s; extending through George Handel "Yankee" Hill's successes in the United States and abroad, and through the innovations of Danforth Marble during the 1830s and 1840s; and fading with the death in 1855 of Joshua Silsbee, the principal Yankee actor after Hill and Marble died in 1849. Although these were not the only impersonators of Yankees on the stage, their creative lives exactly span its period of greatest development and popularity. Any stock actor before midcentury could expect to support a Yankee piece; after 1850, however, the Yankee was more likely to appear as a secondary character – as, for example, in *Uncle Tom's Cabin* (1852), *Ten Nights in a Bar-Room* (1858), or *Our American Cousin* (1858). The extent to which the Yankee entered the repertory of American society by the Civil War was spatial as well as temporal, in that the type had toured not only London and Europe, but also from the Atlantic to the Pacific.[23]

From "Jonathan's" appearance in Royall Tyler's *The Contrast* (1787) to his absorption into the stock repertory by the mid-nineteenth century, the Yankee is consistently offered as independent, self-assertive, rural, uncouth, and witty. Those who achieved star status as actors of the type made of it a role that, ideally, only an American could or (ultimately) would perform. In dialect and songs, through Yankee stories and eccentric movement, and in distinctive love and trickery scenes, the Yankee man of the town offered audiences a recognizable and compatible enactment, an American both real and ideal. In Boston physician and theatre manager Joseph Stevens Jones's *The People's Lawyer* (1839), which may be taken as illustrative, the Yankee character (Solon Shingle) is a supporting player in a central action revolving around a false accusation of theft against the poor but honest heroine's brother. That brother is successfully defended by the hero of the play, Robert Howard, the wealthy but unpretentious people's lawyer.[24]

Formally, the Solon Shingle role retains marks of its origins (both socially and theatrically) in the regional folktale and monologue, which had a performance life on various antebellum stages. The language – "sartin"

for "certain," "winder"/"window," "keer"/"care," "jest"/"just," "druv"/
"drove," many of the regionalisms American speech retains, plus tran-
scriptions that are the inheritance of printing conventions for popular literature – hardly bespeaks transcendental eloquence, but it does capture
its vigor:[25]

These city folks will skin me out of my old plaid cloak, that I bought ten years
ago; hat, boots, and trowsers, tu, far as I know. I've been here long enough. I'll
follow the Squire, find my Nabby, buy a load of groceries, and get home as quick
as my team will go it. When I'm in this 'ere Boston, I get so bewildered I don't
know a string of sausages from a cord of wood. Jest so.

Solon's description of his clothing – the Yankee was traditionally garbed
in top hat, striped high-water trousers over boots, a tailcoat and/or duster,
vest or suspenders, and a loose tie (the Uncle Sam costume) – is more generous than his view of the city. In this play, the city is home to a northeastern natural nobleman, Robert Howard, the titular people's lawyer who
claims the title of a gentleman even though his "hands are hardened by
labor." Higgins-fashion, speech makes this man; he sounds like one who
"has studied in the halls of science," as indeed he has. Nonetheless,
Howard insists he has accomplished no more than less privileged men
might do in America: "What should hinder the son of toil, when genius
stimulates, from acquiring the highest fund of knowledge that science
gives? Our country is a free one, and education flows from the public fountain for all who thirst for its refreshing streams." In a deft solution of the
question of whence America's (dramatic) heroes were to originate, Jones's
protagonist is endowed not with a wealthy, classist, foreign father, but with
a wealthy, unpretentious American one who "was governed by caprice
and insisted upon my learning a mechanic trade, besides educating me for
his own profession, that of the bar, which I have practiced with success."
No snob, Robert Howard, but the best of all possible democratic leaders:
a horny-handed, well-educated son of toil "who never pleads [or needs
to financially] except where he sees oppression preying upon poverty and
innocence." Moreover, Robert Howard is master of an urban village where
everyone knows everyone, and highborn and low, rich and poor mingle
and intermarry. How could it be otherwise in a transcendent town where
"our laws are just, our judges honest men, [and] our jurors are our
equals?" In such a world, "a poor mechanic dares to thwart the wishes of
a merchant," the play's villain, a bad Yankee who is, in the bargain, "too

religious to believe in dancing" and "head horse in the temperance team."
Bold words for playwright Jones's Boston, birthplace of *The Drunkard*
(1844) with its Yankee William and New England setting, yet the villain of
The People's Lawyer is nonetheless a latter-day puritan, the sort indicted
both by the transcendentalist Margaret Fuller and by the class (-conscious)
enemy of her colleague Orestes Brownson's mediating civil society.[26]

In the hands of artists like Hill and Owens, "you might as well try to
back a heavy load up a hill as stop [Solon's] thoughts coming right out in
homely words," nor do the other characters in the play "doubt [his] meaning is good." Despite his particularity, however, the staged Yankee is not
the center of the play's action; a claim to authenticity is. As a local character, the good Yankee has a peripheral place in the transcendent town.
As a villain, the conceited and foxy peddler spinning his yarns and charming the gold out of your teeth, the bad Yankee of foreign travel accounts
and regional American rivalries is too authentic and must be counterfeit-
ed into an icon of Republican virtues (Yankee Doodle). The rustic ideal
is then transformed into the gentrified hero Howard. As a primitive, the
Yankee of theatre culture draws, transcendental fashion, on difference
and individuality. These traits, limned in a number of late-eighteenth and
early-nineteenth-century plays and sketches, rose to a floodtide of vastly
popular stories reprinted nationwide between 1830 and 1860. The staged
Yankee, however, not only provides the audience rejoinders to foreign
criticism or homegrown resentments of New England's political and cultural power, but makes evident there are conflicts in Eden at the intersection of "class."[27]

"Class" in *The People's Lawyer* is less a matter of economics than an inscription of speech, dress, and manners. Solon Shingle lacks both the inherited wealth of Howard and the ill-gotten riches of the pious merchant
villain Hugh Winslow, but he is far more prosperous than Winslow's
clerks. Still, unlike Emerson's redeeming elite, the bourgeoisie of this
staged town amalgamates and tames the civilly disobedient Yankee. The
genius of Hackett, Hill, Marble, and Owens did not reconcile the conflict
between the transcendental individual (personal liberty) and opposing society (collective rights and collective prejudices), even within the seemingly benign boundaries of the ideal town. As Alexander Saxton suggests of
The Forest Rose, this ideal forced a "leveling up" of class difference and
did nothing to transcend racism in American village plays. (Such contests
become exacerbated in the urban contexts of class discussed in Chapter 2.)

In satirizing Jacksonian politics and the Mexican War, the pretensions of the village and the risible peculiarities of native manners, indeed even in their cavalier racism, male and female staged Yankees were perceived to run true to the American grain. From the perspective of Brownson's view of civil society or Thoreau's civil disobedience, the staged Yankee's offer of frankness as a national characteristic leaves much of transcendental philosophy in the dust of village streets. For all these losses, however, there is yet a transcendental legacy in the character's inscription of authenticity. Indeed, this simulacrum for "authentic American" was well established by 1848, when "Yankee" was referenced in *Bartlett's Dictionary of American-isms.*[28]

The staged Yankee is as great a field of combat as the transcendental town and the intersection of individual with civil society or state. We may be less ready, from the perspective of the twenty-first century, to join earlier cultural historians in seeing the Yankee as the "real" American or to take Jonathan as the essential Jacksonian, white, male, racist, and sexist though he be. Moreover, the town that he represents, celebrates, and contests was, by the opening of *The Forest Rose* in 1825, beginning its long decline. The status of perfect laboratory lent to the town by transcendentalism gained anachronistic coloration as the populations of towns displaced to cities and frontiers and the transcendental village began its retreat into nostalgia. In the end, the American hero would not be a Yankee (nor a southerner nor a westerner), but the regionless resident of every place and no place. An emphasis upon the ethical in individual and communal natures, however, remained a sanctified part of the "national" character, in performances both in and out of playhouses, wherever the "American" space of representation was located.

The City

The sonorous roll of statistics chronicling the expansion of cities in antebellum America has lost none of its impressiveness with time. Between 1825 and 1860, the proportion of people living in cities rose from perhaps half a million to 3.8 million. Where only 12 cities in 1820 had over ten thousand inhabitants, by 1860 101 cities did, representing an increase of more than eightfold. The growth of American cities each decade between 1820 and 1860 peaked in an urban population increase in the 1840s of 92.1

percent, three times the rural growth rate. As a result, the urban population by the Civil War had increased 25 percent nationwide, although in
some states (Massachusetts, Rhode Island, New York) more than 50 percent lived in cities. The arrival of four times as many immigrants (five
hundred and forty thousand) in the 1830s as in the 1820s, many concen-
trating in cities, both swelled the population and changed its composition.
Not only did Americans move to cities, however, they moved endlessly
within them. The annual population turnover in Boston between 1830 and
1860 is estimated at 30 percent to about 1845 and 40 percent from 1845 to
1860. Numerous antebellum sources discuss New York's infamous moving
day (1 May), when each year half the city's population may have disap-
peared and been replaced. Those at the lowest income levels (as in Boston) moved several times a year. Americans were well aware they were
"living through an age of fundamental change in the technology, organization, and environments of daily life," and in nothing more than in the
phenomenal growth and importance of cities. In urban spaces particularly, as Emerson observed, the people were on the move.[29]

The antebellum American city offered a variety of representations and
readings. Just as the transcendentalists could read the town as both nurturing and claustrophobic, the city could be the paradise of the future or
the inferno itself. The titles of postbellum "city books" betray the ambiguity: for example, Matthew Hale Smith's *Sunshine and Shadow in New
York* (1868; Fig. 4) and James Dabney McCabe's *Lights and Shadows of
New York Life* (1872). City dwellers agreed that the urban landscape (de)-
constructed itself dramatically and as rapidly, Philip Hone woefully observed of 1839 New York, as "the ruin occasioned by an earthquake." This
was change not at nature's steady and inexorable pace, but at the speed
and seemingly chaotic whim of human desire. The imputation of human
rather than divine agency made the city particularly susceptible to qualitative analyses colored by perceptions of numbers of people, of crowding,
and of varieties of customs as these pertained to a host of social issues.
These qualitative analyses continue to define our perceptions of many aspects of antebellum culture.[30]

A city expresses a philosophy of social organization in where it positions
home, work, social services (hospitals, fire houses, prisons), and voluntary
associational spaces (churches, taverns, clubs, theatres). Integral to this scenario in the antebellum decades is the concentration of urban property in
the hands of a few owners, who (myths of "self-made" men aside) had

usually inherited or married it. These rentiers, as well as the substantial merchants and large manufacturers who were their peers, prior to 1825 had often combined living quarters and counting rooms, locating (as needed) in proximity to the warehouses, suppliers, or natural resources (water, power, high ground) necessary to coach making, shipbuilding, and their other manufactures. This post-Revolutionary pattern did not at once give way to others, but there was a clear imposition of "ordering" upon urban development in the early nineteenth century, of which that in New York City (Fig. 5) may be taken as illustrative.[31]

The Tontine Coffee House had been New York City's "stock exchange" from its erection in 1792. A new building in Wall Street opened in 1827. It contained the Chamber of Commerce, brokers' and merchants' offices, and a central oval room where notices were posted, chiefly the arrival and departure of ships. Known as the Merchants' Exchange, the building stood in proximity to City Hall, which, once located on Wall Street, had moved to Broadway and Park Row in 1812. The center of business and government activity, the blocks surrounding these institutions took in a variety of live–work spaces, churches, schools, clubs, banks, and theatres that mixed income groups but subjected all to a competitive real estate market that deliberately kept housing in short supply. Purposive too was the proposal by New York officials of a grid system, to control development, consisting of standard-sized lots and streets that adjusted the natural landscape or forced it into symmetry. Contesting this ordering were the clusters of "nuisance" industries (brewing, candle making, stables, slaughterhouses, gasworks, smithies, wood shops) concentrated in the sixth, seventh, and fourteenth wards, between Broadway, the Bowery, and the East River, that had constituted the outer reaches of the Revolutionary city and recalled a more fluid concept of land use.[32]

The contest between ordering and clustering in Manhattan produced a variety of spatial patterns. The "nuisance" industries were absorbed and bypassed as the city developed northward, creating progressively more congested spaces in which it was progressively less desirable to live. The wealthy could, and did, respond by uncoupling home and workplace; those less affluent could preserve the older live–work pattern (shopkeepers, shoemakers, out-workers) or reside near if not actually in the workplace. Intense crowding – by 1850, New York had 135.6 persons to the acre, Boston 82.7, Philadelphia 80.0, London (by comparison) 116.9 – was only selectively alleviated by mass transportation, which, at six cents a ticket in

Fig. 4. "Sunshine and Shadow in New York"; the lower image shows the notorious Old Brewery in Five Points (frontispiece to Matthew Hale Smith's *Sunshine and Shadow in New York* [Hartford: J. B. Burr, 1868]).

New York, Boston, and Philadelphia, was not in reach of the majority of low-income workers before 1860. Affected by market factors (New York's exports, for example, did not equal those of 1806 until about 1825), by wages (the real income of journeymen plummeted between 1800 and 1825, and with it the ability to save money, buy property, and raise business credit), and by urban planning and land manipulation, a reduction in the value of labor contributed to the creation of a "class" dynamic. So fluid did neighborhoods remain, however, that it was communal space that became the major public staging ground for this dynamic.[33]

Clustering concentrated crafts, benevolent associations, and social services that both contested and participated in large-scale urban ordering and its promise of eventual upward – though not traditionally outward – mobility. In the antebellum decades, these neighborhoods became a jumble of "foreign" (including domestic) populations in various crafts and trades, and of what would come to be identified as different classes. Intermixture of races was universal in New York, as in the other fourteen cities examined in Leonard P. Curry's study of free blacks in urban America from 1800 to 1850. Block by block in otherwise heterogeneous wards (with neighborhood concentrations in race and religion), the characteristic support businesses of the neighborhood – its taverns, groceries, and small shops – discriminated by ambiance and patronage rather than by address, since up- or down-scaling in a "walking city" is, for the patron of those shops, a matter of locution rather than location. More ambiguous than saloons or even fire stations or churches, however, were public spaces such as theatres, which functioned in neighborhoods (where their managers and personnel often lived) but serviced entire cities. To whom did such spaces belong and what representations did they offer?[34]

Urban theatres were built largely by the rich as business investments, though the effects of fire and age would cause theatrical managers to build playhouses on leased land as the antebellum years wore on. These theatres were intended to serve as gathering places, not only for profit – testaments to native culture and sociability. An 1827 guidebook to New York listed three theatres in operation: the Park Theatre (owned by John Beekman and John Jacob Astor), fronting City Hall Park on the south for eighty feet along Park Row, about two hundred feet east of Ann Street, and back to Theatre Alley; the Chatham Garden Theatre (owned by the heirs of rentier George Janeway), fronting Chatham Street between Duane and Pearl streets and extending back to Augustus Street/City Hall Place; and the

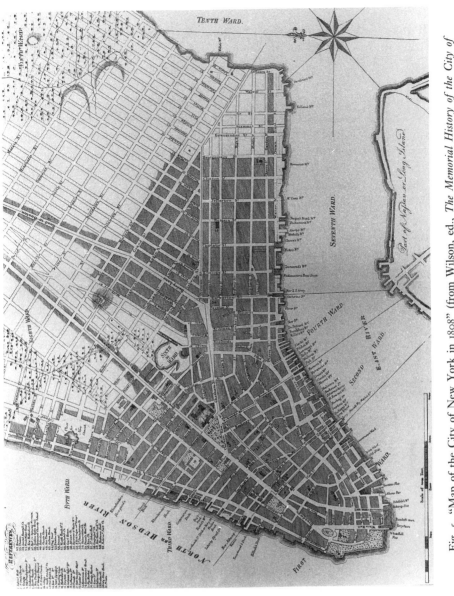

Fig. 5. "Map of the City of New York in 1808" (from Wilson, ed., *The Memorial History of the City of New-York*, vol. 3).

Bowery Theatre (owned by Henry Astor and his associates), fronting the Bowery and stretching to Elizabeth Street between Canal and Hester. The theatres were rivaled by three circuses – often incorporating dramatic performances, ballets, and farces – of which the longest-lived, the Lafayette Circus (in Laurens Street [now West Broadway] near Canal Street) was located far from the old city's financial and governmental center. Circus and theatre amusements were supplemented by three museums offering natural history, art, panoramas, music, and curiosities: Barnum's American Museum (Broadway and Ann Street), Peale's Museum (advantageously located on Broadway opposite the Park), and the Chatham Museum. Three public gardens (Castle, Vauxhall, and East River) rounded out regular diversions, to which were added boat excursions, balloon ascensions, and other seasonal amusements. By the 1837 financial panic, there were eight theatres reported in operation in New York; the number would rise and fall to the Civil War, but overall increase.[35]

Class issues relative to theatre have a text in where a theatre is located and how it is appointed; indeed, cities map achievement in terms of successful competition for space. Frances Trollope's five-week flying tour of Gotham and its theatres from late April to the end of May 1831 identified the valuations New Yorkers gave to theatre spaces, which she reports in her *Domestic Manners of the Americans* (Fig. 6):

There are three theatres at New York, all of which we visited. The Park Theatre is the only one licensed by fashion, but the Bowery is infinitely superior in beauty; it is indeed as pretty a theatre as I ever entered, perfect as to size and proportion, elegantly decorated, and the scenery and machinery equal to any in London, but it is not the fashion. The Chatham is so utterly condemned by *bon ton*, that it requires some courage to decide upon going there; nor do I think my curiosity would have penetrated so far, had I not seen Miss Mitford's *Rienzi* advertised there. It was the first opportunity I had had of seeing it played, and in spite of very indifferent acting, I was delighted. The interest must have been great, for till the curtain fell, I saw not one quarter of the queer things around me; then I observed in the front row of a dress-box a lady performing the most maternal office possible, several gentlemen without their coats, and a general air of contempt for the decencies of life, certainly more than usually revolting.

A few lines later, Mrs. Trollope concludes her theatrical observations with a final theatre visit to hear Mrs. Austin in an "extremely well got up" production of the opera *Cinderella*, observing:

Fig. 6. "Box at the Theatre" (by Auguste Hervieu, from Trollope, *Domestic Manners of the Americans*).

we saw the Park Theatre to advantage, for it was filled with well-dressed company; but still we saw many "yet unrazored lips" polluted with the grim tinge of the hateful tobacco and heard, without ceasing, the spitting, which of course is its consequence.[36]

Mrs. Trollope's remarks are concerned with "fashion," a word antebellumites used for what was popular or in vogue. Though her meaning implicates dress and behavior, her remarks are given an economic reading in a number of recent theatre and cultural histories. Indeed, transformed

into a sociocultural "fact," Mrs. Trollope's not-so-innocent observations
are used to authorize a view that "in New York in the 1830s the Park Theatre was associated with the upper classes, the Bowery with the middle,
and the Chatham with the lower." From this point, it is a short step to
the position that

during the 1830s and 1840s . . . entire theatres became associated with specific
classes. In New York the Park became a fashionable theater, while the Chatham
served a distinctly working-class audience. The Bowery was superior to the Chatham, but by the 1840s . . . had become a raucous center of working-class entertainment.

As a tripartite class-containment system emerges, with the Bowery slipping over time from the upper middle to the lower middle (the "raucous"
working) class, some historians speak with confidence of highbrow and low
and the emergence of a cultural hierarchy in antebellum America. Others
note on reflection that "in truth it is difficult if not impossible to docu-
ment the extent of the separation of classes in the theater" of these decades.[37]

Theatre as a manifestation of achievement rests not alone on the wealth
to build one or the disposable income to buy a ticket, but upon a conven-
tion of theatres as places for staging the self. As a result, antebellum urban theatre architecture offered white patrons spacious lobbies (heated or
cooled, in season), generous balconies, expansive second-floor salons with
large windows framing the street, and comfortable, generously appointed
third-floor punch rooms from which to see and be seen by the town. Seats
in boxes, pit, or gallery carried access to often richly caparisoned public
lounge and refreshment areas, competitively advertised and relentlessly
(often ruinously) remodeled by theatre managers. If the box bars of the
1820s fed genteel vanity, exclusive use of such facilities proved difficult to
maintain; even separate entrances for differently priced seats were contested as undemocratic. More successful was the nearly universal segregation
of urban free blacks, who, Curry's study reveals, were "excluded from
most of the 'public gardens,' museums, and galleries, and from some individual theaters" (in Cincinnati as well as Charleston). Usually, urban
free blacks, subject in various places and times during these decades to
curfew laws, riding outside on horsecars, and other segregationist practices, were similarly restricted in (rather than excluded from) theatres to
upper galleries or colored sections – restrictions that they and some whites

protested. How public a public theatre could be in antebellum America was subject to constant negotiation.[38]

No comparative analysis of antebellum theatre ticket prices nationwide, which fluctuated during the period, has yet been undertaken, and even within cities it is difficult to determine what prices represented in purchased pleasure. When Mrs. Trollope visited America (1827–31), for example, Park Theatre prices varied between 75 cents and $1.00 for a box seat, $37^1/_2$ to 75 cents for a seat in the pit, and 25 to 50 cents for a gallery seat, depending upon business. The Bowery charged 75 cents for a box seat, $37^1/_2$ for the pit, and 25 cents for the gallery, while the Chatham had only box (50 cents) and pit ($37^1/_2$ cents) seats, with half price for children in boxes. These amounts were charged in other northern cities during the period and in Baltimore, Norfolk, and Richmond as well. Bruce McConachie estimates that almost all theatres built in the 1820s – as these three New York theatres were – had more box seats than any other kind, close to twice as many as elsewhere in the house. Selling out these highest-priced seats could triple the revenue brought in by selling out all pit and gallery seats. By the 1830s, however, the correlation between seat and number appears to have favored the gallery: less income, but more constant patronage.[39]

Mrs. Trollope does not tell us what price seats she occupied in her New York theatre visits, nor how much time she spent in them rather than, like her peers, chatting with acquaintances in salons or drinking in coffee or punch rooms. Like them, she may well have seen the offered play before (except for her friend Miss Mitford's *Rienzi*); certainly, constant repetition of recent and older works was characteristic of the antebellum theatrical repertory. Except for newer pieces, like *Cinderella*, for which seats were highly sought, there were several other places in theatre besides one's seat to see and be seen. There were also places where one could avoid being seen, and theatre spaces where "any topic [might be] discussed, without molestations or interruptions." Given numerous reasons to be in the theatre other than to see the performance, Mrs. Trollope's fashion-conscious reading suggests arguments for and against attending specific theatres in 1831 New York. The Park Theatre was convenient to the old centers of power (Exchange and government offices). The Bowery Theatre was some five blocks distant from the Park, and though at the time its proprietors Henry Astor and Matthew Reed lived within a block of the theatre, and its association members Samuel Gouverneur, Daniel

Ingraham, and Prosper Wetmore (prominent business and professional men) lived only a few blocks away, the district was considered "the upper part of the city." That Manhattan would grow northward exactly as the rentiers expected and the urban planners dictated would make the handsome Bowery Theatre the fashion in the early 1830s.[40]

The depiction of New York's aristocracy attending the Park Theatre in John Searle's famous 1822 painting celebrates the lords and ladies of commerce, the venue they chose for self-display (the theatre had been newly rebuilt), and their support of American culture (though the actor onstage in Searle's recreation is the Englishman Charles Mathews in *Monsieur Tonson*). That the painting is a simulacrum of wishful thinking on a number of levels is suggested in actor-manager Joe Cowell's description of the Park at the time as a badly ornamented, dingy, prisonlike building that debouched into an alley "knee deep in filth," from whence he wound his way past the adjacent brothels to the street. The Park was not alone in its proximity to houses of ill fame: The Bowery and Chatham Theatres, as well as the Lafayette Circus, shared their blocks with brothels; indeed, the leading historian of prostitution in New York in these decades locates 34 percent of its whorehouses in the 1830s within 2.5 blocks of a theatre. Searle's patricians surely knew and ignored these proximities, so troublesome to subsequent moral reformers and genteel advocates of social control. Rather, theatre managers in the 1820s and 1830s attempted to capitalize upon the exclusivity issue (Edmund Simpson at the Park, for; Thomas Hamblin at the Bowery, against). In this context, fashion becomes a matter of what is patronized rather than who does the patronizing.[41]

The management of the Park would eventually fail in its attempt to ally its rat-infested and dilapidating structure with *bon ton*, with the earlier high Republican period of George Washington and Thomas Jefferson, indeed with the term and substance of culture itself. The democratized Bowery would fare better in the 1830s and 1840s, but at the price of theatre as it had been known in the early century and of previous definitions of culture. The Chatham, two blocks from City Park but the same distance from Five Points – soon to become a legendary slum and haunt of vice – would not survive Mrs. Trollope's visit by a year, transforming in 1832 into a Presbyterian chapel. Though historians situate the Chatham as a "lower-class" resort, it seems largely to have sought a family clientele (to which Mrs. Trollope was exposed in a most telling way), and in its prices to have been within norms for theatre patronage throughout the city.

Fig. 7. The interior of the Chatham Garden Theatre in 1825 (lithograph, courtesy of the Museum of the City of New York, gift of Stephen C. Clark).

What made it so condemned by fashion may have been its architecture rather than its proximity to a low-income housing area.[42]

Functioning as a theatre during March–June 1831, when Mrs. Trollope was in New York, the Chatham offered would-be patrons a cartographic challenge. Indeed, the *New York Mirror* felt obliged to supply its readers a road map to the theatre, advising that "the *enterance* [*sic*] to the theatre is through the Hall of [a] dwelling house in Chatham Street." One walked through this hallway into a garden: "[Y]ou proceed onward to the fountain, which throws up a refreshing column of pure water directly in front of the folding doors to the Theatre. Passing through these doors you ascend, by a double flight of stairs (to the right and left) to the lobby of the first circle of boxes" (Fig. 7), which, with the second tier, was home to an estimated nine hundred people. These sat in cubicles open to the air at the ceiling and at the back, where "a person can witness the performances without taking a seat within." Obscured from the street and overhung by strangers, the *bon ton* could retreat to the lobby-level balcony fronting the garden for refreshment and to escape from the heat of summer – if not from the cold of winter, which permeated their boxes as a result of perforated walls and doorways covered only by blinds.[43]

Nursing babies, coatless sprawling men, the smell of onions, noise, and the ceaseless spitting of tobacco haunted Mrs. Trollope's visits to the theatre in Cincinnati, Washington, and Philadelphia as well as in New York. Indeed, the freedom of antebellum audience behavior in America is well documented and constitutes one of the dominant cultural myths of the city. Play texts, novels, and nonfictional accounts nurture other images: the city of high life and low, of aristocrats and folk heroes, of greenhorns and city slickers, but most particularly of success and failure, images that stage the city as resolutely as *The Forest Rose* stages the transcendental village and *The People's Lawyer* the town hero. Significantly, the urban space would produce not one hero equal to all situations, such as the Yankee (couth or uncouth), but varied heroes who compete successfully in diverse urban spaces. To these heroes we turn in Chapters 2 and 3, but it is useful to take space here to consider two stagings of the city itself: the worlds of *Fashion* (1845) and of *The Poor of New York* (1857).[44]

The city materialized by Anna Mowatt's *Fashion* – which premiered 24 March 1845 at the Park Theatre, then on its last legs – devolves from the common comic text of virtue led astray by affluence. The play's author was the daughter of a substantial New York merchant and the child bride of a financially imprudent lawyer. Her French upbringing and boarding-school education served well in her financial reversals, but nothing as well as her status as a lady of quality. Simpson, the manager of the Park, was a family friend and neighbor who not only gave her play its premiere but burked the traditional steps in an acting career to start Mrs. Mowatt as a star at his theatre. In her public life, Anna Mowatt combined "quality" with self-reliance in a manner exemplary of the heroines of novels and of her own character Gertrude, product of a genteel education in upstate New York but committed to independence as a governess-companion to the fashion-driven Tiffanys. This text of class and democracy is given a distinctly American reading in *Fashion:* Gertrude reminds the importuning French "count" that she is an American (virtuous), albeit a servant and an orphan; meanwhile, the wealthy moral arbiter of the play, the merchant and rentier Trueman, creates nature's nobleman and woman out of the native (white) clay, saying, "But we *have* kings, princes, and nobles in abundance – of *Nature's stamp*, if not of *Fashion's* – we have honest men, warmhearted and brave, and we have women – gentle, fair, and true, to whom no title could add *nobility*." Trueman also articulates a traditional racism, characterizing Zeke, Mrs. Tiffany's liveried free-black footman, as "a grinning nigger tricked out in scarlet regimentals."[45]

The nationalistic sentiments in Mowatt's play have analogues in the town plays discussed earlier in this chapter, but *Fashion* also speaks the urban creed for achievement in antebellum New York: that money makes fashion and position in the city, and that it is acquired "on the true American high-pressure system." In an environment where self-exertion drives out reflection, fashion becomes a cloak for vice and prompts its slaves "to substitute etiquette for virtue, decorum for purity, manners for morals" (Mrs. Tiffany, Seraphina, Count Jolimatre). The urban rush for success can produce a "mad descent . . . to ruin," as the merchant Tiffany discovers when he finds himself both pandering his daughter and blackmailed by his clerk Snobson. Mowatt's *Fashion* sends a double message, however: It extols good character traits, such as independence and self-reliance (in the heroine Gertrude and as "punishment" for the country-exiled Tiffany women), yet provides salvation by good luck (that Gertrude is Trueman's heir, that Trueman will cover Tiffany's forgery, that Seraphina does not marry the bogus Count, etc.). "Achievement" here is driven by the kind of "fortune" that fueled nineteenth-century urban success myths. In such landscapes of desire, even villains go unpunished: Importunate counts become haute-cuisine pastry chefs, overweening clerks look forward to becoming "men of genius in the West," and dishonest urban merchants are told,

You must sell your house and all these gewgaws, and bundle your wife and daughter off to the country. There let them learn economy, true independence, and home virtues, instead of foreign follies. As for yourself, continue your business – but let moderation, in future, be your counsellor, and let *honesty* be your confidential clerk.[46]

The business of America is not to be impeded by the pursuit of fashion – or by the odd forgery.

Fashion depicts a world of privilege, a universe in which dreams have come true, and the very benignity of its ending betrays a view of reversals of this privilege as temporary and readily foiled. Dion Boucicault's *The Poor of New York*, derived from Brisbarre and Nus's stage hit *Les Pauvres de Paris*, had many subsequent incarnations: as *The Streets of London*, *The Streets of Philadelphia*, *The Poor of Liverpool*, *The Streets of Dublin*, and (reincarnated) as *The Streets of New York*. As the play text and contemporaneous accounts of its staging make clear, the play offered New York a double shot of entertainment. One barrel dispensed local references to Union Square, Five Points, Fifth Avenue, the Astors and "Livingstones," the *Herald*, the Academy of Music, the Union Club, the panics of 1837 and 1857, and an all-too-typical blaze in the "full-of-fire city." The other barrel aimed at a moral tale of virtue succeeding through hard work and self-reliance. *The Poor of New York*, like *The People's Lawyer*, foregrounds a text of authenticity. In the city, with so many indigenous types, the native may be anyone in "the high-pressure system," contested again at the intersection of class, but without *The People's Lawyer*'s text of controlling the civilly disobedient. Authenticity in the urban space is a matter of morals, not speech, dress, and manners. Boucicault shrewdly both erases and underscores class differences by positioning the struggle for success within dual economic crises (the panics of 1837 and 1857) and among forces larger than claims to space: good and evil themselves.[47]

Legitimacy in the urban environment of *The Poor of New York* is a matter of authenticating claims, without which the ethical speaks as only one word against others. Boucicault's legitimator is "the receipt," material witness to a $100,000 deposit that the corrupt banker Bloodgood uses to save himself in the panic of 1837. Evil saves good when the blackmailing clerk Badger returns twenty years later (via a vigilante-enforced exit from California – the escape valve imploding eastward) to milk more from Bloodgood's second and much larger panic-driven fortune. The original depositor, (sea) Captain Fairweather, dead of apoplexy shortly after the transaction, leaves a buffeted family behind: Son, daughter, and wife hang onto Brooklyn Heights gentility for twenty years until economic crisis drives them to the by-now well-developed slums of Five Points. Capable of looking both up and down the economic scale, the Fairweathers are witness to speculation everywhere. Among the upscale, rich Mark Livingstone, school chum of young Fairweather and heir to a square mile of Manhattan real estate, first wastes an inherited fortune "made in those days when fancy stocks were unknown," then "beggars" his mother and himself of all but the precious real estate by speculating in the market and losing. Among the downscale, Puffy the baker relates the saga of many middle-class entrepreneurs in the boom and bust economy of antebellum America:

[O]ver speculated like the rest on 'em. I expanded on a new-fangled oven, that was to bake enough bread in six hours to supply the whole United States – got done brown in it myself – subsided into Bowery, expanded again on woffles [*sic*], caught a second time – obliged to contract to a twelve foot front on Division Street. Mrs P. tends the indoor trade – I do a locomotive business in potatoes, and we let our second floor. My son Dan sleeps with George Washington No. 4, while Mrs. P. and I make out under the counter; Mrs. P., being wide, objects some, but I says – says I, "My dear, everybody must contract themselves in these here hard times."[48]

When speculation switches rich and poor at whim, authenticating virtue requires some hard evidence. Fortunately, Badger knows that the truth is worth the paper it's written on.

With money (and legitimacy) restored, noblesse can be obliged to extend itself to the less fortunate – Livingstone to his Fairweather friends and the Fairweathers to the Puffys. Class remains class: The Puffys have to be dragged onto the carpets of their rich friends, while Livingstone bemoans the poor *middle* class and dismisses beggary as bogus. Nonetheless, class does not authenticate virtue in the urban environment; that is a matter of deeds, of moral evidence as material as Badger's receipt. For Livingstone and Puffy to speculate with their own fortunes hurts no one but themselves, as Puffy observes (though Mrs. Livingstone and Mrs. Puffy might be less sanguine). The moral impact of Bloodgood's speculations, on the other hand, is the stuff of the tabloids: "Wall Street is a perch, on which a row of human vultures sit, whetting their beaks, ready to fight over the carcass of a dying enterprise." Acts that authenticate are described in the play (largely by the cynical Badger) as stagings – "worth fifty cents," "the scene opens in a bank" – performed in some cases, the play suggests, in theatre boxes and supper clubs. Authenticity distinguishes not only true and false (as love from not love), but relationships as well, such as those among love, riches, and happiness. The view is not ingenuous: Poverty and want are bad, and one saves loved ones from them. To pray "God bless us, and pity the Poor of New York" is heartfelt enough when that fate may readily be yours.[49]

By firing both barrels in one entertainment, Boucicault's *The Poor of New York* localizes and authenticates a fictional city in which, as in Mowatt's *Fashion*, there is ample opportunity for staging both the self and the

"American." Not surprisingly, and perhaps least because Boucicault was British, the signals given off are mixed ones. The morally corrupt Bloodgood creates by his very example a depraved, cold, and self-centered child. Such is the legacy, we are taught, of greed to succeeding generations, and certainly the play reinforces self-sacrifice, charity, and honesty in adversity as the social virtues to be transmitted by caring parents to children, families to families, and urbanites to each other. Accordingly, the blackmailing Badger can be reformed by poverty into the Fairweathers' champion (and a bank dick), and the unrepentant Bloodgood gets off with the restoration of the Captain's original fortune.[50]

Still, acquiring money, not giving it away, is the focus of Boucicault's play. Counterfeiting the name of one of New York's most prominent families (Livingston) to suggest the complicity of wealth and tradition in speculation, Boucicault gives Mark Livingstone a speech in support of the shabby, genteel middle class, a discourse staged as a stump speech that attracts (perhaps satirically) both a crowd and a reporter from the sensation-seeking *New York Herald*:

The poor! Whom do you call the poor? Do you know them? Do you see them? They are more frequently found under a black coat than under a red shirt. The poor man is the artist who is obliged to pledge the tools of his trade to buy medicines for his sick wife. The lawyer who, craving for employment, buttons up his thin paletot to hide his shirtless breast. These needy wretches are poorer than the poor, for they are obliged to conceal their poverty with the false mask of content – smoking a cigar to disguise their hunger – they drag from their pockets their last quarter, to cast it with studied carelessness, to the beggar, whose mattress at home is lined with gold. These are the most miserable of the Poor of New York.

Indeed, it is difficult to find the poor in this play. We, like Puffy, must ask of the supposedly impoverished young scion, "You, poor; you who own a square mile of New York?" and wonder how the Puffys, reduced to selling potatoes on the street and subletting rooms, can still put a full-course dinner for seven on the table. Finally, though in their tenement garret the Fairweather women play out a suicide scenario written by want, their poverty is temporary; indeed, help is already on the way.[51]

By 1840, most of the area below Fourteenth Street in Manhattan was occupied, leaving behind in the inexorable march of progress along its confining grid many of the poor of New York. When Boucicault's melodrama opened seventeen years later (in 1857) at Wallack's on Broadway at Broome, the playhouse was well above the still-operating Bowery Theatre and close to the site of the once outlying Lafayette Circus; yet Wallack's was itself some fourteen blocks south of the 1840 mark for "the upper part of the city," a leading edge that had long since left behind the Exchange and City Hall as centers of culture. Like his competitors, the enterprising Wallack would soon chase the edge northward, just as antebellum American cities like Manhattan swept past the exploding problems of vast and sudden growth without solving them. The lure of sunshine and shadow would call more and more players to the urban stage to contest for control of the real or imagined city. The resulting competition is tellingly expressed in displays of theatrical opulence and in the incessant tobacco spitting that defaces them, in plays that trumpet equal opportunity and in segregated seating policies that mock them. It is not the compartmentalization of theatres that speaks this text, but the very clustering of customs, behaviors, and interests that defies ready hierarchizing, a culture repositioning itself in space over and over again as the antebellum decades wear forward.[52]

The Frontier

The history that was already written in America, which the antebellum decades would overwrite with their own characteristic energies, has been told largely in terms of white men and their visions of town and city, of philosophy and social responsibility, of materiality and success. To be sure, the universalizing tendencies in these writings of history evoke the skepticism articulated in the Prologue, but the concepts they embrace and the language they use remain inhabited and in play in America. In historical studies, the undermining of dominant antebellum myths of town and city and the denial or renegotiation of claims has shifted the historical gaze from "great" to working men, from men to women, from middle to working class, from genteel to working women, and so on, via excellent studies over recent decades written predominantly by white revisionist historians. Theatre culture participates in these shifts by offering to view contesting claims for authenticity in, for example, the Solon Shingles and the unfashionables in their theatre seats, in the heterogeneous communities caught in the city's clusters and grids, in the constantly revised relationships among a host of performances produced by the relentless movement out and about that characterize antebellum demographies.[53]

"The frontier" is arguably American history's largest totalizing myth. It descended to white antebellumites bracketed by two commanding narratives: the tales of Pocahontas and of Roanoke. The first tale is that of the supportive, nurturing, assimilating wilderness; the second is the untold tale of promise cut off by malice, of rejection, and of loss. If America, as in Locke's imagining, was paradise, it offered equal potential for salvation or for damnation – in material terms, success or failure. The comfortable but confining town with its familiar hierarchies and customs, the invigorating but terrorizing city with its status signs and fluid rules – both had precedent in European experience. The American wild was unique and unknown in Europe for centuries. As part of the great experiment, the descendents of "the Old World" would write their dreams and nightmares upon the frontier. As is suggested by the phrase from Turner that frames this chapter, the frontier, more than any other indigenous space, would write back.[54]

When Andrew Jackson was sworn in as seventh president of the United States (1829), there were twenty-four states in the Union, augmented by three territories: Michigan (including Wisconsin), Arkansas, and Florida (organized in 1822). Both the northwestern (Oregon) and northeastern (Maine) boundaries were disputed by Britain. By 1860, toward the end of James Buchanan's presidency, northern and southern national borders had been established and there were thirty-three states in the Union, occupying the land from the Atlantic Ocean to the western shore of the Mississippi River, plus the areas now Texas (1845), California (1850), and Oregon (1859). Despite the fifteen-year hiatus between the admission to the Union of Missouri in 1821 and of Arkansas in 1836, few eyes could fail to notice that the homelands of the continent's indigenous peoples had been erased from over a third of what was becoming the national map. Few white Americans in 1825 believed indigenous cultures would survive contact with the expansionist ethos. Indeed, in 1802, John Quincy Adams had articulated development as the new errand into the wilderness, a national mission he had pressed against the British at the Ghent meetings ending the War of 1812, pursued as secretary of state under James Monroe (1817–25), and furthered as national policy during his own presidency (1825–9). When Andrew Jackson took office, the forty-year-ratified U.S. government exhibited a schizophrenic persona toward Indians, alternately extorting land from them by means of treaties and promising assimilation to those whom the alienating law dispossessed. The removal of Indians, given their "failure" to adopt Euro-style enterprise, supplied a self-justifying text to the fatality argument ("nothing to be done," "God's will," "inevitable," "march of progress"). Though President Jackson's views were not unprecedented among occupants of the White House, his administration marks the advent of a "policy" – signaled in Jackson's address of 6 December 1830 to the U.S. Congress, asking who would elect a country covered with forests and a few ranging savages over a republic of cities, towns, and farms, improved by art and industry, "occupied by more than 12,000,000 happy people, and filled with all the blessings of liberty, civilization, and religion?"[55]

On 9 February 1822, a delegation of Pawnee, Kansa, Missouri, Omaha, and Oto hosted a farewell celebration on the north lawn of the White House in thanks to President Monroe for his hospitality in inviting them to Washington. From their arrival in the city on 30 November 1821 – the year the last state prior to Jackson's election entered the Union – the delegates had been entertained, fêted, outfitted and gifted, stared at, painted, given medals, invited to teas, balls, and official receptions, and taken to visit theatres, circuses, churches, museums, farms, military installations, civic organizations, and dignitaries, all with the purpose, according to the president's formal reception speech on 4 February 1822, of exposing them to the comforts and might of white society. Responding in turn to this address, the delegates affirmed their own way of life and their hope of keeping white people off their land so they could continue to enjoy it. Thought to be the most remote tribes with whom the government was then in contact, the trans-Mississippi Indians related a full awareness of the encroachment of white cultures on their own and a desire to preserve their history. To that end, they left behind numerous artifacts and presented at their farewell celebration to "half of Washington" a mock council, a vigorous dance (in paint and breechcloths) with full weaponry, "and exhibited the operation of scalping and tomahawking in fine style." The three-hour theatrical was an enormous success, and contemporaneous accounts repeatedly describe the western visitors as dignified and impressive. The delegates' views of their white hosts were not solicited.[56]

Ceremonial presentations of this sort appear to have been the earliest red–white cultural interaction of the performer–audience type. These had been followed by white stagings of "Indian" ceremonies in theatres, dating in post-Revolutionary America to (at least) 1804, though there are accounts of Native Americans in London theatres from colonial times. It is often uncertain whether those performing the advertised songs, dances, and scalping exhibitions were red or white, though they were usually publicized as the former. These exhibitions were staged throughout the antebellum decades in museums and halls, where they formed parts of cultural exhibits (of paintings and artifacts). On at least two occasions (in 1828 and in 1834), "Indians" were exhibited as a circus act, though this venue does not appear commonplace until after the Civil War. A characteristic theatricalized exhibition of the antebellum decades was offered 1 April 1828 by Peale's Museum in New York, an art gallery and natural history museum established by Rubens Peale (of the celebrated family of painters) of the kind subsequently typified by Barnum's. The exhibition offered, "for a short time, two young Indian chiefs of the Onondaga tribe" chanting, doing war dances, displaying native costumes and artifacts, and enacting a scalping ritual.[57]

On 5 April 1828, Sagoyewatha (1756?–1830), known as the "celebrated Indian Chief, Red Jacket, [took] leave of his white bretheren [*sic*]" at Masonic Hall in New York, a gathering place for the city's (chiefly Whig) gentlemen of property and standing about five blocks from Peale's Museum, at the other end of City Hall Park. With the aid of an interpreter, the Seneca leader "addressed the audience, and other warriors danced and sang and revealed the customs of their people." Recently removed by the Seneca tribal council – an action he had protested in Washington the preceding year, where his likeness was taken by Charles Bird King for a War Department portrait (1828) – Red Jacket was a skilled orator and opponent of assimilation. The Iroquois League (which included both the Seneca and Onondaga) had largely supported the British in the Revolutionary War and was internally divided in the matters of Christianization and land sales, both of which Red Jacket opposed. By 1828, the elderly Seneca had achieved iconic status as a "natural Indian" among whites, yet portraits of him and the New York leave-taking tell the story of a collision of stagings influencing both cultures. On the one hand is George Catlin's 1828 painting of Red Jacket near his upstate New York home, "standing there in the attitude of deep thought, dressed with much care in complete Indian costume, a very interesting memorial," a biographer opined, "presenting evident marks of being one of nature's noblemen." King's portrait of the same year shows Red Jacket in "white" clothing, whereas Robert

Weir's 1828 New York studio portrait, perhaps taken during the April visit, shows Red Jacket full figure, dressed "in the costume which he deemed most appropriate to his character," a fringed coat, with tomahawk and Washington medal. A simplified version of the costume in Weir's likeness was common dress for white frontier figures; it can be seen in paintings (see Ranney's 1849 *Daniel Boone's First View of Kentucky*) and in the famous woodcut from the 1830s of the actor James H. Hackett as the frontier character Nimrod Wildfire (see Fig. 8, below), often connected with Crockett's *Almanacs.*[58]

Red Jacket was in failing health and near the end of a hard life, reason enough for his farewell, but his visit to New York has inescapable political colorings in the climate of 1828, the year Andrew Jackson gained the presidency. Pursuant to the 1823 Supreme Court ruling that indigenous peoples held their land by right of occupancy, the Cherokee had adopted a constitution of sovereignty (1827) to forestall state intervention in their affairs. Emboldened by Jackson's election, the Georgia legislature, in December 1828, declared jurisdiction over all tribal residents. The federal government's refusal to enforce the Supreme Court ruling paved the way for numerous bogus and coerced treaties "voluntarily" ceding tribal lands to the government for sale to the states. Land gone, Native Americans would be removed "for their own welfare." Much of this scenario lay beyond Red Jacket's lifetime, and despite general removal of other eastern tribes by 1848, the Seneca would continue to inhabit portions of their lands in upstate New York, though much pressed by white assimilationist tactics against their traditions of landholding and governance.[59]

Amid mounting pressure for a policy of removal, Red Jacket's leavetaking from the prominent Masons of New York, though essentially a private gathering, constituted a diplomatic visit of a sort still common in official circles. Taken in context with the exhibition at Peale's, however, the entertainment provided by Red Jacket's associates becomes indistinguishable to white audiences in most of its externals from theatrical stagings of the Indian. In one venue (Masonic Hall), indigenous culture is displaced to alien environments by Native Americans; in another (Peale's Museum) the "alien" is inserted by whites into contexts defining white culture. Overarching these displacements is the staging of Red Jacket and his confederates as unreconstructed, "unspoiled," "natural," "originary" Indians. White admirers and promoters of these traits, such as the painter George Catlin, labored ceaselessly in these decades to create and preserve their vi-

sionary Indian while accepting assimilation and/or removal of the surviving embodiments of their ideal. At the same time, Native Americans
staged that originary figure in an effort to secure a heritage for their pos-
terity, which such stagings themselves marked as permanently altered.[60]

   The venue of choice for white stagings of Indians in the 1830s and 1840s
was the theatre. These were the decades of the greatest popularity of the
Indian play. Not surprisingly, then, historians of the drama, in theatre
studies and out, have concentrated upon these plays, cataloguing their
stereotypes of noble savages, Indian princesses, red devils, squaws, drunkards, victims, and emblems of nature, relating these to the general characteristics of heroes, heroines, and villains in antebellum melodramas as
well as to the political events with which the plays' premieres and revivals
often coincided. So well-told a tale need not be rehearsed here, but there
is a useful caution in noting that binary readings of these plays in terms
of positive and negative stereotypes fail, as contemporary historians right-
fully note, to restore agency to the study of the oppressed of the past. To
read John Augustus Stone's *Metamora; or, The Last of the Wampanoags*
(1829), for example, as an extension of U.S. government Indian removal
policy at once empties out "the Indian," reinscribes the myth of the omnipotent state, and reinserts the white man as the center of the reading
(even though it concerns red men, or, as in G. W. Parke Custis's *Pocahontas* [1830], red women). The project of recentering "the Indian" in the
theatrical historical narrative without proposing a "real" (or "self") against
which an "imaginary" (or "other") can then be pitched is a study in its
own right, but it may be useful to that discourse to chart here some intersections between red and white in the U.S. theatre of the earlier nineteenth century.[61]

   In 1832, the U.S. government fought a war, along that part of the Mississippi River bordering Illinois, Iowa, Wisconsin, and Minnesota, against
Makataimeshekiakiah, a Sauk (or Sac) known as Black Hawk (1767–1838).
The brief war, occasioned by government sale of Sauk and Fox lands,
ended in a massacre of his greatly outnumbered forces at Bad Axe, Wisconsin, following which Black Hawk was imprisoned near St. Louis.
Through the fall and winter of 1832–3, Black Hawk and the other Sauk
prisoners continued to make news (popular journalism developed during
these decades) and were visited in jail by luminaries like Washington Irving, who found them "forlorn . . . emaciated and dejected" (not surprisingly, though a disappointment to Irving). Indeed, Irving's quest for the nat-

ural Indian was mirrored in George Catlin's visit, when the artist declined to paint the prisoners in chains, as they were kept, rendering Black Hawk instead in full regalia and as though he were free. In the spring, the 66-year-old leader and his allies were transported by steamboat, stagecoach, and railroad to the East in order to absorb fully the extent of white might. A hostile audience with President Jackson in Washington on 25 April preceded reincarceration in nearby Fort Monroe. There Black Hawk was painted by the leading romantic portraitist of the period, Robert Sully, in the attitude of a southern politician, and by John Wesley Jarvis and Charles Bird King in a quasi-regimental costume supplied by Andrew Jackson.[62]

The Sauk prisoners of war were a media event everywhere they were displayed. Already influential in the elections of 1832, the Black Hawk War became a theme in the staging of Jackson's second inaugural year, which involved a progress through the East that overlapped Black Hawk's tour as a prisoner of war. On 6 June 1833, both "distinguished lions" attended the Front Street Theatre in Baltimore, where, "it is said, that the attention of the house was very equally divided between them." Black Hawk, having thus both discharged his role in a public forum frequently used for such stagings and confirmed his character as a worthy and dangerous foe, was released from jail by Jackson to complete his tour. The Sauk trailed the president into Philadelphia (10–14 June) and arrived in New York (14–22 June), two days after a visit by Jackson that, complained former New York Mayor Philip Hone, attempted to rival the progress of Lafayette as the nation's guest. In New York's media circus, the Sauk "were conducted with ceremony to the theatres, the public gardens, the arsenal, and other places of interest." Pressed by mobs and subject to countless invented and demeaning newspaper stories, the beseiged Black Hawk persuaded his military escort to shorten the tour, bypassing Jackson's progress through New England. Final humiliation followed the Sauk return to Rock Island, Illinois, 1 August 1833, the first anniversary of the massacre at Bad Axe. Black Hawk was there subjected to a mortification feast before the peace chief Keokuk, into whose custody he had been paroled.[63]

The staging of the defeat of Black Hawk and the Sauk was not unlike the triumphal display of prominent prisoners in ancient Rome. Indeed, Black Hawk's fame and popularity among whites followed him for years. In 1837, when the now 70-year-old leader was taken by Keokuk to Washington (where Charles Bird King again painted him) and then upon a second tour of the major eastern cities, Black Hawk "was waited upon by a great concourse of citizens." Like Red Jacket, Black Hawk was a "natural" Indian, but of military rather than oratorical repute. Moreover, like the Indian play hero Metamora, his fame rested upon defiance of authority and limitation; but it also rested upon the acknowledgment of defeat. As the antagonist in a production not of his choosing, the hostage Black Hawk staged an Indian wanting only, like white men, to be free. From this, culture staged Black Hawk as an icon, to be circulated but never possessed, the counterfeit of individual freedom on the boundary of the expanding frontier.[64]

A further staging in red–white interactions in the American theatre of the 1830s concerns Coowescoowe, the Cherokee known as John Ross (1790–1866), son of a Scottish immigrant and a part-Cherokee mother, who led a party opposing removal of the Cherokee and their confederates from the southeastern states and their confinement on reserves in the trans-Mississippi West. Cherokee removal had reached crisis point by 6 February 1836, when the revival of George Washington Parke Custis's play *Pocahontas; or, The Settlers of Virginia* was offered at the National Theatre in Washington. In their success at coexistence by adopting and modifying white customs, the Cherokee most clearly indicted Indian policy in the eyes of whites, being neither "naturals" (like Red Jacket), requiring protection, nor warriors (like Black Hawk) to be handled as a military threat. Symbolically perhaps, the likenesses of John Ross made by Catlin in 1837–8 and by King in 1837 show him in "European" clothing; nor does there appear to be a portrait of him otherwise attired.[65]

The vogue for Indian drama has been attributed to Custis's 1827 *Indian Prophesy*, though his 1830 *Pocahontas* was the more popular play. If Stone's *Metamora* (1829) is the archetypal dramatization of the Indian warrior, *Pocahontas* staged the ultimate assimilationist Indian. One can hardly imagine a worse simultaneity than the Cherokee antiremoval cause, at that time being protested by a Ross-led delegation to Washington, and a revival of Custis's propacifist Indian drama. The coincidence of the two does not surprise, given the topicality of Indians in 1836, but the staging of this particular red–white cultural intersection tells several stories. The play's author was the foster step-grandson of George Washington, a Federalist aristocrat as close to American royalty as it was possible to come, whose name legitimated the Pocahontas myth of the supportive and assimilating Indian. Indeed, in his thank-you speech at the opening of the National's revival of *Pocahontas,* Custis described the New World as "a wild and savage desert" transformed by the arrival of gallant cavaliers into a magnificent empire. It was a view synchronous with Jackson's, toward whom, despite different political affiliations, Custis entertained friendly feelings and about whose military exploits Custis had earlier written a play.[66]

A second *Pocahontas* story derives from a competition for authenticity between the actual Cherokee then in Washington and the actors playing Indians in the drama, who were outfitted in native costumes loaned by the Commissioner of the Indian Bureau and a private military collector. Not content to *look* Indian, the National promised eager audiences to *be* Indian, advertising in the *Globe* that, in the second act,

TEN CHEROKEE CHIEFS, the Delegation of the tribe, having been much gratified by the performance of the National Drama, and anxious to give it full effect, have most liberally offered their services and will this evening appear and perform their real INDIAN WAR DANCE, exhibiting Hate, Triumph, Revenge, etc., and go through the CEREMONY OF SCALPING.

A fews days later, the 13 February *Globe* ran a "news" item (not far from the latest dispatches concerning the Florida War against the Seminoles), reporting:

The fifth representation of Mr. Custis's splendid melodrama *Pocahontas* brought together a very large audience, the interest of which was increased by the introduction of John Ross and his "merrie men," who performed their real Indian war dance, exhibiting hate, triumph, revenge, etc., and went through the agreeable ceremony of scalping, all of which seemed to give great satisfaction to a crowded house. The white men forming the *dramatis personae* were determined not to be outdone by their red allies, and their exertions were so effective that the whole went off with much *eclat*.[67]

The denial of appearance that John Ross subsequently issued, in protest of his commodification, suggests a third *Pocahontas* story. Ross's letter was printed as news in the 15 February 1836 *Globe* (I quote the entire article):

Among the theatrical communications thrust into our columns without our knowledge was one saying that "John Ross and his 'merrie men' performed their real Indian war dance," etc. We believe some such notice was also contained in the play bills. We have received a letter from Mr. Ross in which he says that "neither I nor any of my associates of the Cherokee delegation have appeared on the stage. We have been occupied with matters of graver import than to become the allies of white men forming the dramatis personae. We have too high a regard for ourselves – too deep an interest in the welfare of our people, to be merry-making under our misfortunes," etc.

The unchastened National responded with an advertisement that the Cherokee delegation had "been respectfully invited to attend" the last performance of the revival, "and the majority have accepted the invitation."[68] It seems unlikely appearance followed announcement, for John Ross clearly sought to stage a different kind of Indian: serious, self-regarding, preoccupied with important national affairs. In dress, speech, and customs, Ross distanced himself and his cause from the nostalgic staging of Red Jacket and the show-trial reifications of Black Hawk. A living embodiment of the interactions of red and white, Ross was skilled at establishing analogies that brought enormous white support to his antiremoval efforts, a rhetoric of resistance that refused theatrical appropriation at the same time it sought the national stage. It was a discourse subject to assimilationist interpretations of the sort that equated John Ross and the real-life displacement of the Cherokee with Custis's melodramatic staging of the mythologized tribe of *Pocahontas*.

The many staged Indians of the antebellum decades offer numerous texts of America as whites interpreted it and of Native American responses to contradictory white and red translations of the shared national experience. Historian Anne Norton argues that the southern states, site of the most systematic eastern removal efforts, absorbed the image of the rebellious but independent Indian as the embodiment of regional loyalty and resistance to national hegemony – a southern equivalent of the North's staged Yankee. As the Civil War approached (and with considerable historical irony), the federal government would characterize southern whites as violent and rebellious savages. From the vantage of the frontier, the sale of tribal lands to pay for removal prefaced a doctrine of consumption as conquest, the commodified text of manifest destiny. Coined in 1845 by *New York Morning News* editor John L. O'Sullivan and promoted by William Gilpin as history, "manifest destiny," like "the Indian," is a discourse larger than the present study can encompass. It intersects significantly, however, with depictions of the frontier and how white Americans, secure in the government's solution of the eastern "Indian problem," came to claim "by right of our manifest destiny to overspread and possess the whole of the continent which Providence has given us."[69]

Recent art-historical reassessments of the frontier suggest the futility of defining it in terms either of heroic images or national sins, since such binary readings deny the complexity of the ideological content depictions of the frontier contain. Antebellum art – whether styled in buckskins inside the frame (as in George Caleb Bingham's 1851–2 *Daniel Boone Escorting Settlers* or William S. Jewett's 1850 *The Promised Land*) or depicted on the receiving end of expansionist bulletins (as in Richard Caton Woodville's 1848 *War News from Mexico* or William Sidney Mount's 1850 *California News*) – vividly projected the America "out there" and its reception "in here." Art's role in the orchestration of expansionist ideology is traceable in the views of artists, the content of their paintings, and in the rhetoric of the American Art-Union, which created a taste for American art by defining what it should be and distributing samples to its membership (e.g., Woodville's *War News*, Bingham's 1847 *The Jolly Flat Boat Men*, Kensett's 1851 "Mount Washington," illustrations of American landscapes, and Cole's 1850 *Dream of Arcadia*). Literary and nonfictional accounts of the frontier, rather than direct observation, inspired many of these renderings. Cole drew on *The Last of the Mohicans*, for example; other antebellum artists referenced travel books as well as novels and poems. Indeed, most of the paintings of Boone and other iconic figures were drawn from printed accounts rather than from life.[70]

Appropriated and redistributed in multiple spaces, the frontier of novel-cum-painting-cum-engraving-cum-penny sketch references complex imaginings. More often than depicting expansion, however, or the "last stand of the Indian," antebellum art and literature depicts the American landscape as paradise. As the site both of earthly delight and primal conflict, of Eden and Armageddon (like the antebellum decades, "the beginning in rebellion and the end in war"), antebellum depictions of paradise America intersect and promote a frontier that is both "in here" and "out there." The Hudson River school of landscape artists, but still more the luminist painters and photographers devolving from them, often depicted "settled" areas – the Catskills, the forests of the East, the coastal marshes, and the sea – painting out or dwarfing the human figure and centering relics or witnesses of human presence in a still, vibrant space. Similarly, writers were taken by the tension between active and still, wild and tame, that came to characterize depictions of America in the antebellum decades. Fitz

Hugh Lane's 1864 painting *Brace Rock, Brace's Cove* and Hawthorne's novel *The Scarlet Letter* (1850) mirror this sense of space, of which Hawthorne says:

Glancing at the looking-glass, we behold – deep within its haunted verge – the smoldering glow of the half-extinguished anthracite, the white moon beams on the floor, and a repetition of all the gleam and shadow of the picture, with one removal further from the actual, and nearer to the imaginative.[71]

From Emerson's perspective as a "transparent eyeball," the overseeing artist took in the horizon but also the small-scale form – Thoreau's promise to "cut a broad swath" but still "shave close." At once a space for still and silent reflection to the men of the town and a space of possession and habitation in the grand scale of the city, "frontier" shifts from its European signification of a separating border to indicate a threshold one lives in and on. So viewed, a culture can see the Native American next door as alien yet treat him or her as a symbol of a mediated self, see the sale of tribal lands in a constituted state of the Union as "settling the frontier," and stage both the Indian and the white pioneer as civilized and savage, simultaneously "in here" and "out there." These boundary disputes locate the political in contradictory, constantly shifting and changing territories. The James Kirke Paulding's *Lion of the West; or, the Kentuckian* (1831) and Louisa Medina's *Nick of the Woods* (1838) offer two of those opposing sites.[72]

The Lion of the West was written by James Kirke Paulding without direct contact with Kentucky or other Old Southwest areas. Crafted from tall tales, phrases, and Davy Crockett anecdotes solicited from friends, Paulding's farce won James H. Hackett's competition for an American play and premiered at the Park Theatre in New York on 25 April 1831. Subsequently redrawn by John Augustus Stone (who had won Edwin Forrest's American play contest in 1829 with *Metamora*) – and perhaps by William Bayle Bernard for its 1833 London production as *The Kentuckian; or, A Trip to New York* – *The Lion* joined Hackett's repertoire of Yankee plays, and its success throughout America and in Europe consolidated his status as America's first comedian. Like the later *Fashion*, *The Lion of the West* concerns a bogus nobleman (this time English) out to snare a wealthy New York merchant's daughter. Since the interest of the piece is Nimrod Wildfire, considered the first "stage frontiersman" – the ring-tailed roarer of popular antebellum fiction and drama (Fig. 8) – the fortune hunter is

"Come back, stranger! or I'll play you like a watermillion!"

Fig. 8. James H. Hackett in his backwoods character of Nimrod Wildfire in *The Lion of the West* (engraving, courtesy of the Hoblitzelle Theatre Arts Library).

readily foiled. Instead, attention focuses on the buckskin-clad Nimrod's gaucheries and his collisions with "Mrs. Wollope," who views most Americans as savages. Because his parents "emigrated to the heart of the Backwoods when they were much less settled than at present[, t]his Nimrod was born a thousand miles from good society, and if his manners are abrupt, they convey a native humor." A land baron, a militia colonel, and a former congressman, the Nimrod of this drama is nonetheless uncultured; indeed, even his relatives acknowledge that his "exuberance of spirits, and his total ignorance of conventional restraint" render him unfit to stand as "a specimen of American gentility."[73]

As the "human cataract from Kentucky," Nimrod Wildfire is a natural force whose vitality and innate goodness need civilizing. However, despite its success – Congressman Crockett is said to have bowed to the likeness Hackett (re)presented in Washington in 1833 – the Nimrod staging of the backwoodsman, with his Paulding-derived racism, was quickly subordinated in antebellum theatre, the type relegated to secondary character status and his broad humor employed to alleviate the rectitude of more genteel frontier heroes. Such a configuration is evident in Louisa Medina's *Nick of the Woods*, which premiered at the Bowery Theatre in New York on 5 February 1838. Set in the Kentucky frontier of 1782, Medina's adaptation of Robert Montgomery Bird's popular and virulently anti-Indian novel was a considerable success and offered in the Jibbenainosay (Nick or Satan of the Woods) a lifetime starring part for the actor Joseph Proctor (Fig. 9).[74]

Its inhabitants dressed in frontier regalia, the environment staged as a wilderness of stockades, encroaching forests, rocky passes, and as a roaring cataract down which the Jibbenainosay is precipitated in a canoe of fire, the frontier of *Nick of the Woods* is the site of civilization gone savage. What in Nimrod Wildfire is crude virtue becomes in Roaring Ralph Stackpole of Medina's *Nick of the Woods* the scruples of a horse thief, however colorful. Similarly, the competent romantic lead in *The Lion*'s New York becomes a life-threateningly incompetent woodsman in *Nick*'s Kentucky. It is the Jibbenainosay, however, who most confounds both civilization and the idea of the frontier as paradise, for he is the renegade Quaker Nathan, a madman crazed by the murder of his family, who has become (although their deadly enemy) a "white Indian." Like the savage red men who populate the tale and those in the demimonde of race (Tellie Doe, the Pocahontas-like half-breed), the woodcrafty Nathan serves his purpose in the play and is erased. The frontier needs and uses survival lore, but there is no thanksgiving for vengeance in the service of destruction. The forest primeval is civilization's legacy, and Nick/Nathan embodies the contradictions of the "out there" in the "in here" of eastern theatre culture.[75]

* * * * *

AS HISTORICAL SITES, the antebellum town, city, and frontier suggest real and ideal constructs that both constitute and contest one another. Often, experience is violently bracketed by conflicting ideology. The town, for example, constrains individuals via class and race at the same time it is home to transcendental texts of personal liberty. In a similar way, American cities exemplify transcendental texts of individualism at the same time they stage widening socioeconomic gaps among the cities' many peoples. Nor in pitting the individual against the communal are frontiers im-

Fig. 9. Joseph Proctor in Louisa Medina's *Nick of the Woods* (lithograph from Odell, *Annals of the New York Stage*, vol. 4).

mune from restaging the contests characteristic of the town and the city, simultaneously taking in and rubbing out Indian and frontier cultures alike. The inconsistency in all these stagings is ironically summarized in depictions of Edwin Forrest as the staged Indian Metamora, whose costume, early and late (see Fig. 10), traverses antebellum history in moving the native across time from northeastern forests to trans-Mississippi plains, just as Forrest made him the hero of town and city theatregoers and the archtypically independent and individualistic "American" figure. In the process of contesting each other, oppositions of these sorts recombine into new stagings. In this interplay, the real and the imagined exert equal force, continuously interact, and attempt to accommodate contradictions as extreme as closed village communities and expansionism, white supremacy and democracy, elites and egalitarianism, frontiers and development, slavery, genocide, and economic exploitation and a rhetoric of equal opportunity, freedom, and prosperity. These stagings are extended in other chap-

Fig. 10. Edwin Forrest as Metamora (*left,* from a picture by F. S. Agate, from *Annals of the New York Stage,* vol. 3; *right,* photo by Matthew Brady, in Richard Moody, *Edwin Forrest: First Star of the American Stage* [New York: Alfred A. Knopf, 1960]).

ters, other theatres of culture. There, to cite a few examples, Bowery B'hoys transplant themselves to California, the same control agendas exerted against Indians are applied to workers and women (and are similarly unsuccessful and transformed), and the constitutents of "American" culture are further multiplied and divided. For these readings of the past, we look further on.

2

Liminal Spaces

Wealth is in application of mind to nature; and the art of getting rich consists not in industry, much less in saving, but in a better order, in timeliness, in being at the right spot.
— Ralph Waldo Emerson, "Wealth" (1860)

The old Bowery, pack'd from ceiling to pit with its audience mainly of alert, well dress'd, full-blooded young and middle-aged men, the best average of American born mechanics . . . to me as much a part of the show as any.
— Walt Whitman, "Booth and the Bowery" (1885)

The bourgeoisie have constantly been rising since the twelfth century.
— Lawrence Stone, *The Past and the Present Revisited* (1987)

IN 1847, DANIEL WEBSTER commemorated the inauguration of the railroad from Boston to Lebanon, New Hampshire, by observing, "It is the spirit and influence of free labor, it is the indomitable industry of a free people, that has done all this." Witness to the "extraordinary era in which we live," Webster thought it "altogether new" and unprecedented, "miraculous" and wonderful, yet presaging an unknown and unspeakable future. Like the railroad Webster celebrated, movement in the antebellum decades is often characterized geographically – locomotion across a terrain to "fill" and "settle" a landscape – the linking of town, city, and frontier in that developmental chain lauded by Andrew Jackson and mandated in "manifest destiny." There are spaces above the ground, however, that Webster's dynamic railroad does not traverse. One of these topographies or climates is mapped in Webster's 1832 *Dictionary*, which locates three classes in America. This chapter takes up relationships between class and work, which are considered as liminal spaces – threshold areas without fixed extents or durations – characterized by movement and multidirectionality, and, in the antebellum decades, by racial, sexual, and ethnic inequity.[1]

In addition to an awareness of fundamental changes in the technology and organization of daily life, antebellum Americans have left evidence of "a sharp increase in confusion over social roles." Some of this confusion escapes from Chapter 1's transcendental visions of paradise ribbed with sociopolitical inconsistencies, from Yankees, frontiersmen, and Indians as icons of freedom yet social outcasts, from fashions in theatres, materialism, and morality, and from dramatic shifts in the town, city, and frontier as spaces of representation. Constructs of work and class in the antebellum decades pose further ambiguities, signaled, for example, in the many words used in those years to identify a middle social stratum: "great middle stripe of population," "great middle working class," "middle class," "middling ranks," "middling sorts, "middle classes," "people of the middle condition," and "middling classes." Historians have joined class and work in further distinctions: business class and working class; the existence (or not) of an intermediate class between proletariat and ruling class; class consciousness versus class awareness; handwork (mechanics and artisans) versus headwork (clerks and management); bourgeois as distinct from middle class; petit bourgeois; upper, middle, and lower class; class versus stratification; skilled workers as distinct from laborers; and the viability or inviability of class as a concept.[2]

Though the temptation remains strong among historians to construct if not definitions for all time, then at least a tripartite class structure for nineteenth-century America, theorists have increasingly suggested that class "is not a thing but a relation; it is seen in the activities of people, and refracted in the way that they view the world." Recent histories of antebellum America engage relationships of religion, association, work, aspiration, consumption, ethnicity, race, gender, and residence as readily as they do ideology and income. Just as these change our notion of class, the relational approach alters our views of work, race, associations, and the rest. For all this, viewing class as a historiographical construct (structure, formation, hegemony) remains seductive in historical work and colors even antebellum researches that are relational in what they study – as can be seen in tripartite containments such as those attributed to Mrs. Trol-lope and in binary constructs like highbrow versus lowbrow culture. So ideologically loaded does "class" become that it is tempting to abandon the word; yet, despite its imprecision and contradictions, "class" remains an inhabited construct in virtually all discussions of antebellum culture. It spills into discussions of work ("working class") in ways that bind work and class together. How theatre culture is both influenced by and influ-ences some of the relationships characterizing the liminal spaces of work and class in antebellum America is the concern of this chapter.[3]

Work

The antebellum decades were a period of dramatic change in the nature and perception of labor in America, change that had profound effects up-on working men and women. Two aspects of work, how and where work was done, directly affect how labor is regarded. The waged-labor system of workers and managers with which we are familiar was a new configu-ration in the early nineteenth century, replacing the model of live-in ap-prenticeship followed by a journeyman period and then advancement to the rank of master of the trade. In Philadelphia between 1820 and 1860, the number of master craftsmen in the work force dropped from over 34 percent to approximately 16 percent. The depression of upward mobility meant an increase in manual wage earners competing for jobs, "from a mi-nority of 38.6% to a majority of some 55%" during these years.[4]

Despite twentieth-century images of vast New England textile factories, with their controlling agendas for women workers, and middle-state roll-ing mills consuming male laborers, the antebellum manufacturing para-digm was the small shop. In the 1820s, for example, the largest Manhat-tan firms (12) employed twenty-five workers, whereas the next largest (35) employed only ten to twenty-five. In Philadelphia in 1860, 58 percent of firms still had six employees or fewer. Although numbers of employees in shops did grow between 1825 and 1860, typical manufactures in both large and small cities and in towns (perhaps 60 percent) were not heavy industries (toolmaking, gas production, brewing, sugar refining) but small tailor shops, shoe manufactures, carpenter shops, and bakeries of perhaps ten to twenty-five workers apiece in more populated areas. The workers and proprietors of these small shops were extremely vulnerable to market forces – the former to "sweating" (lower wages for higher productivity) and the latter to the ability to wait for payment, store goods, get credit, or secure business support. These forces had profoundly affected manufacturing by midcentury, well before the factory system's dominance of the workplace.[5]

Small-shop manufactory was complicated in urban areas throughout these decades by the practice of outworking, piecework done in homes and workrooms at progressively lower and lower wages. Estimated in New York, for example, at 48.6 percent of craft labor by 1850, outwork conditions in major cities were often appalling. They were also largely "invisible to most customers and chroniclers, hidden from view in the backroom cutters' bureaus and in the outworkers' cellars" scattered throughout the city. Although the invisible, sweated outworker represents the worst aspects of antebellum labor practices, even better placed workers experienced a business infrastructure increasingly characterized by specialization and effacement. Manufacturing in a competitive market – and over longer distances accessible via the Erie Canal and a multiplication of steamboat and railroad lines – required complex activities, including buying, selling, shipping, managing, promoting, subcontracting, estimating profitability, and calculating wages, sales, and other expenses. These proprietary tasks and jobbing and slopping to wholesalers contributed to the growth of a largely young, white, and male clerical segment among workers acting as or dealing with brokers, commission merchants, agents, auctioneers, jobbers, credit reporting agents, advertisers, insurance agents, and freight haulers. Largely invisible workers doing largely invisible work, these clerks were economically and culturally liminal but conspicuous components of antebellum audiences, crowds, and other informal associations.[6]

The segregation of customer and manager from producer in the antebellum decades (Fig. 11) was mirrored not only in a separation of home and workplace (except in some forms of outwork), but in a diversification of workplaces. By 1855, for example, specialists in a single line of goods made up 81 percent of retail advertisers in Philadelphia, 90 percent in New York, and 79 percent in Charleston (Fig. 12). If manufactures became dirtier and more crowded, stores and offices became cleaner and more elegant, emphasizing the separation of headwork and handwork and contrasting sharply with the often grim environments of sweated labor. Better working conditions in, for example, the block-sized show-windowed department stores introduced in the 1850s did not mean higher salaries;

Fig. 11. "Trades and Occupations: Tailor," 1874 (lithograph by Louis Prang, courtesy of the Library of Congress).

Fig. 12. Interior of Charles Oakford's hat store c. 1855 (engraving, courtesy of the Library Company of Philadelphia).

clerks were generally paid less than craftsmen, and craftsmen continued
to lose ground. A *New York Tribune* account of 27 May 1851 and a *New
York Times* report of 8 November 1853 estimated that a skilled worker in
New York City needed $500 to keep an average-sized family (i.e., five) and
made $300 a year, whereas Philadelphia workers averaged $288 in 1850
and needed $500–$600 to sustain modest family life. "Modest family life"
may be variously defined, but historians agree that neither the wages of
skilled nor unskilled workers in antebellum America kept up with rising
costs and that the percentage of poor in the population steadily increased.
Financial panics accelerated the decline in earning power; the crash of
1837, for example, that figures so prominently in *The Poor of New York*,
threw out one-third of the work force. Wages fell 30–50 percent between
1839 and 1843, remaining stationary from 1843 to 1850, while the cost of
living rose nearly 50 percent. Although there is evidence that workers
moved in and out of poverty on a seasonal scale, estimates of 195,000 destitute people in New York City alone in 1855 – a year capping a decade-
long 23 percent drop in real wages – suggest that for many the liminal
space of poverty had become a permanent address.[7]

Despite its clear erosion, the myth of an American artisan system persisted in white American cultures. Trades at which one could prosper and
retain the traditional perquisites of a craftsman – shipbuilding, some forms
of printing and carpentry, and butchering – remained highly visible in politics, clubs, civic celebrations, and in numerous labor and benevolent associations for workers. The impoverishment of the working class and its
mistrust of the wealthy were specifically recognized as political issues as
early as 1829; indeed, the political party system that formed during these
decades appropriated the rhetoric of "the artisan republic" and organized
(pro or con) around it. Many of the wealthy whose fortunes resulted from
a combination of marrying well, having prestigious family names, inherited wealth, kinship ties, and some personal ability, were staunch public
supporters of the notions that they were self-made and that any (white)
man of character and ambition could do the same. Advice books for young
men nourished similar views, as did the successes of artisans in manufac-
turies of locomotives, iron, and machinery, who rose to proprietorships
of large, new enterprises during these decades.[8]

As work became piecemeal, invisible, and dead-ended, and as the cultural and economic gap between workers and their masters widened, worker separated from worker along racial, ethnic, and gender lines. Leonard P.

Curry's researches reveal that competition for housing and jobs between urban free black men and immigrants was "of very limited importance before 1850"; indeed, African Americans constituted an increasingly small percentage of urban populations as the antebellum decades wore on. Despite the reality, however, "black competition" was raised as a labor issue by politicians, workers, nativists, and others. Accordingly, African Americans were forbidden at various times and places during the first half of the nineteenth century to operate shops, haul goods, or to work as artisans in border South and northern cities (opportunities for free black skilled male workers, Curry's data show, were best in the deep South). Free black men and all women were also refused admission to trade organizations in the 1850s. Although the poverty, even pauperism, of sweating was most tellingly experienced in the antebellum decades by free black and foreign-born common laborers, nativists saw competition from these groups, not outwork and other shifts in manufacturing, as causing the decline of the artisan paradise in America. Increases in immigrant workers (male and female) and the prospect of a flood of freed slaves into urban job markets gave antebellum nativists a ready text. Politicians were quick to exploit division among "the productive classes," to indict "parasitic" bankers and mercantilists and "idle" blacks and Indians, in their quest to secure an electorate lacking traditional leadership allegiances. The "facts" of immigration were marshaled to support nativist claims. When the Erie Canal opened in 1825, for example, about 20,000 (11 percent) of Manhattanites were foreign born; by 1860, 384,000 (48 percent) of the city's 805,000 inhabitants were immigrants. The influx of large numbers of German craftsmen to Manhattan in the late 1840s provided some competition for native artisans, though also support for trade standards and labor organizing. Among antebellum whites, many themselves the result of in-migration to cities, it was the 950 percent increase nationwide of unskilled immigrant (largely Irish) labor between 1844 and 1856 that fueled nativist fears of strike breaking, lower wages, and erosion of the apprenticeship system in the skilled trades.[9]

As workers began to individuate *as* workers, to identify themselves as what historians call a class, a white masculine mechanic "culture" began to emerge, taking up some and replacing other artisan conventions of behavior. This culture embraced organizations devoted to amateur sports, dining and drinking, singing, dancing, and drama, while other societies developed, both within and across ethnic lines, to promote professional sports, religious celebrations, politics, labor issues, and many other interests. Publications of all kinds during these years, from inexpensive metropolitan dailies and ethnic newspapers to sporting papers, fashion journals, etiquette books, storypapers, instructional books, and police gazettes, promote (among clerks no less than craftsmen) the artisan ideal: character joined to effort producing financial success. They and the increased social organizations of antebellum America also point, however, to diverse cultures and life-styles among workers.[10]

Elliot Gorn has suggested that "by the antebellum era, the lower wards of Manhattan were dominated demographically by young single males, wage earners who earned their livings with their muscles." Though the number of such men is difficult to determine, their perception as a national urban presence is widely attested in contemporaneous sources, where the regulation of the manly mechanic and the clerk (often boys as young as 14) becomes a text. Volunteer fire units in particular (professional fire and police forces were not common in cities until the Civil War) were viewed as magnets for rowdyism; many of the loosely organized young toughs known as Bowery B'hoys became volunteer firemen, and rivalry among companies often expressed itself in fights and sabotage of equipment. This behavior was exacerbated by companies' ties to taverns, where political groups conducted their affairs (with what effects upon fire control the antebellum press was quick to point out). The mechanic cultivated a distinctive style identifiable (and perceived) as *not* middle class (genteel), but drawn from ethnicity, religion, gender, work, consumption, residence, voluntary associations, and family organization.[11]

As a simulacrum of an urban type, the antebellum manly mechanic suggests not only acceptance but cultivation of difference. Touted as king of the city wards that he dominated, wards that included theatres he patronized, the manly mechanic defined a street culture for antebellumites (Fig. 13); both the public performance and its stage analogues defied gentrification. Numerous reports of audience behavior in antebellum America make clear that acting out was part of attending the theatre. Washington Irving wrote early in the century of patrons in the pit being pelted with foodstuffs from the gallery and of general audience inattention to the performance. Joe Cowell marveled at hats on in the pit and coats off in the boxes. The *New York Mirror* of 24 March 1827 bemoaned the confusion of attire among box patrons. Mrs. Trollope complained of lounging, undress, nursing babies, and spitting (see Fig. 6). The 14 April 1832 *Spirit of the Times*

Fig. 13. Intersection of Cross (now Park), Anthony (now Worth), and Orange (now Baxter) Streets, 1827 (lithograph, collection of the New-York Historical Society).

condemned the peanut crunching that was ubiquitous in New York's theatres. That same year, the *New York Mirror* of 29 December recounted
that Junius Brutus Booth, the father of the subsequently famous (and infamous) family of actors, played Richard III at the Bowery Theatre while
onstage spectators fingered the kingly regalia displayed on a table in Richard's tent. The Bowery came in for even sharper criticism of its audiences'
unruly behavior in the 9 February 1833 *Mirror:*

We wish to say a word about the police of this theatre; although there are, perhaps, more constables in the house than at any other theatre, there is at times a
great want of order and respectability in the conduct of the pit audience, which
is owing altogether to the lack of decision on the part of the officers. A dirty looking fellow a few nights since, taking it into his head that the pit was hardly comfortable enough for him, coolly stepped into the dress circle, and there seated
himself very much to the discomfiture of some well-dressed females in the same
box. One officer after another attempted to reason with him, but to no purpose;
he combatted all their arguments, and there he sat – while his comrades in the
pit, seeing that he was not to be moved, gave him three cheers.[12]

As a would-be cultural arbiter, the *Mirror* supported gentility and furthered the depiction of the noisy gods of the gallery raining peanut shells
and pork-chop bones down upon the habitués of the pit, often depicted
as but a more affluent and no better behaved form of the "rough." Actors
encouraged audience participation, trading remarks like "Is that so, boys?"
and "Don't you, boys?" in order to elicit roars of appreciation from on
high, a rupture of the dramatic illusion consistent with scoring "hits,"
breaking character to take bows, and similar conventions of antebellum
acting. Even those sympathetic to workers could bemoan their behavior;
thus Charles H. Haswell, a well-to-do New York theatre lover, reports of
a visit to the antebellum playhouse:

Clambering to the mephitic fourth tier, we watched, as long as untrained lungs
could last in that atmosphere, the crowd of rough youth there compacted. Plenty of native sharpness was noticeable in speech and looks among those skyward
seats, which doubtless contained also much native good, some of which would
work itself clear in time and do something of account in the world; but the main
expression of the crowd was of nursing vulgarity and vice with an indescribable
air of sordid ignorance and brutal, fierce impatience of all lovely, graceful, delicate things.

Fig. 14. "The Soaplocks" (watercolor by Nicolino Calyo, collection of the New-York Historical Society).

In response to such criticism, manly mechanics might give over cheering, booing, or calling out to one another or the actors, but to do so, John F. Kasson suggests, was to submit to a gag rule and surrender "their role in a powerful arena of cultural expression."[13]

The emblem of the manly white mechanic is New York City's Bowery B'hoy, who emerges in accounts from the 1830s and was frequently illustrated in the 1840s (Fig. 14). He was fondly recalled by one observer in later years:

At the back of the head [the hair] was cropped as close as a scissors could cut, while the front locks, permitted to grow to a considerable length, were matted by a lavish application of *bears grease*, the ends tucked under so as to form a roll, and brushed until they shone like glass bottles . . . a black, straight, broad-brimmed hat, polished as highly as a hot iron could effect, was worn with a pitch forward . . . a large shirt collar turned down and loosely fastened, school boy fashion, so as to expose the full proportions of a thick, brawny neck; a black frock coat with skirts extending below the knee . . . . A profusion of jewelry as varied and costly as the b'hoy could procure. His rolling, swaggering gait on the promenade on the Bowery; his position, at rest, reclining against a lamp or awning post; the precise angle of the ever-present cigar; the tone of voice, something between a falsetto and a growl; the unwritten slang which constituted his vocabulary cannot be described.

The colors of the B'hoy's clothes were startling – blue coats, brick red vests, green striped trousers. Charles Haswell considered the B'hoy

a class in dress and conversation . . . not an idler and a corner lounger, but mostly an apprentice, generally to a butcher, and he "ran with the machine" [i.e., fire engine] . . . a smooth face, a gaudy silk neck cloth, black frock coat, full pantaloons, turned up at the bottom over heavy boots designed for service in slaughterhouses and at fires.

The Bowery B'hoy of these descriptions was as wiley as his Yankee counterpart and, like him, staged American virtues – of labor, patriotism, and resistance to affected "swells." The manly mechanic was performed in politics as well – for example, by Mike Walsh in the 1840s, who sought political support from what one contemporary disparaged as the "muscular Christians" of the Bowery, "the class of rowdy New Yorkers who run with the Forty and Kill for Keyzer" (the first a fire company, the second a prominent butcher).[14]

Students of antebellum theatre know the Bowery B'hoy as Mose. Beginning in February of 1848, Frank Chanfrau, a stock actor at Mitchell's Olympic Theatre in New York, began to play Mose in *A Glance at New York*, a play crafted by Chanfrau and Benjamin A. Baker, the theatre's prompter. Seven Mose plays followed, at the Olympic and at Chanfrau's National Theatre (formerly the Chatham), until July of 1850. The plays were phenomenally successful both in New York and on tour. Audience response was vociferous from the opening of the first play and rose to a furor when *New York as It Is* appeared in 1848. The *New York Herald* of 26 April reported a crowd so large it forced the stage, roaring, laughing, and shouting, obliging the police and theatre employees to clear the (obviously oversold) house of excess patrons, some of whom walked over the pit audience to their seats. Amazed, one reporter observed that "never did a scene of this kind pass off with better humour. We did not learn of a single accident."[15]

Fig. 15. Francis S. Chanfrau as Mose (courtesy of the Harvard Theatre Collection, the Houghton Library).

Chanfrau, born and brought up on the Bowery, had been a volunteer for the legendary Old Maid fire company, and his Mose both captured the street type and quickly came to elaborate it (Fig. 15). Indeed, the Bowery Theatre had forged such a street connection in the 1830s by lending its orchestra to parades of the "Hamblin Guards" militia, while fire companies often featured banners of theatres burning or portraits of prominent actors on their machines. The street type, heightened by popular journalism, found embodiment in the staged type and returned again to the street (Fig. 16), as the *New York Herald* records:

> There never was such a theatrical hit as Mose has made; the lithographers are multiplying his likeness throughout the city. The boys in the street have caught his sayings, and yesterday morning, while waiting at one of the North River docks for the arrival of some friends per steamboat, we were quite amused at seeing a squal [*sic*] of youngsters enacting *New York as It Is* on their own account to the unbounded delight of the bystanders.[16]

It was not solely in his dress, slang, demeanor, and courage that Mose followed and flattered the manly white mechanic; wisely, Chanfrau made him by trade a butcher, one of the elite crafts where the artisan ideal was preserved. Moreover, the streetwise Mose not only holds his own in wit or brawn, but operates as an equal with his gentrified former schoolmate, who remembers Mose fondly as his defender and is proud to meet and socialize with him despite their obvious "class" differences. Nonetheless, for all this, Mose is a liminal figure: He is subject to a boss (master); he is one of the often criticized fireboys – "a little rough outside, but they're all right here *(touches breast)*"; and though he is upwardly mobile enough to cross his neighborhood turf line (Broadway), his residence is a boardinghouse, bemoaned by antebellum conservatives as a resort of "those whose systems are saturated with whiskey, tobacco juice and foul diseases, and whose minds are still more impure" – Bowery B'hoys, in short – whose company would prompt naïve youths from country villages "to accept invitations to the theater, the concert saloon, and other places of low amusement, where they may be induced to take their first step in vice."[17]

The contest between Mose's liminality as worker in a shifting market, as civic-minded volunteer fireman yet hooligan, and as outwardly mobile artisan yet man of no place is transformed by *A Glance at New York* into sentimentality and promotion of artisan ideology. It is a shift evident not only in Chanfrau's play(s), but in published illustrations of city life that reflect urban problems but simplify and romanticize them. Chanfrau's Mose has gentrylike responses to babies and reads sentimental popular fiction with his Bowery G'hal Lize, whom he squires to Vauxhall Gardens, a popular genteel resort. The upwardly mobile Mose disparages "outsiders" (loafers), saying, "I feel as much for a poor fellow as anybody livin', but not for a lazy one. There's plenty of work in this village for every-

Fig. 16. "Dancing for Eels at Catharine Market, N.Y.," scene from *New York as It Is* (courtesy of the Hoblitzelle Theatre Arts Library).

body, if they're of a mind to look for it" – sentiments hardly reflecting the labor problems antebellum workers were facing. An arriviste Mose, more swell than mechanic, would run contrary to type, however, and in the end his proletarian credentials are reaffirmed in Mose's love of a "muss" (fight) and his inability to stop "runnin' wid de machine." The slicks and confidence men who frame the play and populate the city mandate tough guys like Mose, both to stand up for the naïve and defenseless and to affirm the nobility of work and civic-mindedness. Accordingly, it is not alone the appeal of known locales (Steamboat Pier, Front Street and Broadway, St. Paul's Church, New Street), popular references (current songs, Christy's, the Bowery Theatre), and contemporaneous theatrical conventions (dame impersonations, women in pants, minstrel numbers) that made the play a hit, but Mose's insistence upon cultural individuation.[18]

Antebellum theatre reciprocally staged mechanic culture and culture for the mechanic. As early as 1831, New York theatre manager Thomas S.

Hamblin specifically appealed for the native audience by naming his house
the American Theatre, Bowery, and adjusting ticket prices to the proletarian purse, forcing his competitors to do the same. As "the nursery of
native talent," the Bowery used American stars and American plays to appropriate and create a "national culture." Essential to this process was the
manly hero, alternately cast as the vernacular Yankee, frontiersman, Indian, or Bowery B'hoy, and impersonated by Edwin Forrest, James H.
Hackett, Frank Chanfrau, and (as we saw in Chapter 1) George Handel
Hill, Danforth Marble, and Joshua Silsbee. Among these characters, the
Yankee and the Bowery B'hoy extol the virtues of the American worker
in portraits as diverse as Mose the butcher-fireboy, the mechanic–people's
lawyer, and the laboring Puffys and Fairweathers slipping into the liminal
poor of New York. Like the staged Yankee tamed by the bourgeois town,
the artisan myth kept the Bowery B'hoy economically fastened to his place
while celebrating his cultural independence. As skillfully as he had captured and projected the virtues of the mythical Yankee in *The People's
Lawyer,* playwright J. S. Jones elevated the urban worker to near deifica-
tion in his 1840 *The Carpenter of Rouen:* "A mechanic, sir, is one of God's
noblemen. . . . The Supreme Ruler of the universe is himself the Great
Mechanic." The displacements of selling divorced from producing, of invisible, fragmented, racially restricted, and dead-ended work, bespeak a
reality that those who lived it likely found less palatable than the politics
of staged labor. Among those workers, the most overlooked of laborers has
often been the antebellum working woman.[19]

Acting out of the sort creating the Bowery B'hoy totalizes diverse cultural placements and affixes them to specific locales – the white, urban,
young, not genteel, male "on the Bowery." The Bowery G'hal focuses the
tensions in these images of working, since for a woman to be "on the Bowery" carried additional significations for antebellum urban society beyond
those associated with her fondly remembered, swaggering male companion. The Eliza (or Lize) of *A Glance at New York* is a shopgirl (we don't
learn what kind) who speaks in street dialect, reads storybooks, and sings
Christy (minstrel) songs (but only if there is no one around). She has a
residence (no mention of family), and though Mose introduces her as Lize
to "Mr. Gordon," his grammar school chum, she is "the lady" to the
waiter who takes her order for "coffee and nine doughnuts," and is presented with pride to Gordon's genteel friends. As Mose's "gal," she holds
his coat when he fights, but their relationship is otherwise left unclarified
(in a later Mose play, the characters are married with children).[20]

Fig. 17. Mary Taylor and Francis S. Chanfrau in *A Glance at New York* (courtesy of the Hoblitzelle Theatre Arts Library).

Engravings of Lize show her well but conventionally dressed (Fig. 17). In contrast, a contemporaneous account reports of the midcentury urban working woman she represents:

Her dress is "high," and its various ingredients are gotten together in utter defiance of those conventional laws of harmony and taste imposed by . . . the French mantua makers of Broadway. The dress and shawl are not called upon . . . to have any particular degree of correspondence or relationship in color – indeed, a light pink contrasting with a deep blue, a bright yellow with a brighter red, and a green with a dashing purple or maroon, are among the startling contrasts which Lize considers "some pumpkins."[21]

So flamboyant a costume joined with a frank gaze and distinctive gait – Mrs. Trollope thought American women might be fashionable, "were it not for [their] peculiar manner of walking" – would not pass muster among the antebellum genteel and could be mistaken at will for the bright, uncovered dress and open manner of the prostitute. Indeed, Susan G. Davis suggests of these decades that "working women became prostitutes, if only metaphorically, by their economic activity." Christine Stansell discerns a female culture deriving from economic exigencies wherein a woman's "wages alone could not have financed nights on the Bowery." Working-community mores in antebellum New York, Stansell speculates, may have tolerated "casual prostitution, exchanging sexual favors with male escorts for money or food and drink (what a later generation called 'treating')." The fact that sexism closed wage work to women or relegated them to low-paying jobs, rewarding even their industry with condemnation and exploitation, should not obviate the range of options open to antebellum working women for performing the self.[22]

How badly exploited women were comes clear in comparing their wage work to that of men. The "manly man's" income at midcentury, clerk or mechanic, is located in the previously cited *Tribune* and *Times* accounts of 1851 and 1853 as $300–$600 annually needed to sustain a family of five. A weekly wage of $6.00 at the low end would still leave luxuries like a theatre ticket within a skilled laborer's means. Unskilled laborers and women earning half the skilled rate, $3.00–$3.50 for a six-day workweek, would find a twenty-five-cent gallery ticket half or more of a day's wage, and hardly any entertainment – circus, exhibition, or theatre – cost less than a quarter. Wages discriminate at the poverty end of the labor scale, where a sweated seamstress between 1830 and 1850, working from sunrise to nine at night for between $1.00 and $3.00 a week, could ill afford to spare theatre money from her scant earnings. Above the poverty zone, theatre was in reach; indeed, Haswell reports that midcentury playhouses "contained a good number of women, rough-clad but of decent looks, some mothers of families, with the families small and great together, and a few 'children in arms.'" That entire working(-class) families could attend the theatre bespeaks numerous strategies for cutting expenses – adult workers living at home, boarders, and shared flats, for example – in the face of inequitable wages, particularly for women, and exploitation by bosses and jobbers. Domestic service at midcentury, a major employer of women, held wages steady nationwide at $6.00–$7.00 a month and found, little changed from an estimated 1830 average of $1.20–$1.75 a week. In comparison to needle-women, domestic workers saved room and board and had steady employment; indeed, live-in servants may have been among the few waged women who could save money. Domestic work during these decades had a clear racial and gender profile in urban areas, where a dominance of black applicants in New York in 1830 gave way by 1855 to 74 percent Irish women servants, 14 percent German women, 4 percent native white women, 3 percent black women, and 5 percent other.[23]

In the absence of a satisfying cost-of-living index, it is difficult to ascertain what ticket prices really signify in terms of workers' wages and audience composition, suggesting the appropriateness of withholding the assignment of antebellum theatres to "classes." Similarly, our understanding of what the wages of those who worked in theatres represent about the industry overall is limited by an absence of labor histories of theatre workers, although we know some things about salaries at specified times and places. As a mode of production, the dominant organization of theatres during these decades is the repertory company, consisting of actors (hired according to lines of acting or business) and of management: the actor-manager, scene painters (perhaps employed on a job basis), carpenters-machinists (not only to construct but to move scenery, furniture, and props during performances), gas table operator, orchestra leader, dance master or mistress (probably part-time or add-on jobs), stage manager, prompter, treasurer, wardrobe mistress, and front-of-house personnel (ticket sellers and takers, house police, bill posters, press agent). These were augmented throughout the period by supernumeraries, hired play by play, and by stars (introduced to the United States in 1810) who visited for a few days to two weeks at contracted salaries and sometimes ruinous benefit nights; refreshment staff contracted independently to sell food and drink in the theatre. Those unconnected to the creative side of theatre work were salaried or (if lower management employees, such as ticket takers, house police, or cleaners) part-time daily workers. The acting company and upper management (actor-manager, stage manager, orchestra leader) were hired by the season with "benefits," consisting of the profits from a specified number of performances after house expenses were subtracted. (Benefits were negotiated by contract; one night's benefit could equal several weeks or months of salary for a popular actor or stage manager.) Where necessary or profitable, jobs were doubled (actress-wives of company managers took salaries for keeping the theatre's wardrobe, actors doubled as dance masters, orchestra leaders composed music, stage managers prompted performances). Lengths of contracts varied over these years for seasons extending from the beginning of September through December and December to June (later, September to June), when the theatres were closed for the summer and seasonal layoffs put actors on the road, into other work, or into their savings.[24]

Some controversy surrounds interpretations of lines of acting: utility, walking ladies and gentlemen, heavy (tragic) old men and women, light (comic) old men and women, juveniles, and leads. In general, American actors, like old-style artisans, served an apprenticeship, moving from super or utility to responsible utility, to walking lady or gentleman, and then to juveniles or seconds in the various lines. The apprenticeship might take a specified time in an established company: Kate Ryan's at the Boston Museum in the 1870s lasted four years and was followed by a "journeyman" period of two years, during which she was paid $6.00 a week; only at the end of this six-year trial period did Ryan receive her first season-long contract. Clara Morris was paid $3.00 a week as a 13-year-old novice dancer-actress in Cleveland during the Civil War, with which she supported herself and her mother. After only one season, Morris was given a contract and access to the theatre's wardrobe, typically supplied to supernumeraries and low-paid beginners. American stock actresses provided their own costumes in the nineteenth century, a considerable expense either of cash or time at needlework; special clothing required of male actors was supplied, though experienced repertory actors of both sexes amassed wardrobes as a selling point in hiring them. (Hamblin valued his personal star wardrobe at $5,000 in 1836, when it burned in the Bowery Theatre fire.) Other tools of the trade seem not to have been costly.[25]

Salaries in the antebellum decades appear similar to Ryan's and Morris's from later years; one-time child star Louisa Lane Drew cites a joint salary for herself and her mother of $16.00 a week in Boston in 1833. There were national variations (lower salaries but possibly lower expenses outside major urban areas) and some week-by-week hires (and layoffs) in hard economic times or when specialties were required by certain plays. Stressing that my reading of sources is not systematic, and hence that these figures should not be taken as robust, the following weekly salaries appear customary: $3.00 to $6.00 for beginners; $7.00 to $15.00 for utility players; $15.00 to $30.00 for walking ladies and gentlemen; and $35.00 to $100 for leads. Traveling stars might command $150 to $500 plus benefit for a

week to ten-day engagement. By comparison, in 1857 the Wallack treasurer in America's highest-waged city, New York, was paid $20.00 a week
plus one benefit, the orchestra conductor $30.00 and benefit, and the car-
penter $15.00 per week (all three positions were held by men). This pre-
liminary reading suggests that, except at the lowest ranks, antebellum theatre work paid better than other craftwork. This was markedly true for
women (who appear to have been paid less than men for the same types
of theatre work). In comparison with other wage work, then, performing
provided women greater economic opportunity - a point actress-author
Olive Logan emphasized in inveighing against the postbellum "leg business," which made performing, she thought, a tainted occupation closed
to women seeking "respectable" work.[26]

The repertory company system just described was subject to considerable stress in the antebellum decades. In order to avoid the drain of profits
by expensive but popular stars, managers like Thomas Hamblin, William
Mitchell, Laura Keene, Louisa Lane Drew, J. W. Wallack, and Moses
Kimball tried to hold together good repertory companies and to find popular new plays. Playing certain types of successful plays for longer and
longer periods, however, created long runs, starting with Hamblin's
monthlong consecutive runs in the 1830s. By the 1870s, fewer, longer-
running plays, in combination with the continued popularity of stars and
economic pressures of the postbellum period, would destroy the repertory company as the dominant productive mode in theatre. In this respect,
actors would share the fate of many artisans whose work after the Civil
War was to become more specialized in product, less diverse in craft, and
subject to a larger (national) marketplace. In earlier decades, however, a
season was varied and demanding, typically thirty-nine weeks of 40–130
plays (approximately two-thirds old to one-third new), changed nightly.
Utility men in companies carried the largest number of roles – over a hundred different parts in plays and afterpieces in a season was not unusual
by the Civil War – but not the longest parts; these often belonged to stars
who, like Charlotte Cushman, could offer managers to play (and dress)
two hundred different roles. The premium repertory put on memory produced labor traditions limiting the amount an actor could be expected to
memorize overnight; thus Frank A. Stull, who served his apprenticeship
in Philadelphia in the 1860s, recalled, "I expected, usually, to break the
back of a new part in an afternoon, and it was a giant of a role that the
average actor of the old stock company could not conquer within forty-

eight hours." A new play rehearsed about four hours a day for a week, and while there was instruction in fencing, singing, dance, and role interpretation, the majority of the craft was mastered on the job by acting and watching other actors. As in other artisan trades, performing in the antebellum decades was usually varied (comedy, tragedy, melodrama, singing, dancing), and the work stressed memory, imitation, and repetition of well-worn favorites. The introduction of stars disturbed traditions of training and advancement, while the lengthening of runs of single successful plays produced sporadic unemployment and eliminated the variety and quantity of playing that had been the company's hallmark both as a training school for theatre personnel and as a continuous occupation throughout the artisan's lifetime.[27]

The mode of production represented by the antebellum urban American repertory theatre, with its standing acting companies of perhaps twelve to eighteen men and four to six women – the ratio of three to one is consistent, though size varies – and its management staffs of perhaps a dozen more salaried workers, represents a large employer by antebellum standards. Thus far, scholarly attention to these companies has chiefly concerned the quality of dramatic and acting work it produced, while its nature as a workplace remains localized in studies of individual theatres and (auto)biographies of prominent individuals. The archives utilized by labor historians seldom inform theatre scholarship, just as their researches remain silent about theatre workers in these decades. Chronically underrepresented in theatre histories is the presence of antebellum free blacks either as theatre performers or as audience members. Local laws, such as the curfew against which a Washington theatre manager petitioned in 1833, may have made nighttime theatre work in some locations as difficult for free black performers to do as for free black playgoers to attend. In antebellum Charleston, Curry reports, blacks "were prohibited by law from attending theatres unless serving as attendants to whites," and some Cincinnati theatres excluded blacks by custom. The majority of antebellum city theatres admitted but segregated free black patrons, a practice New Orleans law required. Admission could also be selectively denied, as in Washington in 1838, when *Othello* was deemed "unsuitable" for black spectators, and in 1839, when performances of *The Gladiator,* based upon the Spartacus rebellion, were considered too incendiary for black ears. Segregation laws and customs verify the presence of a black audience; that audience, in turn, supported a black theatre. In New York, for example, the African (Grove) Theatre offered black actors in Shakespeare and melo-drama and showcased Ira Aldridge, who left the United States for Euro-pean fame after the African Grove was destroyed by a white mob in 1823. Eight years later (in 1831), Mrs. Trollope reports of New York's free blacks:

They have several chapels, in which negro members officiate; and a theatre in which none but negroes perform. At this theatre a gallery is appropriated to such whites as choose to visit it; and here only are they permitted to sit; following in this, with nice etiquette, and equal justice, the arrangement of the white theatres, in all of which is a gallery appropriated solely to the use of the blacks.[28]

Labor histories have established high percentages of male professional musicians within the antebellum free black work force, including Phila-delphia's famous military and dance band composer-conductor-performer Francis Johnson. Initially, traditional cultural institutions in America, such as playhouses and concert halls, seem to have numbered few blacks among their performers. Exclusion of "legitimate" (nonmusical) actors like Al-dridge appears nearly total throughout the period. At the same time, black musicians and dancers have left a history of performances in antebellum marketplaces, taverns, dance halls, circuses, and in theatres. This complex subject awaits detailed exploration elsewhere, but a few examples from New York suggest what performing may have offered free blacks in the way of employment. In his 1862 *The Market Book*, Thomas De Voe reports that early in the nineteenth century, Long Island and New Jersey slaves were on certain occasions allowed by their masters to sell goods of their own and did so at the Catharine Street Market in New York City; there, butchers hired them and free blacks to draw trade to the butchers' stalls by dancing on boards or shingles (see Fig. 16). In these years (c. 1806) and after state manumission in 1827, dance contests among free blacks were staged at this market. Accounts from the frontier (Kentucky, Ohio, Mis-souri) in the 1820s describe similar black street dancers who "patted Juba." In the same decade, the vogue for black songs, popular in English and American theatres since the mid-eighteenth century, acquired a new lease in white-authored sheet music drawn from market and street performances (see, e.g., Fig. 2). White British actor Charles Mathews assembled sever-al American "types" in his *A Trip to America* (staged in the United States in 1822 and published in 1824), including a staged Negro. New York–born T. D. "Jim Crow" Rice is certain to have made use of all three traditions (market, regional, and staged), as is reflected in the title to his blackface "Ethiopian opera," *Long Island Juba; or, Love by the Bushel*, in which the white Rice played at the Bowery Theatre in January 1833 (see the section "Displaced Play" in Chapter 3). The song and the dance forms that grew out of these exchanges employed both black and white musicians and dancers, outside and inside theatres. Marion Winter identifies free black New Yorker William Henry Lane, who took the stage name "Juba," as a pupil of "Uncle" Jim Lowe, an established dancer in New York City saloons. "Juba" was reviewed by the *New York Herald* when he performed at a local dance hall, and Charles Dickens is thought to have seen him dance in a similar Five Points setting during the English author's 1842 visit to New York. Winter locates Lane's Juba on tour in New England in 1845 in a minstrel act with four white performers, and finds him subsequently advertised with the Georgia Champion Minstrels as having played at the Chatham and Bowery Theatres in New York. Theatre performances of this kind in the 1840s appear simultaneously with records of challenge dance matches by black performers, reminiscent of the Catharine Street Market, that were held in integrated concert saloons, often indicted by reformers (along with biracial brothels) as disruptive of the peace.[29]

The location of theatre culture in the streets of America's antebellum cities exercised would-be arbiters of taste like the *New York Mirror* to condemn "vernacular" performances and performers, whether black or white, as vulgar and suited only to markets and taverns. As antebellum actresses knew, performing was desirable and profitable work when other forms of higher-paid waged labor were closed off. How much money such work represented to free blacks we have yet to discover, but white male performers were quick to appropriate and commodify black street and tavern forms. The condemnation of these as vulgar opens a text of class, which is evident in a larger reading of theatre culture, such as Mrs. Trollope's of 1831 New York:

I have often, particularly on a Sunday, met groups of negroes, elegantly dressed; and have been sometimes amused by observing the very superior air of gallantry assumed by the men, when in attendance on their *belles*, to that of the whites in similar circumstances. On one occasion we met in Broadway a young negress in the extreme of fashion, and accompanied by a black beau, whose toilet was equally studied; eye-glass, guard-chain, nothing was omitted; he walked beside his sable goddess uncovered, and with an air of the most tender devotion. At the window of a handsome house which they were passing, stood a very pretty white girl, with two gentlemen beside her; but alas! both of them had their hats on, and one was smoking![30]

How these stagings connect to Zip Coon, the city dandy of minstrelsy, to the Jim Crow figure visible and condemned by white characters in plays like *Fashion* and *The Lion of the West,* and how the free black market dancer relates to the Bowery B'hoy butcher, suggests the complex relationships among work, class, and race to which Alexander Saxton points in *The Rise and Fall of the White Republic.* In addition, the location of these types in conflict-ridden cultural contexts and of performers in a liminal labor market suggests the high degree of imbrication of "work" and "class." Indeed, when work itself becomes a class and workers "the productive classes," liminality moves and shifts so thoroughly and permanently as to achieve a spatial locality all its own.[31]

Class

Just as Tocqueville believed that Americans were happily ignorant of philosophy and did not honor intellectual (or artistic) labor, so the young French aristocrat argued there were no very affluent people in the United States, that all had equal opportunity, that wealth was self-made and not inherited, that riches were seldom held more than a generation, and that work in America was more important than (class) status or family. The researches utilized here concerning the city and work make clear the emptiness of Tocqueville's egalitarian assumptions. While histories written in the latter twentieth century about the earlier nineteenth use religion, taste, ethnicity, and aspiration as well as occupation and income as components of "class," they have not always escaped the pressures that ideologies exert to naturalize representations of history even when historical practice seems to contradict belief. "The emergence and consolidation of the culture of the middle class" as a nineteenth-century phenomenon may represent such a naturalization. Just as the presence of hereditary wealth and the creation of a permanent poor reproach Tocqueville's estimate of America, a view of class as a type of performance, as a staging of the self, points to the fragmentation rather than cohesion of the construct in antebellum culture. This section of Chapter 2 utilizes income/occupation-driven factors to explore the public and private performances implicated in "class" and "culture." These performances are seen as liminal roles – fluid, multidirectional, and of varied duration – played in the larger performance arena of theatre culture.[32]

The separation of workplace and home parted not only masters and artisans but members of families, dividing them into those who worked outside the home and those whose work was in it. Accordingly, different relationships emerge among family members and toward family itself. Where the home-work arrangement persisted (in the surviving crafts and those industries characterized by outwork and sweating), families might remain intact in a home during the workday, though they were likely to share space with other workers or boarders. In such environments, children worked full-time as soon as they were able (as young as age 7, if there was no apprenticeship pattern and there was need), supervised by a parent or controlling adult. Similarly, all able-bodied adults worked; indeed, working men disapproved of the "idle wives of the masters" and preferred everyone in a family to contribute to the common stock, a practice customary on farms and sanctioned by artisan traditions for centuries. (Male support did not extend, however, to admitting women to higher-paying jobs or unions.)[33]

Contesting views of the home began to emerge in the 1830s and most tellingly affected the lives of women and children. One view constructs the home as the woman's sphere, where children and dependents who did not produce income were sheltered from "immoral" marketplace conditions. This view ignores the fact that many women in these decades worked in the home for wages, both in their own homes as "common stock" or outworkers and as servants in the homes of others (the latter an estimated 50 percent of employed women). Moreover, the view of the home as a private, market-divorced sphere ignores the widespread antebellum practice of unwaged, income-producing work, such as taking in related and nonrelated boarders. In Philadelphia, for example, such work is estimated to apply to 60 percent of unskilled (white) householders, 50 percent of skilled manual householders, and 45 percent of clerical families in these decades. Boarders produced income that, taken together with home teaching, sewing, writing, and similar hidden wage work, locates "working women" even in "genteel" homes – not only in housing-tight, expensive cities, but also, as studies increasingly reveal, in smaller communities as well.[34]

Despite these realities, Harriet Martineau accurately observed in 1837 that "the encouragement and rewards of labor are not provided" women, whose wage work and other income-producing activities were devalued by "private sphere" distinctions. Indeed, white Americans could extend the sphere construct even to Native American women, whose lives were organized around communal income-producing and landholding principles, in seeking to remove land from their control and force them into domestic and low-paid occupations. Even among whites, the home-as-temple view and the devaluation of wage work by women was an uneasy fit, since it demanded that the paid and income-producing work women did in the home as well as outside it remain invisible. As a result, since socioeconomic problems affecting labor and working conditions could not exist in the "private sphere," reformers were licensed to ignore outwork abuses and focus upon the morality of the home, in such matters as the respectability of (especially women) workers.[35]

Children's lives were very much affected by the (re)construction of the home as an identifying space. Women who worked for wages in their homes perforce solved matters like nursing babies, supervising young children, and caring for ill or dependent family members. The addition of laundry, cooking, and cleaning to these tasks when joined to dawn-to-dusk wage work required as much delegating as possible and a common-sense approach toward too many demands. The "style" of child rearing that emerged was often decried by social reformers as neglect or abuse, a perception exacerbated in the "roaming" of children of women working outside the home. Indeed, many children aged 4 to 14 were out of school: In New York in 1830, twelve thousand children were not enrolled (perhaps two-thirds of their age group); in 1856, half of poor children (thirty thousand) did not go to school, and manual laborers kept their children in school less long than did clerical and other workers.[36]

Control of children was also a text in homes where the mother was presumed not to work for wages or income. Indeed, historians suggest "childhood" was created in the nineteenth century, though clearly not for all children, with play, special clothing, toys, and activities intended to assist in the child's moral formation by the matriarchal nurturer. Instrumental to the creation of both childhood and the home as moral center was the proliferation of a large (often religious) literature early in the antebellum decades advocating woman's assumption of the parenting role in the home and of moral leadership outside it. Fueled by an 87 percent literacy rate at midcentury among white women over 20, popular publications soon joined the chorus. Indeed, Catherine Beecher's frequently reprinted *Treatise on Domestic Economy* (1841), in addition to turning housekeeping (as opposed to housework, which was done by servants) into a full-time occupation and dirt and disorder into moral foes, demanded that the trade-off to women in exchange for subordination to men politically and economically be that "in matters pertaining to the education of their children . . . in all benevolent enterprises, and in all questions relating to morals and manners, they have superior influence."[37]

The vision of the antebellum home as a genteel moral fortress, evoked in Beecher's creation of a place for women, inspired twentieth-century scholars to locate a "cult of domesticity" in antebellum America, little suggesting the extent to which Beecher's identification ran contrary to how most women (and men) actually lived in those days. Domestic housing, for example, provided a number of alternatives other than the idyllic cottages of Catherine Beecher and her sister-in-law, Harriet Beecher Stowe. A contract for rowhouses in New York in 1831, for example – appropriate to homes with live-in strangers and fewer children (5.42 in 1850 as compared to 7.0 in 1800) – divided an $18^3/_4$-foot-wide by 40-foot-long building into a basement kitchen and room (dining or bedroom), a first-floor back and front parlor (or dining room), three or four bedchambers on the second and third (if any) floor, and an attic or half story for servants or boarders. Such a home would rent for $275 a year. Midcentury advice to budget 16–25 percent of income for rent would require an annual income over a thousand dollars. An artisan earning $400 to $600 a year would have to augment his wages considerably via an income-producing wife, rent-paying children, boarders, or some other means in order to afford the home described. Indeed, so pressed were renters in housing-short cities that even doctors, lawyers, and merchants boarded or rented rooms to boarders.[38]

Visions of gentility-obsessed women and the fetishization of domesticity recede even further in the face of the $300 average annual wage of a skilled male worker with a family in the 1850s. For him, the Beecher–Stowe cottage or New York rowhouse was out of range, even with boarders. Multifamily housing, not routinely constructed in most cities until the 1840s, rented by the room – 8 by 10 to 12 by 14 feet, at an average of $4.00 to $9.00 a month for two rooms in 1857, each with a "closet" for sleeping. Unlike the rowhouse described above or a Beecher–Stowe cottage, multifamily spaces were minimally segregated in function. Renting without utilities, both houses and apartments required water to be carried in from neighborhood or backyard pumps, and though gas was introduced in New York in 1825 – and quickly came to illuminate new theatres like the Bowery – it was not laid into any but the richest homes until the 1880s. Washing, reading, cooking, sewing, and the like took place in other than architecturally designated spaces. Moreover, developers began to narrow and deepen urban houses in the 1850s, which cut down on light to the interior rooms of city flats and often to whole apartments in tenements. Indeed, privies (still serving 53 percent of New Yorkers and 73 percent of Chicagoans in the 1890s), in combination with bad drainage, overcrowding, the effluvia from nuisance industries, and poor ventilation, caused the cellars, courts, and rear houses in which, for example, more than fourteen thousand poor New Yorkers lived in 1842, to be judged unfit for habitation. The garret home of the Fairweathers in *The Poor of New York* was sumptuous by comparison.[39]

Many aspects of the home as a manifestation of "class," of conventions of child rearing, and of the work and behaviors expected of women find expression in Sidney F. Bateman's play *Self*. Bateman was the daughter of the actor-manager Joe Cowell (who had performed with the Drakes at Mrs. Trollope's Bazaar in Cincinnati in 1829), and her career reflects the cross-pollination of influences evident in the dramatic and performance work of most American theatre workers. Born into the theatre trade and brought up in Ohio in the 1820s, Bateman acted with her husband, H. L. Bateman, throughout the "West" (Missouri, Ohio, etc.). The mother of eight children, she led a full life – quite the opposite of the "idle wives of the masters" or of the white female characters she drew in *Self*. In addition to acting and playwriting, she coached her daughters Kate and Ellen to childhood stardom, managed the London Lyceum with her husband (where in 1871, they presented Henry Irving in his star vehicle *The Bells*), and, after her husband's death, managed Sadler's Wells Theatre.[40]

Bateman wrote *Self* for a theatre her husband managed in St. Louis in 1855; it subsequently played in New York at Burton's Chambers Street Theatre (opening 27 October 1856). She used her knowledge of country characters and city fashions to craft a melodrama that offered a major comic part, John Unit, to the Yankee actor John E. Owens (1823–86). Owens, who had acquired the rights to and successfully toured the deceased George Handel Hill's role Solon Shingle (from J. S. Jones's *The People's Lawyer*), had become the chief actor in the Yankee line after

Hill's death in 1849, and Bateman's John Unit suggests the metamor-
phoses the type was undergoing as it intersected urban dramaturgical
conventions, such as the local-color references of the Mose plays.[41]

Bateman's *Self,* both in its examination of the ill effects of extravagant
spending and in its last-minute rescue from forgery charges, bears a superficial resemblance to Mowatt's *Fashion* (1845). It is, however, a much more
detailed account of a culture based upon self-appearance. The play opens
in a dry-goods store on Broadway, where two enterprising New Yorkers
merchandise overpriced fabrics to wealthy female customers, daughters of
immigrant sawyers and boardinghouse operators, and widows of taverners.
Upholders of the ethic that "a man to succeed in our business must be
forgetful of everything but the main chance," the merchants conclude that
"with liberal advertising, handsome clerks, and good goods, we can laugh
at the caprices of fashionable ladies" and cheerfully flatter even the "ugli-
est old frumps in the city." "Frump" fails to describe Mrs. Radius, whose
shopping has been delayed by a street accident in which

a dray-load of emigrants – dirty dredful wretches! – ran against a wagon full of
barrels; the horses slipped on the Russ pavement; some of the people were
thrown down and hurt; three of the animals were killed, and I was obliged to wait
until they removed the bodies – a most provoking circumstance.

From the outset, Bateman draws a sequence of class lines with her characters: the overindulgent, spendthrift mother who excuses her son's drunkenness because he "was with friends, whose position in society insures
them respect, even in their excesses"; the overdressed matron who sniffs
that "only the lower class patronize the flaunty style of dress" which she
herself flaunts; and the overcultured son of a successful tailor, who is now
above buying "a suit of clothes in Chatham Square" or "a hat in Catharine Market" yet not above dyeing his hair and aping Paris fashions. In deft
strokes, using the grand shops of the midcentury city as her setting, Bateman depicts the joint ills of work and class signaled by clerks who flirt instead of serve, proprietors who compete at any cost to outwit their rivals
in the mutual deception of the public, tastes created through false advertising, and customers prepared to run up $6,000 bills they cannot settle
with no thought to the tradespeople they might ruin or the servants whose
wages thereby go unpaid.[42]

At the vertex of Bateman's self-centered melodrama is a family appro-
priately named Apex. Mr. and Mrs. Apex – it is the second marriage for

each, she for his money and he for her looks – are enmeshed with her son and his daughter in a tangle of excess and insincerity of the sort inveighed against by countless moral tracts and child-rearing manuals. Alone in her fashionable parlor, Mrs. Apex sees herself as a woman leading a false life to impress false friends, presuming on superficial accomplishments to style herself a patron of the arts and a leader of *ton*. These faults she excuses, however, because she believes them necessary to the social advancement of her son, Charles, a wastrel who has been expelled from college and has gambled his mother to the brink of ruin. Despairing of his own useless- ness, Charles points the moral of his mother's indulgence:

For what should I be grateful to you? For the fine clothes and dainty ruffles that decked my little limbs in childhood, and forbade free motion and joyous play? For the silly fondness that pampered me with unwholesome sweets, that winked at my neglect of useful study, that laughed at my deceptive arts, until low cun- ning was engrafted on my boy nature? For the false reasoning that taught me to believe industry and economy were low, and that enjoyment consisted only in a feeble attempt to ape the follies of a corrupt aristocracy, the very follies that are causing the tottering kingdoms of long centuries to tremble before the onward step of a republic created and sustained by the very labor you have taught me was degrading.

Chastened by his own excesses, Charles resolves to "get a situation as a clerk" and "spend only what I can earn." Such will indeed be his fate, but not before he courts ruin through forgery.[43]

From the luxurious public display of the antebellum department store to the luxurious private display of the antebellum parlor, Bateman moves the action to the simple bedroom of the heroine of the melodrama, some- where on an upper floor. Here Mr. Apex's daughter, Mary, dresses plain and lives plainer, giving away her money, first to her step-mother then to her father, in a futile attempt to keep peace in the family. Thereafter, Mrs. Apex, rather the worse for wear after a late-night party, uses that talisman of genteel new beginnings, the antebellum breakfast room, to coax her son into forgery. The scene gives way to a sumptuous, well-mirrored draw- ing room, where the tension between melodramatic illusion and reality is drawn by the play's *raisonneur*, John Unit:

Upstarts here make money by cheating government in contracts, swindling In- dians with glass beads and bad whiskey, lucky investments in old cabbage gar- dens – all ends in the same thing: children grow up and are the "first people," ride in carriages with livery servants, take daughters to big hotels – Saratoga and Newport – on exhibition to be knocked down to the highest bidder! Sons are idle spendthrifts, and bring the family down again in poverty.

Mary Apex will be subject not to the marriage market but to expulsion from the family bosom: A draft she has given her neglectful father against her own fortune bounces because Charles's and Mrs. Apex's forged check has already cleared out the account. Mary's fate is an even plainer room in a boardinghouse where, accompanied by her loyal black servant Chloe, she plans a future of music teaching and needlework in that fiction of female sustenance so beloved by dramatists. The more realistic Chloe offers her savings and labor as a domestic instead.[44]

Both mistress and maid are saved from the boardinghouse – where spinsters eat thin bread and, Bateman suggests, live out lives of quiet desperation – by removing themselves to the tasteful study of Mary's (fairy) godfather, John Unit, who lives up to his charge to make miracles (and offers that people cannot refuse). Unit's age (60) and crusty analyses of the world around him dispossess this nominal hero of Bateman's *Self* of any romantic connection to the heroine, Mary. His response to her appeal for funds to loan her father takes a self-conscious look at the drama they are playing:

If you had come here to-night and gone into hysterics like the heroine of a novel or a melo-drama, I should have sent you away with a scolding; but you came like a girl of sense, poured out my tea, told a straight-forward story, and only showed, by emotion you could not repress, the deep interest you felt in getting my aid.

Actually, Mary has behaved exactly like the heroine of a gentility melodrama. Her reward is to return to her rightful place, the Apex's sumptuous drawing room ("brilliantly illuminated, mirrors, chandeliers, etc. – chandeliers reflected on large mirror at back"), to force the assembled partygoers (and the audience) to take a look at themselves. In contrast to the hardness of Unit's own heart in choosing the self-interest of business over the "assets that benevolent actions towards our fellow-beings leave in the shape of love, respect, and sympathy," the play extols the loyalty and generosity of the black servant Chloe, "the honest, faithful heart that . . . should make you the welcome inmate of a royal palace."[45]

As *Self* reflects, in work, child rearing, and education, in the removal of fathers as parents, and in the constitution of domestic housing as both a public and a private sphere, antebellum America stages circles of difference that make the emergence of a uniform middle-class culture difficult to locate. Mary P. Ryan suggests that a strategy for coping with unstable economic times emerged from these tensions, one mandating later marriage, controlled family size, multiple incomes, and extended residence of adult children with parents (sometimes involving schooling) as means of maintaining or improving a family's position despite the shifting of male work from the artisan trades and small shops into lower-paying, lower-status clerical posts. In this view, the move from proprietary to employed work involved parents in "a sustained battle to maintain middle-range occupations for themselves and their children." Studies of advice books and cautionary literature find compatible agendas for securing middle-range social status commensurate with income and occupation-driven aspirations. Such strategies do not rule out "the substantial tradesmen, mechanics and artisans" George G. Foster identified as middle class in 1850 – a definition he extended to Mose, the Bowery B'hoy.[46]

It is difficult to find Mose and Lize (or Nimrod Wildfire) in the advice books that proliferate between 1830 and 1860 – approximately seventy etiquette manuals were published, many through several editions. If class is to encompass varying standards of behavior no less than varying standards of cleanliness and sobriety, however, then novels, advice manuals, associations, plays, newspapers, religious sources, periodicals, public rhetoric, and the like open themselves as performances of class rather than the creators of it. The valorization of acting-out class, a taking over and defining of liminal spaces, may be antebellum America's distinctive cultural signature. The interactions between social and cultural melodramas help clarify how varied that signature could be.[47]

As gentility, "middle-class behavior" performs the scenario of conventional melodramas: that there are villains (painted women and confidence men, social gaffes, intemperate behavior, and the like) prepared to spring from concealed spaces (ignorance of "the right thing to do," setting the wrong fork, eating with your knife, speaking to an unknown man in the street, naïvely entering a tavern or brothel) and fall upon virtuous (but unsophisticated, unprotected by church or family, unsupervised by masters or mistresses) young heroes and heroines. Youth on the loose had been a theme for religious leaders in the 1820s, and their advice to young men aspiring to retain the virtues of the town yet succeed in the city often betrays the clerics' own fears of slipping power. The ideological and manipulative agendas of this literature are, indeed, clear and reflected in New York merchant Arthur Tappan's rules for his clerks: temperance, chastity, church attendance (twice on Sunday) and reports about it, prayer meetings (twice a week), and dormitory hours (10 P.M.). Rule number 3 held "no clerk was permitted to visit any theater, and no forgiveness was accorded if he added to the crime by becoming acquainted with members of the theatrical profession." It is unclear how general such controlling behavior was among merchants – certainly employers restricted the personal activities of household servants – but an anxiety about the vulnerability of (especially male) young people was frequently expressed in these decades. The parental protection afforded heroes and heroines who lived at home was extended by a battery of voluntary organizations that provided genteel outlets for socializing – professional societies, political clubs, bible classes, *sangen Vereine* ("singing societies" – immigrants also "clubbed"), athletic tourneys, educational and charitable associations – and served as stages for "a society increasingly aware of role-playing and backstage secrets, as a result of the disruptions and discontinuities of accelerated mobility."[48]

The desire to club with like-minded people, whether informally in their homes or through structured meetings or socials, multiplied the number of opportunities for gentility-inclined antebellumites to perform. For this, one must be properly costumed (no heavy perfumes, no frayed skirt hems or shirt collars), get the stage directions right (how to walk, mask a sneeze, avoid staring), know one's lines (making conversation, handling introductions), and deliver them with appropriate emphasis (controlling emotion, remaining polite, projecting animation). The advice to "behave always as if one were observed" erases the distinction between gentility toward strangers and toward one's spouse or children. Accordingly, the genteel family in private performance was encouraged to formalize routine activities like eating, banning children from the dining room until they had mastered table manners and could keep silent. Similarly, parlors – as *Self* demonstrates – were decorated like stage settings for the performance of "character," "respectability," and other genteel virtues. Indeed, genteel antebellum domestic architecture, hung with many mirrors, conspired to feature dining in someone's home as "the highest social compliment" gentility could offer its own.[49]

The performance of gentility rehearsed in advice manuals, in new views of what constituted news (social activities, gossip, scandal), and in the structures of voluntary associations reflects the dynamics of commodification, of the publishing/reading industry, and it reflects the search by historians for the origins of control strategies they find in postbellum America (bent on such agendas as sanitizing vaudeville or sacralizing the orchestral concert). The antebellum decades give clear evidence that if a gentrification campaign was under way, it was not working. Dickens, for example, reports that "substantial tradesmen, mechanics, and artisans" were still eating with their knives in 1842, and Mrs. Trollope indicts a lengthy list of ungenteel behaviors in her *Domestic Manners* (significantly) *of the Americans*. Numerous critiques by Americans attest to the persistence of "country manners," producing such ambivalent evaluations as Federalist Theodore Sedgewick's 1825 celebration of "the happy union of labor, knowledge, and manners," or Emerson's extolling of the refinement of farmers in his 1837 "Manners." Wealthy diarists of these decades, like Hone and Haswell or the younger George Templeton Strong, expressed concern about material display and rising levels of consumerism and ostentation. The amusements of "society" now reported in antebellum newspapers – musical evenings, tableaux vivants, balls, fêtes, and dinner parties – were also the amusements (though presumably at lower cost) of genteel ("middle class") socializing. Just as pastimes, manners, and fashions in theatres (see Chapter 1) crossed "class" lines, higher education in antebellum America also fails to distinguish class clearly. College was not considered appropriate training for the professions or business (either for self-taught clerks or for those who would become merchant princes). With its chaotic curricula, lack of entrance tests or written examinations, bad texts, and shoddy teaching, the antebellum university may have influenced its male students less than extracurricular literary societies or volunteer associations. Certainly it was a rowdy environment ill-suited either to reforming the spoiled Charles of *Self* or to furthering the ethics of the hero and heroine of the gentility melodrama: products of self-conscious self-study, trained from infancy to defer gratification, control themselves, work hard, and "get on."[50]

If the fluidity of tastes, training, and behavior in antebellum America are added to economic fluidity, "class," like "work," becomes a liminal concept. Gender and cultural constructs – such as "the cult of true womanhood," "the ideal of real womanhood," "the new woman," "the masculine achiever," "the Christian gentleman," "the manly man" (mechanic or backwoodsman), the transcendental man (clerk or businessman), and their female counterparts in the lively girl (Lize) and the transcendental woman (Gertrude, Lucy Fairweather, Grace Otis, and the white "roses") – though they reflect held values of conduct and cherished aspirations, do not provide a consistent barometer of "character." As antebellum melodramas make clear, refinement may cloak evil (Count Jolimaître, Snobson, the Bloodgoods, or Bellamy), while good (Nimrod, the Puffys, Solon, Mose, and Lize) may be dressed in country manners. The deceptiveness of appearance is also the moral of countless etiquette books and the popular literature of the era, both celebrating self-performance. Heroes and heroines in the city – amid the hazards of boardinghouses and crime, beset by filth, noise, and disease – test themselves as moral forces as readily in a changing and deceptive world as those in the transcendental town do through its more familiar ethical dilemmas.[51]

The appeal of melodrama as an aesthetic and psychological mechanism has been explored in a number of literary studies; indeed, that it functions as a form of imagination, of imaging (seeing) or conceiving, has considerable appeal as a reading of American art. Similarly, explorations in recent scholarship of the cultural and political force of the form give to this imagining missing texts of race, gender, and class. Viewed as theatre culture, the centrality of performance to melodrama fragments its functioning as a totalizing construct by emphasizing that melodrama is not a fixed position – a political, social, or even moral testament – but a way of acting and a legitimation of performing outside as well as inside playhouses. As such, as we've seen, a play can extol the very democratic virtues it subverts, urge conformity to social values it both lauds and undermines, and appeal to the diverse membership historians have characterized as the antebellum middle class. When the insistence that one not only can but should perform is located by scholars in social, cultural, and political arenas as diverse as antebellum parlors, clubs, dining rooms, streets, churches, taverns, fire companies, apartment houses, public offices, families, jobs, and child rearing, as well as in the content of newspapers, constructs of gender, and "character," there is little likelihood of the undifferentiated acting out constructs of class have usually demanded of playhouses. This cultural signature – the insistence on performance – authorizes bewildering, even perverse inconsistencies.[52]

In theatre, the shift in repertories during these decades from a dominance by comedy and tragedy to two-thirds melodrama and one-third comedy (with the near-disappearance of tragedy) nurtured a critical dispute concerning what kinds of performances constituted culture and who was to control its expressions in playhouses. On the one hand, critics condemned melodrama as too pat or too sensational in its staging of the ethical, though almost all acknowledged its potential to uplift and teach virtue – moral and educational agenda consistent with goals of genteel child-rearing and with self-improvement. By 1825, organized religions "no longer exercised any certain influence over the censuring or regulation of amusements," though the informal influence of religious leaders is still evident in their remarks, sometimes vituperative, about theatre. Significantly, these objections were attacked by the press in the 1830s and 1840s on the ground transcendentalists staked out: that theatres should be rid of vice, not shuttered. In the place of ministers, editors asserted their own authority as cultural arbitrators, bestowing – in the process of attempting to control theatre – an importance upon the acting out of a larger social melodrama in which theatre in America had seldom previously participated. The control of theatre in the United States, unlike that in Europe, had no text in a national law regulating theatre, and antebellum municipal statutes seldom extended beyond establishing license fees, controlling overcrowding, or providing for fire safety. Indeed, American playhouses were presumed to operate according to an "informal contract" of civic control, summarized at the time of the Astor Place riot:

The public and magistrates have been accustomed to look upon theatrical disturbances, rows, and riots, as different in their character from all others. The stage is presumed to be a correction of the manners and morals of the public, and on the other hand the public has been left to correct, in its own energetic way, the manners and the morals of the stage; and magistrates, looking upon it as a matter between the actors and the audience, have generally refused to interfere, unless there was a prospect of a violent breach of the peace, when they have usually ordered the house to be closed.[53]

As fora for acting out the larger social melodrama and for performances of the self, antebellum playhouses demonstrate marked instabilities as containers of class divisions. While serving as neighborhood phenomena, playhouses also operated as urban institutions (symbolized in the Astor Place

Theatre riot of 1849) and assume national readings as well in the decades prior to the Civil War. As neighborhood and citywide performance spaces, playhouses and the entertainments they offered were intimately caught up in the growth of American publishing. In 1825, news publishing followed a classic, undifferentiated, small-shop format. The owner was also the editor, reporter, advertising and subscription manager, typesetter, and press-(wo)man. News was a jumble of old and copied commercial and political items to which businessmen following the trade and those interested in politics subscribed. In 1833, publishers began to sell newspapers on the street at a much lower price than the six- or seven-cent subscription papers. The "penny presses" reported theatre and police court news, local human-interest stories, fiction, and the like, as well as politics and business news, in a format that was better organized and easier to read. The influence of newspapers grew with increased readerships, aided by technological changes during these decades – cheaper paper, better impression cylinders, steam and rotary presses, telegraph lines – that put a mass market within reach. As big businesses requiring heavy capitalization, the penny presses of the 1840s and 1850s were subject to local pressures by advertisers and to national politics concerning such matters as postal-rate changes. They were vulnerable as well to a host of market forces. Influential among those forces was one affecting not only newspapers but also antebellum journals, storypapers (beginning in 1839), and pamphlet novels (from 1842) – whose combined circulation in these decades far exceeded that of newspapers: the need for wide distribution among a literate readership.[54]

Under the editorship of those who, like James Gordon Bennett of the *New York Herald,* believed themselves responsible for public morals, the antebellum press was not slow to exert itself as an arbiter of public taste and could resemble, where theatre was concerned, a cross between a modern-day scandal sheet and the nightly news. At its most extreme, such papers might charge, as Horace Greeley's reform-minded *Tribune* did on 11 May 1841, that "each theatre contains within its walls a grog-shop and a place of assignation" and that "a large proportion of those connected with the Stage are libertines or courtezans." Greeley's condemnation resurrects moralist arguments that have a genteel text of contamination by association. To this, reviewers of theatre as of novels added complaints that melodramas lacked the grandeur, ideals, and universality of other genres. Displeasure with the repertory intensified as melodrama succumbed (steadily in the 1840s) to dog and pony shows, slack-wire walkers, monkeys and elephants, giants and dwarves, and a host of other devices for attracting audiences and competing with carnivals, parades, executions, ship launchings, and other free fare, with hosts of low-priced exhibitions in museums (including theatrical performances), and with concerts, lectures, and other kinds of presentations. The theatre entertainments of the variety type were not ennobling; they were "vulgar," tasteless, perhaps even violations of moral decorum. What did such a theatre have to offer the hero and heroine of the genteel melodrama, of "the middling class," "the masses," "the common people," since only they, reporters argued, and not the rich, made it possible for theatre to survive?[55]

Attempts by antebellum newspapers or journals to establish a cultural diktat for theatre failed to eventuate in either local or national cultural policies. Because newspapers and journals form the chief data bases for influential studies of single playhouses or of multiple urban theatres, however, their definitions have been prominent components of scholars' class profiles for nineteenth-century American theatre audiences. These profiles often follow the leads of antebellum newspapers in erasing women and free blacks from theatres in the course of advocating a progressive gentrification foregrounding the genteel melodrama as the speaking text in both audience composition and its selection of amusements. As we saw in Chapter 1, class location via gentility is difficult even for white men, whose rowdiness took place in the pit and the box as readily as the gallery (unless all rowdies are presumed to be middle class or all theatres with boxes, pits, and galleries to be genteel). Women defy class containment theories even further. For example, Patricia C. Click, cultural historian of amusements in antebellum Baltimore, Norfolk, and Richmond, discovered that, in those cities, "women, particularly young single women, also attended theater productions with other women, without a male escort" and that "contemporaries did not consider this scandalous." Indeed, women cued for popular actors, and "theater managers often reserved a row or two of front seats for women" – whether gallery, pit, or box seats is not clear – and "these were especially coveted." Was the border South radically different from a border North city like Cincinnati where, Mrs. Trollope assures us, "the larger proportion of females deem it an offense against religion to witness . . . a play?" Similarly, when the actor Tyrone Power laments that the well-filled Tremont Street Theatre in Boston in 1833 consisted "chiefly of men, as on my debut in New York," were women absent because they were reticent to attend the theatre, or were they watching the popular Miss Pelby at a nearby theatre rather than the unknown Power making his first U.S. tour specializing in comic Irish characters of unproven quality or relevance to women? Like newspapers, diarists – especially Mrs. Trollope – often insist upon the gentility scenario as means of furthering their own centrality to culture, particularly where there is a reading of failure by Americans to control behavior.[56]

The frequency with which women are erased from antebellum theatres at the same time they are identified in antebellum theatrical records recommends a certain caution about accepting the image of reluctant femininity, with its removal of agency from women, in the prosecution of their attenuation and subjugation by gentility and class. The argument of fashion and taste did not keep women (or men) from attending antebellum playhouses in ever-increasing numbers. Not only did theatres multiply since Mrs. Trollope's day, but other places of entertainment also proliferated – museums, concert saloons, opera houses, variety halls, minstrel houses, and so on – and competed with playhouses for an audience. Throughout the United States between 1825 and 1860, the number of theatres, like the nation's cities and population, grew at a phenomenal rate. The labors and stresses of antebellum life merited relaxation, advice books argued, and by the Civil War there was a nationwide delivery system prepared to provide it. At the neighborhood and urban level, theatres provided one of the best staging areas for the genteel melodrama. Here, boxes offered excellent places to frame self-performance, miniature dining rooms and parlors blazing with gaslight, with splendid foyers and lounges to provide yet other stage settings. Galleries were excellent settings too, for more communal performances. That women utilized what were for them rare and coveted public fora shines through even James Gordon Bennett's 19 September 1838 editorial fulmination in the *New York Herald* that "63 virtuous and respectable ladies" had to mix at the Park Theatre with "83 of the most profligate and abandoned women" he could imagine – testimony to the presence of those very wives and daughters of respectable New Yorkers not at all reticent to perform their gentility in a presumptively male theatre. Moreover, in order to force his authority, Bennett must erase the women "rough-clad but of decent looks" of whom Haswell speaks, subsuming them in the eighty-three profligates whose passage to their gallery seats Bennett's diatribe seeks to segregate. The sexist, classist, and racist erasures that profiles like these of antebellum theatres and audiences force should cause us to examine "the antebellum gentrification campaign" as a reinscription of some of the more perverse readings of the melodramatic scenario.[57]

Class impinges not only upon the patrons of antebellum theatres, but also upon the on- and offstage lives of those who worked there. Editor Horace Greeley's charge in the 11 May 1841 *Tribune* that "a large proportion" of theatre workers were "libertines or courtezans," while it resembles the much older criticism of theatre – that performers were depraved and plays immoral – represents a significant repositioning of the "theatre debate" in the United States in the nineteenth century. Aesthetic criticism demanded a larger-than-life stage posture identifiable with Romantic and transcendental views of genius and nature. Charged with uplifting and relaxing the antebellum audience member, yet with being exceptional and always public, actors shared with both stage and company managers a vulnerability yet an aloofness to criticism. On the one hand, as numerous "theatre riots" in the 1830s and 1840s attest, theatre people and theatre buildings could quickly become foci for nationalist sentiments, disputes in taste, antiabolitionism, or other issues with which they were casually, directly, or coincidentally connected (*vide* the Kean riot of 1825, the Anderson riot of 1831, the Farren "riot" of 1834, the Wood riot of 1836, the Vestris–Mathews disturbance in 1838, the Timm–Taylor affair of 1844, and the Astor Place riot of 1849). On the other hand, the nature of theatre as work – with its late hours, higher pay, transience, and visibility – conveyed a prominence and popularity that could as readily excuse as accuse. Responses by the Park and the Bowery theatres in New York prior to 1848 to issues of class and gentility help focus the playhouse's involvement in the larger arena of antebellum American theatre culture.[58]

Built in 1798, the Park Theatre was tied by association to the remnants of the Old American Company, an acting troupe dating to the colonial period and, though past its prime, still venerated at century's end as a symbol of national culture. In 1808, Stephen Price became manager of the theatre, a post he held until his death in 1840. Often absent in London, where he lived and, for a time (1826–30), managed the Drury Lane Theatre, Price was assisted from 1812 by Edmund Simpson, who actively oversaw the Park Theatre until shortly before his death in 1848. By 1826, when the Bowery Theatre opened, the Park had, not unsuccessfully, associated itself with "culture" in the European (chiefly British) tradition, a posture buttressed by Simpson's reputation as an exemplary husband and father and Price's association as a college man and lawyer with prominent New

York families. The Park had sustained this reputation despite disturbances of the peace, audience behavior of the sort Washington Irving describes (patrons of the pit serving as targets for missiles hurled by occupants of the galleries), its proximity to brothels, and reliance upon English plays and actors, regularly dispatched to New York from London by Price. This curious blend of English, colonial, and American is captured in Searle's 1822 watercolor reconstructing New York's elite at play.[59]

As we saw in Chapter 1, the Bowery Theatre was built by wealthy New Yorkers near their homes. It burned in 1828 and was immediately rebuilt, its lease passing in 1830 to Thomas S. Hamblin, a British-born actor. Hamblin brought the Bowery – "infinitely superior [to the Park] in beauty," Mrs. Trollope reminds us – to its greatest fame in the 1830s and increased its popularity in the 1840s despite the prolonged depression following the economic crisis of 1837. Hamblin's strategy was to identify his house with the call, issued by literary journals like the *New York Mirror*, for American dramas and actors. Capitalizing upon the Anderson riot at the Park in 1831, occasioned by British singer-actor Joshua Anderson's supposed slurs against Americans, Hamblin that year renamed his playhouse "the American Theatre, Bowery." He hired unknown American actors and made them stars, commissioned American plays, and offered these new and well-produced entertainments for longer runs. These policies allowed the Bowery to compete successfully with (indeed, surpass the popularity of) the Park until 1836, when the Bowery Theatre was a second time destroyed by fire. Hamblin, who lost everything in the blaze, discharged his debts, bought out the lease and regrouped, remaining interested in an interim Bowery others erected on the site. When investment capital loosened after the panic of 1837 and the interim Bowery burned in 1838, Hamblin organized a third Bowery (the fourth theatre on this site since 1826), opened in 1839, which he saw through another round of hard financial times until it, too, burned (in 1845), this time insured. Hamblin rebuilt again and remained the nominal, though not the active, manager of this theatre until his death in 1853, living long enough to have a Pyrrhic victory in assuming the Park lease after Simpson's death (in 1848), until that theatre burned a few months later.[60]

Many of the tensions of antebellum America are manifested in the rivalry of the Park and the Bowery. That those tensions were in a measure orchestrated is attested by Simpson's neighborhood-style management tactics, attempting to cultivate an urban elite (which abandoned him), and

Hamblin's nationalist tactics, attempting depiction of the Park as pro-British and aristocratic and his own house as pro-American and democratic. For all this, there is little to tell the two theatres apart. Their ticket prices were nearly the same, each had the sort of financial success that indicates patrons in all parts of the house, and each experienced the same slumps in attendance. The repertories of both theatres are similar in a preponderance of melodramas; equestrian plays and spectacles featuring elephants, dog acts, giants and dwarves, raging cataracts, the last days of Pompeii, or the battle of New Orleans; plays by Shakespeare, Sheridan, Garrick, and other British dramatists, along with those by Mordecai M. Noah, Jones, Bird, Mowatt, Medina, and other American playwrights. Both theatres alternated star visits with company vehicles run as long as public interest could sustain them, and both theatres offered similar settings for audiences, the Bowery's auditorium consistently newer and frequently refurbished (assisted by fires). Both theatres suffered fights and disturbances ("riots"), and both were considered deficient in decorum: Mrs. Trollope complains of the incessant tobacco spitting at the Park; the *Spirit* reproves peanut crunching at both theatres; the *Spirit* in 1835 condemns the noisy, filthy, and ill-mannered Bowery pit audience (the same year the *Mirror* speaks of the theatre's fashionable audience).[61]

Despite similarities in prices, successes and failures, patrons, repertory, architectural amenities, and criticisms, the positioning of the Park as aristocratic and the Bowery as democratic in the 1830s took playgoing in the United States beyond the rival tactics of managers in one American city and into the arena of a developing national antebellum theatre culture. New York City played an active role in what was staged in this arena because of its centrality to developments in many aspects of the gentility melodrama, among them publishing (defining fashions, needs, knowledge, behaviors), manufacturing and marketing (commodifying and redistributing those needs and behaviors), and theatre (providing representations in its plays, buildings, and performances of how those needs, desires, and behaviors function in life). To be sure, one can overstate the effectiveness of Simpson's and Hamblin's rival tactics by seeing in them, as did some of their contemporaries, the documentation of an actual division between elite and plebeian, high cult and low, native and foreign, of the sort represented in George Pope Morris's declaration in the *Mirror* in 1828 that "in the present corrupted state of the drama [the Park] has been the stronghold of taste, talent, and respectability; its decline argues the decline of similar qualities in the play-going public." Yet within a decade, Morris's associate editor Theodore S. Fay would have his novel *Norman Leslie* dramatized at the Bowery (1836), and Morris's *Briar Cliff* would earn similar author benefits when it was adapted and played at Wallack's Theatre in 1838. In moving to support the Bowery and Wallack's and the melodramas they (and the Park) produced, the *Mirror* editors recognized not only their own advantage as native authors but reflected a repositioning of theatre in America that neither reconciled nor stood at odds with "taste" and "respectability." Rather than a single operationalization of "class" promulgating self-control and a binarized clash between "classes" for control of culture, the licensed acting out of theatre became proximate with the gentility melodrama.[62]

From the perspective of class viewed as a relationship among a host of associations (work, gender, race, religion, family, recreations, income, education, and the like), the melodrama scenario does not require heroes to be rich or heroines well-educated in order to take center stage; they only need to claim liminal spaces that provide the room to perform. It is a scenario of self-creation open to those who believe in the way things ought to be – the well-paying job, the comfortable home, self-education, work to do, and a society of which to be a part. In the main, the liminal spaces where this scenario is acted out are conventional, but even conventional space is dramatic, fraught with danger, challenging, yet full of opportunities to be noticed and to perform successfully. In this, eating with one's knife, getting into a "muss," claiming the vernacular, or staging tableaux vivants have equal merit respective to the play. No one paradigm for behavior completely captures the potential of a liminal space, where the next scene may demand a different kind of playing, such as valorizing country manners and denigrating refinement. These truths heroes and heroines know because they embody "character"; no matter if others report them as profligate and make news of their affairs, the drama must come back around again to their place, a place of performance. In melodrama, class plays out character as it ought to be, creating that middle range for self-exposure between the unreachable and the unacceptable, an enabling rather than a controlling scenario, at once acknowledging and denying – as staged performances do – the environments in which they take place.

* * * * *

AS THE NUMBER OF THEATRES in the United States increased in the 1840s and 1850s and competed with painting, photography, and Indian exhibits, wax and freak museums, spectacula, circuses, castle gardens, dioramas and panoramas, balloon ascensions, ship launchings, balls, parades, and the like, many of the dynamics that fueled attempts to hijack culture evident in the Park–Bowery rivalry faded into insignificance. Elites would continue to subscribe to exclusive staging sites like Astor Place, but these could not survive as restricted spaces. The performance of class in public developed its own referentiality (as in the Bowery G'hal and the genteel heroine), becoming a coded presentation signaled by costume, diction, and manner even when performed in towns, where such information as one's wealth or family position might be known. As a form of identification in liminal spaces emptied of the automatic associations wealth, occupation, gender, and position might once have carried, "location" in the antebellum decades devolved upon such larger issues as those driving melodrama: the content of one's character and involvement in the moral enterprises of society. As the old locations (home, occupation, longevity of residence, associations) failed, the tensions in the melodramatic scenario began to strain against its confining paradigms. Could employers legislate the nonwork lives of their clerks? Should newspapers determine, as some ministers still hoped to do, what was and what was not publicly acceptable? Did stories, plays, and etiquette manuals create values that life could not perform? Who would determine which liminal spaces, public and private, were suitable for staging the larger issues, and thus the constantly redistributed performances of antebellum selves?

3

Spaces of Legitimation

Things are in the saddle
And ride mankind.
 – Ralph Waldo Emerson, "Ode Inscribed to W. H. Channing" (1847)

There is nothing which pleads so strongly against the flagrant injustice
which has closed the doors of productive industry against women, as the fact
that when forced to fall back upon their own resources, so many of them
have been compelled to choose between prostitution and destitution.
 – Edward Crapsey, *The Nether Side of New York* (1872)

Things fall apart; the center cannot hold;
Mere anarchy is loosed upon the world.
The blood–dimmed tide is loosed, and everywhere
The ceremony of innocence is drowned;
The best lack all conviction, while the worst
Are full of passionate intensity.
 – W. B. Yeats, "The Second Coming" (1921)

W hat is the meaning of all this?" James Gordon Bennett asked
in a *New York Herald* editorial (1 September 1835) questioning
the national "hysteria" that appeared to have overtaken paradise
America. Bennett was speaking of the disturbances that, to some antebellumites (and some historians), denominate these decades as years of civil
disorder, a "turbulent era," a time of "mob," "riot," and "demagogues."
In this view, it is not a visionary frontier or the topography of the city,
not economic developments and wrenching changes in work, not the artic-

ulations descriptive of individual senses of "class" that characterize the years from 1825 to 1860 in America, but discourses of control that have as their subject regulation of group action and social life. A wide range of voluntary and legally vested associations are included as staging sites for these discourses in the antebellum decades; religious, temperance, health-oriented, sexual, abolitionist and racial, charitable, utopian, police and fire, asylum, and civic improvement associations name some of them. Control discourses both "create" the thing named by focusing attention upon it – "riot," "drunken disorder," "mob," for example – and color it ideologically, condemning or applauding the practice that the discourse would regulate or implement. Historical studies of the aims and tactics of the person or group that "had social control as one of its implicit goals or . . . latent functions" legitimate the issue around which the control discourse organizes itself (e.g., that there were riots, that prostitution was a problem), but not necessarily that control of a given kind was needed or that attempts at it were successful.[1]

The "mental maps" constructed to locate the tensions between attempts "to create symbolic order out of social multiplicity" (legitimation) and the creation of multiplicity out of symbolic orders (delegitimation) are the subjects of this chapter. Not infrequently in recent years historical studies have been unable to locate the great "stable historical myths" around which histories have in the past been organized: myths of Puritan control, of cults of domesticity, or of the ascendancy of a "mobocracy," for example. Despite controversy about them, legitimating myths retain a seductive hold on U.S. historical studies even in the face of changed historical subjects – nonmale, nonwhite, nonbourgeois, for example – whose presence destabilizes the uniform applicability of great myths as historical explanations of American culture. The continued search for commanding narratives and historiographical paradigms, new myths of legitimation, seems likely to continue as long as historical studies are prized for "coherence," and "comprehensibility" – and contested for totalization and erasure.[2]

Spaces of legitimation in antebellum America disclose not only different actors but different strategies of play where regulating sociocultural agenda are concerned. In some instances control results from *not* exercising wide-scale social regulation. For example, the Boston Athenaeum (a private antebellum library) regulated only its own prosperous subscription members, members who, in turn, sponsored the creation of a separate, public library for Boston. Similarly, legislation, such as the married wom-

en's property acts passed between 1839 and 1862 – which established a
woman's entitlement to her wage and income but not to equity in common law – was prompted by concern not necessarily for working women
but rather for the property of upper- and middle-class women. Social control by exclusion as well as by wide-scale regulation can appear as strategies in connection with the same cultural issue. The regulation of women
in antebellum theatre audiences, for example, sought the wide-scale control of female behavior and dress by excluding those who failed to satisfy
an unstaged code of conduct that self-defines the general case (morality)
in each instance of exclusion (a prostitute). The instability of these strategies and what they proport to legitimate or delegitimate suggests the presence of a discourse of regulation rather than the fact of control, still less
of hegemonic control. What is authorized, valorized, suppressed, contested, or appropriated in antebellum spaces of legitimation is examined in
this chapter via cultural constructions of women, of sensation, and of social play. Like inscriptions of antebellum towns, cities, frontiers, work,
and class, these constructions facilitate the social performance of the self
– not only the performances scripted by author(itie)s, but those valorized
by the actors themselves.[3]

Bodying Forth

Antebellum towns and cities alternated regulation and liberty and provided numerous opportunities for both observation and self-display. Although
etiquette and advice books stress behavior indoors among known compan-
ions, antebellum life multiplied occasions to escape the home. For women,
these included marketing (previously done by men literally "bringing
home the bacon"), lunching out, attending lectures or public balls, using
library and religious reading rooms, out-working, visiting parks, shopping,
riding public transportation, and attending theatrical or musical matinees.
In short, communal contact was expanded, not contracted, by the shift
away from live–work patterns. Some of these out-going activities were sex
segregated – women-only lunchrooms, ferry compartments, even portions
of park lawns – but many more were not; nor were working women unable to enjoy them, given flexible working schedules. Overwhelmingly,
women used the city – alone, in groups, and accompanied by men, children, or servants – moving freely through communal spaces. Men moved

continually through these spaces as well: in the course of their work (e.g., carters, butchers, delivery personnel); to watch entertainments like balloon and ship launchings; by walking home for extensive dinners around two in the afternoon; or in the course of lunching out in taverns, clubs, parks, oyster bars, or on doorsteps. It has been argued that "the street was shared more equitably than any other space" in antebellum cities and towns, and neither women nor men appear to have avoided public spaces despite complaints about being pushed, insulted, forced off the sidewalk, pickpocketed, solicited, and about the congestion and noise of foot and horse traffic. Pleasure as well as business brought people forth, as suggested by a lively tradition of parades and communal public activities of many sorts in these decades. For women in particular, as Lydia Maria Child observed of her free use of New York in the earlier 1840s, there was a choice: to circulate or not. "They who think exclusive gentility worth the fetters it imposes," Child counseled, "are welcome to wear them. I find quite enough conventional shackles that cannot be slipped off, without assuming any unnecessary ones."[4]

While the free movement of women in the marketplaces where Bowery B'hoys "fetched down de cleaver" underscores the public nature of antebellum life, there was also a freer circulation of "private" information and behavior in these decades than postbellum American society tolerated. Histories of antebellum sexuality, for example, disclose both that contraceptive information was widely available in the earlier nineteenth century via marital guides, almanacs, medical journals, physicians, word of mouth, and newspapers (e.g., in 1830s ads for syringe douches, vaginal sponges, cervical caps and diaphragms, and ads in the *New York Times* in 1861 for condoms), and that both information and devices were priced within the range of most working Americans. Contraception via these devices, abstention, coitus interruptus, or abortion was not by custom treated as news (though sex crimes and the activities of alleged abortionists were), but neither were antebellum editors and publishers reluctant or constrained from publishing diatribes, advertisements, or pamphlets about them. Similarly, homosexual practice among men between 1796 and 1873 came to court in New York City only twenty-two times in sodomy indictments that usually cited force or a disparity in ages; indeed, the city did not criminalize (male) consensual same-sex practice until the end of the century.[5]

Conjoined with these framings of the private is the creation of a public discourse of individual control concerning sexual behavior, marked by an increase during the antebellum decades in cautionary sex literature that linked sexual practice to health. This literature posits "normal" women lack a sexual drive and charges men with controlling theirs. It views masturbation, ejaculation, and pregnancy as injurious to health, and advocates chastity as the solution to all "problems" except procreation. Compounding the tension between public discourse and "private sins" was the imposition upon sexuality of romance – a "quest for emotional intimacy and even spiritual union" – driving a wedge of language, expectations, and behaviors between desire and action. The "romance" text appears to have been disparately interpreted by antebellum social groups; indeed, Christine Stansell argues that views of sexual practice (specifically, female behavior) among working people varied according to "the context of particular situations" rather than corresponding to an absolute moral standard.[6]

The relating of sex to health contextualizes the former in an interesting way. Health reformer Sylvester Graham, for example – popularly remembered for his whole-wheat crackers – sought to stem a variety of excesses he indicted as injurious to health, authorizing fresh vegetables and grains, more frequent bathing, daily exercise, abstention from alcohol and other stimulants (such as red meat), and a regular and quiet life. Graham's advice was consistent with literature in the 1830s that urged (especially sexual) restraint, and its wide appeal in part resulted from offering a comprehensive explanation of ill health (excess) about which the sufferer could do something. As Stephen Nissenbaum notes, "ailments did not originate in the confusing array of external circumstances over which they had no control, but rather in that single area of their lives for which they could assume total responsibility: the ordinary routine of private habit." The Graham regimen (and boardinghouses offering it), water cures, and fresh-air therapy appealed to builders, grocers, machinists, and bookbinders rather than to wealthier or poorer men and women, and wide publication of Graham's works and his lectures found ready reception among young adults in their twenties, who constituted 45 percent of white populations in large U.S. cities in 1840 and 30 percent nationwide.[7]

Graham's sexual agenda derived from his view that "persistent sexual desire was neither healthy nor natural." In his *Lectures to Young Men on Chastity* (1834), Graham held that "health does not absolutely require that there should ever be an emission of semen from puberty to death." Graham argued not celibacy (he was himself married) but rather that sexual activity, which dissipated energy as readily as a rich diet or the use of alcohol, needed to be controlled. That the view was general (though we cannot know how widely held) is signaled by a substantial body of cautionary sex literature after 1830, where previously (despite the high profile of Puritans in our mythic past) there had been hardly any. In the main, this literature argued against masturbation, promoted contraception in marriage and abstinence outside it, and considered prostitution a scientific (health) concern as much as (or more than) a moral one. The conflation of issues of health and morality made strange bedfellows: Scientists (like health reformers) argued frequency of intercourse from once a week to once a month, depending upon "constitutional stamina, temperament, occupation, habits of exercise, etc."; ministers (citing scientists) promised onanism would cause debility, insanity, and weak offspring; sex advocates like Oneida's John Humphrey Noyes promoted Graham's dietary regimen while interpreting sexual "self-restraint" not as regulated monogomous intercourse but as contraception via the control of ejaculation with a variety of female partners; and Magdalene Societies, in allying with diet, temperance, and exercise reforms, promoted a return to "normal" female sexuality that subverted their own moralist agendas by connecting prostitution more closely to science than to god.[8]

Scientizing sexual activity problematized prostitution as a social concern with a text in disease but furnished no social program to address it. As a health issue, prostitution initially paled by comparison to the epidemics of cholera (1832–4, 1849, 1855), typhoid/typhus (1837, 1842, 1855), and yellow fever (1832) that ravaged populations already weathering tuberculosis, scarlet fever, dysentery, diphtheria, whooping cough, measles, and other contagious or infectious diseases. Such plagues killed fifty to seventy thousand people in London in 1848–9, and though their effects were less concentrated in the United States, epidemics were greatly feared. Slums and poverty were linked by reformers in these decades to health and environmental causes (frequently temperance, but also concern for clean water and adequate sewerage and waste removal). By comparison, sexually transmitted diseases did not become a dominant text until midcentury, when they were perceived as epidemic both in England and the United States. At that point, health concerns appear to have joined with existent moral and communal texts, simultaneously privatizing and socializing prostitution. On one hand, the ideology forged from the health text made the individual responsible for his or her own improvement. Harassment of the Mayhew and Comstock sort, with their agendas in the 1860s and 1870s of examination, surveillance, and legislation, was not the social program of the antebellum decades; on the other hand, the privatization of prostitution as a health issue did nothing to redress its social causes. That prostitutes in the United States were far more likely to be made from poverty than from weak characters, for example, was underscored by William Sanger's landmark 1858 study, yet its scientific framing could "regulate" the "problem" only via individual (educational, therapeutic) means. Coupled with the notion that wage work for women was unnatural, prostitution in antebellum America became a problem without a solution.[9]

A considerable difficulty for reformers of the time (and for historians since) lies in locating "prostitute." The leading historian of prostitution in ninetenth-century New York City, Timothy J. Gilfoyle, makes clear that there, as in other American cities and towns,

there was no statutory definition of prostitution. It was a condition of vagrancy and of being female; men patronizing prostitutes were rarely arrested. When prosecuted, prostitutes were usually treated as disorderly persons or vagrants, and if convicted, it was a misdemeanor, not a felony. Prostitution was only a crime in a public street. No law prohibited soliciting in a saloon, dance hall or furnished room[ing] house.[10]

Gilfoyle and Christine Stansell argue that the most typical form of prostitution in antebellum American cities was casual or occasional, the exchange of sexual favors for food, drink, entertainment, or money by women who had other jobs but were subject to periodic unemployment or slave wages. (Indeed, Stansell asks, would such behavior be considered prostitution by the women involved or by the communities in which they lived?) "Prostitutes" of this definition could be found in most city neighborhoods and defied statistical enumeration since they were not identifiable as inhabitants of brothels (Fig. 18). Antebellum reformers, however, locating prostitution as habitual and occupational, inflated the number of its perpetrators, setting the figure at ten thousand in New York City in 1833 – a number even they agreed was too high but that they continued to use throughout these decades. Prostitution of the sort more usually associated with the term – involving full-time sex workers and brothels – was not located (as in Europe) in red-light districts or tenderloins (characteristic of the later century), but existed in all parts of Manhattan; moreover, the lack of residential segregation in other antebellum American cities suggests

Fig. 18. *New York by Gas-Light*, "Hooking a Victim" c. 1850 (lithograph, courtesy of the Museum of the City of New York, gift of Karl Schmidt).

this dispersion may have been general in, at least, northern cities in the earlier nineteenth century. Even the most exclusive neighborhoods – for example, the West Wards in New York, where John Jacob Astor, Philip Hone, and brothel rentier John R. Livingston lived – were within one to four blocks of brothels, though there were far more in less affluent neighborhoods like New York's Five Points.[11]

As a space of legitimation – an activity to be regulated – antebellum health texts joined with moral ones to view prostitution as a threat to the young, in particular to the hero and heroine of the city-life melodrama, put most at risk by sexual activity. Recalling the flood of young men into cities, to whom advice books, health regimens, and voluntary associations reached out, sex literature positioned men as both victims and victimizers. On the one hand, Verranus Morse, Arthur Tappan, novels, plays, and countless tracts asserted that youths would be corrupted by boarding-houses, theatres, bad habits, and out-and-out villains (male or female) if they were not on their guards. On the other hand, young men were depicted and described as seducers. With a consent age of 14 for males and 10–12 for females in these decades, sex with "women" even before the onset of menarche (variously estimated at 14–15 in 1835) was not statutorily prohibited, further confounding definitions of adulthood, consent, seduction, and morality among the young. A similarly ambivalent portrait characterized antebellum young women. On the one hand, they were at risk for seduction or rape, particularly if in domestic service, the "respectable work" most often urged on them by reformers. On the other hand, young women between 15 and 29 were the "whoreacracy," the seducers of youth, the sewers (to follow Parent-Duchâtelet) into which (male) society poured its corruption and which "it" in turn spewed forth to corrupt generations yet unborn.[12]

Not surprisingly, the theatre emerges as a staging ground for antebellum sexuality and with it a discourse that sought to control audience behavior. As we saw in Chapter 2, the arguments of clerics concerning immoral plays and players largely lost effectiveness in these decades. In their stead, a legitimating discourse emerged (articulated largely by moral reformers and publishers), with social control agenda that questioned the morality of audience members. Though Claudia D. Johnson, the historian of "that guilty third tier" (where prostitutes are said to have sat), attempts to locate her text as an abiding one in early American theatre, no strong claim for regulation appears to forward itself prior to the 1832 publication of prominent art and theatre historian (and one-time [1796–1805] Park Theatre manager) William Dunlap's influential *History of the American Theatre*. Dunlap's call for the regulation of theatres was prompted by his desire for government control and support of American theatre on the models of early-nineteenth-century "national" theatres in Germany and France. In order to make that argument, Dunlap had to establish private theatre management as inadequate. Accordingly, his history identifies several problems, which he writes on the body of women. He says:

The evil we mean, and shall protest against, is that which arises from the English and American regulation of theatres, which allots a distinct portion of the proscenium to those unfortunate victims of seduction.

Dunlap's *History* depicts "the problem" by extending the frame of performance (the proscenium) to the auditorium and by moralizing the prostitute (here as "unfortunate victim,' though quickly less benignly). "Prohibition of the immoral display would remove a just stigma from the theatre, and would further the views of managers by increasing their receipts," he argues, since the return of those who object to "the display" would more than make up revenue lost from the displayers. To Dunlap, it is an outrage that a "separate place should be set apart, to present to the gaze of the matron and virgin the unabashed votaries of vice, and to tempt the yet unsullied youth, by the example of the false face which depravity assumes for the purpose of enticing to guilt." So beset, "those who wished to support, as a mode of improvement, the representation of good dramatic works, have been driven from the boxes by the spectacle presented, not on the stage, but on seats placed opposite to them, and attracting their attention from the stage."[13]

Perhaps realizing that he is painting theatres as brothels, Dunlap extends the metaphor into a broad condemnation of American culture:

The improper, indecent, and scandalous practice of setting apart a portion of the boxes for the most disgusting display of shameless vice, has no connexion [*sic*] with the question of the utility of theatres. The prostitution of the pencil, the graver, or that mighty engine, the press, to the purposes of vice, immorality, or irreligion, might with equal propriety be charged against those modes of ameliorating or instructing society.

The "problem" is thus triangulated by Dunlap into a moral, aesthetic, and legislative one. What can explain the "meagre, mean, and despicable" plays – in comparison to Shakespeare and (ironically, he cites) Congreve – brought out in America (several of which Dunlap himself authored or adapted) except star-tailored plays, women of ill fame, hack dramatists, huge playhouses, and shows of monsters and animals? Until these evils are removed, only "such audiences as are fit for such exhibitions" will attend the theatre.[14]

Dunlap's approach to this knot of origins creates a causal perplex that singles out the most visible, intimidable object, the person of the rogue female. As an insolvable site for action, the prostitute stands in for the general problem of audience morality: that in America, "It is not practicable to exclude the impure and the vicious from public resorts." Neither does Dunlap advocate such exclusion. Attending the drama might, after all, reform the corrupt, whereas segregation merely exacerbates the evil – as witness the Federal Street Theatre in Boston (1793–1852) which, says Dunlap,

provided a separate entrance for those who come for the express purpose of allur-
ing to vice. The boxes displayed the same row of miserable victims, decked in
smiles and borrowed finery, and the entrance could only, by its separation from
those appropriated to the residue of the audience, become a screen inviting to secret guilt.

Dunlap's solution is the heterosexual date: "If a regulation was enforced
that no female should come to a theatre unattended by a protector of the
other sex, except such whose standing in society is a passport to every
place, the evil would be effectually remedied." It is a solution that pro-
poses, ironically, to control prostitution by universal inclusion, distributing "impurity" throughout the playhouse.[15]

Dunlap's regulatory text was quickly appropriated by respectability-
hungry managers and by those who used it as an argument against rather
than for external regulation. Noah Ludlow, for example, boasts in his
memoir that his St. Louis theatre in 1837 refused admission to unescorted
women and used "a private policeman, well acquainted with such kind of
persons by sight" to eject "women notoriously of the *pave*" and their bul-
lies. Ludlow enacted Dunlap's plan, insisting a "gentleman, or someone
having the appearance of a man of respectability" accompany his female
audience members, "even in the third tier." Actress and playwright Olive
Logan also drew attention to prostitutes in playhouses, writing of "that
dark, horrible guilty 'third tier'" in Cincinnati playhouses when her father
managed a theatre there (1844–54). "None but the most degraded of prostitutes" sat in this section, she vividly recalls, where they swore, shouted,
and solicited, until public opinion compelled managers to regulate the of-
fenders. Chronicler of city life George G. Foster expanded the control text
in his 1850 consideration of Niblo's Theatre in New York, arguing that the
regulation of women contained the behavior of men:

The secret was simple – no woman is admitted to this house, unless accompanied by a gentleman. The consequence is that rowdies avoid the house, or if they
visit it, have no inducement for misbehaving – and respectable and quiet people
freely come, with their wives and children, sure of being neither shocked by ob-
scenity nor frightened by violence.

Accounts insisting that "a portion of each house has been set aside for
public prostitutes, has been converted into an arena of assignation" appear
frequently in histories of antebellum theatres and society and contribute

Fig. 19. "A 'Bowery' on a Lark" (from Jennings, *Theatrical and Circus Life*).

to the perception both of prostitutes as a "problem" and of their presence as localized to designated seating ("that guilty third tier"). Contextualized in terms of "class" and antebellum working women on the whole, however, the evidence may seem both less robust and more directed.[16]

As we saw in Chapter 2, the profound shifts in the nature and location of work that characterize the antebellum decades produced an increase in the number and visibility of women working outside the home for wages. Social histories of nineteenth-century Britain emphasize that "certain forms of working-class behavior which offended bourgeois norms – rough voices, garish dress, drinking, and swearing" (indeed, the mere fact of work for wages) – often prompted the equation of working women with prostitutes. Historians of nineteenth-century America similarly point out that "popular perception identified . . . the prostitute, as much by her demeanor in public as by her actual sexual behavior," a behavior costumed in dress that could be conflated with that of working women, particularly with the Bowery G'hal, who deliberately elected bright colors, slang, a distinctive walk, open manner, and the absence of deference to "swells" (Fig. 19). Consideration of the wages of G'hals "in smiles and borrowed finery" (as Dunlap characterizes young single women) or the wages of the "rough-clad [woman] of decent looks" (whom Haswell identifies *en famille* in the antebellum theatre), suggests that the seating they could most likely afford was in the galleries. There, they offered a ready target for those prepared to extend the text of prostitution to all women who, by reason of dress, behavior, or employment offended the sensibilities of male critics, authors, reformers, and those women and men who would or did manage theatres. Despite these voices, theatres (as noted in Chapter 1) were traditionally self-regulating spaces with which managers did not interfere unless the peace was sufficiently disturbed to warrant calling up the watch. Regulation of prostitutes in theatres was particularly difficult since it was not against the law to solicit in a public place, increasing the chance that the unlucky doorman or manager who, right or wrong, labeled a woman a prostitute and tried to eject her might create the very disturbance regulation was interested in preventing. In addition, separate entrances to the third tier, such as those in Ludlow's St. Louis theatre and in the Federal Street Theatre in Boston, affronted the sensibilities of people who sat in gallery seats, denying them access to ornate lobbies and well-furnished lounges, and even imperiling their lives in the event of (frequent) theatre fires (Ludlow, e.g., describes "a flight of winding stairs having no connection with the other entrances"). In a day in which, as George Templeton Strong observed of the Castle Garden Theatre in New York in the 1850s, "Nob and snob, Fifth Avenue and Chatham Street sit side by side fraternally on the hard benches," sentiment did not favor exclusivity among whites in theatres, beyond that imposed by ticket prices.[17]

"The guilty third tier" is a discourse that forces classist and racist texts in explorations of antebellum American theatre history. Classism conflates working women with prostitutes. In addition to middle-class antebellumites like Dunlap, Ludlow, Logan, and, to a degree, Foster, who are prepared to erase the difference, there are those who would reinscribe it, which can encourage a reading of working women as "bourgeois at heart" and in turn erase the sexism and economic conditions that drew some antebellum women into occasional prostitution. Stansell, on the other hand, argues that working(-class) communities took a different and more tolerant approach toward sexual activity than that advocated by critics for genteel women and their communities, a view of mores and behaviors that accommodated the economic and social conditions of their lives. As spaces of legitimation, antebellum theatres staged these differences in their auditoria while offering melodramas of chaste sexuality on their stages, plays whose heroines may well have represented the dream lives of some antebellum working women. While a feminist history rightly notes the injustice of conflating working women with prostitutes, prostitutes are also working women, and the erasure of the fluid line between the one and the other in these decades only expunges the historical positioning of waged work for women and its poverty, and reinscribes prostitution as a moral issue.[18]

The racist text in the "guilty third tier" discourse operates yet more perversely in its conflation of segregation and prostitution to erase both black men and women from theatre spaces. The nearly universal segregation in white-operated theatres, the historical circumstance of these decades, is evident in relationship to sex as early as Moreau de Saint-Méry's account of the New Hall on Chestnut and Fourth Streets in Philadelphia, which he visited during his 1793–8 tour of America: "Women go in the pit like men; but these are not women of any social standing. The upper gallery admits women and colored people who can't sit anywhere else." Although women are, in this account, plainly seated in the pit – a practice also substantiated by a 1759 playbill for Cruger's Wharf Theatre in New York – Johnson's "guilty third tier" discourse assumes that "the fact that they were segregated on a tier with blacks suggests that the writer is speaking of the same women whom Dunlap describes as prostitutes." Setting aside the migration of an eighteenth-century account to the very different historical circumstances of the nineteenth century, the discourse's equation of black women (and men) with prostitutes not only extends a common racist text, but denies the presence of segregation laws or customs as specific historic circumstances conditioning the stigmatization of unescorted women. Antebellum racial conditions suggest both less and more fluid readings of theatre attendance in cities where black populations were numerous. At Caldwell's Camp Street Theatre in New Orleans in 1825, for example, black patrons had access to third-tier box and gallery seats, and there was one night a week when integrated audiences were seated (to accommodate, John S. Kendall states, white men escorting quadroon women). To read all "colored people" as prostitutes allies race itself with morality, a familiar text in antebellum racist literatures. The historic circumstances of race, taken with gender, legitimate exclusivity in ways theatre historians have, thus far, barely explored.[19]

While it is not wholly clear what parts of the theatre "that guilty third tier" designated – a "third row" in a gallery, a box in the third tier, or the whole of the third gallery – attempts at containing women were not limited to "the most degraded of prostitutes," nor to the unescorted women, poorer women, nor (all) women of color (mis)taken for them. "Ambiguous women" are located throughout the antebellum playhouse. Theatre architecture in these decades, as we've seen in Chapter 1, generally divided the auditorium into a pit, boxes, and galleries. Pit seating was gentrified taxonomically before the Civil War into the "parquette" (orchestra seating to the balcony edge) and the "parterre" (orchestra seating under the balcony); it was also made more comfortable via padded chairs to replace backless benches or, elsewhere in the house, hard stall seats. A city-life handbook of St. Louis theatre recreates an evening in which "a *nymph du pave*" and a wayward wife in orchestra seats keep an assignation (arranged via a newspaper ad) with two salesmen from a hotel. In addition, the handbook's author describes well-appointed women in the dress circle (presumably not prostitutes) who have come to the theatre to flirt, while box and gallery seats give place to both nonworking and working prostitutes. Charles Haswell's less sensationalized reminiscence looks out from the box circle upon

two gloved women in the audience; they, by force of their attire, I suppose, felt a certain application of the saying *noblesse oblige*, since they went much out of their way to be agreeable to us and were very courteous and hospitality-minded.

If Haswell's is a coy description of prostitutes, the editor of the *New York Herald* (19 September 1838) was anything but reticent bluntly to take a body count:

On Friday night the Park Theatre contained 83 of the most profligate and abandoned women that ever disgraced humanity; they entered in the same door, and for a time mixed indiscriminately with 63 virtuous and respectable ladies. . . . Men of New York, take not your wives and daughters to the Park Theatre, until Mr. Simpson pays some respect to them by constructing a separate entrance for the abandoned of the sex.

"They" were everywhere.[20]

How good a contact point a theatre was in comparison to ferry landings, hotels, taverns, the streets, and other places of free public congregation remains at present uncertain. For example, prostitutes and clients would have both to buy tickets and leave the theatre to turn a trick (solicitation in a theate was not a crime, but public intercourse was) – unless there was a reduced price or free admission once the play had progressed, of the sort invoked by Oscar Wilde's reference in *The Importance of Being Earnest* to "trot[ting] "round the Empire [Theatre in London] about ten." Despite the appeal of "ambiguous women," lounges were the crux of the "regulation" agenda. They are luridly described in George G. Foster's 1851 study of Gotham, trenchantly entitled *New York Naked:*

[The upper galleries of the Bowery] are filled with rowdies, fancy men, working girls of doubtful reputation, and, least of all, the lower species of public prostitutes, accompanied by their "lovyers" or such victims as they have been able to pick up. The central point of this stratum is the punch room, where a continual flood of poisoned brandy, rum, and whiskey is poured down the reeking throats of these desperate wretches until, steam being up to the proper point, they take their departure one by one, to the haunts of crime, debauchery and robbery, whence they issued at nightfall like broods of dark ill-omened birds.[21]

Two decades earlier, in its 2 April 1834 number, the *New York Sun* had cited a Chapel Street prostitute's endorsement that "we girls always patronize the Bowery – moreover the manager here is a very clever man," a report that cannot have intended any credit to Hamblin, the theatre's manager. Stygian portraits and testimonials to vice were not exclusive to the Bowery Theatre or to New York. Ludlow reports closing his second-floor "saloon for gentlemen" in St. Louis before the end of its first (1837–8) season because "it was found to be an annoyance to the occupants, not only of the second, but of the first tier" because "the loud talking that frequently took place there disturbed many persons who came to hear and enjoy the performance on the stage." Clearly, ticket prices and architecture had an impact upon regulation. So did longevity: An 1838 report to the Society for the Reformation of Juvenile Delinquents indicted the smaller saloon or concert theatres (Fig. 20) then springing up as "more injurious to the morals of the city than the older establishments," where prostitution and (in some houses) the "grog shop" were regulated.[22]

That regulating women was not universally attempted by antebellum theatres is suggested by the infrequency of ads requiring women to be escorted and by the presence of ads encouraging their "unregulated" attendance (offers of special seating, matinees, and the like). The recourse of choice for theatre managers (although Ludlow was not the only exception) seems to have been to eject only those patrons who behaved inappropriately inside the theatre. In this, closing or regulating the theatre saloon may have played a greater role than attempts to exclude "prostitutes." The futility and ambiguity of attempts to regulate women is nicely captured by William Sanger in his 1858 study of prostitution: "It is right to say here, that many of the managers of our best theatres have abolished the third tier, so called, and if any improper woman visits them she must do so under the assumed garb of respectability and conduct herself accordingly."[23]

In its juxtaposed class, sex, race, legislative, aesthetic, social, and economic agendas, "that guilty third tier" in both antebellum theatres and recent research has fetishized prostitution into a legitimating discourse involving all women, inside playhouses and out. Not only did city-centered storypapers and handbooks of city life like Foster's forge a link between theatres and vice, but also sexual guidebooks led the randy antebellumite to institutionalized prostitution – "Butt Ender's" *Prostitution Exposed; or, A Moral Reform Directory* (1839), "Charles DeKock's" *Guide to the Harems; or, Directory to the Ladies of Fashion in New York and Various Other Cities* (1855), or "Free Lovyer's" *Directory of the Seraglios in New York, Philadelphia, Boston, and All the Principal Cities of the Union* (1857–9). Brothels and theatres were not infrequent neighbors in the antebellum urban landscape. Gilfoyle's study locates 93 of New York's brothels (34%) within 2.5 blocks of a theatre between 1830 and 1839, 87 (42%) at that proximity between 1840 and 1849, and 181 brothels (53%) within 2.5 blocks of a theatre between 1850 and 1859. While brothels were scattered all over antebellum New York City, they also concentrated close to centers of transient population. In addition, Broadway and the Bowery, avenues adjacent to theatres, were favorite promenades of *femmes du pave*. The chance of encountering "them" was, then, threefold: One had to walk through "prostitutes" to get to the theatre, one encountered "them" among the audience, and "they" used the theatre as a place to contact clients.[24]

The Chatham, Bowery, Broadway, and Lafayette theatres in antebellum New York City all shared their blocks with brothels. "Sarah Brady's establishment on Church Street and Mrs. Brown's on Leonard Street advertised their proximity to the National Theatre"; indeed, when the National burned in 1841, one of its walls fell on a newly opened "temple of Venus." Reinforcing Joe Cowell's description of the Park Theatre as a theatrical dive, an erotic roadmap charts that theatre's association with whorehouses as being long, if not distinguished:

Fig. 20. "Harry Hill's 'Free and Easy'" (from Jennings, *Theatrical and Circus Life*).

In addition to the dressing rooms for performers [behind the Park in Theatre Alley], Rebecca Fraser ran a brothel in the early 1820s before moving around the corner at Ann Street in 1825. For nearly a decade, from 1831 to 1839, [Sarah McGindy and] Mrs. Newman ran a house with at least eight girls only a few doors behind the Park Theatre [that specifically catered to performers and patrons alike].[25]

Not surprisingly, then, *Harper's Weekly* complained in 1857 that the mere erection of a theatre ushered gambling, prostitution, and drunkenness into a neighborhood, ruining "that quarter for any decency of life." When even a tolerant theatregoer like Lydia Maria Child decried "the low, unsatisfactory, and demoralizing character of popular amusements" inside theatres that served as a "sensual stimulus and fierce excitement [to] every little vagabond of this city," how much more might a powerful journal condemn not only the "regulation" of conduct in such places, but the sensual stimulus that the simple presence of a theatre injected into the communities of the matron, virgin, and youth?[26]

The campaign against "that guilty third tier" and prostitutes in theatre extends the gender antagonism evident in debates concerning women as wage workers (see "Work" in Chapter 2) beyond the workplace and into shared cultural arenas. The antebellum theatre was an opportune setting for staging the hostility that altered constructs of working in these decades often carried, but those constructs implicated others – racial, economic, gendered – that spread strategies of legitimation to a variety of aesthetic, publishing, social, and sexual locales. In refusing Dunlap's argument for regulation by the state (as the United States has to the present day), antebellum theatres were left to the legitimating agendas of managers. Their solution to "the problem" of prostitution in the playhouse and rowdy men in the saloons was either to ignore it, to act only to maintain public order (the "contract" discussed in "Class" in Chapter 2), to redistribute theatrical space (architectural changes), or to invoke performance criteria – most frequently "the garb of respectability" or "the appearance of a man [or woman] of respectability." Social historians have made much of the gentrification campaign in nineteenth-century America (again, see "Class"), but it is perhaps a uniquely theatrical approach to meet the titillating and moralizing text of the "guilty third tier" with an invitation to perform the appearance of respectability.

Sensation Scenes

The liminality of antebellum spaces provides ready transition from one representative space to another. As reformers and a popular press made the erotic a discourse, so sex readily gave way to violence; indeed, Gilfoyle suggests that "the widely publicized trial of Richard P. Robinson for the brutal murder of the glamorous prostitute Ellen Jewett in 1836 initiated the era of the sex scandal in the penny press." If sex was news, violence was bigger news, as can be discerned in an antiprostitute campaign driven less by morality than by a perceived need to regulate "disturbances." (You could be immoral in the playhouse auditorium if you went about it in an orderly way.) The antebellum decades, however, were not adjudged to be orderly years; in fact, the major voluntary associations had as their movement goals the regulation or reformation of some "disturbing" aspect of

American life: temperance for the inebriate, abolition for the slave, education for the ignorant, religious revivals for the unregenerate, charity for the indigent poor, or asylums for the lost. Regulation extended texts of personal reform (diet, sexual conduct, exercise, manners, and the like) into the body politic. The uneasy relationship between personal and public control was constantly renegotiated in these decades – a tension acted out in the antebellum theatre, where the two could readily escalate into conflict.[27]

European playhouses had frequently served as staging areas both for newsworthy events, such as touring dignitaries or public celebrations, and for civic unrest. Their centralized locations and public natures in American cities continued these traditional associations. As a playground for public opinion, antebellum American theatres were often located near city hall, the custom house or stock exchange, jails, marketplaces, banks, or other cultural institutions. While theatre managers encouraged, even vied for visits by public figures (e.g., Lafayette or Black Hawk), they were less sanguine when their playhouses were preempted as civic fora for staging public issues. Of the seventy-seven disorders reported nationwide in the "decade of riots" (1834–44), twenty-five occurred in or around theatres but few had directly to do with theatrical matters. Among those that did during the antebellum decades, the largest disturbances in theatres involved claques formed in support of or in opposition to specific actors or theatre managements over slights to Americans or American artists by foreigners. Theatrical disorders of this type fell within the self-regulating text (see "Class" in Chapter 2) wherein the public was permitted, as one judge lectured misbehavers in 1822, to applaud or hiss but not to "make the theatre a scene of riot or confusion." The house management was expected to endure disturbances of this sort without calling in the public watch or constabulary and thereby escalating matters. Moreover, the "contract," to use the legitimating language for this unbounded and constantly contested relationship, had clear spatial limits: the interior and exterior of the theatre building. Beyond these confines, "regulating" was a civic matter and in hands other than those of a theatre's management.[28]

Civic regulation of disturbances, within theatres and out, became news from the earliest years of these decades. Paul O. Weinbaum suggests antebellum newspaper editors were entirely willing "to use the mob to influence public policy and opinion," and certainly newspaper accounts present disturbances as the concern of editors as much as of civic or religious authorities. Advocacy could be both brazen and censured. When the *Gazette and General Advertiser* of 2 October 1833, for example, urged "a firm but discreet interference [with an abolition meeting to] put a stop to the injudicious and ill-advised course of these deluded individuals," the journal was rebuked by the press as inciting the public to riot (a condemnation issued by newspapers that themselves took an advocacy course in other causes). What emerges is a context for action couched as "sensation": "a strong impression (e.g., of horror, admiration, surprise) produced in an audience or body of spectators, and manifested by their demeanour." News reports that sensationalized scenes of disorder sought an emotional response from readers, in that perception via the senses ("sensation") was held to be a form of cognition. To "know" disturbances was, then, to "feel" them and to manifest or stage that response in perceptible ways.[29]

Like vice, violence lent itself to sensationalization. Conspiracy theories were ready to hand. In these scenarios, theatres became "an adjunct to the political stage," while plays served "political exigencies." Antebellumites focused upon the leaders and goals of disturbances: "Mobs" were led by "demogogues"; the disorders they orchestrated – whether against the price of flour, a foreign actor, or an unpopular cause – were "riots" carried out by "rabble" ungoverned by principle. Actions without discernible causes were irrational and primitive, the stuff of lunatics, drunkards, and savages. Civic dramas, on the other hand, had plots and agents to conduct them. Performatively expressed, sanctified struggles for power (which is how the Revolutionary War had come to be seen by 1825) exalted the ordinary actor. Indeed, humble life itself had become news in the explosion of weeklies and dailies during the 1830s and 1840s. At the same time, the power of individual presence diminished before a crowd of unknown faces, as magistrates who tried traditional tactics of mass control in these decades soon discovered. Where there was no economic or social advantage to good behavior – an observing boss or approving congregation, for example – deference to communal authority diminished in importance before status within the crowd itself.[30]

Antebellum traditions of gathering, most visible in parades, furthered the exhibition of symbolic civic value performed by the empowered individual. Parade celebrations of labor, militia, fire control, religion, patriotism, race and ethnicity, political affiliation, public order, and holidays paralleled the nominal content of disturbances. In addition, parades could be orderly (costumes, drill order, bands, a program) and respectable (affluent), or disorderly (spontaneous) and without costly display. The ordered, respectable parade separates performers and audience; the less orderly display reduces that distance, offering the choice to participate by observing or to appropriate the text prompting the gathering and perform it.[31]

The distinction between audience and participant in antebellum America was flexible, both within theatres and out. The view that riots and disorders in the streets occurred because there were no professional police in America's major cities (until the 1850s) was extended by antebellumites to absent or ineffectual policing inside theatres. Both contexts reflect an investment in the possibility of consensus – that is, that there would be voluntary compliance with visible and firm authority – a view requiring interpretations of individual rights and constituted law of the sort questioned by Orestes Brownson and the transcendentalists. Both civil life and "acceptable" activity in theatres lacked such a consensus. The search for rational cause in consensus-free behavior pulled spectator and performer in opposite directions, one stressing commonality and the other individuality. Antebellum theatre attempted conflation of these two via "sensation" in sociodramas like *The Drunkard* (1844) and *Uncle Tom's Cabin* (Aiken version, 1852). Disturbances inside or proximate to theatres of the Farren (1834) and Astor Place (1849) sorts affected a similar conflation of the individual into the communal that proved greater than sensation could contain.[32]

The health movement readily extended to temperance and harmonized with advice manuals encouraging moderation in all aspects of behavior. Socially, however, the violence excess drink visited upon the body of men (in particular) warred directly with the communal nature of the antebellum saloon. Traditionally, taverns had been centers for transport, news, business, nourishment, politics, and recreation. In these functions, they shared importance as communal centers equal to churches. Churches, on the other hand, could not fulfill all these functions, and initially did not seek to do so; but the religious revivals beginning in 1831 promulgated an activist faith that mandated intervention in a number of human affairs and the end of gradualism as a tactic against alcohol, slavery, and other reform issues. That some of this activism was motivated by retrograde desires to slow the course of change and to reinforce reformers' social and political power seems likely, but such fear-driven concerns may have been less compelling to antebellumites than the single-cause explanation (inebriation) that sensation (reason) then required be addressed. In one stroke, one could both understand and effect that understanding. Historians of temperance describe a three-phase evolution of the movement in the antebellum decades: first to the habits of business managers and professionals (1826–40), then to those of craftsmen and laborers (1840s), and only in the decade just prior to the Civil War to prohibition. Turning alcohol into a legitimating discourse reflected material changes in post-Revolutionary America that turned grain into more easily shipped and less likely to spoil alcohol, manufactured it in quantity in frontier Pennsylvania, Kentucky, and Tennessee, and priced it cheaper than food.[33]

The change in attitudes and behaviors toward alcohol in these decades seems dramatic. In the first quarter of the nineteenth century even ministers drank at social gatherings, workers drank on the job, meals featured several kinds of alcohol, and entertainments made liquor available to patrons or guests; yet within twenty years (1830–50) liquor consumption nationally was cut by two-thirds (from an estimated seven gallons per capita annually to two) and its presence in work or home settings was deemed by more than a few to be inappropriate or actually evil. These were voluntary reductions affected largely without prohibitionary statutes. The temperance message, carried by print rather than through lectures by worthies, extensively relied upon the organizational service of women and youths. It explained a wide variety of evils, provided villains (distillers, traders, tavernkeepers), victims (drunkards and their families), and heroes (the abstainer), and valorized self-reliance: Anyone (it was argued) could be temperate. More important, temperance organizations and the voluntary associations with which they coincided – the YMCA, mercantile libraries, church groups, clubs, athletic associations, speakers groups – provided alternatives to the tavern as places to interact, gather news, eat, make business or social contacts, relax, and discuss or attend to the larger affairs of the world. Social infrastructures of this sort could not address the economic problems of the laboring drunkard, but temperance orders, such as the Washingtonians, tried to foster alternatives to alcoholic fire companies and a more tolerant understanding of the problems of workers – meanwhile keeping alive the artisan myth that hard work and temperate habits could still make the (white) mechanic the master. Such rhetoric did not obviate the perceptions of inequality often focused in negative characterizations of temperance, such as this in the *Liberal Advocate* of 3 March 1832: "Who are the most temperate men of modern times? Those who quaff the juice of the grape with their friends . . . or the cold-water, pale-faced, money-making men who make the necessities of their neighbors their opportunity for grinding the face of the poor?"[34]

Numerous entertainments were pressed to serve the temperance cause – poems, short stories, minstrel sketches, tableaux vivants, songs, skits, and plays – giving performance in the process the "respectability" of an instructive medium with social importance. The noble cause of temperance licensed enactments by both amateurs and professionals, extending texts of self-performance for the former beyond health, etiquette, and advice books. Moreover, the temperance "drama" was tailor-made for sensation, given its highly charged content of blasted lives, its "ordinary" heroes and heroines, socioeconomic threats, d.t.'s, villainous plots, and heartwarming reforms and reunions. From a regulatory perspective, the individual temperance melodrama ("the world as it ought to be," the fallen saved) legitimated the existence of a national danger requiring broadfront action to save the Republic. From a perspective of personal legitimation, the wide number of amateur temperance plays and the half-dozen professionally successful American ones held out to audiences the promise of self-determination, the "happy ending" of lifetime self-control agendas.[35]

W. H. Smith's *The Drunkard; or, the Fallen Saved* has become a legend in nineteenth-century American theatre history. It opened in February 1844 at the Boston Museum and reached perhaps 140 performances by the next year. Its production at Barnum's Museum in New York, beginning 8 July 1850 and ending 7 October, is considered the first uninterrupted run of a hundred consecutive performances – a steady advance from Hamblin's monthlong hits of the 1830s. Smith, stage manager and actor at the Boston Museum from its first season with a permanent acting company (1843) until 1859, was said to have written the play from his own battles with the bottle; he is principally known for playing Edward Middleton, the drunkard of the piece. Certainly, *The Drunkard*'s subject matter harmonized with proprietor Moses Kimball's alliance of his "Museum" with morality and education (the building offered paintings, stuffed birds, curios, live animals, wax statuary, and other items of interest en route to the theatre auditorium). The play's nationwide success, however, well into the postbellum decades, is said to have brought to the playhouse patrons who did not otherwise attend the theatre, perhaps persuaded by advertisements of it as "a moral lecture," sometimes "with sacred music."[36]

Even in its day, *The Drunkard* stirred the urge to burlesque in John Brougham (famed for his satires *Po-ca-hon-tas; or, The Gentle Savage* and

Metamora; or, The Last of the Pollywogs) and in satirists of lesser note. The delirium scene was extracted for serious and comic presentation along with other sketches; indeed, so powerful was the movement against alcohol that "temperance companies" appeared in the 1840s to advance its cause and help the intemperate to the pledge. Pertinent here is the drawing together of religion, temperance, politics, health reform, publishing/news, and social agenda through the agency of sensation to legitimate abstinence, a campaign that can locate control goals in both temperance advocates and antitemperance supporters. The optimistic agenda that saw in temperance a unique opportunity to make a better future for individuals and for society also consistently identified intemperance as the cause of inequity and social disorder, accepting punishing market conditions as inevitable and beyond human control. The social doctrine of resignation offered little motivation to sobriety for the laboring poor, but it was a powerful text for a newly created generation of clerks anxious to stay even with the artisan ideal of advancement. *The Drunkard*'s Edward Middleton was their hero. A product of the transcendental town, college graduate Middleton is a country squire and the heir to position; he is cast opposite the poor, equally fatherless, rustic, charming, and virtuous heroine. Her fortune is to marry him, his to repair his family inheritance in the embracing village. As in *The Forest Rose,* songs and dances celebrate the rustic paradise and the marriage of the virgin bride to the hero of the clerks' dream.[37]

The specter of ruin that looms over Eden is drink-driven; without it, could the villainous Cribbs succeed in deceiving Edward as to his (the villain's) true nature? Where authority imbibes, however – "Deacon Whitleather, he never sits down to dinner without a stiffhorn of something to wash it down" – and where the Sabbath is not kept, who shall guide even fortunate youth in the traditional pathways that had nurtured the sons of merchant families, apprenticed at age 14 to those clerking posts that educated them for proprietorship? Through four years of menial and upscaled labor, and with the father-master ever a proper role model, the merchant prince proved himself diligent and temperate. Buttressed by a wide network of religious and benevolent associations, nothing was uncertain or uncontrolled. Edward Middleton – in that "middle" place with no patriarch to guide him – lives, on the other hand, not the destiny of a future king of commerce, but the peril of the lowly clerk, without family, connections, or a formal network to conduct him through his career and life. His fall is swift: Two acts and hardly more years to descend from paradise

to Five Points. Instead of advice manuals to substitute for absent authority – William Alcott's *Young Man's Guide* (1833) or Daniel Wise's *The
Young Man's Counsellor* (1854) name two among the pamphlet army – or
voluntary associations with his improvement at heart, Edward becomes
one of those ten thousand clerks adrift in New York in 1845. Unguided, he
is prey not to corruption by amusements but, as YMCA official Charles
Tracy told a gathering in 1854, to the "fatal snare of business," a danger
far worse, Tracy knew, than "to suppose that the theatre and the gambling house were the main things to guard against."[38]

The inevitable fall occurs: corruption in the marketplace. The destitute
Middleton is urged by the villain Cribbs to commit forgery against Arden
Rencelaw, "the princely merchant! the noble philanthropist! the poor
man's friend! the orphan's benefactor!" The evils of drink, however, lie
not alone in temptation to defraud but in the public disorder inevitably
following upon drink: tavern brawls, street singing, crime, rowdiness, and
noise, the disturbances that kept city fathers in arms against the taverns,
hotels, theatres, and circuses that shattered domestic peace. At crisis point
– wife reduced to taking in washing then to beggary, child starving – the
clerks' dream at last comes true. The kindly king of commerce, Rencelaw,
lifts Edward from his drunken stupor and pledges to raise him "once
more, to the station in society from which you have fallen." A reformed
drunkard himself, Rencelaw is the perfect master: a good example, in deed
not only exemplary but providential, "an instrument of heaven." With
such intervention, sanity is regained by a village maid in time to recall
Middleton's grandfather's will, secreted by the villain, and to reinstall the
reformed hero in Eden. With him temperate, wealthy, restored to home
and hearth, useful, pious, and respected by society once more, what sacred
hymn could crown the final domestic tableau in Middleton's transcendental village but "Home Sweet Home?"[39]

Though melodrama exactly suits the temperance theme, here its form
is mediated to accommodate a flawed hero. Vitiated by drink, it is not
Middleton who rescues the imperiled heroine from the villain's erotic designs but the Yankee character William, and it is Rencelaw who must
supply the detection of evil that Middleton's befuddled mind cannot
encompass. William, the comic spinster Miss Spindle, and the play's frequent songs and dances are hard pressed to desacralize the heavily pietized world of *The Drunkard*, whose pieties are thrown into high relief by
sharp contrasts: good–evil, town–city, calm–disorder, quiet–noise, peace–

unrest, health–delirium tremens. Modern psychiatry might make much of the villain Cribbs, driven to intense hatred of Middleton's father by his forgiveness of Cribbs's early "act of vile atrocity"; the antebellumite would recognize that revenge, avarice, and hatred in return for pardon and pity (even if seasoned with contempt) was irrational and bereft of legitimating cause. Agents so lost to sensation, to knowing and feeling, were incapable of right action; they, as Cribbs concludes, live and die villains. To the temperate, the imposition of behavioral controls upon themselves and others was no more than acting upon their sensation of disobedience and disorder as spiritual problems with both material and moral components. As such, for all temperance advocates, the new governors of behavior were not the artisan masters but internalized controls externally manifested.[40]

As an ideal, Edward Middleton is an uneasy role model because he is flawed by drink. In addition, he is not a worker but a manager of (inherited) money; we never see him do anything with either his education or position except alternately waste and enjoy them. Middleton does not serve as a hero, however, either by being perfect or by sharing the socioeconomic status of the clerks and artisans he is intended to inspire; his service is to be saved, to receive benevolence merited solely because accepted. The gift of grace was equally available to all, whether that meant being awakened to religion, eating a Graham cracker, refusing alcohol, rejecting seduction, dining with a fork, being polite on the street, or talking quietly in a theatre. Middleton's counterpart in the sober and honest William converts the Yankee to mechanic and maximizes the character's availability as a role model to lower-grade clerks and workers. William will never be the focus of the drama, but his actions are brave and heroic, and his steadfastness and industry are accordingly both recognized and rewarded. He is a role model not least – like Woodworth's William before him – in knowing his place in his antebellum world. A third male hero is offered in Rencelaw, on the one hand the master to be emulated, on the other someone who has known travail and failure. To emulate him is to accept grace and, like him, to accede to the thrones of commerce. Women, too, have counterpoised heroes in this play: Mary Middleton, the long-suffering wife whose heroism through good deeds and perseverance (like Rencelaw and William) is rewarded; and Agnes, William's sister, crazed by the death of her fiancé through drink, who is restored by grace (like Middleton) to "take her place among the singers at the old meeting-house again." In offering these different models of heroes and heroines, *The Drunkard* interweaves the texts of individuality (self-reliance) and communality (in this case, the availability of grace to those who will accept it) in the powerful space of sensation.[41]

A similar sociocultural dynamic fuels other theatricalizations of regulating texts. Aiken's 1852 dramatization of Harriet Beecher Stowe's novel *Uncle Tom's Cabin* is perhaps less studied than the novel itself, but it has been a regular stopping place for examinations of abolition sentiment, concessions to antiabolitionism, domestic versus market economies, and the offering of religious values in place of the complex incentives underpinning slavery. The brief consideration here of Aiken's play as a space of legitimation cannot engage a now extensive Uncle Tom scholarship; nor does it suggest the space of representation is other than a complex of appropriations of slavery by free whites for white audiences through white actors. As a regulation of abolition via sensation, delegitimizing slavery in Aiken's *Uncle Tom's Cabin* engages both representative and liminal spaces.[42]

We have seen (in Chapter 1) antimaterialism in the transcendental town, whose daughter Harriet Beecher Stowe was. Stowe's inheritance, however, was that of organized religion and its legacy of intolerance, against which Emerson and his fellows inveighed and on whose behalf Stowe wrote in an 1852 letter to a would-be dramatizer of her novel:

It is thought with the present state of theatrical performances in this country, that any attempt on the part of Christians to identify themselves with them will be productive of danger to the individual character, and to the general cause. If the barrier which now keeps young people of Christian families from theatrical entertainments is once broken down by the introduction of respectable and moral plays, they will then be open to all the temptations of those who are not such, as there will be, as the world now is, five bad plays to one good.

Stowe is also implicated in the liminal space of gender, discussed in Chapter 2 (see "Class"). Her sister-in-law, Catherine Beecher, had proclaimed of women in her 1841 *Treatise* that "in all benevolent enterprises and in all questions relating to morals and manners they have superior influence." It was an influence Beecher and Stowe applied to the structures of women's lives via their 1869 *The American Woman's Home,* legitimating architecture, domestic economy, and home furnishing in minute detail. The combination of moral and domestic influence was extended to spaces legitimating abolition in Stowe's 1852 novel.[43]

Uncle Tom's Cabin is considered the most popular play of the second half of the nineteenth century. The extent of that popularity dwarfs superlatives: Uncle Tom dishes and crockery; songs, board games, and restaurants; an Uncle Tom street in Berlin; a word in French (*l'oncletomerie*); an initial run in Troy, New York, of a hundred consecutive performances (attracting twenty-five thousand people when only thirty thousand lived in the city); lantern-slide versions, minstrel versions, burlesques, a southern variant, equestrian versions, a diorama; forty-nine Tom companies on the road in 1879 and five hundred in 1899; theatres hung with scripture for performances, seating added for blacks, and (as for *The Drunkard*) attendance by patrons who would not otherwise, it is said, have visited the theatre – including, in 1854, Harriet Beecher Stowe herself. Aiken's adaptation was made at the request of his cousin-in-law, George C. Howard, who managed a theatre at Troy, New York. Howard and his wife, who had met and married as part of the original Boston Museum cast of *The Drunkard* in 1844, premiered the roles of St. Clare and Topsy in *Uncle Tom's Cabin*, with their daughter as Little Eva and Aiken joining in blackface as George Harris. With other members of their family, the Howards "Tommed" for the next thirty-five years in this most commanding of numerous adaptations of Stowe's novel.[44]

Recent scholarship emphasizes the antebellum humanitarian sensibility that undergirds the play; indeed, Aiken's *Uncle Tom's Cabin* is strongly representative of both artisan rhetoric and the charity debate. In the first case, as Mrs. Stowe observed, "The slave holder can whip his refractory slave to death; the capitalist can starve him to death." Aiken endows George Harris with the (white) manly mechanic's greatest fear and loathing ("My master! . . . What right has he to me?") and his most passionate conviction ("I'll be free or die!"). To a working(-class) audience that had never and would never own slaves, the communality becomes, as Eric Lott's study of the play suggests, the right to work for a (fair) wage. To be denied the text of self-reliance is to be denied individuality, a sin against Providence from whence such blessings flowed. In the case of charity, voluntary associations formed to alleviate poverty and related social ills juxtaposed causes with cures: drunkenness–sobriety, improvidence–saving, poverty–employment. Slavery in Aiken's *Uncle Tom's Cabin* represents the inversion of these values as they apply to the workplace. The aged, the infirm, and the child were entitled to charity (of the sort to be given a loyal, lifetime dependent like Uncle Tom), but the extension of something for nothing corrupts others (as it does Simon Legree). Slavery is also the inversion of family life. To Stowe and Catherine Beecher, to whom women's superior moral influence extended beyond the homeplace into "benevolent enterprises," there was no anomaly in opposition by churched women to male economic interests if these related to morals (and what economic interests did not?). Accordingly, Stowe created several strong female characters who voice either opposition to slavery or support of abolition. These Aiken's play eliminates, pitching the melodramatic heroine, Eliza, against the economic evil (slavery/Legree, et al.) in the interest of morality and its cornerstone, the family.[45]

Eliza's partner in heroism is her husband George Harris. In their dramatic flights from slavery, Aiken links them with Phineas, the slaveowner-Quaker, Yankee-frontiersman. Eliza, George, and Phineas are strong characters and potential heroes and heroine, but all three escape the drama at the end of Act II; this consigns these characters, like *The Drunkard*'s William, to their fates as self-reliant but secondary dramatic agents. Indeed, throughout its six acts, thirty scenes, eight tableaux, and underscoring music, songs, and dances, Aiken's *Uncle Tom's Cabin* scrupulously erases each potential hero or heroine. George Shelby sells Tom, separates both a mother and child (Eliza and Harry) and a family (Tom and Chloe), and remains unredeemed by an unsuccessful eleventh-hour attempt to rescue Tom that leaves Shelby still a slaveowner. The patrician St. Clare fails to free Tom despite a deathbed promise to Eva. We are clearly called to reject Shelby and St. Clare, not to have them as heroes. Similarly, Ophelia's love of Topsy does not reposition and connect her to the play's central dramatic question, slavery. The replacement of Phineas by Gumption Cute (Aiken's creation) in the second half of the play substitutes schemes and foolery for the moral force of the staged Yankee. The drunken and brutal slave catchers give us not reformed villains of the Badger sort in *The Poor of New York*, but rather living justification for temperance and charity arguments that corrupt individuals make corrupt societies.[46]

Like Edward Middleton in *The Drunkard*, Uncle Tom is an uneasy role model. It has been argued that Tom's long suffering and perseverance are characteristic of the heroines of melodrama, offering audiences a "feminized" (in the sense of passive) heroism. The analogy is a peculiar one for the stage, where heroines like Mary Middleton are far from inactive, for all their endurance of misfortune. Rather, Tom, like the fallen hero of *The Drunkard*, is the subject of grace – not, in his case, the charity extended to the flawed but a mercy earned by action. Because grace comes too late, Tom's is not the world "as it ought to be"; his is a world that is unjust. Tom's fate, then, is that of a victim – a character insufficiently manifest – not that of the hero of the play. Though audiences know and feel for Aiken's Tom, the cause to which his life responds is outside himself, outside reason in this sense, so that the character loses agency in the world of the play. In the world of nineteenth-century American melodrama, because Tom is faithful and struggles, he should survive. By making Legree a force beyond the human pale, however – one who despises the counsel and reproof even of his mother, drinking before her, swearing at her, and finally throwing her senseless to the floor – Aiken pits Tom against a demon impervious to reason or appeal by human agents. If antebellumites were to scorn Legree, as surely Aiken's play intends them to do, the cause is not in Tom's actions but in Legree's nature.[47]

A "feminized" Tom is uneasy as well because it essentializes, displacing the "manly man" with the "womanly woman," erasing one stereotype and inscribing another. Hierarchies are reversed without being displaced. If "feminized" traits (tenderness, loyalty, faithfulness, nurturance) are valorized, the genders switch without altering the game. As Foucault notes, discourses "circulate without changing their form from one strategy to another, opposing strategy"; here the resisting slaves of the first two acts (George and Eliza) change into the submitting slave of the last four acts. As Foucault further points out, however, discourses can also hinder power, inserting "a stumbling block, a point of resistance and a starting point for opposing strategy." If a strategy of peaceful resistance emerges from Uncle Tom, the play contrasts it in George Harris's affirmation that "a man" must fight for liberty "to the last breath"; the forefathers did so, George argues, escaping both the Indian captor (equated with slave master) and the British oppressor who would have enslaved "Americans."[48]

The cabin of Aiken's Uncle Tom, as Eric Lott notes, is a schizophrenic site in which the character/hero is alternately masculinized and unmanned: He is presented as a class hero to workers professionally aloof both to integration and abolition, a hero at once blackened and whitened, a cause for action transformed in the (play's) end as beyond action. The alternate personalizing and communalizing of Aiken's *Uncle Tom's Cabin* vitiates abolition and inserts benevolence in its place, as ennobling to audiences practicing charity as the uplifting apotheosis that ends the play. The melodrama's effectiveness, its ability to manifest sensation, is sited with its weakness as a delegitimation of slavery, rehearsing all the reasons for wide-ranging intervention – broken families, exploited workers, beaten and seduced slaves, corrupted whites, and racism (vested in degrees of color and in depersonalization) – but leaving emancipation suspended with Eva, somewhere overhead in the realm of Providence.[49]

Displaced Play

Antebellum spaces of legitimation provide a number of opposing texts for staging. One is to create order as a means of containing disorder. In 1849, New York City introduced a structure of city departments – Police, Finance, Streets, Almshouse, Water, City Inspector, and the like – with elected heads reporting to an elected mayor, aldermen, and to state representatives. Running parallel to these, in New York and in larger antebellum communities, was a webwork of voluntary associations, varying from Magdalen societies, school boards, business associations, social clubs, and charitable and abolition groups, to music, art, and cultural support groups. Through these, Edward Pessen suggests, the urban rich maintained an influence that after the 1840s they no longer directly sought in politics. Indeed, the modest goals and sedate methods of these associations, taken with economic control, allowed the rich to maintain "vast influence" over "every aspect, every problem of urban life" without seeming to do so. In this view, associations had three power spheres: control of the intended clientele, direction of those who joined and staffed the associations, and cooperation in the "plebeianization" of governments, which left real governing with the leaders of special-interest and social associations. In the realm of the subjects of care, then, governments were alleviated from providing service; indeed, many aid societies argued their own methods were preferable to those of asylums (i.e., prisons, orphanages, reformatories, madhouses, or almshouses), which featured tactics of starvation, isolation, and physical abuse. In the realm of the agent, association members found identity, individuation, and fellowship in such groups, all of particular importance to antebellum women. In the realm of agency, antebellum management and distribution techniques could make the influence of issue-oriented voluntary associations national as well as local, much as organized religions had exerted their influence from the local to the national scene in earlier decades. On all three levels, associations assumed the self-actuating characteristics of their joining members, holding that delinquency, poverty, alcoholism, prostitution, and even slavery had "causes" in individual human behaviors.[50]

Control agendas implicated the rich, poor, and middle "classes." Charity volunteers who did the work of associations usually lived in the wards they visited, which in the larger cities remained ethnically and economically heterogenous throughout these decades, despite some heavy ethnic and racial concentrations by neighborhoods. Heterogeneity appears less typical of smaller cities away from the northeastern seaboard, such as Rochester and Utica, where vigorous zoning efforts sought to segregate work and leisure spaces from homes, or in the slave and border states, where law or custom segregated by race. Though volunteers' interference with family and support networks in working and poor neighborhoods may have been less than welcome by those in need, the in-migrating do-gooder with her middle-class agenda is a postbellum icon that erases the local cultural structures characterizing even the poorest antebellum neighborhoods. For example, early-nineteenth-century fire companies were lodged in communities and reflected their ethnic and religious mixes, partook of and contributed to neighborhood culture (street, theatre, club), interacted with other semiprofessional groups (such as the watch) to control crowds at fires, and vied with municipal authorities for political control of their companies. How important the total network could be was suggested by the *New York Commercial Advertiser* of 26 September 1836, which charged that the mass resignation of forty-four of forty-eight fire companies over the removal of a chief played a role in the destruction of the Bowery Theatre. Similarly, the 5 June 1850 *New York Tribune* insisted upon the communal integrity of Five Points (see Fig. 13), arguing against its depiction as a legendary slum, "the scene of more monstrous stories (at a distance) than any other spot in America" (see, for example, the lower image in Fig. 4). Instead, the paper asserted, Five Points was "not such an awful spot, after all"; it was a neighborhood, a network of relationships lacing a community together in the face of poverty, crowding, and exploitation. The perceived disorders of the fire company and the low-income neighborhood were rather, as Mary Ryan suggests, a different kind of order, one in which the fire company as a communal agency was so jealously guarded that despite (or, perhaps, because of) the danger and expense of being a volunteer fireman, there were usually waiting lists among its overwhelmingly working(-class) membership.[51]

Associations, official, unofficial, and local, had a high potential for socialization: They absorbed excluded or transient populations, such as in-migrating urban male clerks, and provided opportunities for those populations to perform and exert influence. Women were repeatedly used to legitimate causes that their voluntary work alternately reinforced and undermined – as in temperance work, with the goal of preserving the very homes the work freed women to leave. Similarly, associations could stimulate cross-cultural interaction. For example, Catholic opposition to largely Prostestant reform movements, Jay Dolan argues, created a major social issue for Catholics in the antebellum decades: how to demonstrate their compatibility with the U.S. voluntary system. The need to perform in the theatre of volunteerism produced a wealth of Catholic aid and cultural societies that by the Civil War had begun to diversify the religious composition of voluntary efforts. Official regulatory bodies were also subject to cross-cultural pressures in this period, as Michael Holt and others have seen in the displacement of consensus politics and the emergence of political parties that legitimated opposition and competition. Issue-oriented political organizations reached beyond traditional membership pools, forging more inclusive constituencies in the very process of pursuing (as with nativist parties) exclusionary goals. Because the issues organizations valorized could be press- or party-created discourses furthered for political purposes, political machines like Tammany Hall, as Jerome Mushkat documents, blurred internal party differences into "united front" platforms that preserved their political power at the expense of principle-driven policies.[52]

For all this, the "decade of riots" reminds us that heterogeneity is not synonymous with brotherhood. Urban space, for example – the most heterogeneous of antebellum social sites – is the locus of social problems and of attempts to solve, contain, or ignore them; yet, as Mary Ryan suggests, the city is also the site of diversity most representative, in America, of change. The conflicting legitimations evident in the antebellum city are productive of culture; they empower spectators to become creators of experience, as is evident in the self-performances of theatre audiences, fire companies, associations, or community relationships. Antebellum theatre culture developed and emerged in cities, legitimating an acting out of behaviors and attitudes that (as Eric Lott has demonstrated regarding the co-optation and redistribution of minstrelsy) were indicted outside the cultural field of play. The varieties and inconsistencies of these forms of cultural performance find a focus in the Farren "riot" of 1834, in which cultural play was displaced to antiabolition demonstrations in the streets, reified there, and returned to the theatre as a valorization of racism and black culture, authority and rebellion, exclusion and inclusion.[53]

Abolitionists never tired of accusing "gentlemen of property and standing" of playing prominent roles in creating disturbances against them. Antiabolitionist presses in the 1830s, like William L. Stone's *Commercial Advertiser* and James Watson Webb's *Courier and Enquirer,* similarly targeted agents of disruption, indicting the "mad impertinence" of those who opposed slavery – not "gangs of black fellows . . . threatening to burn the city, and . . . overcome the whites," but wealthy abolitionist merchants like "Arthur Tappan and his troop of incendiaries" – singling out such ringleaders and arguing that they needed to "be put down by the strong arm of the law." In selecting "sinister men" (rather than Satan) as causal, both mobs and associations moved from religious to secular modes that spoke to vaguely defined fears and aspirations: loss of self-determination, control by others, tyranny, destruction of the family, selfishness, and the like, contradictory "sensations" also dividing such individual reform agendas as health and sex. That such "sensations" crossed socioeconomic lines is suggested both in who signed abolition petitions between 1829 and 1839 (large numbers of artisans and shopkeepers, declining numbers of merchants and professionals) and in the composition (according to arrest records) of antiabolition mobs (higher in commercial and professional men than among abolitionists, but also high in percentages of artisans and tradesmen). Moreover, not only did both sides of a disturbance share compositional elements, but also some of their respective members shared "principles"; for example, both pro- and antiabolitionists advocated colonization of blacks and held that African and Native Americans were separate races and inferior to Americans of European descent – a position held by the "American School" of ethnology in the decades preceding the ascendancy of Darwin's theory of common origin.[54]

Conspiracy theories of subversion have lost little of their appeal since the antebellum decades. The "human cause" approach valorizes performance; indeed, David Brion Davis notes that "numerous participants in the slavery controversy, without sensing the full implications of their choice of words, adopted the imagery of the stage." On the most evident level, the "performance" was of a melodrama, with evil intent cloaked by a seemingly virtuous exterior. In this scenario, a merchant like Tappan, with his control of his clerks' behavior and his opposition to organized labor, was tailor-made for the role of villain even when it entailed the most implausible accusations – for example, that Tappan was part of a British abolition-fronted conspiracy to undermine the U.S. government. Similarly, institutional agencies became personal villains to abolitionists, as when the New York City Postmaster and the U.S. Postmaster General suppressed a huge mailing of antislavery materials in 1835 – actions that, while undoubtedly unconstitutional, were supported by President Jackson and his cabinet (star villains in the abolition scenario) and fueled abolitionist perceptions that their opposition was widely organized and institutionally led.[55]

On 2 December 1833, more than seven months before the disturbance that would become known in the annals of American theatrical history as the Farren "riot," the Bowery Theatre advertised that Edwin Forrest would play *Metamora* for the first time at that playhouse. Later that month, a company actor named D. D. McKinney failed to be off book at the last rehearsal of the play; this being contrary to house policy, he was fined. McKinney refused to accept the penalty and was then fired. An attempt to disturb the theatre during Forrest's visit having failed, McKinney fostered a claque at Tammany Hall that got up a petition on 16 January 1834 against the Bowery manager Thomas S. Hamblin and his stage manager, George Farren, both English born. The petition, published in the *Evening Star* on 18 January, alleged that the theatre had no right to regulate actors or expel disturbers. It further accused Hamblin of anti-American statements and Farren of despotism, conduct condemned as proud and insolent. Hamblin and his remaining actors rejoined (in a reply also published in the *Evening Star*) that the theatre's rules were of long standing in the profession. Hamblin asserted his right to govern his theatre, admitting, without apology, that he had damned public opinion in the matter. The Park Theatre, hoping to profit by the brouhaha, hired McKinney to perform, but Forrest's popularity at the Bowery continued unabated, and there the matter, for a time, rested.[56]

Farren's theatrical benefit on 9 July 1834 proved the incident had not been forgotten. Hot on the heels of an abolitionist celebration at the Chatham Street Chapel (formerly Theatre) on the Fourth of July, broken up by antiabolitionists, a butcher named Sentis filed a police complaint alleging that on 5 July Farren had damned Americans and struck the butcher when he had objected to the statement. Farren was arrested but denied the charge, and the incident was again reported, this time in the *New York Sun,* on the day before Farren's benefit. On Monday, 7 July, a black abolition meeting at the Chatham Street Chapel was disturbed. A fight ensued and police cleared the building. Three of the next day's papers – the *Commercial Advertiser, Courier and Enquirer,* and the *Sun* – gave the week's events wide (in some cases incendiary) coverage. Fires broke out in abolitionists' stores, African Americans were beaten, an abolition meeting at the Chapel (for 9 July) was canceled, and the crowd that had assembled to break it up was instead harangued by a procolonization speaker. From the Chatham Chapel to its former rival, the Bowery Theatre, was, as we saw in Chapter 1, a matter of blocks.[57]

Forrest was again on the stage in *Metamora* on 9 July 1834 when the Bowery Theatre was rushed by a crowd the *New York American* estimated at over a thousand. The crowd, which may have been a splinter group of the much larger (perhaps five thousand) antiabolition mob at the Chapel or a group separately gathered for the purpose, broke down the front doors of the theatre and "pour[ed] in their swarms until every nook and avenue of the theatre was filled, and the females of the stage and the audience . . . [escaped] from the house through the rear door of the building." In possession of the theatre, the crowd, according to former New York Mayor Philip Hone, "took possession of every part of the house, committed every species of outrage, hissed and pelted poor Hamblin," notwithstanding, Charles Haswell reports, "an American flag which he employed, as a buckler against the missles projected at him." It was announced either (wording varies) that Farren had left or been dismissed from the theatre – the usual course of action with actors accused of offending audiences (*vide* Kean in 1825 and Joshua Anderson in 1831). Hamblin made the apology that tradition required for his earlier wayward statements, and either Hamblin or Forrest appealed to the mob, as a final show of contrition, to let the players please them by presenting a native actor singing the popular favorite "Zip Coon." In a trenchant reflection on this moment, Eric Lott remarks the bizarre juxtaposition of antiabolition rioters and nativists "calmed by one of the several minstrel songs about the miscegenating proclivities of black dandies." In the end, however, a show of force rather than a musical number was the performance necessary to persuade the crowd to quit the house. It took the form of a parade of civil authority in which a hundred watchmen trooped into the theatre, directed by the mayor and city aldermen and augmented with police. The 10 July 1834 *Ameri-*

can reports that because "violence had not been resorted to by [the crowd]" – trashing Hamblin's theatre and threatening actors fell within the bounds of "legitimate" audience behavior – "it was resolved that no violence should be exerted against them." Still the invaders resisted leaving the theatre until the mayor and aldermen led the watch onto the stage itself, an act that encouraged the crowd to disperse.[58]

Abolitionist Lewis Tappan's house was sacked the same evening as the Bowery Theatre; indeed, rioting continued for two days, stitching separate events together in the minds of contemporaneous witnesses like Hone into what Peter Buckley has called "a seamless organism." Though available evidence falls short of conspiracy, it is sufficient to Leonard Richards to suggest purpose and plan: "From the beginning," Richards argues, "potential rioters knew where to meet, when to assemble, and whom to attack. Such information made the rounds at the marketplace. Occasionally, it appeared in a handbill, but usually it spread verbally." As we saw earlier in this chapter (see "Bodying Forth"), skilled workmen – to whom historians have attributed much of the rioting over these eight July days in New York in 1834 – moved freely about the city through all its public spaces. What emerges from these sensation scenes is a complex and contradictory web of relationships, not the script of a simple melodrama with its clear agents and agencies. The Farren "riot" touched labor relations: McKinney's responsibilities to his boss, Hamblin, and that boss's highly visible agent, Farren; Arthur Tappan's regulation of his clerk's leisure activities, religious practices, and political views (see "Class" in Chapter 2); the depressed employment market of 1834 and fears of (black) labor competition and the indifference of bosses. The Farren "riot" touched technology: The *New York Sun*'s new printing press could turn out a thousand penny copies an hour in 1834, providing a blow-by-blow account of the "riots" with which it met the quantum increase in need for news; similar technological growth enabled abolitionist presses in the later 1830s to publish twice as many antislavery tracts at half of what it had cost to print them earlier in the decade. The Farren "riot" touched "class" and nationalism: Hamblin and Farren, "in denying to the audience of that [the Bowery] Theatre the right of expressing their approbation or disapprobation of an actor's performance," had been despotic and "aristocratic," conduct that McKinney's Tammany Hall supporters condemned as "by no means congenial to the feelings of American citizens," and "not to be tolerated by an American public." The Farren "riot" touched issues

of governance: The "contract" that legitimated disturbances and the destruction of property as rights of protesting citizens was set against Hamblin's right to pursue "a manly, independent course" befitting "the conductor of an American theatre." The "riot" touched gender in linking
sex, race, and violence on all sides of the dispute: in Arthur Tappan's
alleged miscegenation and "assaults" upon the sexual virtue of female
abolitionists (by his encouraging them to discuss issues like miscegenation); in women forced by threats of male violence to flee the Bowery Theatre; and in mob assaults targeting African Americans, especially in New
York wards with 10 percent black populations – the Fifth, the "bloody
ould Sixth" (containing Five Points and the Bowery Theatre), and the
Eighth.[59]

The displaced play acted out on the Bowery stage returned from the
theatre to the streets, where rioting continued in New York for several
days, with blacks and white abolitionists as favored targets, then finally ran
its course. Hamblin's American Theatre, Bowery, its doors repaired, continued to prosper and played host to McKinney in November 1834, when
he appeared for Hamblin's benefit night. George Farren was exonerated
by the Court of Sessions of the charges leveled against him and left New
York for the South, where he was for many years associated with the theatrical firm of Ludlow and Smith. His replacement as Bowery Theatre
stage manager was Thomas Flynn, a British-born actor in the company at
the time of the riot, who appears to have had the "popular" touch Farren
lacked. The Chatham Street Theatre/Chapel and the Bowery Theatre as
communal symbols physicalized a number of the above-listed tensions in
New York during a hot July week in 1834. Hamblin was able to withstand
the challenge to his legitimacy as a theatrical manager in the slippery context of antebellum American theatre regulation. He did so with the sympathetic (if bemused) support of patrician patrons like Hone and Haswell,
who condemned plebeian patrons who assaulted Hamblin and his theatre,
and with the assistance of the city's highest officials, who supported Hamblin's right to control audience behavior. At the same time, Hamblin successfully negotiated the minefield of interests that lay between the "authorities," whose support he courted, and the larger number of patrons,
whose attendance was essential to his financial survival. The Farren affair
suggests that Hamblin, despite the nativism (and opportunism) of rechris-
tening his venue "the American Theatre" in the wake of the anti-English
Anderson riot of 1831, sought designation neither as an elite, middle, nor

proletarian playhouse, but as a cultural site for the performance of all of these, and other, valuations.[60]

The complexity of the cultural exchanges produced by antebellum riots finds a singularly rich expression in the staged Negroes "Zip Coon" (a player in the Farren affair) and "Jim Crow," appropriations by white song-and-dance men of black street and concert saloon performers, modifications of European traditions of folk and stage humor, music, and dance, and (in the originary tale traditions of the type character) the products of white actors' field research. No performer was more anxious to authenticate his creation of the staged Negro than its foremost popularizer T(homas) D(artmouth) Rice. "Daddy" Rice, as he was known, was born in the seventh ward of New York City in 1806 and served as a supernumerary at the Park Theatre and as a member of the Lafayette Theatre company, afterward joining Noah Ludlow at Mobile and the Chapman and Drake companies at Louisville and Cincinnati, where he worked from 1828 to 1832. It was in Cincinnati, according to tradition, that Rice observed a crippled black stableman from whom he appropriated a song and dance named, after its progenitor, "Jim Crow." In Rice's return New York appearances at the Bowery Theatre (beginning 12 November 1832), he "jumped Jim Crow" forty-nine times during the 1832–3 season and introduced other Negro songs and characters, such as Gumbo Cuff in *Oh! Hush! or, The Virginny Cupids* and Guffee in *Long Island Juba; or, Love by the Bushel*. Premiered 9 January 1833 and billed as "an Ethiopian Opera," *Long Island Juba* was a clever commodification of the traditions of New York City black market performance (see Figs. 2 and 16), the Ohio frontier legacy of "patting Juba," and expanding urban concert saloon venue that integrated black and white performers, techniques, and audiences. Rice played thirty-two times in his second (1833–4) season at the Bowery Theatre in New York, reprising his popular and widely pirated blackface songs and dances.[61]

In the spring of 1834, the Bowery Theatre began to advertise "a new Local Entertainment" by its house playwright, Jonas B. Phillips, entitled *Life in New York; or, The Major's Come*. Premiered 24 April 1834, *Life in New York* was a four-act farce whose main attraction was a variety of local types in a series of comic and topical sketches. These were continuously revised to accommodate new performers and topics. The major of the title was Yankee Major Jack Downing, drawn by Phillips from Seba Smith's enormously popular humorous sketches, augmented by a cast of

Yankee characters and a "Mrs. Trollope, a well-bred lady of foreign distraction." An heir of Moncrieff's 1821 London farce *Tom and Jerry, Life in New York* was one of the early (Theodore Shank argues the first) popular entertainments of the type to originate in the United States. Hamblin's publicity explained:

The object of this Entertainment is to afford some glances at home. Among its various phases will be exhibited, Life in Wall Street, or, the Major among the Brokers – Tattersall's – Palmo's – Visions of Life – Life on the Pave – Five Points, etc., etc., etc. And if occasionally features of personal identity should exhibit themselves, the author disclaims all intention of offence, personal or otherwise.

With fresh scenery and new music, *Life in New York* played twenty times in its first season, initially as the main piece, then shortened to a prelude or afterpiece. On 20 May 1834 new scenes were added featuring T. D. Rice as "Jim Crow" in what appears to be the character's first incorporation into a play.[62]

The provenance of "Zip Coon" is a subject for a historiography concerned with origins, a matter less integral to this study than are relationships of the kinds the characterization produces. One of these associates "Zip Coon" with Natchez-Under-the-Hill, a rough waterfront area of the Mississippi city where boatmen, gamblers, pirates, and prostitutes gathered. The character was claimed by several performers, among them George Washington Dixon who, according to Odell, first appeared in New York at the Lafayette Theatre (Fig. 21) in July of 1828, the theatre where Rice, a month later, played his first prominent character. While Rice served his Ohio and Mississippi River Valley apprenticeship, George Washington Dixon continued to develop his staged Negro songs and dances, particularly "Coal Black Rose," which became his signature. Ironically, the lyrics of this song, which concern Gumbo Cuff's and Sambo Johnson's competition for Black Rose, formed the plot of Rice's 1833 success *Oh! Hush! or, The Virginny Cupids* (Rice played the mechanic Cuff against the dandy Sambo). Dixon appeared as "Zip Coon" in a benefit at the Park in August of 1834, less than a month after the Farren affair, having, Odell notes, "recently appeared at the Bowery." Indeed, as the foremost performer of the staged Negro in New York until Rice began to eclipse him in 1833–4, Dixon at once focused and displaced race and class tensions in the crucial place of contestation, the cultural arena.[63]

Fig. 21. The Lafayette Theatre, New York, in 1827 (engraving, from the Cooper–Hewitt, National Design Museum, Smithsonian Institution; courtesy of Art Resource, NY).

Unlike "Jim Crow," the southern slave, "Zip Coon" emblemized the northern dandy. Lott sees sectionalism, class, and conflict in these characters, written to be sure upon the appropriated and commodified body of the black man but in a displaced space where white attitudes toward class as well as race could be reconfigured and played out. The American singer, summoned to the Bowery stage to perform "Zip Coon" before the Farren rioters, sang (in the 1834 version preserved in the Harvard Theatre Collection) these verses about then-current events:

> Dat tarnal critter Crockett, he never says his prayers,
> He kill all de wild cats, de coons, and de bears,
> And den he go to Washington to help to make de laws,
> And dere he find de Congress men sucking of der paws.

If I was de President of dese United States,
I'd suck 'lasses candy and swing upon de gates,
And dose I didn't like, I'd block 'em off de dockett,
And de way I'd block 'em off would be a sin to Crockett.

I tell you what's a goine to happen now very soon,
De United States bank will be blown to de moon,
Den all de oder bank notes will be mighty plenty,
An' one silver dollar will be worth ten or twenty.

O glory be to Jackson, for he blow up de banks,
An' glory be to Jackson, for he many funny pranks,
An' glory be to Jackson, for de battle of Orleans,
For dere he gib de enemy de hot butter beans.[64]

The slant of this version of "Zip Coon" supports a populist view of Davy Crockett and Andrew Jackson; both politicians are features of "Jim Crow" lyrics as well, which also touch on U.S. Bank deposits, feats of the ring-tailed roarer sort, and "swinging on de gates." The "Zip Coon" persona, however, is a mockery of the populist. The character was dressed to the pink of fashion – tight pantaloons, "long tail blue" coat, lacy shirt, *lorgnon*, curled hair, baubles, and top hat, judging by the cover of Atwell's 1834 sheet music to the song – his stance affected, if not effeminate, his claim to be "a larned skoler" belied by the Jim Crow dialect of the lyrics. "Zip" is an urban street type referenced by antebellum European travelers like Mrs. Trollope, Fanny Kemble, and Lady Emmeline Stuart-Wortley, simultaneously referencing the aristocrat and the arriviste, the master and the man, the lover and the misogynist, the royalist and the republican.[65]

In the context of the Farren "riot" and the antiabolition disturbances with which it coincided, the enactment of "Zip Coon" is clearly racial. Lott combines this text with that of class, seeing the black dandy as a fig-uration both for white mechanics' fears of black labor competition and for wealthy white abolitionists like Arthur and Lewis Tappan, whose alleged amalgamationist views find expression in the dandy's characteristic wom-anizing. We have repeatedly traversed the intersection of gender, class, and race, which form a strong text in Lott's reading of blackface minstrel-sy. Indeed, the contests among these gain definition in the wide adoption by antebellum women as well as men of staged Negro tunes, as evidenced by Lize, the Bowery G'hal (see "Work" in Chapter 2). Though his ac-count is somewhat overwrought, James Kennard, Jr., was not much off the mark when he observed, in 1845, of the Crow and Coon mania of the 1830s:

"Even the fair sex did not escape the contagion: the tunes were set to music for the pianoforte, and nearly every young lady in the Union, and the United Kingdom played and sang, if she did not *jump*, 'Jim Crow.'" The text Kennard writes upon the (mass) cultural body of the (chiefly white) woman is that of the inauthentic, since to him blackface tunes were "base counterfeits" of "genuine negro songs." To transcendentalist Margaret Fuller, on the other hand, street performances of the theatre dance tune "Jim Crow" by black children were an example of "native" culture.[66]

From the vantage of our own time, Fuller's "native" seems a profound displacement of Kennard's "genuine," yet in commodified cultures the counterfeit is also true performance. Here, the text is not that the representation stands for the real, but that the representation (counterfeit) is itself real. Cultural performance can only enact (represent, symbolize, counterfeit) subjects, an enaction that is the product of the resistance between subjects and performances. In this sense, the performance space is always a space of delegitimation. In it, "legitimate" subjects (people, things, values) are endlessly appropriated in a constant movement from street to stage and back again, as the fashions, sheet music, dance steps, slang, engravings, and stage-to-stage transfers of "Jim Crow," "Zip Coon," and their minstrel heirs demonstrate. Such displacements accommodate wrenching historical appropriations: accounts of slaves who knew and performed many minstrel songs, and of black theatre and concert hall performers like "Juba," who both exploited and transformed the tradition; nineteenth-century white abolitionists and twentieth-century black civil-rights activists, who equally have found such music authentic, as well as nineteenth-century black abolitionists and twentieth-century white cultural historians, who equally have found it inauthentic; and always the press of historical circumstances in the antebellum decades that staged the Negro in the broader arena of theatre culture, as the *Spirit of the Times* suggested 11 March 1854:

The slavery agitation has been augmented by the passage of the Nebraska–Kansas bill, and a little zest is given to the votaries of negro freedom by attendance at the Bowery or National. . . . We have nothing to do here with the matter, politically, but we can perceive what the drama may do to foster or eradicate passions and prejudices of high or low degree.[67]

Street forms lent a carnivalesque topicality and participatory format to Rice's and Dixon's staged Negroes, still visible in the mid-nineteenth-century minstrel show and its highly formalized postbellum successors.

Social historians grant these stagings "common" cultural targets: burlesques of pretensions, of upper-class arrogance, of middle-class imitativeness and sanctimony, and vindication of native canniness. Nonetheless, the sexism of their "dame" characters and the racism of their grotesque white stagings of stupid or pretentious negroes belie talk of commonality; indeed, discourses of commonality often serve to affirm the dynamism of the center and its ability to accommodate (and safely contain) change. With this caution in mind, what remains evident in the antebellum staged Negro are multiple cultural [de]legitimations: A black dandy called Mose in an 1852 minstrel song transforms from a rail fireman into a Bowery fire B'hoy; sanctified or valorized culture is satirized in Negro sketches (Shakespeare parodies, send-ups of romantic novels, burlesques of politicians and authorities); themes of displacement of country and town to city common to melodrama feature in minstrel songs; patriotic sentiments, customs, and class tensions evident in white characters in plays reprise in minstrel characters, making these, Eric Lott argues, reflective of "a profound white investment in black culture." As simple white-to-white transfers, proven stageworthiness seems to drive use of these subjects and values. Claims to authenticity, however, suggest a projection of sociocultural norms wherein performances, as "unauthentic" appropriations, displace the literal to create something else. In those other spaces of "something else," where subjects are multiply positioned rather than given binarized readings, the most contested topics in antebellum society – slavery, race, gender, and morality – remain intact and in contest. Here, as Henry Louis Gates has observed, concepts of black and white "are mutually constitutive and socially produced." These spaces of something else, of the [de]legitimated, bespeak the simultaneous universes of theatre culture.[68]

* * * * *

ANTEBELLUM SPACES of legitimation focus the tension between attempts at uniformity and manifestations of multiplicity. The secularization of legitimating authorities in these decades creates human heroes, heroines, and villains to replace providential forces – or suggests social amelioration is beyond human intervention. The insertion of agency and audience-created experience opens spaces of representation to liminal subjects and inevitably problematizes customary legitimations. Authority presses to retain the rules in play, offering subordination to ideology as the price of enfranchisement of liminal subjects. Simultaneously, those subjects alter the field of play, clarifying that all spaces are liminal, while revealing the distance between discourses of regulation and the absence of control. In these ways, a plethora of antebellum entertainments defied would-be cultural arbiters, women eluded agendas of domesticity, theatres evaded official regulation, and cultures escaped into and out of the streets. Moreover, the search for and embrace of sensation in these decades gives a distinct coloration to what antebellum America bodies forth, and to the displaced play of perceptions as diverse as America-as-Eden and America-as-Armageddon.

In the publication of significant local histories in recent decades exploring antebellum control agendas, historians have made available a wealth of material that challenges the exclusionary tendencies in our readings of American history. Studies of what I have called antebellum theatre culture, the performance of culture in a variety of social venue, now grapple with the historiographical implications of escaping totalizing "myths" (to rehearse Jeff Mason's and Philip Fisher's identification of these explanations) that assume historical experience is the same for all participants (often white, male, and of a particular socioeconomic status or "class"). For a generation of historians seeking to reinsert workers, nonwhites, and women into the antebellum cultural record there now exists the further task of considering how these historical subjects when taken with a poststructuralist/postmodern/deconstructionist historiography compel us to change the rules as well as the players, that is, to reconceive what we think history is and how it operates as well as who or what it is "about." Antebellum [de]legitimations force this discourse because these historical spaces concern attempts at control that immediately bring historiogrphical constructs into play, for example, mainstream and margin, highbrow and low, bourgeois and proletariat, and tripartite class structures. The search for more satisfying [hi]stories can readily reenact controlling narratives that are as fixed or exclusive as the totalizing theories of history we seek (if we do) to evade. Theatre culture provides a way to see antebellum destabilization and change in other than binary or hegemonic terms, to regard it as a performance involving a variety of relationships and dynamics rather than as a structure. The caution in this is to avoid creating a ghetto of alterities (delegitimation) and an omnipotent center (legitimation) which safely contains resisting subjects within the confines of historical theories that acknowledge the subjects while erasing their resistance and operations. Local researches have done much to supply the historical locations out of which positionality grows, while at the same time exposing the appropriations and destabilizations that have constituted and continue to affect cultural practice.

Epilogue
Simultaneous Spaces

The retrospective is never anything but a category of bad faith.
    – Roland Barthes, *Preface to Critical Essays* (1964)

We shall not cease from exploration
And the end of all our exploring
Will be to arrive where we started
And know the place for the first time.
    – T. S. Eliot, "Little Gidding" (1942)

The return to the past is impossible.
    – Tzvetan Todorov, *The Conquest of America* (1984)

IN 1851, G. P. PUTNAM PUBLISHERS of New York issued a travel guide to London, advertised to Americans contemplating the tour as "the first book of the kind published in this country." Entitled *Memories of the Great Metropolis; or, London, from the Tower to the Crystal Palace*, the guide begins with its culminating event, the Crystal Palace exhibition (officially, the Great Exhibition of the Works of Industry of All Nations), inaugurated 1 May 1851. Plans for the fair, marked as the first international exposition in modern European history, had been afoot since 1849 when H.R.H. Prince Albert, Chairman of the Commission producing the exhibition, determined that it would extend beyond its British trade-fair predecessors to embrace foreign productions. In keeping with this plan, invitations were issued to foreign commissions to select and forward exhibits, to which half the space in the exhibition hall would be allocated. The American Committee, derived from members of the National Institute, the Smithsonian Institution, and trade-oriented agencies, promptly applied "for greater floor-area than any other nation except France." Industrial in bias, the 1851 exhibition was closed to the fine arts (though sculpture was included); even so, its greatest impact upon spectators was cultural rather than commercial. This assessment by the author of America's "first" travel guide suggests some of the exhibition's effects:

It is impossible to compute the important advantages which must result from this magnificent enterprise. That it must exert a most potent and beneficial influence in stimulating to emulation the artist, the mechanic, and the artizan [*sic*], is a matter beyond doubt; while it will tend to combine in friendly alliance the collective genius and skill of the civilized globe. It affords the greatest demonstration of the rapid progress of civilization, in its tendency to remove the jealousies and false estimates which obtain among men, and in inspiring them with a more liberal charity and fraternal spirit. The servile restrictions which are imposed between the patrician and the plebeian, have thus become ameliorated – the pride of the peer yields to the power of genius, though in rags; and under the same roof, the monarch has mingled with the mechanic in doing homage to its wonderful creations. Thus labor is dignified, the race elevated, and enlightened philanthropy universally diffused. Such an exhibition of the products of skill also essentially aids in educating the popular taste.

In a similar vein, the London *Times* observed that, "By the favor of Heaven, we shall continue to improve, and, as we improve, to throw down the clumsy barriers within which barbarism has for so long intrenched itself and divided the nations of the earth."[1]

An exposition is a symbolic universe in which the material of a culture is offered in a modeled space to vicarious travelers. These "universes" market both objects and commanding views of cultures as they have been, are, and will be. Exhibitions, Robert W. Rydell argues, propagate "the ideas and values of the country's political, financial, corporate, and intellectual leaders," who in turn offer these ideas and values to the public "as the proper interpretation of social and political reality." Most of these values are on display in the eyewitness assessments by the authors of *Memories of the Great Metropolis* and of the *Times* article, which underscore as well the way the Crystal Palace exhibition organized potentially troubling experiences into an order that affirmed class, race, gender, and national supremacy. So instructed, consumers of the fair's intellectual, social, and cultural materials were "organized" (and colonized) by the very notions implying comparative superiority in a global cultural hierarchy: enterprise, collective genius, progress, civilization, class difference, race elevation, improvement, and the defeat of barbarism. At the same time, however, the exhibition, rather than validating the "universal" spaces of the Prologue to this book, institutionalized the differences evident in the representations, liminalities, and delegitimations that form the subjects of this book's intervening chapters. This Epilogue considers those differences from the perspective of their simultaneity, first in the London Exhibition and its satellite entertainments, then in the New York Crystal Palace of 1853 and the cultural issues it raises about antebellum America. As in much of this work, the investigation of fairs takes a view of cultural diversity as simultaneous, not simply oppositional or, still less, developmental. From these expositions, the Epilogue moves to an assessment of the shifts in historical space mapped in this book as a whole. First, however, it is useful to reprise briefly the concept of simultaneous spaces, evoked in the image of Borges's garden that opened the Prologue.[2]

The idea of multiple, coexistent "universes" is located in modern physics. Derived from Werner Heisenberg's uncertainty principle and the researches of Louis de Broglie, Niels Bohr, and Erwin Schrödinger, the theory of parallel universes in physics attempts to escape the dualistic quality of early quantum measurement theories, which posed two modes of behavior for quantum waves ("jump" or "collapse") ultimately dependent upon the observer. Instead, as Hugh Everett, John Wheeler, Eugene Wigner, John Cramer, and other postwar physicists suggest, a quantum wave branches (or flows) simultaneously in multiple spaces that both object and observer occupy. No space or world is more "real" than another, and each continuously transforms and grows. When quantum measurement is viewed in this way, "The past," as Nobel physicist Eugene Wigner has put it, "has no existence except as it is recorded in the present." Although views of flow, transformation, and simultaneity are located in twentieth-century physics in the context of atomic particles, they have parallels (and prefigurations) in our century's philosophy, history, and art, as well as in other nonscience disciplines. These fields do not require physics in order to think relatively, but are, I believe, enriched by the analogies that quantum research has generated. In spatial arts (such as theatre) and social relationships (such as culture), a simultaneous historiography questions the universal view espoused by enthusiasts of the Crystal Palace exhibitions and the developmental binary opposition that is its conveyance. The expositions' confident locutions from "barbarism" to "civilized" and from "past" (primitiveness) to "present" (improvement) to "future" (greatness) are, from the perspective of the other spaces taken up in this work, an organization of culture at once dependent upon its diverse stagings and a refusal to give diversity a role in the script it produces. Denial is not the full cultural scenario, however, since diversity both resists attempts to hegemonize and simultaneously creates alternative "universes" out of the colonizing experience. A number of these relationships among historical spaces were on display in the exhibitions of 1851 and 1853, to which we now turn.[3]

* * * * *

THE GREAT EXHIBITION of the Works of Industry of All Nations was a subject of public debate from its inception in England because it required both government and public support to succeed. Aided by skeptical newspapers, politicians protested that even though the exhibition was to be chiefly funded by contributions from industry and private individuals, it would have ruinous effects upon London. Hyde Park, the building site, would, the 25 June 1850 *Times* fulminated, "be turned into the bivouac of all the vagabonds of London." The park would be denuded of trees; visitors to the fair would create insuperable traffic problems in the neighborhood, raise prices, and increase the liklihood of plague and crime; anarchists and foreigners would overrun London, the working poor would waste their shillings journeying to the fair, and British trade would be forever degraded by an influx of cheap foreign goods. The focus of wider-based opposition to the project was the initial design for the exhibition hall, which the Royal Commission's Building Committee assembled from among the 245 plans submitted to its competition, none of which was in itself considered good enough for adoption. From this doubtful dealing came a brick-domed design for a building four times the length of Westminster Abbey and twice the width of St. Paul's Cathedral, to be made of sheet iron and stone. The plan was hardly consistent with promises to the public that the exhibition hall would be easy to remove once the fair was over and Hyde Park little disturbed by its temporary presence. In addition, the committee design was universally disliked – and too expensive.[4]

Fig. 22. Exterior view of the London Crystal Palace (from Gibbs-Smith, *Great Exhibition of 1851*).

The commission survived a division of the House of Commons to halt the fair on 4 July 1850, but sentiment did not swing the exhibition's way until Joseph Paxton, builder of the Chatsworth Conservatory and a director of the Midland Railroad, gave his late-submitted plan for the exhibition hall (which the Royal Commission had been dilatory in approving) to the *Illustrated London News*. Printed 6 July, Paxton's design, a nineteen-acre stepped glass and iron construction with no interior walls, comprising prefabricated parts that could be erected and dismantled with relative ease, quickly gained popular support and (in a form modified to accommodate some of the Hyde Park elms, whose destruction fueled objections to the exhibition) subsequent commission approval (Fig. 22). The light and airy design (essentially an elaborated greenhouse) was assisted to popularity by Paxton's friend, the playwright and *Punch* columnist Douglas Jerrold, who dubbed the proposed building (2 November 1850) "The Crystal Palace." Opposition did not, of course, wholly disappear. Paxton, who in his youth had been head gardener to the Duke of Devonshire, had risen to national prominence as a builder through that mixture of ability, luck, and patronage forming the stuff of nineteenth-century success stories, despite the lack of training as either an architect or engineer. The *Times* predicted that his Crystal Palace would leak, be subject to intense heat from the sun, and vastly overrun its budget. Critics charged foundations or flimsy walls would give way, that vibrations from machines and traffic would cause the building to collapse, and that hail would beat it or winds would blow it down. Mr. Airy, the providentially named Astronomer Royal, wrote a pamphlet on the matter predicting that Paxton's building would inevitably fall.[5]

Dire prophesies notwithstanding, Paxton's design went forward without a hitch, from groundbreaking in August 1850 to the grand opening in May 1851. The timely construction of the Crystal Palace was followed avidly in the press, which published numerous illustrations of men at work on the building, of glass and iron being fabricated for it in factories, and of such newsworthy events as the first ribs of the transept being raised or Prince Albert visiting the site to the cheers of workmen. These illustrations in time included daguerreotypes and collotypes taken of the exterior and interior of the building on days when it was closed to the public, official paintings, woodcuts, lithographs, sketches, and "aeronautic views" of the great ferrovitreous expanse. As interest in the exhibition mounted, Londoners prepared for a new entertainment industry: tourism. Exhibits began to arrive in February 1851 to remain on display until 15 October, when the exhibit was officially to close. Between 1 May and the last day it was open to the public (11 October), the more than a hundred thousand exhibits on view at the Crystal Palace were seen by 6,039,195 paying visitors, considerably more people than lived in Greater London and representing perhaps 17 percent of the total population of Great Britain. Their entrance fees produced an after-expenses profit of £186,437. In addition, Exhibition Year stimulated more entertainments than London had ever seen and contributed to enormous attendance increases at public institution exhibits (visitors to the Tower of London Armory, for example, numbered 32,313 in 1850 and 209,000 in 1851). Special trains were put on all over England. Thomas Cook's Midland Railway Excursions alone brought 165,000 visitors to the fair from outside London, providing them with train and entrance tickets plus a free copy of Cook's weekly *Exhibition Herald and Excursion Organizer,* describing the rail journey to London and "suitable" temperance hotels in the city. (Queen Victoria noted a subscription group at the exhibition [12 June] of eight hundred parishioners from Kent and Surrey, "walking in procession 2 and 2, the men in smock frocks, with their wives looking so nice" [Fig. 23].) Peripatetic Americans turned to the Appendix in *Memories of the Great Metropolis* for descriptions of

Fig. 23. "Agriculturalists at the Exhibition" (from the *Illustrated London News*).

London accommodations, restaurants, theatres, shopping, museums, hospitals, and railway stations.[6]

The path of cultural tourism had been prepared by those material developments that the Crystal Palace exhibition of 1851 was intended to celebrate. The British had been at peace for thirty-six years when the fair opened; trains, steam heat, gas lighting, safer water, the telegraph, and John Loudon McAdam's "macadamized" roads had all changed daily life. Even in the United States and Canada, where such developments had yet to cross the continent, exhibits bore ample testimony to North American technological advances. In England as in America, however, development was not without contest, as the Chartist march in London on 10 April 1848 and political events in Europe in that revolutionary year had shown. In times of demonstration, public buildings like the British Museum were placed under guard, and those wary of the sizeable public gatherings likely to be prompted by the 1851 exhibition hinted at the disparities the exposition itself encouraged. For example, despite the American travel guide's allusion to the amelioration of restrictions between patrician and plebeian characterizing the fair (an idea furthered by a June 1851 cartoon in *Punch*

showing farm and mechanic families mingling with wealthier ones – Fig.
24), the exhibition offered patrons segregated admission options: There
were 141 days reserved for season ticket holders, two "pound days," 28
five-shilling days, 30 two-shilling-six-pence days, and 70 one-shilling days.
The scheme clearly anticipates, as the attendance figures bear out, that
there would be many more visitors on "shilling days." These, wealthier
patrons of the fair might totally avoid simply by paying a higher admission price for selected days or portions of days.[7]

The organizing commission for the Great Exhibition of 1851 had as part
of its task the valorization of material craft as well as design. Accordingly,
numerous classes of goods were established and international juries constituted to award medals in each class for inventions, novel applications of
known principles, and for excellent workmanship without regard to originality. To be sure, these awards were given not to workers but to manufacturers, whose support of the Great Exhibition had been solicited not
only by making participation competitive (and thus selection meritorious),
but by promising a chance at international recognition through prize medals. For craftsmen, that recognition began with construction of the Crystal Palace itself, a job that needed to be accomplished competently and on
time, under the eye of a watching world. Indeed, the building was itself a
giant display box, offering a large ground floor and surrounding second-
floor galleries as a splendid showcase for often drab and banal material.
The success of the men who built "the Palace" in completing it on sched-
ule prepared the way for "plebeians" to invest, as they appear to have done
in great numbers, in the fair as "their" exhibition of class and nationality.
This investment was assisted by British employers, since, according to the
London *Times* (13 October 1851), the Great Exhibition

induced masters to send their servants, manufacturers their hands, bankers and
merchants their clerks, tradesmen their apprentices, railway companies their men,
and last, most wanted and most common of all, induced the owners and occu-
piers of the soil to send up, by subscription among them, their agricultural la-
bourers.[8]

Their generosity (and mistresses' in sending their maids), one contemporary suggested, produced "a better feeling between the employers and the
employed." Charity school pupils and charity recipients were sent to the
Great Exhibition by benevolent societies to see goods "of immense interest and quite something new for the generality of people," Queen Victoria
noted, especially "articles having hitherto only come over as presents to

"Whoever Thought of Meeting You Here?"

Fig. 24. "The Pound and the Shilling" (from *Punch;* by permission of the British Library).

the Sovereign." Henry Mayhew, in a novelized version of the 1851 exhibition, hoped that its valorization of craftsmen as "artisans," while it did not put more money in pay packets, would have the effect not only of dignifying toil to those who did not labor but of inspiring self-respect in those Britains who did. Wholly outside these labor and class framings, foreign exhibitors began at a disadvantage. Since they had not been part of making the enveloping display box, they and their work could only be the recipients of transferred British accomplishment, evidenced both in the organization of the fair and the erection of a beautiful and original building. Indeed, Henry Cole, chief mover of the exhibition, boasted that its success grew in part from confidence that exhibits would be secure, easy to transport in England, and otherwise enjoy the benefits of a civilized society.[9]

Displays from the United Kingdom at the Crystal Palace exhibition were chiefly organized by types of goods; the British Empire and non-British portions of the building were indexed by the name of the country or colony. The *Official Catalogue* lists 534 American exhibits. By comparison, France is credited with 1,737 exhibits, Belgium with 512, and Austria with 746. Though exhibits were added after the catalogue was printed, it was evident that the United States, whose section of the "palace" was decorated with an eagle rampant, had failed to fill all the space it had claimed. *Punch* gleefully suggested using the excess space as a hotel, at "the sign of the Spread Eagle," and speculated about the American exhibits rumored to be on the way – "the Leg of a Multiplication Table . . . the tremendous Wooden Style that separates the American from the English Fields of Literature." Even the more charitable *Tallis's History and Description of the Crystal Palace* observed, "The number of articles sent from the United States to the Exhibition was neither what was expected of them, nor, we believe, did it adequately represent their capabilities." Horace Greeley, a juror on the Exhibition Award Committee, sent home to his paper letters describing the exhibition in which he objected to *Punch* and *Times* criticisms about the meagerness of the American section. While Greeley agreed with *Tallis's* assessment that there were many things in the U.S. collection "which presented features of peculiar interest, and which did credit to [U.S.] industry, ingenuity, and skill," he was obliged to conclude upon reflection that, while the U.S. exhibits were indeed "creditable to us as a nation," they "fell far short of what it might have been, and did not fairly exhibit the progress and present condition of the Useful Arts in this country." New Jersey commissioners to the exhibition believed more displays would have followed the opening had ridicule of American ambitions not deepened earlier opinions in the United States that American exhibits would not get fair play in London. Postfair American assessments, however, concluded that the U.S. had "made signal triumphs in just those arts which most distinguish civilized man from the savage," and had lost honor only in those arts separating "a luxurious nation from the hardy energy of practical workers."[10]

Although the U.S. government provided transportation to England for exhibits, it did not, unlike the governments of other foreign exhibitors, make appropriations money available. As a result, cargo languished dockside and the American section remained undecorated until banker George Peabody, resident in England, provided a $15,000 grant for these purposes. The American exhibits, despite their inauspicious arrival and paucity of numbers, won both popular and press support as the fair wore on. Positive publicity resulted from practical demonstrations in the English countryside of McCormick's agricultural machinery. American lockmaking was boosted when an exhibitor was able to pick two of England's most highly touted locks but no one could pick his. Colt revolvers and Robbins and Lawrence rifles, American sewing machines, rubber goods, printing presses, daguerreotypes, and locomotives were much admired. Queen Victoria, previewing the exhibition hall, reported in her diary that the American section was beautiful, but she subsequently found its contents "not very interesting," remarking only upon its locks, reaping machine, and "'Bowie' knives in profusion, made entirely for Americans who never move without one." Five American firms were awarded Council Medals – out of 170 given – including McCormick's reaper, Goodyear's rubber products, Dick's printing press and tools, Bond's astronomical instruments, and Borden's meat biscuit. The yacht *America* capped these successes by winning the coastal race and thus the cup that has since borne its name. The Liverpool *Times* of 27 August 1851 concluded that American industry ought "no longer to be ridiculed, much less despised" and that U.S. enterprise would "assuredly pass us unless we accelerate our speed."[11]

In addition to displaying America's six thousand fossils, mechanical instruments, stuffed birds, furniture, apparel, and other trade-fair goods from the international exhibitors, the Crystal Palace offered participants an opportunity to stage their cultures. The *Official Catalogue* of the exhibition indicates that the main avenue east, which ended in the American section, featured a model of Niagara Falls by George Catlin (one had been part of his Indian Gallery since at least 1841), a mass of ore, Hiram Powers's marble statue *The Greek Slave*, a railway bridge, and Peter Stephenson's sculpture *The Wounded Indian*. Illustrations of the American section, however, indicate that its focal display comprised Powers's statue and an Indian teepee on a raised platform (the bridge?), with two modeled figures in Indian dress beside it (Fig. 25). *The Greek Slave* (1843) was one of the most popular exhibits in the building. *Tallis's* describes Powers as "an American sculptor of great talent" who "has executed many admirable works," and says of this statue that "the modest dignity expressed in this figure, its beauty, and the delicacy of its execution, are deserving of the highest praise." The sentiment was general, though not universal, among critics; their responses and the sculpture's popularity with the public suggest the extent to which Powers's fame had increased since the days when he modeled wax figures for Mrs. Trollope's Bazaar in Cincinnati.[12]

Fig. 25. The United States section of the Great Exhibition (lithograph by John Absolon, from *Recollections of the Great Exhibition of 1851* [London: Lloyd Bros. & Co., 1851], courtesy of the Hilyer Art Library of Smith College).

If Powers's statue evoked a narrative from antiquity – the female figure depicted was to be viewed as a Christian slave in the marketplace being appraised for purchase by barbarians, a serviceable metaphor for American slavery – Catlin's Indian exhibit was exactly contemporary and harmonized with American displays of Indian corn, canoes, Indian saddles, and the subject of Stephenson's sculpture. The United States was not alone in offering uniquely North American stagings of culture; Canada's display of a birchbark canoe and other Indian artifacts caused one spectator to remark upon "the somewhat curious . . . mixture of the works of a savage population with the clearest evidence of English civilisation." British cartoonists not infrequently depicted the United States as an Indian, intending no compliment in associating "Americans" with "savages." The contiguity was long-lived in London entertainments. George Catlin had taken his Indian Gallery to England in 1840 (Fig. 26). It was by that time a large collection

Egyptian Hall, Piccadilly.

MANNERS AND CUSTOMS

OF THE

NORTH AMERICAN INDIANS.

Twenty Living Figures, arrayed in beautiful Indian Costumes, fully armed and equipped, illustrating Mr. CATLIN's LECTURES in his NORTH AMERICAN INDIAN MUSEUM, forming the most thrilling and picturesque *groups* and *tableaux vivants* descriptive of Indian life.

Programme for Monday Evening;
COMMENCING AT EIGHT O'CLOCK.

A brief **Lecture** on the Customs and Condition of the North American Indians, *with several Figures, in full-dress, of different Tribes.* After which

A Beautiful Group of Warriors and Braves in full-dress, reclining round a fire, regaling themselves with the pipe and a dish of pemican which are passing around. In the midst of their banquet the Chief enters, in full-dress; the pipe is extended to him—he smokes it in sadness, and then breaks up the party by announcing that an enemy is at hand, and they must prepare for war!!

TABLEAUX VIVANTS.

No. 1—Warriors Enlisting, by "*smoking through the reddened stem.*" The Chief sends "*runners*" or "*criers*" through the tribe with a pipe, the stem of which is painted red; the crier solicits for recruits, and every young man who consents to smoke through *the reddened stem,* when it is extended to him, is considered a volunteer to go to war.

No. 2—Council of War. Chiefs and Doctors deliberating in Council. The Doctors are considered the Oracles of the Nation, and are always consulted by, and seated in council with the Chiefs.

No. 3—War Dance; the ceremony of swearing in the warriors, who take the most solemn oath, by dancing up to and striking the "reddened post."

No. 4—Foot War-Party on the March. "*Indian File,*" armed with shields, bows, quivers, and lances—the Chief of the party, as is generally the case, going to war in full-dress.

No. 5—War-Party Encamped at Night, wrapped in their Robes, with their weapons in their arms; sentinels at their posts.

No. 6—An Alarm in Camp; sentinels rousing the party to arms.

No. 7—War-Party in Council, consulting as to the best mode of attack.

No. 8—Skulking, or advancing cautiously upon the enemy to take them by surprise.

No. 9—Battle and Scalping; the Chief wounded.

No. 10—Scalp Dance, in celebration of a victory; the women in the centre of the group holding up the scalps, and the warriors dancing around them, brandishing their weapons, and yelling in the most frightful manner.

No. 11—Treaty of Peace. The Chiefs and Warriors of the two hostile tribes, in the act of solemnizing the treaty of peace, by smoking mutually through the calumet or pipe of peace, which is ornamented with the Eagle's quills; the calumet resting in front of the group.

No. 12—Pipe of Peace Dance, by the Warriors, with the pipes of peace or calumets in their hands, after the treaty has been concluded.

ON THURSDAY EVENING, numerous *Groups* and *Tableaux* will be exhibited at the same hour, descriptive of DOMESTIC Scenes in Indian Life in times of *Peace;* representing their Games—Dances—Feasts—Marriage Ceremonies—Funeral Rites—Mysteries, &c.

Admittance to the Tableaux and also to the Gallery, One Shilling.
Catalogues, at the Door of the Exhibition, explaining the whole collection, One Shilling.

PRINTED BY C. ADLARD, BARTHOLOMEW CLOSE.

Fig. 26. Broadside for Catlin's Indian Gallery and *tableaux vivants,* Egyptian Hall, London, 1840–1 (courtesy of the Gilcrease Museum).

(weighing about eight tons) of both paintings and the artifacts Catlin had obtained from Indians during his travels. He had arranged his materials around a twenty-five-foot Crow teepee erected in the Great Exhibition Room in Egyptian Hall in London and had augmented admission receipts with sales of his books and engravings. Like the 1851 fair, Catlin's Gallery the previous decade had been couched as an educational enterprise, with a docent at hand to answer visitor's questions. Three evenings a week, however, white performers in Indian dress would offer war dances and "Indian" ceremonials. In 1843, Catlin allied with a troupe of nine Ojibway being toured through England by showman Arthur Rankin. The "performance art" combination proved a considerable success and was staged for Queen Victoria. In the summer of 1844, the Ojibway were replaced by a band of Iowa Indians imported by P. T. Barnum, who was considering buying the Indian Gallery in that year and operating it with Catlin's nephew. Catlin escorted the Iowa around London, as he had their tribal predecessors, then toured them through England in the winter of 1844–5, during which two of the Indians died of illness. The troupe left for Europe in April 1845 and performed in France into the summer. The Iowa returned to America and were replaced by a second party of Ojibway, who entertained Louis Philippe at the Tuileries, following which Catlin was installed in a gallery at the Louvre. Two Ojibway died on tour in Belgium during the winter of 1845; the remainder left Catlin in January 1846 and continued to tour in Europe and England until 1848.[13]

According to Catlin biographer William H. Truettner, Catlin went out of the Indian exhibition business at this time and "never again attempted to stage these Wild West performances." The Crystal Palace's *Official Catalogue,* however, contains an ad for "Catlin's American Indian Collection," visible at rooms in Waterloo Place, Pall Mall, stating that the Indian Gallery had been reopened "with new and interesting additions from the Rocky Mountains. 600 Paintings. Costumes and Weapons on figures. – Promenade Lectures by Mr. CATLIN, with War-songs, War-whoops, &c., at 2 in the day, and half-past 8 in the evening." Catlin's books and engravings were also offered, along with wax figures. In August 1851, Altick reports, Catlin "added to the show a delegation of Iroquois chiefs and warriors," who used Catlin's premises to sell off moccasins, bags, reticules, caps, bracelets, and other artifacts "which they had intended to display in the Crystal Palace." It is likely these artifacts were Catlin's own – he would be imprisoned for debt in London in 1852 – and it is unclear whether the

"Iroquois" were white men or Indians. The teepee and costumed figures displayed at the Crystal Palace transferred to the American section of the 1851 exhibition the central emblem of Catlin's staging of "American" culture. In its contesting blend of ethnological exhibit and sideshow (a characteristic of much of the Great Exhibition itself), cultural diversity had become the focal performance of the American section's most public display.[14]

Robert W. Rydell links fairs to other forms of entertainment – zoological gardens, minstrel shows, circuses, museums for curiosities, dime novels, and Wild West shows, specifically – that promoted white supremacy in the nineteenth and early twentieth centuries, but the fairs more distinctly so because they were linked to science, art, economic development, and history, and so wore the robes of authority. The Crystal Palace exhibition grew from the Royal Society of Arts; its profits would in turn fund the building of the Victoria and Albert Museum, London's Science Museum, Natural History Museum, and Geological Museum, the Imperial College, and the Royal Colleges of Art and Music. The U.S. and other national committees included scientists and those with an interest in science (the Smithsonian and the National Institute, in the case of the United States). Such organizations had cultural preservation and categorization as their tasks, here (among others) the rescue of "the memory and memorials of the Red Indians from oblivion." The Great Exhibition of 1851, for all that it allowed no selling of exhibited goods, nor even the listing of prices for goods, moved freely between marketing goods and marketing cultures. That combination characterized other exhibitions that year as well. Producers scrambled to win a share of tourist dollars; there were dozens of panoramas and dioramas, including Frémont's "Overland Route to Oregon and California," updated to take advantage of recent gold strikes in California – events perhaps more imaginatively showcased in a Sloane Street flea circus featuring "fleas in California, digging, washing, and sifting gold." James Wyld, who exhibited maps and terrestrial spheres in the Crystal Palace, constructed a "Great Globe" in Leicester Square, where tourists could climb up three stories and review the land masses of the earth, replete with volcanoes, mountains, and surrounding oceans. One He-Sing managed to present himself to the Queen and march with the Duke of Wellington in the ceremonies opening the Crystal Palace, only to prove to be not a foreign diplomat but part of an attraction housed on a Chinese junk moored at the Thames. Lectures at the Polytechnic tied exhibits at the Crystal Palace to an eclipse of the sun at the end of July 1851, more nearly approached by "scientific" balloon ascensions or approximated in fireworks displays connected to outdoor historical, geographic, or geological displays. More conventionally, Londoners and fairgoers could take in *Apartments to Let*, a comedy featuring a gauche "go-ahead Yankee," one of many plays and shows making 1851, according to Altick, the apogee of the London exhibition business.[15]

The commission for the Great Exhibition had promised to remove its building by 1 June 1852, and, despite some sentiment to the contrary, the Crystal Palace closed as scheduled in October 1851. Concerts and similar events were held in the empty structure until it was dismantled, to be resurrected (in an enlarged version) at Sydenham. Extra rail lines were built to it there and, from its opening 10 June 1854 to its death by fire 30 November 1936, the Sydenham Crystal Palace served as both museum and amusement center to an annual average of two million visitors. (To the end, it retained the trappings of "science" and ethnology in its architectural recreations of antiquity and foreign locales, its picture gallery, historical waxworks, displays of the races, animals, birds, and flora of the planet, its galleries devoted to technological advances, and in its concerts, aquatic displays, dog and flower shows, acrobats, pleasure gardens, and outdoor spectacles [with fireworks] like the "Battle of Trafalgar.") In its tenure at Hyde Park, the Crystal Palace had been the cause of none of the disturbances or disruptions its critics had feared (sparing complaints about rude or unscrupulous omnibus drivers) and had avoided both the commercial and the sideshow atmosphere that came to characterize subsequent fairs. The status bestowed by Prince Albert's presence as chair of the commission and Queen Victoria's repeated visits contributed to the 1851 Crystal Palace's commercial success and its highest approval as a place to visit. American exhibitors, judges, and showmen quickly grasped the powerful combination represented by official support, architectural splendor, science, and commodification. As the London *Times* of 2 September 1851 noted, P. T. Barnum "is actually among us, and his presence, like that of Napoleon, in the field, is always ominous of business." Indeed, plans were soon afoot for a New York Crystal Palace, capitalizing on the success of the London original.[16]

Lacking the vision of Henry Cole, the commanding diplomacy of Prince Albert, and the architectural innovativeness of Paxton (who submitted a design that proved too long for the site), the New York Crystal Palace

Association (officially the Association for the Exhibition of the Industry of All Nations) had in view less the civilized exchanges of nations via industry than it did opportunity and profit. Founded by prominent Americans (Horace Greeley among them), the private enterprise began in 1851 with the granting of a charter by the New York State legislature and a five-year lease from the City of New York for Reservoir Square, the five acres bounded by present-day Fifth and Sixth Avenues and Fortieth and Forty-second Streets (home then to the Croton distibuting reservoir, now to the New York Public Library and Bryant Park). P. T. Barnum, who would soon be drawn into the project, thought the distance from City Hall (four miles) "was enough of itself to kill the enterprise." In addition, the city required that the entrance fee not exceed fifty cents and that the exhibition hall itself be made chiefly of iron and glass. Two Danish-born architects, Georg J. B. Carstensen and Charles Gildemeister, were commissioned to plan such a building after Paxton's design was abandoned. Their allegedly fireproof exhibition hall was a ferrovitreous structure two stories high, the first floor octagonal with seventy-foot towers at its angles and the second shaped as a Greek cross. The building had smaller vaulted naves leading (like the committee design for the Hyde Park Crystal Palace) to a large dome, rising 148 feet above the main structure, which housed the Lattig Observatory (Fig. 27).[17]

From the first, the New York Crystal Palace was dogged with problems. The dome leaked, and the discovery that a number of structural ribs were missing delayed the advertised May opening to 14 July 1853. With a building cost that sources put at either $634,880 or $640,000 (the latter representing £130,000 in comparison to £170,000 for Paxton's Hyde Park structure and its fittings), the exhibition would close out receipts at $340,000 (£70,000, against London's £522,179) – receipts "little more than half the expenditure." For all this, theatre historian T. Allston Brown recalls:

This edifice started in its delicate beauty from the earth like the "'magining of happy vision." Viewed at a distance, its burnished dome resembled a half-disclosed balloon, as large as a cathedral, but light, brilliant, and seemingly ready to burst its bands and soar aloft. Nothing like this building, in shape or size, material or effect, was ever before seen in America.

New York Mayor Jacob A. Westervelt called the structure "the most tasteful ornament that had ever graced the metropolis." President Franklin

Pierce and Secretary of War Jefferson Davis (with Greeley, one of the U.S. commissioners to the London exhibition) were present for the opening ceremonies, which began at Castle Garden with speeches to a crowd of some twenty thousand, band music, and then a parade of city, state, federal, and foreign dignitaries up Broadway and Sixth Avenue to the "palace" grounds. A thunderstorm drenched the marchers, and by the time a dried-off president reappeared in the exhibition hall, the audience had dwindled to seven hundred.[18]

The New York Crystal Palace, according to the chief chronicler of the city's theatricals, George C. D. Odell, "was a sort of permanent fair enclosed in glass" that "served to display merchandise to curious visitors." In order to attract spectators to the site, the Crystal Palace Association offered musical, dramatic, and variety events in its main rooms and a penny arcade in one of the galleries. The observatory was serviced by an Otis steam elevator that carried passengers three hundred feet into the air, and the building was brilliantly illuminated at night by (reputedly) more gaslights than in use in the whole of Gotham. For all this, the New York Crystal Palace quickly slipped into debt. On 15 April 1853, three months before its opening, P. T. Barnum had written to association president Theodore Sedgwick, offering the support of his *Illustrated News* to the venture "so long as it maintains its present character of being a national work and calculated to redound to the honor of the American nation." The association turned to Barnum, persuading him to become a board member and then president (in March 1854) against Barnum's better judgment that "the novelty had passed away, and that it would be difficult to revive public interest in the affair." In a letter to Horace Greeley dated 8 March, Barnum assessed the enterprise as too much in debt to be saved but said he would try to cram the Crystal Palace "with visitors for at least another season."[19]

In an effort to stimulate attendance, Barnum arranged a "grand reinauguration" ceremony in May 1854 featuring the midgets General Tom Thumb and George Washington Nutt. A balloon ascension was subsequently held on the grounds. On 15 June, the Crystal Palace featured one of several "musical congresses," monster concerts of fifteen hundred instrumentalists and singers under the baton of Monsieur Louis Jullien, in which Handel's *Messiah* and the *William Tell* and *Tannhäuser* overtures echoed to silence in the cavernous building, the shuffling of forty thou-

Fig. 27. "The New York Crystal Palace" (from Wilson, ed., *The Memorial History of the City of New-York*, vol. 3).

sand feet in the audience a symphony in itself. For the occasion, Jullien composed a "Fireman's Quadrille" with military marching bands and a large chorus singing and urging on the supposed firemen, the whole supplemented by a fireworks display outside the building. Though novel in its way, the event struck George Templeton Strong, who was in the audience, as claptrap not likely to rescue the building, by then nearly empty of exhibits. "Its character has changed," Strong complained to his *Diary;* the Crystal Palace "is now merely an extension of Barnum's Museum." In less than a year, the New York exhibition had lost any national character it might have enjoyed by its name association with the London exhibition of 1851 and had become but another struggling entertainment enterprise. Barnum made a final effort to revive the concern with a Fourth of July celebration. He resigned from the association a few days later, still convinced that, despite the loss to stockholders (himself among them), "the general prosperity of the city has been promoted far beyond the entire cost of the whole speculation."[20]

With the Lattig Observatory already foreclosed, the New York Crystal Palace limped on for four more years. Brown records the sale of goods by auction 31 October, to which visitors were admitted (as at a modern-day flea market) for an entrance fee. Odell records promenade concerts at the building in September 1856, and Brown notes the twenty-ninth annual fair of the American Institute opened there 15 September 1857. (Barnum had tried to interest Moses Kimball in dismantling the building and moving it to Boston because of its value as an exhibition hall.) By January 1858, the association was bankrupt and the ground lease had expired. The city took over the enterprise in hope of reviving it, but on 5 October 1858, two thousand spectators viewing exhibits prior to an evening concert (at which ten thousand were expected) were obliged to flee the Crystal Palace when a fire broke out. Within minutes, the building was totally engulfed, the conflagration providing a final "grand view" for thousands of onlookers. The loss of the building and its contents was estimated at two million dollars.[21]

Though the London Crystal Palace exhibition did not admit live ethnological displays (there were exhibits featuring live operators, such as telegraphers), the New York Crystal Palace did quickly, under Barnum, resort to them. Later American exhibition directors (those of the Centennial Exposition in Philadelphia in 1876, for example) followed the British precedent and excluded "entertainments," but they did include living Amerindians and other "native" people from around the world. Robert Bogdan observes that "although they were not displayed as a paid sideshow, as they had been in dime museums and the circus, the line between 'scientific' ethnological displays of the world's people and sensational exploitation of the exotic for profit was blurred." Following the examples of London showmen and P. T. Barnum, large numbers of American cultural entrepreneurs clustered outside prohibited fairgrounds, until, by the World's Columbian Exposition in Chicago in 1893, the amusement area – the Midway Plaisance – had become part of the fairground itself. Allied to the Department of Ethnology and Archaeology, this midway acknowledged what the Crystal Palaces of 1851 and 1853 had already authorized: that the commodification of culture made "exhibits" equally of spectators and of the materials displayed, of unitary ideologies (about class, work, progress, race, gender, and civilization) and the diversity that constituted them.[22]

* * * * *

CULTURAL DEBATES in antebellum America focused upon the place of art and performance in the creation of an "American" culture. As early as 1816, the patrician John Pintard wrote to his daughter, apropos the New York Academy of Sciences, "We must aim at giving proper direction to young minds, find out new resources for occupation and *killing* time, among which theatres, operas, Academies of Arts, Museums, etc., are to be classed as the means to attract and prevent the growth of vice and immorality." Pintard's cultural agenda was clearly directed toward the instructive capacity of art and to the responsibility of "society" (his elite construction of it) to provide those cultural resources. Twenty-five years later, on 5 November 1841, former mayor of New York Philip Hone confided to his diary that "theatre should come in for a better share of support," suggesting that, in at least one art form, New York's elite had failed to supply either direction or resources; indeed, historians see decreasing elite involvement in the antebellum decades with agendas of cultural control. The reasons for disengagement vary regionally. Chicago, which by the 1850s had become the largest primary grain and lumber market in the United States and the railroad center of the West, privileged the humble origins of its prominent men and a style of "simple living" at war with Harriet Martineau's 1834 description of "educated and refined and wealthy persons" in the Windy City. Here, too, financially successful business and professional men clubbed together in the 1840s and 1850s while scoffing at elite associations in other cities. The articulation of enterprise as the key to success diversified who the wealthy and prominent were in towns and cities both outside and within the Northeast corridor. In southern cities like Charleston, where historians locate a homogenous plantocracy fueled by economic stagnation and the absence of enterprising new blood, antebellumites such as William Gilmore Simms in 1844 identify a cultural "languuour" in patrician support of both art and intellectual activity. The absence of elite direction, patronage, and control, taken together with the identification of the "merely enterprising," locates antebellum cultural production in the manufactories of the workers and entrepreneurs represented by the Crystal Palace exhibitions.[23]

The 1853 New York Association for the Exhibition of the Industry of All Nations and American participation in the Great Exhibition of 1851 in London might be taken as verification of "middle-" or "business-class" agenda picking up where elite hegemonies left off. It seems to me, however, that the aristocracy-oriented models that such a transfer would mimic

– the defined and accepted structures evident in many British statements about class in the context of the Crystal Palace exhibition in Hyde Park – were themselves transformed in the antebellum decades away from the unitary toward the diverse. One such change is embedded in the 3 January 1848 observation by the *New York Herald,* "There is a revolution going on in theatres. The legitimate drama is down forever, buried and entombed twenty feet underground." If the stuff of theatre had become melodrama or the kinds of "edifying" entertainments presented by George Catlin and P. T. Barnum, the shift reflects a view of work and play trouped in the Crystal Palace exhibitions. The *New York Times* of 28 January 1854 urged the new relationship in saying people needed to "make it a duty to play." More radically, the *New York Clipper* (28 February 1860) argued "the end of work is to enjoy leisure." Modern American life (as it was) was unhealthy, sedentary, and/or stressful, mandating exercise for men and women and the rechanneling of competition into sport and a host of "useful" leisure amusements. To be able to afford leisure as the result of work was to tour one's own manufacturing, and what was performed as theatre culture reflects what had been or could be produced. This commodified culture, with its free-fall through social strata and differences, is defined not wholly as a battle of classes but rather of proximities, those areas where simultaneous "universes" overlap. In these spaces, culture was likely to become overelaborate in attempting to be all things to all people, substituting – as Ralph Nicholson Wornum observed in his prize-winning essay "The [1851] Exhibition as a Lesson in Taste" – "ornament itself for the thing to be ornamented."[24]

The antebellum decades in the United States valorized the ornamental, making natural objects (living Indians, African Americans, working men, women) agreeable via an appropriated mixture of things that commercialized yet insisted upon their authenticity: expensive lace fabricated by poorly paid working women or workers displaced by machines; stuffed Indians clothed in a hodgepodge of garments displaced, like performing Indians themselves, from organic tribal contexts; captives mimicking in white marble the enslavements of black people; culture at the extremities of large (the giant orchestra, the great exhibitions) and small (General Tom Thumb and the California flea circus). At the same time, by 1860, these commodifications, degradations, and appropriations had become American culture, a culture characterized by simultaneous, interactive diversities rather than the universal spaces of social control. One sees this process at work in many of the activities that emerge in these decades. The popular lecture, for example, had reached some four thousand American communities nationwide by the early 1840s. In bringing speakers with regional or national reputations, "scientized" by the sponsorship of learned societies, to men and women of even the smaller towns – and fare was to be pitched to the whole community, to be "useful" and "impartial" – the popular lecture, like the exhibition, marketed the worlds of astronomy, biology, physiology, geology, conversation, reading, memory, the Middle Ages, Iceland, the human condition, women, "oriental life," and the Crystal Palace itself to those who had not yet caught "the excursion habit." With attendance at such lectures conservatively estimated at four hundred thousand a week in the 1850s, "the craving for useful knowledge" had itself become a material industry, offering coherent understanding, self-improvement, or a sense of intellectual control to spectators. In a similar vein, the daguerreotype – so popular in the United States that by 1853 there were more studios on New York's Broadway alone than in all of London – offered Americans reproductions of "the authentic," the likeness of a family member or views of contemporary scenes (like the California gold rush or the Crystal Palace), and reproductions of these reproductions in the engravings and paintings made from them (Catlin's Indians or the mass production of Crystal Palace goods marketed via engravings in mass-produced catalogues, newspapers, and magazines).[25]

Herbert Blau, translating Brecht, reminds us that all representation is false and that the critical task is to arrive at estimates of relative truth. When, mimicking Heracleitis, we step into the stream of history, we risk making our subjects too much or too little like ourselves. In addition, the refusal both of totalizing categories (including time itself) and of positions of closure is problematic when writing histories of subjects who accepted or welcomed such categories as normative, as many readers of culture in America still do. The Prologue to this work emphasizes historical relationships. Lafayette's visit in 1824–5 coincided with a growth spurt of traditional entertainments, with the migration of "entertainment" into new areas, and heralded the expansion by 1860 of the concept of entertainment itself (via its linking to instruction) into spaces unimagined by even the most ambitious entrepreneurs in the 1820s. In the United States in the decades between Prologue and Epilogue, authenticity debates often masked both diversity and the effects of diversity upon culture. The chapters of the present study have followed the tensions between individual and group stagings, the "messy" exchanges that constitute antebellum American culture. On the threshold of the Civil War, the testimony of an epilogue of change, appropriation, and commodification stands prologue to the succeeding appropriations, conflicts, and commodifications in American culture characterizing the balance of the nineteenth century. In transforming the small town, city, and regional simulacra of early decades into the national figures troped at the Crystal Palace exhibition (so exquisitely and ironically captured in Catlin's Indian display and Powers's *Greek Slave*), constitutive performances of America's simultaneous cultural universes claim the stage they seem to me to merit.[26]

Viewed as theatre, as a performance at once earnest and assumed, true and false, accepting and contesting, liberating and oppressing, nineteenth-century American culture becomes, I think, much richer than it can be when viewed as a confining structure – as something happening inside cultural monuments (such as theatres) yet outside the bounds of history. At the same time, neglecting performance as constitutive of culture denies to history readings that enrich and inform it. At stake is not the ground of interdisciplinary cooperation, but a way of doing – performing – history that casts subjects in the different roles and scenes they inhabited in the historical past. To return to this place we have known before is to keep faith with memory, not to repair the things that have been broken, but to recognize that we are made by and of the simultaneities that constitute the universe.

Notes

Acknowledgments

1. Tzvetan Todorov considers the act of extended nomination in *The Conquest of America*, trans. Richard Howard (New York: Harper & Row, 1984), p. 28. Jacques Derrida takes up the mutability of speaking in *Writing and Difference*, trans. Alan Bass (Chicago: U. of Chicago Press, 1978), p. 177.

Prologue: Universal Spaces

1. Jorge Luis Borges, "The Garden of Forking Paths," in *Labyrinths*, trans. Donald A. Yates, ed. Donald A. Yates and James E. Irby (New York: New Directions, 1962), p. 28, and in *Ficciones*, trans. Helen Temple and Ruthven Todd, ed. Anthony Kerrigan (New York: Grove Press, 1962), p. 100. For sources in physics and its connection to theatre, see my "Time, Space, Timespace, Spacetime: Theatre History in Simultaneous Universes," *Journal of Dramatic Theory and Criticism* 5, 2 (Spring 1991): 63–84. The essay is indebted to Michel Foucault's "Of Other Spaces," *Diacritics* 16, 1 (Spring 1986): 22–7. The historical and spatial sense of North American tribal peoples is discussed in many sources, autobiographical, historical, critical, and fictional. For a poignant example, see Leslie Marmon Silko, *Ceremony* (New York: Penguin Books, 1979), esp. p. 126.
2. An important early exploration of the impact of positivism upon theatre studies is Bruce A. McConachie, "Towards a Postpositivist Theatre History," *Theatre Journal* 37, 4 (December 1985): 465–86. Other studies in the field appear in Thomas Postlewait and Bruce A. McConachie, eds., *Interpreting the Theatrical Past: Essays in the Historiography of Performance* (Iowa City: U. of Iowa Press, 1989); Sue-Ellen Case and Janelle Reinelt, eds., *The Performance of Power: Theatrical*

Discourse and Politics (Iowa City: U. of Iowa Press, 1991); and Janelle G. Reinelt and Joseph R. Roach, eds., *Critical Theory and Performance* (Ann Arbor: U. of Michigan Press, 1992).

3. See Jeffrey D. Mason, *Melodrama and the Myth of America* (Bloomington: Indiana U.P., 1993); John W. Frick, "'He Drank from the Poisoned Cup': Theatre, Culture, and Temperance in Antebellum America," *Journal of American Drama and Theatre* 4, 2 (Spring 1992): 21–41; and Bruce A. McConachie, "Out of the Kitchen and Into the Marketplace: Normalizing *Uncle Tom's Cabin* for the Antebellum Stage," *Journal of American Drama and Theatre* 3, 1 (Winter 1991): 5–28. A number of historical studies draw the connection between social and cultural performance. See esp. Karen Halttunen, *Confidence Men and Painted Women: A Study of Middle-Class Culture in America, 1830–1870* (New Haven: Yale U.P., 1982); John F. Kasson, *Rudeness and Civility: Manners in Nineteenth-Century Urban America* (New York: Hill & Wang, 1990); and Susan G. Davis, *Parades and Power: Street Theatre in Nineteenth-Century Philadelphia* (Philadelphia: Temple U.P., 1986).

4. Reinelt and Roach, *Critical Theory and Performance*, pp. 10, 293–4. On the science model in American historical practice, see Stanley Aronowitz, *Science as Power: Discourse and Ideology in Modern Society* (Minneapolis: U. of Minnesota Press, 1988); and Peter Novick, *That Noble Dream: The 'Objectivity Question' and the American Historical Profession* (Cambridge: Cambridge U.P., 1988). The nostalgia for certainty, for clear playing fields, identified canons and values in the discipline, and for a controlling historiography that priviledges "facts," suggest the discomfiture of postmodern theatre historians with postmodernity. The valorization of primary materials, of "precise and testable data . . . confirmed or rejected on logical and scientific grounds," data capable of destroying 'unfounded' hypotheses, sounds the echo of positivism. On these issues, see Michael L. Quinn, "*Theaterwissenschaft* in the History of Theatre Study," and Jim Davis and Tracy C. Davis, "The People of the 'People's Theatre': The Social Demography of the Britannia Theatre (Hoxton)," both in *Theatre Survey* 32, 2 (November 1991): 123–36 and 139–70, respectively, but esp. pp. 135–6 in the former and pp. 141–4 in the latter. Joyce Flynn, "A Complex Causality of Neglect," *American Quarterly* 41, 1 (March 1989): 123–7.

5. For the northeastern skewing and an interesting account of tides since World War II in the study of American literature before the Civil War, see Cecelia Tichi, "American Literary Studies to the Civil War," in *Redrawing the Boundaries: The Transformation of English and American Literary Studies*, ed. Stephen Greenblatt and Giles Gunn (New York: MLAA, 1992), pp. 209–31. For gender studies in theatre on theoretical and critical levels, see Jill Dolan, *The Feminist Spectator as Critic* (Ann Arbor: UMI Research Press, 1988); Sue-Ellen Case, *Feminism and Theatre* (London: Macmillan, 1988); and Gayle Austin, *Feminist Theories for Dramatic Criticism* (Ann Arbor: U. of Michigan Press, 1990). See also the essays in Lynda Hart, ed., *Making a Spectacle: Feminist Essays on Contemporary Women's Theatre* (Ann Arbor: U. of Michigan Press, 1989); Sue-Ellen Case, ed., *Performing Feminisms: Feminist Critical Theory and Theatre* (Baltimore: Johns Hopkins

U.P., 1990); and June Schlueter, ed., *Feminist Rereadings of Modern American Drama* (Rutherford, N.J.: Fairleigh Dickinson U.P., 1989). Recent theatre studies recuperate house playwrights, workers, and popular entertainments; see Walter J. Meserve, *Heralds of Promise: The Drama of the American People in the Age of Jackson, 1829–1849* (Westport, Conn.: Greenwood Press, 1986); Bruce A. McConachie, "'The Theatre of the Mob': Apocalyptic Melodrama and Preindustrial Riots in Antebellum New York," in *Theatre for Working-Class Audiences in the United States, 1830–1980*, ed. McConachie and Daniel Friedman (Westport, Conn.: Greenwood Press, 1985), pp. 17–46; McConachie's *Melodramatic Formations: American Theatre and Society, 1820–1870* (Iowa City: U. of Iowa Press, 1992); and Laurence Senelick, *The Age and Stage of George L. Fox, 1825–1877* (Hanover, N.H.: U.P. of New England, 1988). In addition to these, the scholarship of Don B. Wilmeth and Brooks McNamara has been instrumental in legitimating popular nineteenth-century American theatre as a subject worthy of study.

6. Chantal Mouffe, "Hegemony and New Political Subjects: Toward a New Concept of Democracy," *Marxism and the Interpretation of Culture*, ed. Cary Nelson and Lawrence Grossberg (Urbana: U. of Illinois Press, 1988): 89–90. Reinelt and Roach, *Critical Theory and Performance*, p. 163. Mason, *Melodrama and the Myth of America*, pp. 1–12. Homi K. Bhabha, "Postcolonial Criticism," in *Redrawing the Boundaries*, ed. Greenblatt and Gunn, p. 461.

7. T. J. Clark, *The Painting of Modern Life* (New York: Alfred A. Knopf, 1985), p. 6. Tichi, "American Literary Studies," pp. 222–3. Concerning the myth-centered works of Henry Nash Smith, Leo Marx, and R. W. B. Lewis that have served as commanding narratives in American studies, see Philip Fisher, "American Literary and Cultural Studies Since the Civil War," in *Redrawing the Boundaries*, ed. Greenblatt and Gunn, pp. 232–5. For Foucault, see particularly the essays translated in: *Power/Knowledge*, ed. Colin Gordon (New York: Pantheon Books, 1980); *Language, Counter-Memory, Practice*, ed. Donald F. Bouchard (Ithaca: Cornell U.P., 1977); *The Foucault Reader*, ed. Paul Rabinow (New York: Pantheon Books, 1984); and *Michel Foucault: Politics, Philosophy, and Culture*, ed. Lawrence D. Kritzman (New York: Routledge, 1988).

8. "Liminal" is a key term in Halttunen, *Confidence Men and Painted Women*. Several recent works have considered cultural structures, among them Mason, *Melodrama and the Myth of America;* McConachie, *Melodramatic Formations;* Lawrence W. Levine's *Highbrow/Lowbrow: The Emergence of Cultural Hierarchy in America* (Cambridge: Harvard U.P., 1988); and Peter G. Buckley, "To the Opera House: Culture and Society in New York City, 1820–1860," Ph.D. diss. (SUNY–Stony Brook, 1984). These take differing views of class, as do the following historical works that have influenced this study: Stuart M. Blumin, "The Hypothesis of Middle Class Formation in Nineteenth-Century America: A Critique and Some Proposals," *American Historical Review* 90, 2 (April 1985): 99–118, and his *The Emergence of the Middle Class: Social Experience in the American City, 1760–1900* (Cambridge: Cambridge U.P., 1989); Arno J. Mayer, "The Lower Middle Class as Historical Problem," *Journal of Modern History* 47, 3 (Fall 1975): 409–36; Peter N. Stearns, "The Middle Class: Toward a Precise Defini-

tion," *Comparative Studies in Society and History* 21, 3 (July 1979): 377–96;
Michael B. Katz, "Social Class in North American Urban History," *Journal of
Interdisciplinary History* 11, 4 (Spring 1981): 579–605; Mary P. Ryan, *Cradle of
the Middle Class: The Family in Oneida County, New York, 1790–1865* (Cambridge: Cambridge U.P., 1981), and her *Women in Public: Between Banners and
Ballots, 1825–1880* (Baltimore: Johns Hopkins U.P., 1990); Sean Wilentz, *Chants
Democratic: New York City and the Rise of the American Working Class, 1788–1850*
(Oxford: Oxford U.P., 1984); Christine Stansell, *City of Women: Sex and Class
in New York, 1789–1860* (New York: Alfred A. Knopf, 1986); and Elizabeth
Blackmar, *Manhattan for Rent, 1785–1850* (Ithaca: Cornell U.P., 1989). I have also
discussed this issue in "Hustlers in the House: The Bowery Theatre as a Mode
of Historical Information," in *The American Stage*, ed. Ron Engle and Tice
Miller (Cambridge: Cambridge U.P., 1993). Simon Frith, "The Good, the Bad,
and the Indifferent: Defending Popular Culture from the Populists," *Diacritics*
21, 4 (Winter 1991): 102–15. See esp. p. 107, where Frith suggests that taste in
culture plays across the class-containment formations that underpin cultural
studies.

9. For Marx and Engels, see *The German Ideology*, trans and ed. S. Ryazanskaya
(London: Lawrence & Wishart, 1979), vol. 5, p. 229. Histories of associations,
legitimating authorities, movements, and the like are referenced in Chapter 3.
Some of those important to this study and not referenced elsewhere in this Prologue include Paul E. Johnson, *A Shopkeeper's Millennium: Society and Revivals
in Rochester, New York, 1815–1837* (New York: Hill & Wang, 1978); Allan S. Horlick, *Country Boys and Merchant Princes: The Social Control of Young Men in
New York* (Lewisburg, Pa.: Bucknell U.P., 1975); David J. Rothman, *The Discovery of the Asylum: Social Order and Disorder in the New Republic*, rev. ed.
(Boston: Little, Brown & Co., 1990); Burton J. Bledstein, *The Culture of Professionalism: The Middle Class and the Development of Higher Education in America*
(New York: W. W. Norton, 1976); Paul A. Gilje, *The Road to Mobocracy: Popular Disorder in New York City, 1763–1834* (Chapel Hill: U. of North Carolina
Press, 1987); John B. Jentz, "Artisans, Evangelicals, and the City: A Social History of Abolition and Labor Reform in Jacksonian New York," Ph.D. diss. (City
University of New York, 1977); and Ronald G. Walters, *American Reformers,
1815–1860* (New York: Hill & Wang, 1978).

10. The Great Exhibition of the Works of Industry of All Nations of 1851, or more
simply the Crystal Palace exhibition, was the first international trade fair in
western Europe in modern times. It provided a significant staging ground for
"American" culture and introduced ethnological displays, from North America
and other parts of the world, to the trade fair. The impact of this upon subsequent U.S. expositions is explored in Robert W. Rydell, *All the World's a Fair:
Visions of Empire at American Industrial Expositions, 1876–1916* (Chicago: U. of
Chicago Press, 1984). A number of postcolonial debates are relevant to this discussion; see Bhabha, "Postcolonial Criticism," and also the exchanges concerning Bakhtin in the following issues of *Diacritics:* 23, 2 (Summer 1993): 47–70; 23,
4 (Winter 1993): 93–9; and 24, 4 (Winter 1994): 71–7.

11. L. P. Hartley, *The Go-Between* (London: Hamish Hamilton, 1953), p. 9. The Robert Louis Stevenson quote is from *The Silverado Squatters*. For Benjamin on Klee's *Angelus Novus*, see section IX of "Theses on the Philosophy of History," in *Illuminations*, trans. Harry Zahn, ed. Hannah Arendt (N.Y.: Harcourt, Brace & World, 1968), pp. 259–60.

12. In addition to the original thirteen states – Connecticut, Delaware, Georgia, Massachusetts, Maryland, New Hampshire, New Jersey, New York, North Carolina, Pennsylvania, Rhode Island, South Carolina, and Virginia – the following had been admitted as states: Vermont (1791), Kentucky (1792), Tennessee (1796), Ohio (1803), Louisiana (1812), Indiana (1816), Mississippi (1817), Illinois (1818), Alabama (1819), Maine (1820), and Missouri (1821). The three territories in 1830 were Michigan (presently the states of Michigan and Wisconsin), Arkansas, and Florida. Lafayette's itinerary for every day of his visit is given in J. Bennett Nolan, *Lafayette in America Day by Day* (Baltimore: Johns Hopkins U.P., 1934), from which all dates in this Prologue are taken unless otherwise noted. Lafayette's journey from Washington, D.C., around the boarders of the United States in 1825 is detailed in Edgar E. Brandon, comp. and ed., *A Pilgrimage of Liberty: A Contemporary Account of the Triumphal Tour of General Lafayette Through the Southern and Western States in 1825, as Reported by the Local Newspapers* (Athens, Ohio: Lawhead Press, 1944). The authoritative contemporaneous account of the general's return is that written by his secretary, Auguste Levasseur, *Lafayette in America in 1824 and 1825; or, Journal of a Voyage to the United States*, trans. John D. Goodman, 2 vols. (Philadelphia: Carey & Lea, 1829). Studies of the Erie Canal follow in these notes.

13. The New York events are described in Nolan, *Lafayette in America Day by Day*, by dates and in Levasseur, *Lafayette in America*, vol. 1, Chapter 1.

14. A rich visual history of Lafayette's visit can be found in Marian Klamkin, *The Return of Lafayette, 1824–1825* (New York: Charles Scribner's Sons, 1975).

15. For Lafayette's activities in New York, see Levasseur, *Lafayette in America*, and Klamkin, *Return of Lafayette*. For the entertainments available there in 1824, see George C. D. Odell, *Annals of the New York Stage* (New York: Columbia U.P., 1928), vol. 3, pp. 166–7. For Hervieu's panorama, see my "Mrs. Trollope Visits the Theatre," *Journal of American Drama & Theatre* 5, 3 (Fall 1993): 16–27.

16. Lafayette's visits to the theatre are documented by date in Nolan, *Lafayette in America Day by Day*, which also addresses George Washington's preference for *The School for Scandal* (p. 260). Appearances at theatres in New York are confirmed in Odell, *Annals*, vol. 3, pp. 138, 151, 168–9, and 163 (the Lafayette Amphitheatre bill is not given).

17. For the assessment of New York theatre, see Levasseur, *Lafayette in America*, vol. 1, pp. 93–4.

18. Ibid., vol. 1, pp. 97–9.

19. The quotes are from ibid., vol. 1, p. 98. Odell, *Annals*, vol. 3, p. 168, discusses the events and the gale.

20. Levasseur, *Lafayette in America*, vol. 1, pp. 141–50, describes the visit to Philadelphia. Klamkin, *Return of Lafayette*, pp. 77–8, provides an inventory of par-

ticipants. Susan G. Davis discusses the Lafayette reception in the context of parading in *Parades and Power,* pp. 126–7. We may owe the 1828 restoration of Independence Hall to Lafayette's observation that he hardly recognized the building, on account of "modernizations" since his day.

21. Davis, *Parades and Power,* pp. 70, 126–7, and 66–7; and see Klamkin, *Return of Lafayette,* pp. 76–86.

22. Levasseur, *Lafayette in America,* vol. 1, p. 16; gradualist and colonization texts enter Levasseur's account at a number of points. For Roberts, see Odell, *Annals,* vol. 3, p. 135. Market performers are discussed in Thomas F. DeVoe, *The Market Book* (1862; rpt. New York: Burt Franklin, 1969), pp. 344–5; and Peter G. Buckley, "'The Place to Make an Artist Work': Micah Hawkins and William Sidney Mount in New York City," in *Catching the Tune: Music and William Sidney Mount,* ed. Janice Gray Armstrong (New York: Museums at Stony Brook, 1984), pp. 22–39.

23. For Fredericksburg, see Nolan, *Lafayette in America Day by Day,* p. 259, and Klamkin, *Return of Lafayette,* pp. 102–3. Levasseur's account contains a lengthy tribute to Thomas Jefferson's kindness as a slave master (*Lafayette in America,* vol. 1, pp. 218–19) and considers Madison and other prominent slaveholders of his acquaintance to be sensible of the injustice of slavery and enlightened therefore to amend it. Given Levasseur's abolitionist views, there is an inescapable sense of accommodation in these solicitudes, driven perhaps by a desire to have his book received well in the South, or not to offend those who had been hospitable to him, or by a sensitivity to his status as a foreigner; or perhaps this reflects the mediating hand of Levasseur's translator, John D. Goodman, who annotates the text at several points where it deals with race and slavery. (I have not compared the English to the French text for similar mediations in the translation.) Levasseur records roadside stops at black homes by Lafayette as the party moved south.

24. For the Washington reception of the Choctaw and Chickasaw leaders, see Levasseur, *Lafayette in America,* vol. 2, p. 10. For John Quincy Adams's Indian policy, see Alexander Saxton, *The Rise and Fall of the White Republic: Class Politics and Mass Culture in Nineteenth-Century America* (London: Verso, 1990), esp. pp. 84–5, 37–9. Lafayette's progress through Indian territory is detailed by Levasseur in vol. 2, Chapter 6 (with the treaty quotation on p. 71). The general's movements are also tracked in Nolan, *Lafayette in America Day by Day,* and reprised by Klamkin, *Return of Lafayette* (Chapter 16). For press treatment of this part of Lafayette's journey, see Brandon, *Pilgrimage of Liberty,* p. 141.

25. Levasseur, *Lafayette in America,* vol. 2, pp. 74–5, for the quotes. The "Ball Play" is discussed in a letter written by someone escorting Lafayette's party though the Georgia–Alabama Indian territories. Published 5 April 1825 in the *Georgia Journal* (and reprinted in Brandon, *Pilgrimage of Liberty,* pp. 141–2), it is "the only notice concerning the journey through the Indian country that appeared in the public press," according to Brandon. The Ball Play was clearly a cultural staging; the description of it in the letter, however, suggests a performance rather than an athletic event. The relevant portion reads: "The Indians then formed, and, after going through some ceremonies, gave a *Ball Play,* which, to those who

never witnessed one before, was very amusing. It lasted an hour, and the General appeared to be well entertained with it."

26. Levasseur, *Lafayette in America*, vol. 2, p. 81, for the quote. Levasseur appends a counterexample of Indian justice and white injustice, concluding (pp. 82–3), "Poor Indians! You are pillaged, beaten, poisoned or excited by intoxicating liquors, and then you are termed savages! Washington said, 'Whenever I have been called upon to decide between an Indian and a white man, I have always found that the white had been the aggressor.' Washington was right." This defense, however, is immediately followed (p. 83) by the longer passage quoted in the text.

27. Lafayette's visit to New Orleans is detailed in the section headed "Louisiana" in Brandon, *Pilgrimage of Liberty*, pp. 160–97; for the despotism speech, see p. 168. The catalogue of activities provided by Nolan, *Lafayette in America Day by Day*, is fleshed out by Levasseur, *Lafayette in America*. The visit is briefly considered in Klamkin, *Return of Lafayette*, pp. 144–5.

28. For his description of these events and for the quotes, see Levasseur, *Lafayette in America*, vol. 2, pp. 90, 91–2. See also Brandon, *Pilgrimage of Liberty*, pp. 162–97.

29. Levasseur, *Lafayette in America*, vol. 2, pp. 91–2; for the description of the Choctaw, see Brandon, *Pilgrimage of Liberty*, p. 172. Levasseur adds (vol. 2, p. 92) that the Indians had been camped near New Orleans for nearly a month "in order to see the 'great warrior,' 'the brother of their great father Washington.'" "Great white father" rhetoric is considered by Michael P. Rogin, *Fathers and Children: Andrew Jackson and the Subjugation of the American Indian* (New York: Alfred A. Knopf, 1975); Charles Camp, "American Indian Oratory in the White Image: An Analysis of Stereotypes," *Journal of American Culture* 1, 4 (Winter 1978): 811–17; and see Saxton's *White Republic*.

30. For the theatre visits, see Levasseur, *Lafayette in America*, vol. 2, pp. 92–3 (the quote concerning the black veterans is from p. 93). For the newspaper account, see Brandon, *Pilgrimage of Liberty*, pp. 181–2. Nolan, *Lafayette in America Day by Day*, (p. 283) is the only source mentioning the vaudeville; Brandon's otherwise exhaustive account omits it (pp. 192–3).

31. The journey itself is a testament to Lafayette's good health and stamina at the age of 68. In addition, except for Sabbatarian complaints about activities taking place on Sundays, the general emerged from his travels with a good report. Lafayette connected with the Erie Canal at Lockport, New York, whose deep cut and locks he had reviewed the preceding September at a Masonic banquet in New York City, where the centerpiece had been a tables-long model of the waterway, exact in every detail and replete with water and tiny canal boats. He stayed with the slow-moving canal to Rochester, rode by horse relay to Syracuse (bypassing an unfinished section), canaled to Schnectady, and traveled by carriage to Albany and overland through Massachusetts to Boston. Lafayette's route is traced by Nolan, Klamkin, Levasseur, and Brandon (who gives a map). See also Ronald E. Shaw, *Erie Water West* (Lexington: U. of Kentucky Press, 1966), pp. 181–2.

32. On Kaskaskia and Buffalo, see Levasseur, *Lafayette in America*, vol. 2, pp. 141, 186–7. (The Illinois tribal confederacy included the Kaskaskia, the Cahokia, the Michigamea, the Moingwena, the Peoria, and the Tamaroa.)

33. Brandon, *Pilgrimage of Liberty*, pp. 174–5, for the dignitary's quote. Lafayette's visit was not without its material side. In addition to a free (if arduous) ride throughout his sojourn as the nation's guest, Lafayette also gained a good chunk of Florida real estate from his grateful adoptive country. For all that, the affirmation of his centrality to democratic causes, which had not taken his fame or fortune as far in France as in the United States, may have been as valuable to him as as any hope of gain.

34. For the Erie Canal and the Monroe Doctrine, see Shaw, *Erie Water West*, p. 408; for the "holy cause" of republicanism, p. 188; for canal economics, pp. 275–6. By 1860, in the often rehearsed political compromises of the antebellum decades, Iowa (1846), California (1850), and Oregon (1859) had been admitted to the Union as free states, and Arkansas (1836), Texas (1845), and Florida (1845) as slave states. Northern border disputes were resolved by the Webster–Ashburton Treaty with Great Britain in 1842, which established the Maine boundary. A sequence of negotiations ending in 1846 fixed the northwestern boundary with Canada at the forty-ninth parallel. Congress annexed Texas in 1845 and, after war with Mexico (1846–8), a southern border for the United States was established.

35. Ibid., p. 398. For the Indians compromised by the development the canal represented, see pp. 7, 400–10.

36. See ibid., Chapter 10, for an account of these celebrations. See also George E. Condon, *Stars in the Water* (New York: Doubleday, 1974).

37. For the New York City celebrations, see Shaw, *Erie Water West*, pp. 188–92, and Condon, *Stars in the Water*, pp. 100–7.

38. Sources as in previous note. A Vauxhall Garden balloon ascent failed to take place, causing angry patrons to rip the balloon to pieces and trash the grounds (*New York Evening Post*, 5 November 1825).

1. Spaces of Representation

1. The phrase is from Locke's *Two Treatises of Government*. The narcissism that devolves from scholarly projections of America as paradise, of discovery as the most important thing about it, voiding the sense of an America that developed through historical processes, is taken up in Cecelia Tichi, "American Literary Studies to the Civil War," in *Redrawing the Boundaries: The Transformation of English and American Literary Studies*, ed. Stephen Greenblatt and Giles Gunn (New York: MLAA, 1992), pp. 209–31. Historical as well as literary explorations of antebellum America reflect ideological inscriptions of the originary American, who remains unaffected by the two hundred years of interaction that had already transpired in the eastern United States by 1825.

2. Travel literature is extensive. Those with the most direct relationship to theatre and this study include Moreau de Saint-Méry, *Moreau de Saint-Méry's American Journey* [1793–8], trans. Kenneth and Anna M. Roberts (Garden City, N.Y.: Doubleday & Co., 1947); Basil Hall's *Travels in North America, 1827–1828*, 3 vols. (London: Simpkin & Marshal, 1829); Francis Trollope's *Domestic Man-*

ners of the Americans, ed. Donald Smalley (New York: Vintage Books, 1960); Charles Dickens's *American Notes* (1842; rpt. London: Mandarin, 1991); Alexis de Tocqueville's *Democracy in America,* ed. Phillips Bradley, 2 vols. (New York: Random House/Vintage Books, 1990); Fanny [Frances Anne] Kemble's *Journal,* 2 vols. (London: John Murray, 1835), vol. 1; Frederick Marryat's *Diary in America,* 3 vols. (London: Longman, Orme, Brown, Green & Longmans, 1839); and Harriet Martineau's *Society in America* (New York: Saunders & Otley, 1837). For discussion of these and others, see Allan Nevins, *American Social History as Recorded by British Travellers* (New York: Henry Holt & Co., 1923); and Robert B. Downs, *Images of America: Travelers from Abroad in the New World* (Champaign: U. of Illinois Press, 1987). For the British view of the sublime and the uncivilized, see Christopher Mulvey, *Anglo-American Landscapes: A Study of Nineteenth-Century Anglo-American Travel Literature* (Cambridge: Cambridge U.P., 1983), pp. 10–11. Thomas Colley Gratton, British Consul in Boston in these years, observed: "The greatness of the country strongly contrasts with the deficiencies of the people. The magnificent scale of creation seems unsuited to the beings who possess it" (Nevins, *American Social History,* pp. 248–9).

3. According to the *Oxford English Dictionary,* both Addison in 1711 and Robertson in 1777 used the word "American" to mean aboriginal inhabitants, whereas Gale in 1765 and Johnson in 1775 applied it to white colonials. Werner Sollers speaks eloquently of this ambiguity in "Romantic Love, Arranged Marriage, and Indian Melancholy," in his *Beyond Ethnicity: Consent and Descent in American Culture* (Oxford: Oxford U.P., 1986), pp. 102–30. He suggests that the mythic paradigms bracketing the colonial American experience are the Thanksgiving feast at Plymouth and the disappearance (and presumed destruction) of the colonists at Roanoke.

4. A myth-centered scholarship and its location of "stable stories" is taken up by Philip Fisher, "American Literary and Cultural Studies since the Civil War," in Stephen Greenblatt and Giles Gunn, eds., *Redrawing the Boundaries,* pp. 232–50. In order to avoid quotation marks throughout this work around such disputed terms as "American" and "Indian" and constructs like "paradise" and "the American experience," I underscore their provisional status here and use quotation marks subsequently in the work when the words or contexts are at issue. Similarly, I move between race terms (red, black, white) and constructs (Indian, Negro, descendants of Europeans) in a way that is, I hope, clear in context, however taxonomically unsatisfying. In the antebellum decades, such words were as unstable and disputed as they are in our own day – for example, that "Indian" signaled a foreign nation on the continent and "African" those alien to it. Who was entitled by the word "American" was itself at the point of contest. Finally, I use the term "staged" instead of the more traditional "stage" throughout this work in reference to such simulacra as the staged Yankee, Indian, or frontiersman in an effort to emphasize the created nature of these myths and my skepticism that antebellumites regarded them as "authentic" representatives of real people, however much authenticity itself was disputed in those decades.

5. One young transcendentalist said the word was "a nickname which those who stayed behind gave to those who went ahead"; see Donald N. Koster, *Transcendentalism in America* (Boston: Twayne Publishers, 1975), p. 2. For Tocqueville, see *Democracy in America,* vol. 2, p. 3.

6. For philosophical influences upon the transcendentalists, see (among many): Georges J. Joyaux, "Victor Cousin and American Transcendentalism," *French Review* 24, 2 (December 1955): 117–30; William R. Hutchinson, *Transcendentalist Ministers* (New Haven: Yale U.P., 1959), pp. 22–51, for French, German, and other influences; Alexander Kern, "The Rise of Transcendentalism, 1815–1860," in *Transitions in American Literary History,* ed. Harry H. Clark (Durham: Duke U.P., 1954), pp. 247–314; and R. A. Yoder, "The Equilibrist Perspective: Toward a Theory of American Romanticism," *Studies in Romanticism* 12, 4 (Fall 1973): 705–40, for transcendental connections to English Romanticism. For the gathering in Ripley's study, see Koster, *Transcendentalism in America,* pp. 13–15. The antebellum penchant for associations is discussed in greater detail in Chapter 3, but it is germane to note here that of thirty-some transcendentalists analyzed by Kern (p. 250), all were New Englanders, Unitarians, Harvardians (if they attended college), all (except Ellery Channing) one-time clergymen or teachers, overwhelmingly middle class, and, of course, white. Tichi, "American Literary Studies," provides a précis of "individualism" scholarship in recent years (see also her sources in literary studies – she does not mention drama or theatre). In the same volume, Fisher, "American Literary and Cultural Studies," pp. 232–5, notes the appeal, especially to myth-centered scholarship, of periods in American history (e.g., Puritan and transcendental) where intellectuals are presumed to be in charge. For his study of class politics and culture, see Alexander Saxton, *The Rise and Fall of the White Republic: Class Politics and Mass Culture in Nineteenth-Century America* (London: Verso, 1990).

7. For the unitarian response to transcendentalism, see Cameron Thompson, "John Locke and New England Transcendentalism," *New England Quarterly* 35, 4 (December 1962): 435–57, and n. 43 concerning Cousin's influence. Cousin's *Letters on Locke* was published in America in 1834 (under another title) and went to four editions by 1855; Coleridge's *Aids to Reflection,* edited by a Locke opponent, was issued in 1829. Both strengthened the transcendentalist association of Locke with a Puritan (Unitarian) repression of feeling, a view with a very long history in the United States. For Dickens, see the 1842 *American Notes,* pp. 60–1; for Child, see "Letter XIII" (24 April 1844), in *Letters from New-York: Second Series* (New York: Charles S. Francis, 1845), pp. 125–30.

8. Contemplation and intuition allowed the perception, via nature, of wholes as well as connecting parts. These views are expressed by Thoreau in *Walden and On the Duty of Civil Disobedience* (New York: Harper & Row, 1965), and by Emerson, *Selected Writings* (New York: Signet/NAL, 1983). Secondary commentary is extensive: see Koster, *Transcendentalism in America,* pp. 33–5; Kern, "Rise of Transcendentalism," pp. 292–5; and Paul F. Boller, *American Transcendentalism, 1830–1860: An Intellectual Inquiry* (New York: G. P. Putnam's Sons, 1974), pp. 67–8. Coleridge on Edmund Kean is from "Table Talk, 27 April 1823," in *Table*

Talk and Omniana (Oxford: Oxford U.P., 1917), p. 44. The painterly vocabulary is noted in literature and reviewing by James T. Callow, *Kindred Spirits: Knickerbocker Writers and American Artists, 1807–1855* (Chapel Hill: U. of North Carolina Press, 1967); and Nina Baym, *Novels, Readers, and Reviewers: Responses to Fiction in Antebellum America* (Ithaca: Cornell U.P., 1984).

9. For the political aspects of transcendentalism see, in addition to sources already cited, Duane E. Smith, "Romanticism in America: The Transcendentalists," *Review of Politics* 35, 3 (July 1973): 302–25; and Richard Francis, "The Ideology of Brook Farm," in *Studies in the American Renaissance*, ed. Joel Myerson (Bloomington, Ind.: Twayne, 1978), pp. 561–95. Tichi traces shifts in scholarly treatments of Emerson and Thoreau away from trancendentalism as a philosophy of individualism and toward viewing its groundings in economic and social history ("American Literary Studies," pp. 220–1).

10. See A. Robert Caponigri, "Individual, Civil Society, and State in American Transcendentalism," in *Critical Essays on American Transcendentalism*, eds. Philip F. Gura and Joel Myerson (Boston: G. K. Hall, 1982), pp. 541–60. This thoughtful essay discerns a materialist mediation in transcendentalism, particularly in the work of Orestes Brownson.

11. For Emerson, see "Self-Reliance," in *Selected Writings*. Quite a different view of the state is voiced by Novalis, who says, "Ein Mensch ohne Staat ist ein Wilder [A man without a state is a savage]." Other German Romantics (e.g., Herder) personalize the state, often positioning it as the enemy, or make the state organic (as Schelling does), intrinsically unified but compromised by extrinsic interference. For these and other observations, see Smith, "Romanticism in America." For civil disobedience as a moral imperative, see Thoreau's *Walden and On the Duty of Civil Disobedience*, p. 62.

12. For Brownson, see Caponigri, "Individual, Civil Society, and State," esp. pp. 555–7.

13. For Brook Farm, see Francis, "Ideology of Brook Farm," which, although primarily philosophy, raises interesting issues concerning role playing in a variety of Brook Farm amusements. On the education of blacks in antebellum America and related issues, see Leonard P. Curry, *The Free Black in Urban America, 1800–1850* (Chicago: U. of Chicago Press, 1981) (p. 150 for Alcott); and James O. Horton and Lois E. Horton, *Black Bostonians: Family Life and Community Struggle in the Antebellum North* (New York: Holmes & Meier, 1979).

14. The primary study of Brook Farm theatrical activities is Lucille Gafford, "Transcendentalist Attitudes Toward Drama and the Theatre," *New England Quarterly* 12, 3 (September 1940): 442–66. Theatrical histories of the plays performed there are provided in Arthur Hobson Quinn, *A History of the American Drama from the Beginning to the Civil War* (New York: Appleton–Century–Crofts, 1923); and Walter Meserve, *An Emerging Entertainment: The Drama of the American People to 1828* (Bloomington: Indiana U.P., 1977).

15. See Gafford, "Transcendentalist Attitudes Toward Drama," for journal sources. Fuller is primarily associated with the early *Dial* (her reflective piece appeared in July 1842), George Ripley with the *Harbinger* (see esp. the 18 December 1847

issue). Both reviewed drama and considered theatre. Indeed, Sylvester Judd, a Unitarian minister, wrote a play and used playbills to frame a theatre visit by the title character of his novel *Margaret.*

16. For the luminist–transcendentalist link, see Barbara Novak, *American Painting of the Nineteenth Century: Realism, Idealism and the American Experience,* 2d ed. (New York: Harper & Row, 1979); and John Wilmerding's excellent collection (including noteworthy essays by Novak, Wilmerding, and Albert Gelpi), *American Light: The Luminist Movement, 1850–1875* (Princeton: Princeton U.P., 1989), whence the first quote (p. 17). The second quote is from Wilmerding, ed., *The Genius of American Painting* (New York: William Morrow, 1973), p. 121. *American Light* contains reproductions of many of the paintings cited here, as does William Truettner's *The West as America: Reinterpreting Images of the Frontier, 1820–1920* (Washington: National Museum of American Art / Smithsonian Institution Press, 1991). In the latter source, the essays by Patricia Hills, "Picturing Progress in the Era of Westward Expansion," pp. 97–147, and Elizabeth Johns, "Settlement and Development," pp. 191–235, are germane to considerations of the town and "civilization."

17. For Durand, see Bertha M. Stearns, "Nineteenth-Century Writers in the World of Art," *Art in America* 40, 1 (Winter 1952): 31–2; and John Durand, *The Life and Times of A. B. Durand* (New York: Charles Scribner's Sons, 1894), p. 174; for John Quidor, see John I. H. Baur, *John Quidor: 1801–1881* (New York: Brooklyn Museum, 1942), pp. 11–12; for Cole, see (among many) Kenneth J. LaBudde, "The Mind of Thomas Cole," Ph.D. diss. (Univ. Minnesota, 1954). For these artists and others, see Callow, *Kindred Spirits,* esp. pp. 183–91, 224–5; for critical concepts borrowed from painting in reviews of novels, see Baym, *Novels, Readers, and Reviewers,* p. 160.

18. *The Forest Rose* is reprinted, with useful commentary, in Richard Moody, *Dramas from the American Theatre* (Boston: Houghton Mifflin, 1966), pp. 143–74; the quotes here are from p. 155. Samuel Woodworth was the composer of "The Old Oaken Bucket," though the music for the play was the work of John Davies. The history and assessment of the play is Moody's, but generally held. See also Meserve, *An Emerging Entertainment,* pp. 239–40, and David Grimsted, *Melodrama Unveiled: American Theatre and Culture, 1800–1850* (Chicago: U. of Chicago Press, 1968), p. 156, n. 105.

19. The farm is extolled in song by William Roseville (II.ii), Harriet's sweetheart (Lydia's brother). The pretentious father is the property of young Blandford (II.v), Lydia's lover. The "roses" in the play include two Rosevilles (a veritable town of roses) and the black Rose, plus Harriet Miller, who is described as a country rose. Bellamy's threat of literary infamy is from act II, scene v, just preceding the full-chorus song-and-dance finale, a paean to rural life, farmers, domestic harmony, and upright behavior. Saxton, *White Republic,* pp. 121–3, briefly examines the role deference politics played in early Whig republicanism and in its Jacksonian Democrat successor vis-à-vis racism ("hard" and "soft") and class in Woodworth's *The Forest Rose.*

20. Grimsted has taken *Rosina Meadows, the Village Maid; or, Temptations Unveiled*

(c. 1843) as the paradigmatic American melodrama of the first half of the nineteenth century, "the tragedy of the age"; see his *Melodrama Unveiled*, pp. 241–8, for a sensitive reading of the play and the paradise village. On racism in *The Forest Rose* and the Yankee, see Saxton, *White Republic*, pp. 116–23.

21. For the existence of a native drama, see Harold J. Nichols, "The Prejudice against Native American Drama from 1778 to 1830," *Quarterly Journal of Speech* 60, 3 (October 1974): 279–88. For the continued call for one, see (among many) James Kirke Paulding, "The American Drama," *American Quarterly Review* 1 (June 1827): 331–57. For the search for an American novel when one already existed, see Baym, *Novels, Readers, and Reviewers*, esp. pp. 242–7. Walter J. Meserve, *Heralds of Promise: The Drama of the American People in the Age of Jackson, 1829–1849* (Westport, Conn.: Greenwood Press, 1986), pp. 160–1. Many nineteenth-century American actors and theatrical managers were clubmen: the Booths, Thomas Hamblin, the Wallacks, Joseph Jefferson, Sol Smith, Noah Ludlow, and William Warren, prominent among them. Indeed, club membership (esp. Freemasonry) often paved the way for community receptivity to theatricals, particularly in the western antebellum states.

22. Baym, *Novels, Readers, and Reviewers*, discusses tensions between the particular and the universal. An insight into why a similar study has not been undertaken for American plays and production reviews is offered by Joyce Flynn, "A Complex Causality of Neglect," *American Quarterly* 41, 1 (March 1989): 123–7. Though lauded as distinctly American, the staged Yankee was not unique to American actors, as Charles Mathews, Sr., who was British, demonstrated by playing Jonathan W. Doubikin in his *A Trip to America* on tour in 1822–3 and, less benignly, in *Jonathan in England* in 1824. The American Yankee actor James H. Hackett saw and copied some of this work. "Nature to advantage dressed" is, of course, Alexander Pope's definition of "true wit" (*An Essay on Criticism*, pt. II, line 297).

23. The commanding account of the staged Yankee remains Francis Hodge, *Yankee Theatre: The Image of America on the Stage, 1825–1850* (Austin: U. of Texas Press, 1964). A cultural history of the several white male character types – Yankee, frontiersman, Indian, and Bowery B'hoy – would be most useful.

24. The version of *The People's Lawyer* used in this discussion is that reprinted in Montrose Moses, *Representative Plays by American Dramatists*, vol. 2 (1925; rpt. New York: Arno Press, 1978). Moses gives 1839 as Hill's first appearance as Solon Shingle in this play (National Theatre, Boston), the date that Meserve also adopts (*Heralds of Promise*, pp. 97–9). The bibliography in Hodge's *Yankee Theatre* cites 17 December 1842 as the initial play date (Park Theatre, New York). William Clapp does not record an 1839 performance in *A Record of the Boston Stage* (Boston: J. Munroe, 1853; rpt. New York: Benjamin Blom, 1968), see chaps. 24, 25, but the Moses's bibliography (p. 392) may verify the Boston date. John E. Owens, who took over the part in the 1860s (Hill died in 1849), seems likely to have influenced some of the published versions of this play, expanding Solon Shingle's part into the dominant role. (The absence of effective copyright laws afforded Jones no protection, but see Moses on this point, pp. 388–9.)

25. For sources in folktale, see the discussions in Constance Rourke, *American Humor* (1931; rpt. New York: Anchor Books, 1953); and Richard M. Dorson, *American Folklore* (Chicago: U. of Chicago Press, 1959). For comments and reprinted selections, see Walter Blair, *Native Humor* (New York: American Book Co., 1937; rpt. San Francisco: Chandler Pub. Co., 1960). The quote that follows is from act II, scene iv, of the version printed in Moses, *Representative Plays*, p. 422.

26. For a consideration of the Yankee as Uncle Sam, see Rourke, *American Humor*, p. 25. For the lines from the play text, see Moses, *Representative Plays*, pp. 407, 398, 423, 413, 411, 394, and 399, respectively. The title character in *The Drunkard* falls from paradise to the notorious Five Points area of New York City before temperance restores him to the village (see section "The City," below).

27. For the quotation, see *The People's Lawyer*, p. 423. For Yankee stories, see Blair, *Native Humor*, pp. 43–4; Rourke, *American Humor*, pp. 31–4; and Hodge, *Yankee Theatre*, chaps. 2 and 3. Seba Smith's Jack Downing, Haliburton's Sam Slick, James Russell Lowell's "Bigelow Papers," Francis Witcher's widows, and Shillaber's Mrs. Partington are examples of Yankees staged in published fiction during the nineteenth century.

28. For the Yankee as part of the campaign for an "American" literature and drama (largely derived from dialect and regional stories and manners), see, in addition to Rourke, Blair, Nichols, and Hodge, Brander Matthews, "Americans on the Stage," *Scribner's Monthly* 18, 3 (July 1879), p. 331, and the *American Quarterly Review* for June 1827 (pp. 331–57), September 1830 (pp. 134–61), and December 1832 (pp. 509–31). Emerson's views on the redeeming elite are widely referenced. The Yankee as a cultural icon and racist figure is discussed at length in Saxton, *White Republic*, chap. 5, "Theater." See also Baym, *Novels, Readers, and Reviewers*, concerning realism as "American." No actress of the antebellum period made a starring career of female staged Yankees, but few escaped playing them, some notably (e.g., Catherine LeSugg Hackett).

29. A statistical summary of growth in these decades is provided in Lyn H. Lofland, *A World of Strangers: Order and Action in Urban Public Space* (New York: Basic Books, 1973), chap. 1. The growth of urban America during these decades impacts studies in many fields. Those influential to the present work include George Rogers Taylor, "The Beginnings of Mass Transportation in Urban America," pts. I & II, *Smithsonian Journal of History* 1, 2 (Summer 1966): 35–50, and 1, 3 (Fall 1966): 31–54, respectively; population statistics from pt. I, pp. 35–6; Adrienne Siegel, *The Image of the American City in Popular Literature, 1820–1870* (Port Washington, N.Y.: Kennikat Press, 1981), statistics on pp. 3–5; Peter R. Knights, "Population Turnover, Persistence, and Residential Mobility in Boston," in *Nineteenth-Century Cities: Essays in the New Urban History*, ed. Stephen Thernstrom and Richard Sennett (New Haven: Yale U.P., 1969), statistics from pp. 263–4. For comparative statistics for England, Germany, and France, see Eric Lampard, "The Urbanizing World," in *The Victorian City*, vol. 1, eds. H. J. Dyos and Michael Wolff (London: Routledge & Kegan Paul, 1973), pp. 3–57. See both Elizabeth Blackmar, *Manhattan for Rent, 1785–1850* (Ithaca: Cornell U.P., 1989), pp. 213–16, for moving day, and Elizabeth Collins Cromley, *Alone Togeth-*

er: *A History of New York's Early Apartments* (Ithaca: Cornell U.P., 1990). Philip Hone also bemoans moving day in *The Diary of Philip Hone, 1828–1851,* ed. Allan Nevins (New York: Dodd, Mead & Co., 1927), vol. 1, pp. 157–8; and see Seba Smith, *May-Day in New-York; or, House-Hunting and Moving* (New York: Burgess, Stringer, 1845); and Lydia Maria Child, *Letters from New-York* (New York: Charles S. Francis, 1843). Mobility among immigrants is discussed in Jay P. Dolan, *The Immigrant Church: New York's Irish and German Catholics, 1815–1865* (Baltimore: Johns Hopkins U.P., 1975), pp. 36–9; between 1850 and 1870, 55 percent left the Irish parish he studied and 58 percent left the German. For informative essays concerning city life between 1825 and 1860, see *The Memorial History of the City of New-York from Its First Settlement to the Year 1892,* ed. James Grant Wilson (New York: New-York History Co., 1893), vol. 3; and James Hardie, *The Description of the City of New York* (New York: Samuel Marks, 1827), one of many antebellum guidebooks to the city, this one especially useful for its listing of places of public amusement. The quote is from Stuart M. Blumin's engaging and informative "Explaining the New Metropolis: Perception, Depiction, and Analysis in Mid-Nineteenth Century New York City," *Journal of Urban History* 11, 1 (November 1984): 9.

30. For a consideration of nonfictional accounts of urban life, see Blumin's "Explaining the New Metropolis," and George R. Taylor's "Gaslight Foster: A New York 'Journeyman Journalist' at Mid-Century," *New York History* 58 (July 1977): 297–312. On sunshine and shadow, see also John F. Kasson, *Rudeness and Civility: Manners in Nineteenth-Century Urban America* (New York: Hill & Wang, 1990), p. 80. For Hone, see *Diary of Philip Hone,* pp. 394–5. For fictional, review, and newspaper accounts, and for the creation both of the city as the center of literary life and of city literature, see Callow's *Kindred Spirits,* Baym's *Novels, Readers, and Reviewers,* Siegel's *Image of the American City,* and John Paul Pritchard, *Literary Wise Men of Gotham: Criticism in New York, 1815–1860* (Baton Rouge: Lousiana State U.P., 1963), esp. pp. 83–153.

31. See Blackmar, *Manhattan for Rent,* for the proprietary pattern in New York. The creation of class structures via soaring rents and plummeting wages, examined in Chapter 2 of the present volume, forms a text in Edward Pessen, *Riches, Class, and Power before the Civil War* (Lexington, Mass.: D. C. Heath & Co., 1973); Christine Stansell, *City of Women: Sex and Class in New York, 1789–1860* (New York: Alfred A. Knopf, 1986); Sean Wilentz, *Chants Democratic: New York City and the Rise of the American Working Class, 1788–1850* (Oxford: Oxford U.P., 1984); and Howard B. Rock, *Artisans of the New Republic* (New York: New York U.P., 1979). In focusing upon New York, there is no intention to slight other American cities subject in the antebellum decades to "urban planning" of the sort that befell Manhattan. These cities and the impact of social divisions evident there as the result of urban geography and other forces have been studied extensively; see, for example, Stuart M. Blumin, "Mobility and Change in Ante-Bellum Philadelphia," in *Nineteenth-Century Cities,* ed. Thernstrom and Sennett, pp. 165–208; Bruce Laurie, "Fire Companies and Gangs in Southwark: The 1840s," in *The Peoples of Philadelphia: A History of Ethnic Groups and Lower-Class*

Life, 1790–1940, ed. Allen F. Davis and Mark H. Haller (Philadelphia: Temple U.P., 1973), pp. 71–87; idem, "'Nothing on Compulsion': Life Styles of Philadelphia Artisans, 1820–1850," *Labor History* 15, 3 (Summer 1974): 337–66; Ronald Story, "Class and Culture in Boston: The Athenaeum, 1807–1860," *American Quarterly* 27, 2 (May 1975): 178–99; and Taylor, "Beginnings of Mass Transportation."

32. See John Austin Stevens, "The Beginning of New York's Commercial Greatness, 1825–1837," in *Memorial History of the City,* ed. Wilson, vol. 3, pp. 334–63; and Charles Burr Todd, *The Story of the City of New York* (New York: G. P. Putnam's Sons, 1888). Paul A. Gilje provides useful maps and a sense of the growth of the city in his *The Road to Mobocracy: Popular Disorder in New York City, 1763–1834* (Chapel Hill: U. of North Carolina Press, 1987). For the grid system proposed by the Streets Commission of wealthy and prominent men in 1811, and for the clustering of "nuisance" industries, see Blackmar, *Manhattan for Rent,* pp. 95–102. One of the Federalists appointed to this commission, Gouverneur Morris, concurrently (1810–13) chaired the commission recommending construction of the Erie Canal.

.33. For urban crowding and fares, see Taylor, "Beginnings of Mass Transportation," pt. I, pp. 37–9; for exports, see Stevens, "Beginning of New York's Commercial Greatness," p. 336; for wages, see Rock, *Artisans of the New Republic,* p. 237, Wilentz, *Chants Democratic,* p. 402, and Blackmar, *Manhattan for Rent,* pp. 103–4. The pressure of rents dramatically eroded the real value of wages and became an acute problem for working women and children. Historians agree that most housing was shared to reduce expenses (see the discussion of boarders in Chapter 2), which intensified crowding and eroded sanitation. The literature of class as it affects the "middle-level" home is extensive and taken up in Chapter 2. Immigrants to New York in these decades – the Germans in the tenth, eleventh, thirteenth, and seventeenth wards, the Irish in the fourth, fifth, and sixth – lived in some of the worst wards (e.g., the sixth and the seventeenth), where tenements were mixed with slaughterhouses, foundries, coal yards, stables, and a high number of taverns (one for every six people in the Sixth Ward in 1864, according to Blackmar, *Manhattan for Rent,* pp. 30–1).

34. Curry, *Free Black in Urban America,* p. xvii. Curry's sample cities are Albany, Baltimore, Boston, Brooklyn, Buffalo, Charleston, Cincinnati, Louisville, New Orleans, New York, Philadelphia, Pittsburgh, Providence, St. Louis, and Washington. His study of housing patterns in each of these locales reveals increasing concentrations by race in the large northeastern cities, "But nowhere," he concludes of these decades, "did the degree of residential separation of the races approach the levels of the twentieth century" (p. 79). Then, as now, however, "turf control" of public spaces in cities eventuated in street gangs, associational gangs (apprentices in a trade or junior firemen), and voluntary groups with official sanction (firemen and watchmen). The absence through much of the period of a clear separation between official and unofficial control made keeping order in public places, such as theatres, extremely difficult, not because authority was absent but because it was subject to negotiation. This is further discussed in Chapter 3, but see Peter G. Buckley, "To the Opera House: Culture and Soci-

ety in New York City, 1820–1860," Ph.D. diss. (SUNY–Stony Brook, 1984), pp. 162–80, for a listing of sources and a general discussion of the "contract" governing audience "rights" to theatres. See also Bruce A. McConachie, "'The Theatre of the Mob': Apocalyptic Melodrama and Preindustrial Riots in Antebellum New York," in *Theatre for Working-Class Audiences in the United States, 1830–1980*, ed. McConachie and Daniel Friedman (Westport, Conn.: Greenwood Press, 1985), pp. 17–46.

35. For the building of the Bowery Theatre in New York, see Theodore Shank, "The Bowery Theatre, 1826–1836," Ph.D. diss. (Stanford Univ., 1956); for an example from Philadelphia, see William B. Wood on the Arch Street Theatre in *Personal Recollections of the Stage* (Philadelphia: H. C. Baird, 1853); for an example from Boston, see Edward W. Mammen, "The Old Stock Company: The Boston Museum," *More Books* 19 (January-May 1944). Numerous studies, referenced throughout this work, record the history of theatre building in America. For the guidebook, see Hardie, *Description of the City*, pp. 341–5; for theatres operating in New York, see J. Hampden Dougherty, "Ten Years of Municipal Vigor, 1837–1847," in *Memorial History of the City*, ed. Wilson, vol. 3, p. 370; and the standard source, George C. D. Odell, *Annals of the New York Stage*, vol. 3 (1821–34), vol. 4 (1834–43), vol. 5 (1843–50), vol. 6 (1850–7), and vol. 7 (1857–65) (New York: Columbia U.P., 1928–31). For specific theatres in these early years, see Barnard Hewitt, "'King Stephen' of the Park and Drury Lane," in *The Theatrical Manager in England and America*, ed. Joseph Donohue (Princeton: Princeton U.P., 1971), pp. 87–141; Frederic Litto, "Edmund Simpson of the Park Theatre, New York, 1809–1848," Ph.D. diss. (Indiana Univ., 1969); Julia Curtis, "Chatham Garden Theatre Salary Book: 1827–1828," *Theatre History Studies* 13 (1993): 1–16; and Shank. Chatham, originally a tent theatre, was structurally enclosed in 1824.

36. For Mrs. Trollope, see *Domestic Manners of the Americans*, pp. 339–40. I deal more extensively with Mrs. Trollope's visit and how it has been read in my "Mrs. Trollope Visits the Theatre: Cultural Diplomacy and Historical Appropriation," *Journal of American Drama and Theatre* 5, 3 (Fall 1993): 16–27. Some class literature relating to theatre is given in n. 37; the bulk is taken up in Chapter 2.

37. For southern uses of "fashion," see Patricia C. Click, *The Spirit of the Times: Amusements in Nineteenth-Century Baltimore, Norfolk, and Richmond* (Charlottesville: U.P. of Virginia, 1989), pp. 96–7. The tripartite division is David Grimsted's (*Melodrama Unveiled*, p. 56), so often repeated as to have become canonical (see, e.g., the sources that follow, and p. 253 of Gilje's *Road to Mobocracy*). The quotation regarding class-specific theatres is from Stuart M. Blumin, *The Emergence of the Middle Class: Social Experience in the American City, 1760–1900* (Cambridge: Cambridge U.P., 1989), pp. 144–5, as is the caveat against overdetermination that follows. Highbrow and low is, of course, the summary view of Lawrence W. Levine's *Highbrow/Lowbrow: The Emergence of Cultural Hierarchy in America* (Cambridge: Harvard U.P., 1988), which extends Buckley's "To the Opera House" in the matter of cultural hierarchy in nineteenth-century theatre. The literature discussing specific classes and theories of class (esp. of "the middling sorts") is identified in Chapter 2. Works pertaining more directly to cultural contexts, in addition to sources already cited in this chapter, include Karen

Halttunen's *Confidence Men and Painted Women: A Study of Middle-Class Culture in America, 1830–1870* (New Haven: Yale U.P., 1982), and Kasson's *Rudeness and Civility.*

38. For descriptions of the Bowery and Park, see Shank, "Bowery Theatre"; Litto, "Edmund Simpson of the Park"; William C. Young, *Documents of American Theatre History,* vol. 1 (Chicago: American Library Assn., 1973); Joseph N. Ireland, *Records of the New York Stage from 1750 to 1860* (1866; rpt. New York: Benjamin Blom, 1966), vol. 1, pp. 521–2; my entry for the Bowery in *American Theatre Companies, 1749–1887,* ed. Weldon B. Durham (Westport, Conn.: Greenwood Press, 1986); and Odell, *Annals,* vol. 3, p. 377. Shank notes (p. 19) that box and pit seats at the Bowery Theatre were reached through the ornate main entrance in Bowery Street but that the gallery was accessed via the plain entrance on Elizabeth Street. For theatre architecture in other cities (which was comparable in characteristics, if not in grandeur), see Wood's *Personal Recollections* for the Chestnut Street Theatre in Philadelphia, Clapp's *Record of the Boston Stage* for that city's Tremont Street Theatre in 1828, and Young. Wood (p. 291) cites an 1822 handbill protesting separate entrances to different seating areas. On the segregation of urban free blacks, see Curry, *Free Black in Urban America,* pp. 90–1.

39. Admission prices at the Park, Bowery, and Chatham Theatres are mine, as sifted from New York newspapers and read against Odell's *Annals,* Shank's "Bowery Theatre," Litto's "Edmund Simpson of the Park," and other sources. For cities in the south, see Click, *Spirit of the Times,* p. 38. The estimates of seating distribution to income are Bruce McConachie's from the Chestnut, Arch, and Tremont Theatres in the 1820s; *Melodramatic Formations: American Theatre and Society, 1820–1870* (Iowa City: U. of Iowa Press, 1992), pp. 13–14. In the absence of an economic history relating seat prices and types across antebellum U.S. theatres, it is difficult to think through the material bases for "class" distinctions, though I do some relating of these to income in subsequent chapters.

40. Talking and socializing in antebellum playhouses appears to have been a universal practice. Traditional histories, newspaper accounts, dissertations, and similar sources provide no cause to challenge the view that American theatres in these decades produced a standard repertory and featured the same star actors. The similarity in repertory among the Park, Bowery, and Chatham is evident; see esp. the entries in Durham, *American Theatre Companies,* where one notes that the Park hit *Cinderella* was also offered by the Bowery, and that the latter's elephant of Siam also played the Chatham in 1830, when it was an amphitheatre. The Bowery did inaugurate the long-running single play, a practice soon imitated. The quotation concerning privacy is from a description of the Chatham Theatre in the *New York Mirror* of 15 May 1824; it, like many statements from these decades, may be as straightforward as it appears or as duplicitous as McConachie finds it (*Melodramatic Formations,* p. 173). For the Bowery district as the upper city, see the *New York Mirror* of 15 April 1826 (p. 303). For the Bowery Theatre's popularity between 1830 and its burning in 1836, see Shank, "Bowery Theatre"; my entry for the Bowery in Durham; my "Antedating the Long Run: A Prolegomenon," *Nineteenth Century Theatre Research* 13, 1 (Summer 1985): 33–6;

and my "Theatre and Narrative Fiction in the Work of the Nineteenth Century American Playwright Louisa Medina," *Theatre History Studies* 3 (1983): 54–67.

41. For a deconstruction of Searle's painting, see Buckley, "To the Opera House," pp. 85–92. The performance was 7 November 1822. Odell (*Annals*, vol. 3, p. 474) reports the 1821 Park was rebuilt on its original site because merchant homes and businesses were concentrated there. Population increases of seventy-five thousand by 1830 (to two hundred thousand) made New York much less localized by the time Mrs. Trollope visited its theatres. For the unimpressible Joe Cowell, see *Thirty Years Passed among the Players in England and America*, vol. 2 (New York: Harper & Bros., 1844), pp. 56–7. For the history of prostitution as it pertains to New York theatres in this era, see Timothy J. Gilfoyle, "City of Eros: New York City, Prostitution, and the Commercialization of Sex, 1790–1920," Ph.D. diss. (Columbia Univ., 1987), pp. 82–4, 100–7; for his maps of brothels in the antebellum decades, see pp. 46–9. (*City of Eros* was published by W. W. Norton in 1992.) Hamblin made a virtue of accessibility at his playhouse, christening it "the American Theatre, Bowery" for a brief while in the early 1830s. Simpson, like his Park predecessor Dunlap, tried valiantly, and not unsuccessfully, to associate his theatre with wealth, tradition, and culture. Indeed, the impact Dunlap and Simpson exert upon our reading of early nineteenth-century theatre and art is still, I think, underestimated – perhaps the legacy of their "blameless lives" versus Hamblin's sensationalized one. Click, *Spirit of the Times*, p. 97, argues that in the cities she studied the rich set the fashion.

42. For a physical description of the Park, which burned a final time in 1848, see Young, *Documents of American Theatre History*, vol. 1, p. 63–7; for its decline, see Richard Grant White, "Opera in New York, II," *Century Magazine* 23, 6 (April 1882), p. 869. The repertory Hamblin preferred for the Bowery was a company-sustained classical one, but his tastes succumbed to the advantages of long-running melodramas and star turns, either by visitors or his protégés. Carol Groneman-Pernicone's "The 'Bloody Ould Sixth': A Social Analysis of a New York City Working-Class Community in the Mid-Nineteenth Century" (Ph.D. diss., Univ. Rochester, 1973) reads the sixth ward and Five Points against the slum myth, while detailing its poverty and deterioration under the pressure of crowding. Blackmar notes that as early as 1829 campaigns to clear Five Points described inhabitants as vagrants, prostitutes, and criminals (*Manhattan for Rent*, pp. 175–6). While reformers produced some of these characterizations, the commercial interests that sought to profit from clearing the area leave one skeptical about its accuracy.

43. Young, *Documents of American Theatre History*, vol. 1, pp. 72–4, provides a picture and description of the Chatham. The *Mirror* "road map" is 15 May 1824. For the conversion of the Chatham into a chapel, see Odell, *Annals*, vol. 3, p. 591. A Chatham Theatre, located two blocks from the Chatham Garden Theatre, opened in 1839 (see Durham, *American Theatre Companies*, pp. 167–78). McConachie argues that the abolition of gallery seating and democratization of boxes influenced patronage (*Melodramatic Formations*, pp. 9–11, 14).

44. See *Domestic Manners of the Americans*, pp. 133–4, 233–4, 270–2, for Mrs. Trollope on American manners in theatres outside New York City. For images of the city in popular literature, see Siegel, *Image of the American City*, and Baym, *Novels, Readers, and Reviewers*. The text of *Fashion* utilized in this discussion is from Richard Moody's edition, *Dramas from the American Theatre*, pp. 309–47 (which include his introduction and the text). Dion Boucicault's *The Poor of New York* is less frequently anthologized; some collections of American plays omit him entirely because he was British. The edition cited here is that of Daniel C. Gerould's *American Melodrama* (New York: PAJ Publications, 1983), pp. 10–14 (introduction), 32–74 (play text). All subsequent act, scene, and page citations refer to these editions.

45. Details of Anna Cora Ogden Mowatt Ritchie's life are taken from Moody, but see her *Autobiography of an Actress* (Boston: Ticknor, Reed, & Fields, 1854) and Eric Barnes's still dominant biography, *The Lady of Fashion: The Life and Theatre of Anna Cora Mowatt* (New York: Charles Scribner's Sons, 1954). Gertrude upbraids Count Jolimatre in act II, scene ii (pp. 327–8). Trueman's moral is the last line of the play, prior to the epilogue (act V, p. 346); his view of Zeke is given in act I (p. 324).

46. Trueman's recipe for domestic reform is in act V (p. 346). For the previous quotations: The French maid Millinette equates money and fashion at the opening of act I (p. 318); Trueman describes the free-enterprise system in II.i (p. 326) and fashion's connection to sin in III.i (p. 330) and again in IV.i (p. 336); Mr. Tiffany's discovery of the road to ruin and Snobson's escape West are in act V (pp. 342, 346, respectively).

47. See Gerould's introduction for the play's analogues and the "full-of-fires" citation. A paid fire department was introduced in New York City in 1865 and is taken up in Chapter 3. The fashion for local-color references increased with the nineteenth century and is indeed one of melodrama's legacies to the "realistic" mise-en-scène of the fin de siècle. The literature of appearance, such as that affecting gentility, is considered in Chapter 2.

48. Puffy's description of his fortunes is from II.i (pp. 40–1). For the origin of the receipt, see act I; for Badger's adventures out West, see act III (pp. 51–2); for Bloodgood's profiting at the expense of others in the second panic, see II.ii (p. 44); for Livingstone's speculations, see act III (p. 50).

49. For the Puffys' self-abasing behavior in the mansions of the rich, see the end of the play (V.iii, p. 74). The play cites the *New York Herald* as the source of the characterization of Bloodgood and his financial peers as buzzards (act III, p. 48). For Badger's stagings of virtue, see acts I (p. 38) and III (p. 52); for Alida Bloodgood's stagings in theatres and restaurants, see II.ii (p. 44); for the love–money–happiness relationship, see act III (pp. 55–6). The prayer is Mr. Puffy's in IV. i (p. 59).

50. See, for example, Alida Bloodgood's views on marriage in IV. ii (p. 62), typical of "European" aristocratic depravity in antebellum fiction. The Fairweathers provide numerous examples of self-sacrifice, the Puffys of generosity.

51. Livingstone's speech is from II.i (p. 43). Puffy's query is from II.i (p. 42), and his family provides a feast in II.iii (pp. 45–7). Three- to five-story multifamily housing was first systematically constructed in Manhattan in 1843 (Blackmar, *Manhattan for Rent*, p. 206). From the first, apartments were small (subdivided rooms of 8 by 10 feet or 12 by 14 feet) and short on air, light, and sufficient safe plumbing.

52. *The Poor of New York* opened 8 December 1857. There are significant, I believe, historiographical difficulties in hierarchizing theatres along class lines, as the discussions in subsequent chapters, it is to be hoped, suggest.

53. For some of the theoretical and applied work restructuring class and gentility, see n. 13 in the Prologue. Views of the city, class, and gender are considered in sources given in nn. 29 and 31 of the present chapter; these subjects are taken up in detail in Chapters 2 and 3.

54. Much has been made of the paradise analogy; indeed, Judeo-Christian morphology often colors views of America – as errands into the wilderness, pilgrimages, crusades, visions, and so on. In addition to sources already cited, the following have been particularly useful in addressing such ideologies as they pertain to the frontier: Dawn Glanz, *How the West Was Drawn: American Art and the Settling of the Frontier* (Ann Arbor: UMI Press, 1982); and J. Gray Sweeney, *The Columbus of the Woods: Daniel Boone and the Typology of Manifest Destiny* (St. Louis: Washington U. Gallery of Art, 1992). See also Ellwood C. Parry, *The Image of the Indian and the Black Man in American Art, 1590–1900* (New York: George Braziller, 1974); and see Wilmerding's *American Light* and Truettner's *The West as America*.

55. Jacksonian Indian policy has been extensively studied by historians. For some recent views, see Michael P. Rogin, *Fathers and Children: Andrew Jackson and the Subjugation of the American Indian* (New York: Alfred A. Knopf, 1975); and Ronald N. Satz, *American Indian Policy in the Jacksonian Era* (Lincoln: U. of Nebraska Press, 1975). More generally, see Roy Harvey Pearce, *The Savages of America: A Study of the Indian and the Idea of Civilization*, rev. ed. (Baltimore: Johns Hopkins U.P., 1965). For views of expansion and of the Indian in art, see particularly Patricia Hills, "Picturing Progress," and Julie Schimmel, "Inventing 'the Indian,'" both in Truettner, *The West as America* (pp. 97–147 and 149–89, respectively). Saxton, *White Republic*, pp. 36–9, 54, considers expansionism and racism as both structural and ideological aspects of Adams's career. Jackson's address is cited on p. 57 in Pearce and pp. 215–16 in Rogin.

56. For an account of the Indian visit, see Herman J. Viola, *The Indian Legacy of Charles Bird King* (New York: Doubleday & Co. / Smithsonian Institution Press, 1976), pp. 22–43. The quote is from an eyewitness account cited by Viola (p. 31).

57. For a chronology of Indians staged in theatres, see Don B. Wilmeth, "Noble or Ruthless Savage? The American Indian Onstage in the Drama," *Journal of American Drama and Theatre* 1, 2 (Spring 1989): 39–78; and idem, "Tentative Checklist of Indian Plays (1606–1987)," *Journal of American Drama and Theatre* 1, 3 (Fall 1989): 34–54. For an earlier version of these stagings of "the Indian," see

my "Staging the 'Native': Making History in American Theatre Culture, 1828–
1838," *Theatre Journal* 45, 4 (December 1993): 461–86. I am indebted to Stuart
Thayer for sharing his circus research regarding Indians in the antebellum decades. See also his *Annals of the American Circus, 1793–1829* (Manchester, Mich.:
Rymack Press, 1976), p. 202, where Thayer notes a circus company performance
– with Indians – by the Park Theatre, beginning 24 July 1828. An advertisement
from the *Post* is cited by Odell in his *Annals*, vol. 3, p. 368.

58. Red Jacket's leave-taking is provided in Odell, *Annals*, vol. 3, p. 368. For accounts of Red Jacket's life see: J. Niles Hubbard, *An Account of Sa-Go-Ye-Wat-
Ha; or, Red Jacket and His People (1750–1830)* (1885; rpt. New York: Burt Franklin, 1971); Edward Eggleston and Lillie Eggleston Seelye, *Brant and Red Jacket*
(New York: Dodd, Mead & Co., 1879); A. C. Parker, *Red Jacket: Last of the
Seneca* (New York: McGraw–Hill, 1952); and *Transactions of the Buffalo Historical Society, vol. 3: Red Jacket* (Buffalo: Buffalo Historical Society, 1885). White-
authored nineteenth-century accounts of the lives of prominent Native Americans, some claiming to be authorized, are often the only written biographies to
descend to us. Government documents of the times are similarly beset by problems of transcription and translation. For some reflections on the latter, see
Charles Camp, "American Indian Oratory in the White Image: An Analysis of
Stereotypes," *Journal of American Culture* 1, 4 (Winter 1978): 811–17. Gerald Vize-
nor notes that "The formal descriptions of tribal events by outsiders, such as
missionaries, explorers, and anthropologists, reveal more about the cultural values of the observer than the imaginative power of spiritual tribal people"; *The
People Named the Chippewa: Narrative Histories* (Minneapolis: U. of Minnesota
Press, 1984), p. 140.

For Red Jacket's trip to Washington and Bird's painting of him, see Viola,
Indian Legacy, pp. 121, 60; and see Thomas L. McKenney and James Hall, *The
Indian Tribes of North America* (Edinburgh: John Grant, 1933), vol. 1, pp. 6–7.
McKenney, the first head of the Bureau of Indian Affairs (1824–30), commissioned an extensive collection of native artifacts and portraits, many of which
are reproduced in his extraordinarily biased history, first published in 1844. For
Catlin's portraits of Red Jacket and others, see William Truettner, *The Natural
Man Observed: A Study of Catlin's Indian Gallery* (Washington: Smithsonian Institution Press, 1979), p. 13; Weir's very different view of Red Jacket appears on
p. 72. For Senecan women and Red Jacket, see Joan M. Jensen, "Native American Women and Agriculture: A Seneca Case Study," in *Unequal Sisters: A Multicultural Reader in U.S. Women's History*, eds. Ellen C. DuBois and Vicki L.
Ruiz (New York: Routledge, 1990), p. 54. Cole's *Daniel Boone* is reproduced in
Sweeney, *Columbus of the Woods*, color plate 2 (following p. 4); the costume is
very similar to that worn by Joseph Proctor as *Nick of the Woods* (see Fig. 9
of the present volume). For Hackett costumed as Nimrod Wildfire, see Fig. 8
herein.

59. The development of Jacksonian Indian policy in general is taken up in Rogin,
Fathers and Children, and Satz, *American Indian Policy;* for the Seneca, see
Jensen, "Native American Women and Agriculture." Race views are central to

the removal scenario; see Reginald Horsman, "Scientific Racism and the American Indian in the Mid-Nineteenth Century," *American Quarterly* 27, 2 (May 1975): 152–68; for race generally, see William Stanton, *The Leopard's Spots: Scientific Attitudes Toward Race in America, 1815–1859* (Chicago: U. of Chicago Press, 1960). David Brion Davis's *The Slave Power Conspiracy and the Paranoid Style* (Baton Rouge: Louisiana State U.P., 1969) is also relevant to this discourse.

60. For Indian entertainments and exhibits, see Wilmeth, "Noble or Ruthless Savage," pp. 43–54. For Catlin's view of the originary Indian, to which many supportive whites subscribed, see Truettner's *Natural Man Observed*. In Timothy Flint's *Recollections of the Last Ten Years Passed in Occasional Residences and Journeyings in the Valley of the Mississippi* (1826; rpt. New York: DaCapo Press, 1968), a source many antebellum painters rifled for subject matter, the author observed that the French had "as natural an affinity [for indigenous peoples] as there is repulsion between the Anglo-Americans and them" (pp. 163–4). The myth of French affinity is taken up in such recent works as R. David Edmunds and Joseph L. Peyser, *The Fox Wars: The Mesquakie Challenge to New France* (Norman: U. of Oklahoma Press, 1993). For tensions between the real and ideal Indian, also see Schimmel, "Inventing 'the Indian,'" and Sweeney, *Columbus of the Woods.*

61. For the staged Indian, see, in addition to Wilmeth, "Noble or Ruthless Savage": Murray H. Nelligan, "American Nationalism on the Stage: The Plays of George Washington Parke Custis (1781–1857)," *Virginia Magazine of History and Biography* 58, 3 (July 1950): 299–324; Richard E. Amacher, "Behind the Curtain with the Noble Savage: Stage Management of Indian Plays, 1825–1860," *Theatre Survey* 7, 2 (November 1966): 101–14; Kathleen A. Mulvey, "The Growth, Development, and Decline of the Popularity of American Indian Plays before the Civil War," Ph.D. diss (New York U., 1978); Marilyn J. Anderson, "The Image of the Indian in American Drama during the Jacksonian Era, 1829–1845," *Journal of American Culture* 1, 4 (Winter 1978): 800–10; Burl D. Grose, "'Here Come the Indians': An Historical Study of the Representations of the Native American upon the North American Stage, 1808–1969," Ph.D. diss. (U. of Missouri, 1979); and Joyce Flynn, "Academics on the Trail of the Stage 'Indian': A Review Essay," *Studies in American Indian Literature* 2, 1 (Winter 1987): 1–16. For the need to theorize history, see: Harvey J. Kaye, *The British Marxist Historians* (Cambridge: Polity Press, 1984); Elizabeth Fox-Genovese and Eugene D. Genovese, *The Fruits of Merchant Capital* (New York: Oxford U.P., 1983); and Eric Hobsbawm, "Comments," as cited by Kaye (esp. on p. 229). *Metamora* as legislation is taken up in Jeffrey D. Mason's "The Politics of *Metamora*," in *The Performance of Power*, ed. Sue-Ellen Case and Janelle Reinelt (Iowa City: U. of Iowa Press, 1991), pp. 92–110.

A case against binarization is offered by Paula Gunn Allen in "'Border' Studies: The Intersection of Gender and Color," in *Introduction to Scholarship in Modern Languages and Literatures*, 2d ed., ed. Joseph Gibaldi (New York: MLAA, 1992), p. 305, where she observes: "It is not merely biculturality that forms the foundation of our lives and work in their multiplicity, aesthetic largeness, and wide-ranging potential; rather, it is multiculturality, multilinguality, and dizzying class-crossing from the fields to the salons, from the factories to the academy, or from galleries and the groves of academe to the neighborhoods and reservations." A consideration of stagings of the antebellum "Indian" as "citizens of more than one community" living "within worlds that are . . . markedly different from one another" offers rich ground for a decolonized U.S. culture.

62. For Black Hawk and the war, see: Rogin, *Fathers and Children*, pp. 234–5; Cecil Eby, *"That Disgraceful Affair," the Black Hawk War* (New York: W. W. Norton & Co., 1973), pp. 274–80; Benjamin Drake, *The Life and Adventures of Black Hawk; with Sketches of Keokuk, the Sac and Fox Indians, and the Late Black Hawk War* (Cincinnati: George Conclin, 1838), pp. 192–216; William T. Hagan, *The Sac and Fox Indians* (Norman: U. of Oklahoma Press, 1958); and *Black Hawk: An Autobiography*, ed. Donald Jackson (1883; rpt. Champaign: U. of Illinois Press, 1964). For Washington Irving, see Drake (p. 202) and Eby (p. 274). For Catlin's visit, see these sources and Truettner's *Natural Man Observed* (Catlin did sketch the Sauk in chains). Concerning Black Hawk's tour as a prisoner of war, the audience with Jackson, and the paintings, see Eby (pp. 275–7) and Drake (pp. 193–6).

63. For the theatre visit and the rest of the tour, see Drake, *Life and Adventures of Black Hawk*, pp. 196–216 (quote at pp. 196–7) and Eby, *"That Disgraceful Affair,"* pp. 276–9. See also *Niles' Weekly Register* for 15 June 1833 and the *Frankfort (Kentucky) Commonwealth* of 30 July 1833. For Philip Hone's record (for 15 June 1833), see *The Diary of Philip Hone, 1828–1851*, ed. Allen Nevins (New York: Dodd, Mead & Co., 1927), vol. 1, p. 94. The quotation concerning New York events is from Drake (p. 200). The blackface entertainer T. D. "Jim Crow" Rice wrote and performed *Black Hawk* at the Bowery Theatre following this visit (Shank, "Bowery Theatre," p. 372). For Black Hawk's return to the Mississippi, see Drake, pp. 204–16.

64. For the 1837 tour, see Eby, *"That Disgraceful Affair,"* pp. 285–8. For the quote, see Drake, *Life and Adventures of Black Hawk*, p. 217. For King's 1837 painting, see Viola, *Indian Legacy*, p. 93, and McKenney and Hall, *Indian Tribes of North America*, vol. 2, facing p. 58.

65. The Cherokee Nation removal is chronicled in Rogin, *Fathers and Children*, chap. 7, and Satz, *American Indian Policy*, chap. 4. For the *Pocahontas* production, see the *National Intelligencer*, 6–11 February 1836, and Nelligan, "American Nationalism on the Stage." Detailed accounts of the activities of Ross and his party in protesting the treaty and of subsequent events preceding removal in 1839 are provided in Grant Foreman, *Indian Removal: The Emigration of the Five Civilized Tribes of Indians* (Norman: U. of Oklahoma Press, 1953), pp. 268–312, and McKenney and Hall, *Indian Tribes of North America*, vol. 3, pp. 310–23. For Rayna Green's "The Pocahontas Perplex: The Image of Indian Women in American Culture," see DuBois and Ruiz, *Unequal Sisters*, pp. 15–21. For the portrait by Catlin, see Truettner's *Natural Man Observed*, p. 222; for King's portrait of Ross, see McKenney and Hall, *Indian Tribes of North America*, vol. 3, facing p. 312. John Ross's daughter Eleanora was depicted in an 1844 portrait by

John Mix Stanley as "a picture of genteel accomplishment," the Pocahontas stereotype rehabilitated for white consumption (see Schimmel, "Inventing 'the Indian,'" pp. 181–2).

66. For an evaluation of Custis's career as a dramatist and his play as the start of the vogue for Indian dramas, see Nelligan, "American Nationalism on the Stage," pp. 302–3. Custis was the grandson of Martha Custis Washington (via a son of her first marriage) and was raised in the Washingtons' Mount Vernon home after his father died at the close of the Revolutionary War. Extending these aristocratic ties, Custis's daughter married the noted Civil War general Robert E. Lee. For the quotation, part of Custis's thank-you speech at the opening of the revival of *Pocahontas* at the National Theatre, see the *National Intelligencer* of 8 February 1836 and the *Washington Globe* of that date. For Custis's Jackson ties, see Nelligan, p. 315.

67. For the production's costumes, see the newspapers cited in the preceding note. The *Globe* ad appeared 11 February 1836. On the Seminole, the name given to an aggregate of displaced Native Americans, see Virginia B. Peters, *The Florida Wars* (Hamden, Conn.: Archon Books, 1979).

68. The invitation/advertisement to the last performance appeared in the 19 February 1836 *Globe*.

69. For the southern appropriation and northern characterization, see Anne Norton, *Alternative Americas: A Reading of Antebellum Political Culture* (Chicago: U. of Chicago Press, 1986), pp. 145–51; conquest as consumption vis-à-vis the Indian is taken up on pp. 211–18 of her interesting book. A similarly compelling portrait of conquest and commodification is drawn by Tzvetan Todorov in his *The Conquest of America*, trans. Richard Howard (New York: Harper & Row, 1984). For manifest destiny and the quote, see the 17 December 1845 *New York Morning News* and numerous sources already cited (e.g., Glanz, *How the West Was Drawn;* Sweeney, *Columbus of the Woods;* and Truettner's *The West as America* and *Natural Man Observed*). Gilpin's 1860 history, *The Central Gold Region*, was revised and reissued in 1873 as (significantly) *The Mission of the North American People* (rpt. New York: DaCapo Press, 1974).

70. William Truettner addresses binarization in "The West and the Heroic Ideal: Using Images to Interpret History" – a rejoinder to criticism of the exhibition that accompanied *The West as America* – in the *Chronicle of Higher Education* (20 November 1991), p. B2. See also Sweeney's *Columbus of the Woods*. For the Art-Union, see Hills's "Picturing Progress" in *The West as America*, and Charles E. Baker, "The American Art-Union," in *The American Academy of Fine Arts and American Art-Union*, ed. Mary B. Cowdery (New York: New-York Historical Society, 1953), pp. 95–240. Art-Union reproductions for its members are listed on pp. 286–93.

71. The Eden and Armageddon bracketing of post-Revolutionary to Civil War America is Norton's (*Alternative Americas*, p. 2). It is akin to Sollers's framing of the myths of Pocahontas and Roanoke (see n. 3). For luminism's role in the depiction of paradise, see John Wilmerding's *American Light*, wherein the Lane–Hawthorne analogy is suggested on p. 97.

72. For Emerson's eyeball, see *Nature*, in *Selected Writings;* for Thoreau's close shave, see F. O. Matthiessen, *American Renaissance: Art and Expression in the Age of Emerson and Whitman* (New York: Oxford U.P., 1941), p. 95. Sacvan Bercovitch gives "frontier" an American reading of limitlessness rather than restriction in "New England's Errand Reappraised," in John Higham and Paul K. Conkin, eds., *New Directions in American Intellectual History* (Baltimore: Johns Hopkins U.P., 1979), pp. 85–104, at p. 98 – a consideration extended in his subsequent work. Saxton (*White Republic*, p. 147) connects transcendentalism to manifest destiny, the Over-Soul as an expression, via Whitman, of the productive mission.

73. James Kirke Paulding, John Augustus Stone, and William Bayle Bernard, *The Lion of the West*, ed. James N. Tidwell (Stanford, Calif.: Stanford U.P., 1954), provides the text and its history. Paulding calls for a native theatre in his *American Quarterly Review* article "The American Drama." For the play and Paulding's 1842 trip of seven thousand miles with Van Buren to the Old Southwest and Great Lakes, see Larry J. Reynolds, *James Kirke Paulding* (Boston: Twayne Pubs., 1984), pp. 11, 17–18. For an interesting view of Philadelphia publishers Carey and Hart and the publication of Crockett almanacs and autobiography, see Saxton, *White Republic*, pp. 81–2. For the tall tales and so on, see Dorson, *American Folklore;* Blair, *Native Humor;* Rourke, *American Humor;* and Hennig Cohen and William Dillingham, *Humor of the Old Southwest* (Boston: Houghton Mifflin, 1964). For *The Lion* as part of Hackett's career, see Hodge's *Yankee Theatre*. The quotations from the play text are on pp. 21, 22, respectively.

74. The "human cataract" is in Paulding et al., *Lion of the West*, p. 23. For Crockett, see the *Spirit of the Times* for 21 December 1833, and Hodge, *Yankee Theatre*. Saxton, *White Republic*, p. 151, cites Paulding and Thomas Hart Benton as exemplars of a racism linking blacks in the cities to job competition and Indians in frontier areas to competition for land. Louisa Medina, *Nick of the Woods* (Boston: Spenser's Boston Theatre, n.d.) provides the rare play text. A text based on French's Standard Drama is contained in James L. Smith, ed., *Victorian Melodramas* (London: J. M. Dent, 1976). For Medina's career, a comparison of her play and Bird's novel, and a production history of the play, see my "Theatre and Narrative Fiction in the Work of the Nineteenth-Century American Playwright Louisa Medina," *Theatre History Studies* 3 (1983): 54–67. She is contextualized in a discussion of similar "journeymen" playwrights in Walter Meserve's *Heralds of Promise*, pp. 139–45.

75. For Hackett's costume as Nimrod Wildfire and Proctor's as the Jibbenainosay, see n. 58 and Figs. 8–9. There is a text of the assimilating/accommodating woman in Tellie Doe reflective of inabilities of antebellum authorities to deal with cultural differences in the status of women (see Jensen, "Native American Women and Agriculture"). Werner Sollers offers a reading of history as projected on the Indian, a genealogy in which Indians become ancestors who are replaced, their traditions appropriated in a red–white fusion (pp. 121–7).

2. Liminal Spaces

1. Daniel Webster, "Opening of the Northern Railroad to Lebanon, N.H.," in *The Philosophy of Manufactures*, eds. Michael B. Folsom and Steven D. Lubar (Cambridge, Mass.: MIT Press, 1982), pp. 445–6. The concept of liminal space is put to good use in Karen Halttunen, *Confidence Men and Painted Women: A Study of Middle-Class Culture in America, 1830–1870* (New Haven: Yale U.P., 1982), see esp. pp. 25–7.

2. See David Brion Davis, *The Slave Power Conspiracy and the Paranoid Style* (Baton Rouge: Lousiana State U.P., 1969), p. 26, for the quote. There is a wide literature concerning class formation in antebellum America. Those most useful to this study include: Stuart M. Blumin, *The Emergence of the Middle Class: Social Experience in the American City, 1760–1900* (Cambridge: Cambridge U.P., 1989), and its prefigurations "Explaining the New Metropolis: Perception, Depiction, and Analysis in Mid-Nineteenth Century New York City," *Journal of Urban History* 11, 1 (November 1984): 9–38, and "The Hypothesis of Middle-Class Formation in Nineteenth-Century America: A Critique and Some Proposals," *American Historical Review* 90, 2 (April 1985): 99–118; Arno J. Mayer, "The Lower Middle Class as Historical Problem," *Journal of Modern History* 47, 3 (Fall 1975): 409–36; Peter N. Stearns, "The Middle Class: Toward a Precise Definition," *Comparative Studies in Society and History* 21, 3 (July 1979): 377–96; and Michael B. Katz, "Social Class in North American Urban History," *Journal of Interdisciplinary History* 11, 4 (Spring 1981): 579–605. The varying terms for middle class are provided in a number of sources, but see esp. Blumin's "Hypothesis," pp. 310–12. Among many sources exploring class in non-American settings, Norbert Elias's study of the bourgeoisie in nineteenth-century Germany is often referenced: *The Civilizing Process: The History of Manners*, trans. Edmund Jephcott (New York: Urizen Books, 1978), see esp. pp. 26–40.

3. For class as a relation, see Katz, "Social Class," p. 604. Components of class are offered in Mayer, "Lower Middle Class," see esp. p. 424, and in Blumin's "Hypothesis," pp. 312–13. For tripartite divisions of culture, see David Grimsted, *Melodrama Unveiled: American Theatre and Culture, 1800–1850* (Chicago: U. of Chicago Press, 1968), p. 56; and Blumin's use of the concept of class-segregated theatres in *Emergence of the Middle Class*, pp. 144–6. For binary constructs, see Peter G. Buckley, "To the Opera House: Culture and Society in New York City, 1820–1860," Ph.D. diss. (State Univ. of New York–Stony Brook, 1984); and Lawrence W. Levine, *Highbrow/Lowbrow: The Emergence of Cultural Hierarchy in America* (Cambridge, Mass.: Harvard U.P., 1988). Two and three class divisions are discussed in the section "The City" in Chapter 1, where a few of many sources dealing with class ideologies are also referenced.

4. For the decline of the apprentice–journeyman–master system, see, among many sources, Sean Wilentz, *Chants Democratic: New York City and the Rise of the American Working Class, 1788–1850* (Oxford: Oxford U.P., 1984), esp. p. 33; and Bruce J. Laurie, "'Nothing on Compulsion': Life Styles of Philadelphia Artisans, 1820–1850," *Labor History* 15, 3 (Summer 1974): 337–66. See Stuart Blumin,

"Mobility and Change in Ante-Bellum Philadelphia," in *Nineteenth-Century Cities: Essays in the New Urban History,* ed. Stephen Thernstrom and Richard Sennett (New Haven: Yale U.P., 1969), p. 199, for the quote. A number of reports in the 1820s by the General Society of Mechanics and Tradesmen discuss the decline of the apprenticeship system. Wilentz points out that a master continued to labor until he died or retired and, despite standing at the head of his trade, usually owned little or no property. Allan S. Horlick's *Country Boys and Merchant Princes: The Social Control of Young Men in New York* (Lewisburg, Pa.: Bucknell U.P., 1975) notes a parallel pattern for clerks destined to become merchant princes and apprentices learning mastery of a trade, up to the point of controlling the means/profits of production. For downward mobility among workers and immigrants, see Robert Ernst, *Immigrant Life in New York City, 1825–1863* (New York: Columbia U./King's Crown Press, 1949).

5. For Philadelphia, see Blumin, *Emergence of the Middle Class,* p. 75; for New York, see Wilentz, *Chants Democratic,* pp. 31, 112, and Table 11 from the New York County 1850 census. For market forces, see Blumin, "Mobility and Change," pp. 201–3; for outwork in New York, see Table 11 in Wilentz. For the effects of outwork on women, see Gerda Lerner, "The Lady and the Mill Girl: Changes in the Status of Women in the Age of Jackson," in *Our American Sisters,* ed. Jean E. Friedman and William G. Shade (Boston: Allyn & Bacon, 1973), pp. 82–95; Christine Stansell, "The Origins of the Sweatshop: Women and Early Industrialization in New York City," in *Working-Class America,* ed. Michael H. Frisch and Daniel J. Walkowitz (Urbana, Ill.: U. of Illinois Press, 1983), pp. 78–103; and Stansell's *City of Women: Sex and Class in New York, 1789–1860* (New York: Alfred A. Knopf, 1986). The term "sweating" was used, if not introduced, by city-life author George G.Foster in the 1850s; see, e.g., *New York Naked* (New York: DeWitt & Davenport, 1854), pp. 141–2. For Foster, see George Rogers Taylor, "Gaslight Foster: A New York 'Journeyman Journalist' at Mid-Century," *New York History* 58 (July 1977): 297–312; and Blumin's "Explaining the New Metropolis."

6. For the quote, see Wilentz, *Chants Democratic,* p. 128. For new business tasks, see Blumin's *Emergence of the Middle Class,* pp. 70–1, also the source (pp. 79–84) regarding clerk activities in Philadelphia. The outwork and jobbing process is found in smaller cities as well. Paul E. Johnson's *A Shopkeeper's Millennium: Society and Revivals in Rochester, New York, 1815–1837* (New York: Hill & Wang, 1978) states that by 1830, shoemakers, coopers, and construction workers in Rochester were experiencing considerable dislocation in their trades (pp. 39–42), with resulting drops in status and income. Ironically, the opening of the Erie Canal, which ensured the success of communities like Rochester, also displaced the artisan system in many crafts. Similarly, while the use of the telegraph in business by 1847 and the opening of a rail line to Lake Erie in 1851 made it possible for merchants to order goods at will and keep up with demand and changing tastes in specialized lines, these intensified jobbing, outwork, and fragmentation among crafts and trades. See Charles Burr Todd, "Telegraphs and Railroads, and Their Impulse to Commerce, 1847–1855," in *The Memorial History of the City of*

New-York from Its First Settlement to the Year 1892, ed. James Grant Wilson (New York: New-York History Co., 1893), vol. 3, pp. 413–17.

7. For the separation of home and workplace, see "The City" in Chapter 1. Specialization in antebellum stores is discussed in Blumin's *Emergence of the Middle Class,* pp. 79–84, and their layout on pp. 92–8. Clarence D. Long's *Wages and Earnings in the United States, 1860–1890* (Princeton: Princeton U.P., 1960), p. 68, sets the average industrial worker's annual wage in 1860 at $297. The newspaper estimates of $500–$600 may set levels high, since they assert a family of five needed two pounds of meat a day and four pounds of sugar a week. For the crash of 1837 and wages to midcentury, see Ernst, *Immigrant Life,* p. 83. For the fluidity of poverty, see John F. McClymer, "The Historian and the Poverty Line," *Historical Methods* 18, 3 (Summer 1985): 105–10. McClymer advocates using indices that vary by occupation, race, ethnicity, gender, and living standard. For the numbers of destitute, see Ernst, *Immigrant Life,* p. 83; for the drop in real wages, see Robert A. Margo and Georgia C. Villaflor, "The Growth of Wages in Antebellum America: New Evidence," *Journal of Economic History* 42, 4 (December 1987): 873–95.

8. For shifts in elite crafts and working conditions as a political issue, see Wilentz, *Chants Democratic,* pp. 134–41, 200–14. Richard B. Stott argues, in *Workers in the Metropolis: Class, Ethnicity, and Youth in Antebellum New York City* (Ithaca: Cornell U.P., 1990), that the antebellum American working class did not have artisan origins (p. 3) and was more significantly shaped by the immigration of young and senior unskilled laborers in the 1840s. Accordingly, the industries that thrived in New York City after 1840 – for example, printing, clothing, jewelry, furniture, and carriage manufacturing – were, in Stott's reading, those that were labor intensive rather than land or transportation dependent (see pp. 22, 28, 32). For the rich, see Irvin G. Wyllie, *The Self-Made Man in America: The Myth of Rags to Riches* (New York: Free Press, 1954), esp. pp. 35–7; for antebellum success books and the cult of self-achievement, see pp. 152–66. Popular literature reinforced the myths that wealth and family did not matter. For a less optimistic view, see Edward Pessen, *Riches, Class, and Power before the Civil War* (Lexington, Mass.: D. C. Heath & Co., 1973). For examples of self-made men in these decades, see Herbert G. Gutman, "The Reality of the Rags-to-Riches 'Myth': the Case of the Patterson, New Jersey, Locomotive, Iron and Machinery Manufacturers, 1830–1880," in *Nineteenth-Century Cities,* ed. Thernstrom and Sennett, pp. 98–124. The rags-to-riches potential in small cities is discussed in Clyde Griffen, "Workers Divided: The Effect of Craft and Ethnic Differences in Poughkeepsie, New York, 1850–1880," also in *Nineteenth-Century Cities,* pp. 49–97.

9. Leonard P. Curry, *The Free Black in Urban America, 1800–1850* (Chicago: U. of Chicago Press, 1981), pp. 1–2 for the quote and pp. 25–35. For union exclusions, see Wilentz, *Chants Democratic,* p. 249; for the destitute, see Ernst, *Immigrant Life,* Appendix V, Table 20 (1,464 Irish of a total of 2,355 paupers). For nativism, see Wilentz, pp. 266–7, and Ernst, pp. 102–7. Stott argues that, in New York City, "the number of skilled workers who saw their opportunities narrowed by industrialization was probably small" (*Workers in the Metropolis,* p. 66) and that

"the victim of the expansion of semi-skilled work was not the highly trained urban craftsman but the rural artisan and the farm wife" (p. 66). For political exploitation of divisions among workers, see Alexander Saxton, *The Rise and Fall of the White Republic: Class Politics and Mass Culture in Nineteenth-Century America* (London: Verso, 1990), pp. 144–5. For immigration data, see Ernst, p. 184; for the Germans, see Ernst and Wilentz; for the Irish unskilled, Margo and Villaflor, "Growth of Wages," p. 885. See also Carol Groneman-Pernicone's "The 'Bloody Ould Sixth': A Social Analysis of a New York City Working-Class Community in the Mid-Nineteenth Century," Ph.D. diss. (U. of Rochester, 1973), for the three-quarters foreign-born population of New York's sixth ward, the highest in that city. For the most part, however, wards remained heterogeneous, though blocks could be heavily concentrated by race or ethnicity in given cities – see Mary P. Ryan, *Women in Public: Between Banners and Ballots, 1825–1880* (Baltimore: Johns Hopkins U.P., 1990), pp. 60–1. Jay P. Dolan, *The Immigrant Church: New York's Irish and German Catholics, 1815–1865* (Baltimore: Johns Hopkins U.P., 1975), pp. 74–5, reports that the 55 percent German labor force that was skilled in 1850 had risen to 95 percent by 1855; see p. 25 for Catholic, especially Irish, antiblack attitudes. There is a variant of the nativist text in the low intermarriage figures between German and Irish Catholics in Dolan's study – only 4 percent between 1850 and 1870 (see p. 71, n. 14).

10. That workers became "class conscious" in these decades is widely supported by the historians cited here, and see Curry, *Free Black in Urban America*, pp. 213–14. The distinction between "class conscious" and "class aware" in the nineteenth century is taken up in Anthony Giddens *The Class Structure of the Advanced Societies* (London: Hutchinson, 1975). Concerning the "manly mechanic," see Elliot J. Gorn, "'Good-Bye Boys, I Die a True American': Homicide, Nativism, and Working-Class Culture in Antebellum New York City," *Journal of American History* 74, 2 (September 1987): 388–410; and Laurie's "'Nothing on Compulsion.'"

11. For the quote, see Gorn, "'Good-Bye Boys,'" p. 408. For clerks, see Horlick, *Country Boys and Merchant Princes*. For studies of controlling texts and campaigns to gentrify, see esp. Halttunen, *Confidence Men and Painted Women*, and John F. Kasson, *Rudeness and Civility: Manners in Nineteenth-Century Urban America* (New York: Hill & Wang, 1990). The connection between the B'hoy, fire companies, saloons, and politics is drawn in Herbert Asbury, *The Gangs of New York* (New York: Alfred A. Knopf, 1927), pp. 30–1; and see also Ernst, *Immigrant Life*, p. 164, and Wilentz, *Chants Democratic*, pp. 260–2. Firehouse activities extended to stuffing ballot boxes, intimidation, and informal policing of neighborhoods. Fire companies in relation to the Bowery B'hoy and theatre are treated in Buckley, "To the Opera House," chap. 4. For fire companies specifically, see: Stephen F. Ginsberg, "The History of Fire Protection in New York City, 1800–1842," Ph.D. diss. (New York U., 1968); Richard B. Calhoun, "From Community to Metropolis: Fire Protection in New York City, 1790–1875," Ph.D. diss. (Columbia U., 1973); and Bruce Laurie, "Fire Companies and Gangs in Southwark: The 1840s," in *The Peoples of Philadelphia: A History of Ethnic*

Groups and Lower-Class Life, 1790–1940, ed. Allen F. Davis and Mark H. Haller (Philadelphia: Temple U.P., 1973), pp. 71–87. For identification of mechanic culture as not middle class, see Stansell, *City of Women,* p. 100, and Blumin's "Hypothesis," esp. pp. 304–5.

12. For Washington Irving, see Barnard Hewitt, *Theatre U.S.A.* (New York: Mc-Graw–Hill, 1959), pp. 59–61. Joe Cowell, *Thirty Years Passed among the Players in England and America* (New York: Harper & Bros., 1844), vol. 2, p. 60. In addition to newspapers cited in the text and studies of class and decorum generally, audience behavior as a subject in critical reviews of theatres is engaged in Odette Salvaggio, "American Dramatic Criticism, 1830–1860," Ph.D. diss. (Florida State U., 1979), pp. 244–7. Such behaviors are also a text in Buckley, "To the Opera House," and Levine, *Highbrow/Lowbrow.*

13. For actors and audience, see Charles Haswell's *Reminiscences of an Octogenarian of the City of New York, 1816–1860* (New York: Harper & Bros., 1897), pp. 362–3, and see Irving's account from earlier in the century (n. 12). For resistance to gentrification and the quote, see Kasson, *Rudeness and Civility,* p. 251.

14. The Bowery B'hoy in life, literature, and on stage is taken up by Richard Dorson, "Mose, the Far-Famed and World Renowned," *American Literature* 15, 3 (November 1943): 289–300. For the quote, see Abram Dayton, *Last Days of Knickerbocker Life* (New York: G. P. Putnam's Sons, 1897), pp. 164–5; I've conventionalized spelling and punctuation. According to Stuart Berg Flexner, "when one referred to such a Bowery Boy the fad was then to use a contemptuous or humorous mock Irish pronunciation of 'Bowery B'hoy.' A Bowery Boy's girlfriend or female counterpart was called a *Bowery Girl,* often pronounced 'Bowery Ga'hal'"; *Listening to America* (New York: Simon & Schuster, 1982), p. 485. For Haswell, see *Reminiscences,* pp. 270–1. The political context is from Wilentz, *Chants Democratic,* p. 329, and see Buckley, "To the Opera House," chap. 4.

15. For the stage history of Mose, see David L. Rinear, "F. S. Chanfrau's Mose: The Rise and Fall of an Urban Folk Hero," *Theatre Journal* 33, 2 (May 1981): 199–212. For the play, see Benjamin A. Baker, *A Glance at New York* (New York: Samuel French, n.d.). This version appears to date some time after 1857; Rinear assigns 1849 as the publication date to the manuscript of the play in the Harvard Theatre Collection, which has a smaller part for Lize but is otherwise similar to the Samuel French version. For the Olympic and its tradition of well-mounted topical burlesques, see Rinear's *The Temple of Momus: Mitchell's Olympic Theatre* (Metuchen, N.J.: Scarecrow Press, 1987). Stott, *Workers in the Metropolis,* discusses fire companies on pp. 229–31, and Mose, Lize, their worker style and speech, and other entertainments patronized by working men and women on pp. 223–9, 247–76.

16. For the Hamblin Guards, see the 19 November 1849 *New York Clarion* and Buckley's discussion of the connection between these companies and New York theatres ("To the Opera House," pp. 337–42, 345). Hamblin also loaned his theatre at no charge for the annual fireman's ball. Mose Humphreys, who led the Lady Washington (No. 40) company – in which, as in the Old Maid Company (No. 34), Chanfrau had served – had strong nativist tendencies. Paul O. Weinbaum's

Mobs and Demagogues: The New York Response to Collective Violence in the Early Nineteenth Century (Ann Arbor: UMI Press, 1977), pp. 152–3, records a Sunday brawl in Chatham Street in the late 1830s involving Mose Humphreys (see n. 17) and his company and Hen Chanfrau and Engine Company No. 15 that drew an estimated one thousand participants and spectators. In addition to nativism and fighting, the Tompkins Blues Militia was drawn from Engine Company No. 30, a political/police/fire/occupational/cultural relationship that, Buckley observes, merits scholarly investigation (see the *New York Clarion*, 13 October 1839, *New York Aurora*, 7 October 1843, and *New York Argus*, 3 August 1844, for some of the connections). The *New York Herald* review is 26 April 1848.

17. Mose's butcher connection is specified in act II of *A Glance at New York* (p. 29), where Lize praises her Bowery B'hoy to a girlfriend: "You ought to see him in de market once, I tell you – how killin' he looks! de way he takes hold of de cleaver and fetches it down is sinful!" Blumin suggests Chanfrau drew Mose from Mose Humphreys, "apparently a printer on the *New York Sun*" ("Explaining the New Metropolis," p. 21). Printing was also an elite craft and would sustain the play's artisan myth, but for other red-blooded sources, see Rinear's "Chanfrau's Mose." Alvin F. Harlow identifies the B'hoy with shipbuilders and carpenters in his *Old Bowery Days* (New York: D. Appleton, 1931), whereas the more contemporary Cornelius Mathews states, "He is sometimes a stout clerk in a jobbing house, oftener a junior partner in a wholesale grocery, and still more frequently a respectable young butcher" (*Pen and Ink Panorama of New York City* [New York: John S. Taylor, 1853], p. 141; for the colors of the B'hoy's clothing, see p. 134). The butcher connection exploits the power this craft had in controlling the principal markets in Manhattan, all kept below Tenth Street from 1830 until 1870, with one exception in Harlem. Butchers controlled access to these markets via political ties, and their presence in them was very noticeable (see Eugene P. Moehring, "Public Works and the Patterns of Urban Real Estate Growth in Manhattan, 1847–1855," Ph.D. diss. [City Univ. of New York, 1976], pp. 281–95; and Todd's "Telegraphs and Railroads," pp. 445–6, which locates a market opened in 1836, the last of fifteen). Centre Market butchers were connected to the Chatham Theatre. Moreover, Buckley notes ("To the Opera House," chart, pp. 306–7) that butchers were the most numerous (six) among the workers arrested at the Astor Place Riot.

    For the boardinghouse, Broadway, and fires, see pp. 9–10 of the play text for *A Glance at New York;* for the rough but feeling fireman, see p. 20. On boardinghouses, see Verranus Morse, "City Boarding Houses," *Young Men's Magazine* (September 1857): 199. Groneman-Pernicone reports boardinghouses were more favored by native-born young men (30 percent) than by German (25 percent) or Irish (5 percent); moreover, 40 percent of Irish men under age 40 lived at home ("'Bloody Ould Sixth,'" pp. 63–4).

18. Concerning city illustrations in periodicals and illustrated newspapers, see Michael Wolff and Celina Fox, "Pictures from the Magazines," in *The Victorian City*, vol. 2, eds. H. J. Dyos and Michael Wolff (London: Routledge & Kegan Paul, 1973), p. 573. Chanfrau's play has a running gag featuring Mose and a de-

serted baby. For the sentimental novel, see *A Glance at New York*, p. 21; for the work myth, pp. 16–17.

19. For Hamblin, see my entry for the Bowery Theatre in *American Theatre Companies, 1749–1887*, ed. Weldon B. Durham (Westport, Conn.: Greenwood Press, 1986). Theodore Shank notes a city-life sketch by the Bowery house playwright Jonas B. Phillips in 1834, entitled *Life in New York* (see "The Bowery Theatre, 1826–1836," Ph.D. diss. [Stanford Univ., 1956], p. 361); see also Walter J. Meserve, *Heralds of Promise: The Drama of the American People in the Age of Jackson, 1829–1849* (Westport, Conn.: Greenwood Press, 1986). For the quote, see J. S. Jones, *The Carpenter of Rouen* (New York: Samuel French, 1840), p. 9.

20. *A Glance at New York*, II.ii, p. 21, for Lize's shop and storybook; II.ii, p. 22, for residence, song, and reluctance to sing on the street; II.v, p. 29, for a minstrel duet; II.v (actually the sixth scene), pp. 30–1, for introductions, the waiter, and Mose's coat. Mose and Lize are married in the (nonextant) Baker-Chanfrau *Mysteries and Miseries of New York* (1848), the third Mose vehicle (see Rinear, "Chanfrau's Mose," p. 207).

21. The Bowery G'hal is described on pp. 107–8 in George G. Foster's *New York by Gas-Light* (New York: DeWitt & Davenport, 1850), and see his description of servant girls on promenade in *New York in Slices* (New York: William Graham, 1849).

22. For Mrs. Trollope, see *Domestic Manners of the Americans*, ed. Donald Smalley (New York: Vintage Books, 1960), p. 351. Fanny Kemble thought American women waddled, as if their shoes pinched; see her *Journal*, 2 vols. (London: John Murray, 1835), vol. 1, pp. 55, 66. See Susan G. Davis, *Parades and Power: Street Theatre in Nineteenth-Century Philadelphia* (Philadelphia: Temple U.P., 1986), p. 47, and Stansell, *City of Women*, pp. 94, 256 n. 52, for references to working women's fancy dress, and p. 275, n. 53, for prostitutes' dress. The quotation concerning the sexual behavior of working women on dates is from Stansell, *City of Women*, p. 176. Prostitution and its relationship to theatre culture is taken up in Chapter 3.

23. For male income, see n. 7 and related text. The $6.00 figure is optimistic: $312 for a fifty-two-week workyear, assuming the man was never unemployed. An English visitor in earlier years was surprised to find in the pit men who, "should they ever think of seeing a play [in London], must take up their abode among the upper gallery" (Henry B. Faron, *Sketches of America* [London: Longman, Hurst, Rees, Orme, & Brown, 1818], pp. 86–7); workmen sitting where they pleased is not likely to have stopped in the antebellum decades. For female income and hours at the poverty end, see Stansell, *City of Women*, pp. 113, 176, and Groneman-Pernicone, "'Bloody Ould Sixth,'" pp. 141–2. Patricia C. Click, *The Spirit of the Times: Amusements in Nineteenth-Century Baltimore, Norfolk, and Richmond* (Charlottesville: U.P. of Virginia, 1989), establishes laborers' wages in Maryland and Virginia in 1850 at 70 cents a day (p. 96) and provides a decadal breakdown of prices for entertainments in her region of study (p. 95). For women in theatres, see Haswell's reconstruction of a midcentury visit to the Bowery Theatre (*Reminiscences*, p. 362). For servants' wages, see Faye E. Dudden, *Serv-*

ing Women: Household Service in Nineteenth Century America (Middletown, Conn.: Wesleyan U.P., 1983), pp. 90–112; and Stansell's *City of Women*, p. 272, n. 9, where she argues domestics' wages declined from 1800 to 1860. There appear to have been informal wage controls by (female) bosses. For savings and the ethnic–racial breakdown of domestics, see *City of Women*, pp. 156–7; see also Ernst, *Immigrant Life*, pp. 214–15, and Curry, *Free Black in Urban America*, p. 22. Comparatively, Dolan reports Catholic priests were paid $600 annually in 1850, incomes that could be swelled by gifts to $1,000 a year (*Immigrant Church*, pp. 65–6). Frank Luther Mott, in *A History of American Magazines, 1741–1850* (Cambridge, Mass.: Harvard U.P., 1939), p. 506, notes that, as of 1838, $13.00 a month plus board was the highest salary the state of Connecticut had ever paid a teacher; moreover, a college professor in 1843 earned about $600 a year. Groneman-Pernicone notes (p. 12) that half the Irish immigrants were women (compared to 40 percent in other groups), which likely had a bearing both upon their presence in the work force and their cultural visibility.

24. Company compositions are given in Durham, *American Theatre Companies*. For detailed explorations of specific companies, see Edward W. Mammen, "The Old Stock Company: The Boston Museum," *More Books* 19 (January–May 1944); Barnard Hewitt's "'King Stephen' of the Park and Drury Lane," in *The Theatrical Manager in England and America*, ed. Joseph Donohue (Princeton: Princeton U.P., 1971), pp. 87–141; or Shank, "Bowery Theatre." The value of benefits is difficult to assess. David Rinear estimates Mitchell's Olympic in 1848 had a $200 capacity. Its most popular actors contracted for benefits of a clear one-third, equaling $66.00 (more or less) if the house was full; less prominent actors got half of receipts after a $100 house-expense deduction, leaving a maximum benefit of $50.00 if the house was full. Rinear estimates salaries of such beneficiaries at $15.00 a week, valuing the benefit at something between three and one-third and four and a half weeks' pay (*Temple of Momus*, pp. 189–90).

25. See: James C. Burge, *Lines of Business: Casting Practice and Policy in the American Theatre, 1752–1899* (New York: Peter Lang, 1986); Kate Ryan, *Old Boston Museum Days* (Boston: Little, Brown, 1915), pp. 245–7; Clara Morris, *Life on the Stage* (New York: McClure, Phillips & Co., 1901), pp. 27–30; and Louisa Lane Drew, *Autobiography* (New York: Charles Scribner's Sons, 1899), p. 65. For Hamblin's wardrobe, see the *New York Herald*, 23 September 1836.

26. Hamblin hired actors weekly in the 1840s. For salary estimates and their sources, see my entries for the Boston Museum, the Bowery, and Wallack's in Durham, *American Theatre Companies;* see also Rinear's *Temple of Momus*. For Logan, see "The Leg Business," *Galaxy* (August 1867): 440–4. A *New York Times* article of 9 October 1866 identifies an income of $2,500 to $3,000 a year (about $48.00 to $58.00 per week for fifty-two workweeks) as "middle class." These figures would be high for antebellum wages – the Civil War inflated salaries – but they do imply that some prewar theatre personnel could fit the criteria.

27. Hamblin, William Mitchell, Laura Keene, and the Wallacks (James and Lester) managed in New York; Louisa Lane Drew ran the Arch Street Theatre in Philadelphia, and Moses Kimball was the proprietor (though not the active manager)

of the Boston Museum. For Hamblin and the long run, see my note, "Antedating the Long Run: A Prolegomenon," *Nineteenth Century Theatre Research* 13, 1 (Summer 1985): 33–6. Seasonal data derives from the sources supporting my entries in Durham, *American Theatre Companies,* but see esp. Mammen, "Old Stock Company," and Shank, "Bowery Theatre." For Stull, see his "Where Famous Actors Learned Their Art," *Lippincott's Monthly Magazine* 75, 3 (March 1905): 374–5. Otis Skinner discusses his training in the waning days of repertory in *Footlights and Spotlights* (Indianapolis: Bobbs Merrill, 1924), see esp. pp. 41, 80, 108.

28. The personnel figures conflate those of Mammen in "Old Stock Company" for the uncharacteristically stable and long-lived Boston Museum, and reflect also Burge's *Lines of Business* and Rinear's *Temple of Momus* (the ratio of 3:1 in playwriting and casting is still standard at the end of the twentieth century). My support of the ratio, if not specific numbers, derives from the antebellum records previously mentioned in these notes. For segregationist laws and the quote, see Curry, *Free Black in Urban America,* pp. 88–91. For the African Grove, see Jonathan Dewberry, "The African Grove Theatre and Company," *Black American Literary Forum* 16, 4 (Winter 1982): 128–31. For Mrs. Trollope's observations, see her *Domestic Manners of the Americans,* p. 350. The 1855 census identifies 11,840 blacks in New York; fewer than two thousand belonged to churches, according to Dolan (*Immigrant Church,* p. 24).

29. Concerning free blacks working in theatres and concert halls, see Curry, *Free Black in Urban America,* p. 23. On the Catharine Street Market, see Thomas De Voe, *The Market Book* (1862; rpt. New York: Burt Franklin, 1969), pp. 344–5. On "Juba" on the frontier, see Hans Nathan, *Dan Emmett and the Rise of Early Negro Minstrelsy* (Norman: U. of Oklahoma Press, 1974), pp. 71–92. On Mathews, sheet music, and popular songs and icons, see Peter G. Buckley, "'The Place to Make an Artist Work': Micah Hawkins and William Sidney Mount in New York City," in *Catching the Tune: Music and William Sidney Mount,* ed. Janice Gray Armstrong (New York: Museum at Stony Brook, 1984), pp. 22–39. For the use of black music, mannerisms, and dance in minstrelsy, see Alexander Saxton, "Blackface Minstrelsy and Jacksonian Ideology," *American Quarterly* 27, 1 (March 1975): 3–28. Rice's "Long Island Juba" is indexed in George C. D. Odell, *Annals of the New York Stage* (New York: Columbia U.P., 1928), vol. 3, p. 635, and see the last chapter of Shank's "Bowery Theatre." For William Henry Lane, see Marian Hannah Winter, "Juba and American Minstrelsy," *Dance Index* 6, 2 (February 1947): 32–6. Odell (vol. 5, pp. 397, 400) records Juba performing 29 January 1848 at the Broadway Odeon and 8 February 1848 at the New York Melodeon (he does not record engagements at the Chatham or Bowery such as those referenced in Winter's account). Pinteaux's Saloon, through which one entered the Odeon, would constitute a concert tavern of the sort popular in the 1840s. The transition from eighteenth-century northern black festivals to parading by African Americans in the first third of the nineteenth century is charted by Shane White, "'It Was a Proud Day': African Americans, Festivals, and Parades in the North, 1741–1834," *Journal of American History* 81, 1 (June 1994): 13–50.

30. See the *New York Mirror* of 4 December 1824 for a characteristic example of its condemnations of "vernacular" performances in the 1820s and 1830s. For Mrs. Trollope, see her *Domestic Manners of the Americans*, p. 350, and illustration 24, "Black and White Beaux," facing p. 361. Fanny Kemble describes as "grotesque" parading black women dressed "in the height of fashion, with every colour in the rainbow about them" (*Journal*, vol. 1, pp. 75–7).

31. Wilentz suggests (*Chants Democratic*, p. 259) that minstrel shows were aimed at arriviste blacks of Mrs. Trollope's description, as well as at white dandies. General histories of pre-Civil War American theatre, already skewed geographically, seldom describe professional black theatre activity; references in general accounts and specific histories of black professional theatre activity (esp. musical) increase for the later nineteenth and twentieth centuries (the latter, dramatically).

32. See Alexis de Tocqueville, *Democracy in America*, ed. Phillips Bradley (New York: Random House/Vintage Books, 1990), vol. 1, chap. 3, pp. 46–53. His views, the result of nine months in the United States during 1831–2, frame Pessen's discussion in *Riches, Class, and Power* (see esp. p. 303). For the nineteenth-century phenomenon, see Burton J. Bledstein, *The Culture of Professionalism: The Middle Class and the Development of Higher Education in America* (New York: W. W. Norton, 1976), p. 53. For ideology and its relationship to society, see T. J. Clark, *The Painting of Modern Life* (New York: Alfred A. Knopf, 1985), pp. 6, 8. For the perils of the return to a "real" or normal in the cultural performance of power, see Davis, *Parades and Power*, pp. 12–13. Arthur Kroker and David Cook observe in their *The Postmodern Scene: Excremental Culture and Hyper-Aesthetics* (New York: St. Martin's Press, 1986), p. 89: "The 'real' is always prepared to abandon its public disguises and, in a quick reversal of effects, to dissolve." On the public–private debate, see Dena Goodman's "Public Sphere and Private Life: Toward a Synthesis of Current Historiographical Approaches to the Old Regime," *History and Theory* 31, 1 (February 1992): 1–20; for public and private in antebellum America, see Ryan's *Women in Public*.

33. For the conversion of the household into a workplace, see Stansell, *City of Women*, p. 128. For the divorce of home and work, see Mary P. Ryan, *Cradle of the Middle Class: The Family in Oneida County, New York, 1790–1865* (Cambridge: Cambridge U.P., 1981), pp. 44–8, 103; and Johnson's *Shopkeeper's Millennium*, pp. 48–55. Johnson points out that neighborhoods in Rochester segregated work from residence after 1825, and also segregated residences along socioeconomic lines in a way not previously evident in his community (a pattern perhaps more common in smaller than larger antebellum cities). For the working children of immigrants and working-class material standards and consumption, see Stott, *Workers in the Metropolis*, pp. 168–73, 186–90. For idle wives, see Elizabeth Blackmar, *Manhattan for Rent, 1785–1850* (Ithaca: Cornell U.P., 1989), p. 124; and on housework, Susan Strasser, *Never Done: A History of American Housework* (New York: Pantheon Books, 1982). For women viewed by male workers as marketplace competition, see Blackmar; on their exclusion from unions, see Wilentz, *Chants Democratic*.

34. On the immoral workplace, see Elizabeth K. Helsinger, Robin Lauterbach Sheets, and William Veeder, *The Woman Question: Society and Literature in Britain and*

America, 1837–1883, vol. 2 (New York: Garland, 1983; rpt. Chicago: U. of Chicago Press, 1989), pp. 110–13. For Philadelphia boarding, see Blumin, *Emergence of the Middle Class*, p. 363, n. 154; for boarders in Oneida county, see Ryan, *Cradle of the Middle Class*, p. 201, who suggests 20 percent of the families she studied had unrelated boarders in their homes in 1855. Johnson (*Shopkeeper's Millennium*, pp. 46–7 and n. 30) locates lodgers among 26 percent of journeymen, 30 percent of laborers, 24 percent of shopkeepers, 14 percent of businessmen, and 80 percent of master craftsmen in Rochester in 1827. For the relationships among boarding, the inability of workers to own homes, transportation, and the development of worker neighborhoods in antebellum New York City, see Stott, *Workers in the Metropolis*, pp. 191–222. Live-in workers dropped off by 1834, but taking in boarders survived the split of home from workplace. See also Blackmar, *Manhattan for Rent*, p. 137, on boarders.

35. For Martineau, see Helsinger et al., *Woman Question*, vol. 2, p. 110. For antebellum Senecan women and white sexism, see Joan M. Jensen, "Native American Women and Agriculture: A Seneca Case Study," in *Unequal Sisters: A Multicultural Reader in U.S. Women's History*, ed. Ellen C. Dubois and Vicki L. Ruiz (New York: Routledge, 1990), pp. 51–65. The moralizing of socioeconomic problems is considered by Anita Levy in *Other Women: The Writing of Class, Race, and Gender, 1832–1898* (Princeton: Princeton U.P., 1991), pp. 35–7. Significantly, Ryan's careful study of Oneida County, *Cradle of the Middle Class*, makes clear the number of women working for wages (pp. 203–9). Adding in those producing income from boarders would raise the percentage still higher (see Tables E7, · E13, E14 [pp. 271, 274]).

36. On "social worker" responses to working women's child rearing, see Stansell, "Women, Children, and the Uses of the Streets: Class and Gender Conflict in New York City, 1850–1860," in *Unequal Sisters*, ed. Dubois and Ruiz, pp. 92–108. Stansell also notes the transference of social problems (vagrancy, crime, prostitution) to the family, causing reformers to focus on reforming how the poor lived or on the confiscation of children (to asylums, for transportation, etc.). The school attendance figures are from Ernst, *Immigrant Life*, pp. 140–2, and see Blumin, *Emergence of the Middle Class*, p. 190, on shorter overall attendance. Dolan locates five thousand children in parochial schools in New York in 1840 (*Immigrant Church*, p. 105), 20 percent of the school population.

37. On childhood and the mother's role, see Ryan's *Cradle of the Middle Class*, pp. 90–101. For childhood as a creation of the nineteenth century, see Bledstein, *Culture of Professionalism*, p. 211. For female literacy, see Carl N. Degler, *At Odds: Women and the Family in America from the Revolution to the Present Day* (New York: Oxford U.P., 1980), p. 308. Tocqueville claimed there was no adolescence in America because boys began working at 14 (*Democracy in America*, vol. 2, p. 192). For Beecher, see Strasser, *Never Done*, and Beecher's *Treatise on Domestic Economy* (New York: Marsh, Capen, Lyon, & Webb, 1841; rpt. New York: Schoken, 1977), p. 9.

38. Beecher and Stowe proposed their ideal homes in *The American Woman's Home* (1869; rpt. Salem, N.H.: Ayer Co. Pubs., 1972). For a discussion of their work and related issues, see Doris Cole, *From Tipi to Skyscraper: A History of Women*

in Architecture (New York: George Braziller, 1973), pp. 28–51. For the decline in family size, see John D'Emilio and Estelle Freedman, *Intimate Matters: A History of Sexuality in America* (New York: Harper & Row, 1988), p. 58; and Mary P. Ryan, *Cradle of the Middle Class*, p. 36. An Oneida County woman born before 1805 would average 5.1 children; a woman born in 1810, 3.6. For the rowhouse plan in 1831 and rent/income figures, see Blackmar, *Manhattan for Rent*, pp. 193–4; the budget percentages and boarders are from Elizabeth Collins Cromley, *Alone Together: A History of New York's Early Apartments* (Ithaca: Cornell U.P., 1990), pp. 16–17. Land manipulations of the sort reflected in housing shortages concentrated wealth nationwide in these decades (e.g., 10 percent of the population owned 89 percent of New York's income). For wealth, see Blumin, "Mobility and Change," p. 204; Craig Buettinger, "Economic Inequity in Early Chicago, 1849–1850," *Journal of Social History* 11, 3 (Spring 1978): 413–18; and, of course, Pessen, *Riches, Class, and Power*. For the correlation between concentrated wealth and tight housing in New York, see Blackmar, *Manhattan for Rent*, esp. p. 104.

39. For construction trades as employers, see Blackmar, *Manhattan for Rent*, pp. 183–4, and p. 206 for the construction of multifamily housing. For apartment rents, see Dolan, *Immigrant Church*, p. 36, who points out food prices were 20–60 percent higher in tenement stores. For utilities and narrow buildings, see Cromley, *Alone Together*, pp. 27, 35; also Strasser, *Never Done*, p. 70, who observes that though there were many gas companies, their weak and smelly product "primarily lighted city streets and public places" until the end of the nineteenth century. For the introduction of gas in New York, see J. Hampden Dougherty, "Ten Years of Municipal Vigor, 1837–1847," in *Memorial History of the City*, ed. Wilson, vol. 3, p. 372. Gas theatre lighting was introduced in Philadelphia in 1818 and was general in northeastern theatres by 1825, well ventilated at the roof to disperse its odors. For its ability "to display [Bowery] spectators to advantage," see the *New York Mirror*, 23 August 1828. For privies, see p. 97 in Strasser. More prosperous houses with running water piped into them still had no provision for heating it except the kitchen stove; this produced servant complaints about running the stairs to fetch water to bedchambers and made laundry the most hated domestic chore. For the New York City inspector's report concerning housing unfit for habitation, see Blackmar, *Manhattan for Rent*, p. 205 and n. 52; on tenements, see Dolan, *Immigrant Church*, pp. 34–8. Antebellum slums were integrated, though Leonard P. Curry, *Free Black in Urban America*, reports the existence of all-white streets and courts, particularly in New York and Boston, pointing to economic-based discrimination in substandard urban housing.

40. See the introduction to Bateman's *Self* in *Representative Plays by American Dramatists*, vol. 2, ed. Montrose J. Moses (1925; rpt. New York: Arno Press, 1978), pp. 697–703. For more on Cowell, see his *Thirty Years Passed*.

41. Moses, *Representative Plays*, pp. 697–703. For more on Owens, see Chapter 1, n. 24, of the present volume.

42. The quoted passages from Bateman's *Self* in Moses, *Representative Plays*, are on pp. 713, 714, 708–9, 709, 709–10, and 748, respectively.

43. For Mrs. Apex's self-reflections, see p. 717; for Charles's speeches, see p. 730.

44. Unit's speech is p. 741. Mr. Apex is described as a plantation owner and slave-holder, and while the play extols Chloe's virtues, she is also an example of the "Mammy" stereotype.

45. Unit's description of the melodrama he and Mary are enacting is on p. 754; the self-reflective parlor is described on p. 755, which also contains Unit's equation of feelings with business assets; the praise of Chloe and the advice-book virtue are on p. 763.

46. Family planning was facilitated by available birth-control devices (often inef-fectual) and abortion. Ryan's *Cradle of the Middle Class* is key to the construct of middle class as a survival strategy; see especially her summary of its compo-nents on pp. 165–70, the shifts in occupation, pp. 177–8, and the quote, p. 184. Ryan takes up public women in *Women in Public*. Concerning advice books, see n. 47. For Foster, see his *New York by Gas-Light*, p. 69.

47. On advice books, see Halttunen, *Confidence Men and Painted Women*, p. 92, and Kasson, *Rudeness and Civility*, pp. 43–53. For concepts of the natural gentleman and related issues, see Stow Persons, *The Decline of Gentility* (New York: Co-lumbia U.P., 1973), esp. pp. 31–5, 53–70. On varying class standards of behav-ior, see Stearns, "Middle Class," p. 383. In the context of city, frontier, and role playing, David Brion Davis notes in *Slave Power Conspiracy* (p. 28): "Even the simplicity and spontaneity of the man of nature soon became stylized in staged performances which ranged in credibility from Andrew Jackson to Davy Crock-ett, from Henry David Thoreau to Joaquin Miller. In the era of P. T. Barnum, whom could you trust?"

48. The Presbyterian Church inveighed against "the restless and wandering activi-ty of youth" in Utica in 1820 (Ryan, *Cradle of the Middle Class*, p. 65), but the theme was general in the influential works of these religious publishing houses. Ryan sees this literature as the earliest indication of a shift in family order. For the fear religious leaders had that they were losing their power to others, see Halttunen, *Confidence Men and Painted Women*, pp. 5–10. For Arthur Tappan, see Walter Barrett [Joseph A. Scoville], *The Old Merchants of New York*, vol. 1, p. 230, cited by Horlick (*Country Boys and Merchant Princes*, p. 172, note), with the caution that Scoville detested Tappan for his abolitionist ventures, though Horlick thinks the account otherwise consistent with Tappan's views and activi-ties. Wyllie considers Tappan's rules consistent but not typical among merchants (*Self-Made Man in America*, p. 69). For the control of (particularly female) ser-vants' private lives, see Dudden, *Serving Women*. For voluntary associations for young people living at home, see Ryan, *Cradle of the Middle Class*, pp. 106–42, who points out that associations for young men mixed classes but served useful business purposes; indeed, the moral character of men was one of the factors cit-ed in published credit ratings. For associations and similar views in major cities, see Horlick. For immigrant clubs, see Ernst, *Immigrant Life*, pp. 127–8. The quote is from Dudden, *Serving Women*, p. 28, who adopts the image of a stage, performances, and role playing to describe antebellum social concerns, a meta-phor prominent in the material Halttunen considers.

49. Paranoia escapes not only from David Brion Davis's context (*Slave Power Conspiracy*), but from those explored by Halttunen in *Confidence Men and Painted Women*, Kasson in *Rudeness and Civility*, and others. On clubs, see Pessen, *Riches, Class, and Power*, pp. 225–30; Buckley's "To the Opera House," which also takes up dining (pp. 231–3); and Francis G. Fairfield, *The Clubs of New York* (New York: Henry L. Hinton, 1873). On costuming the self and other regulations, see Kasson, pp. 114–73; it is also an extensive text in Halttunen, who situates the parlor as the crucial staging ground (p. 118). Kasson elects the dining room as the genteel coronation site, both in *Rudeness and Civility* (pp. 188–98) and in "Rituals of Dining: Table Manners in Victorian America," in *Dining in America, 1850–1900*, ed. Kathryn Grover (Amherst: U. of Massachusetts Press, 1987), pp. 114–41. It is not clear at what point all-male dinners in the home gave way to sexually integrated ones, but the practice appears to have become general among the wealthy after 1825, when homes moved farther from places of business and all-male dinners transferred from homes to restaurants and clubs. The work involved in preparing and serving such dinners, which ran to multiple courses, was considerable (see Strasser on cooking, *Never Done*, pp. 16–46). The description of the genteel home as a place of compartmentalization and enclosure is upheld in Buckley's dissertation and in Bledstein (*Culture of Professionalism*, p. 61). Clifford E. Clark speaks of the dining room as the center of the (chiefly) postbellum house in "The Vision of the Dining Room: Plan Books, Dreams and Middle Class Realities," in *Dining in America*, ed. Grover, pp. 142–72. The rowhouse floor plan cited earlier sustains the division of functions in genteel domestic architecture, but servants and boarders confute the private–public divisions scholars often make; indeed, the constancy of servant complaints about running the stairs in narrow, multistoried dwellings (see Dudden, *Serving Women*) suggests their ubiquity in the genteel home.

50. For cultural control after the Civil War, see Kasson, *Rudeness and Civility*, p. 245. Dickens reports his observation in *American Notes*. *Tribune* reporters were ejected from the House of Representatives in 1848 for noting an Ohio legislator's gauche lunch-eating habits; see Michael Schudson, *Discovering the News: A Social History of American Newspapers* (New York: Basic Books, 1978), p. 29. See Persons, *Decline of Gentility*, p. 66, for Sedgwick. Complaints about materialism are general in *The Diary of Philip Hone, 1828–1851*, 2 vols., ed. Allan Nevins (New York: Dodd, Mead & Co., 1927), and in Haswell's *Reminiscences*. For a particularly forceful indictment of consumerism, see George Templeton Strong's *Diary*, ed. Allan Nevins and Milton Halsey Thomas (New York: Macmillan, 1952), entry for 31 July 1849; and see Buckley's account of the Knickerbockers ("To the Opera House," p. 237). Thoreau, Poe, Holmes, Hawthorne, and Lowell shared Hone's and Strong's dim views of materialism. For the amusements of the wealthy, see Pessen, *Riches, Class, and Power*, pp. 230–41. On higher education in the antebellum decades, see Bledstein, *Culture of Professionalism*, pp. 227–36.

51. On the untenability of the home as woman's but not man's sphere, see Nancy Cott, "On Man's History and Woman's History," in *Meanings for Manhood: Constructions of Masculinity in Victorian America*, ed. Mark C. Carnes and Clyde

Griffen (Chicago: U. of Chicago Press, 1990), pp. 205–11. The subject forms the focus for Ryan's *Women in Public*. The "masculine achiever" and "Christian gentleman" are taken up by Clyde Griffen (p. 203) in his "Reconstructing Masculinity from the Evangelical Revival to the Waning of Progressivism: A Speculative Synthesis," in *Meanings for Manhood*, pp. 183–204; he supplies the concept of "evangelical males" to Donald Yacavone's "Abolitionists and the 'Language of Fraternal Love,'" in *Meanings for Manhood*, pp. 85–95. For the "tough guy" side of the triangle, see David G. Pugh, *Sons of Liberty: The Masculine Mind in Nineteenth-Century America* (Westport, Conn.: Greenwood Press, 1983); Elliot J. Gorn's "'Good-Bye Boys'" and his "'Gouge and Bite, Pull Hair and Scratch': The Social Significance of Fighting in the Southern Backcountry," *American Historical Review* 90, 1 (February 1985): 18–43; and Bruce Laurie's "Fire Companies and Gangs" and his *Working People of Philadelphia, 1800–1850* (Philadelphia: Temple U.P., 1980). Carroll Smith-Rosenberg considers the "two competing mythic dramas" of antebellum male reformers and the Davy Crockett of the almanacs in her *Disorderly Conduct: Visions of Gender in Victorian America* (New York: Alfred A. Knopf, 1985). For a summary of literature offering the now-displaced "cult of true womanhood" and her own model, see Frances B. Cogan, *All American Girl: The Ideal of Real Womanhood in Mid-Nineteenth Century America* (Athens: U. of Georgia Press, 1989). For popular literature, see Adrienne Siegel, *The Image of the American City in Popular Literature, 1820–1870* (Port Washington, N.Y.: Kennikat Press, 1981); and Michael Denning's *Mechanic Accents: Dime Novels and Working-Class Cultures in America* (New York: Verso, 1987).

52. Peter Brooks, in his *The Melodramatic Imagination* (New Haven: Yale U.P., 1976), observes of melodrama that "nothing is left unsaid; the characters stand on stage and utter the unspeakable, give voice to their deepest feelings, dramatize through their heightened and polarized words and gestures the whole lesson of their relationship. They assume primary psychic roles, father, mother, child, and express basic psychic conditions" (p. 4). In the theatre, Brooks continues, melodrama stages such meanings on several planes and transforms desire into plastic signs (pp. 46–7).

53. For theatre reviewing in these decades, see Vincent L. Angotti, "American Dramatic Criticism, 1800–1830," Ph.D. diss. (Univ. of Kansas, 1967); and Odette C. Salvaggio, "American Dramatic Criticism, 1830–1860," Ph.D. diss. (Florida State Univ., 1979). The ability of ministers to regulate theatre is discussed in Buckley, "To the Opera House," p. 137. For press response to ministers' attacks upon theatre, see Salvaggio, pp. 91–100. For continuing attacks in religious publications, see, for example, Stephen P. Hill, *Theatrical Amusements* (Philadelphia: Baptist General Tract Society, 1830); Robert Turnbull's *The Theatre* (Hartford: Caulfield & Robins, 1837) and his *The Theatre in Its Influence upon Literature, Morals, and Religion* (Boston: Gould, Kendall, & Lincoln, 1839); and E. Digby Baltzell, *Puritan Boston and Quaker Philadelphia* (New York: Free Press, 1979). See also Grimsted, *Melodrama Unveiled*, pp. 26–7, on clerical opposition to the theatre in the 1830s and 1840s. On the informal contract, see H. M. Ranney, *Account of the Ter-*

rific and Fatal Riot at the New-York Opera House, on the Night of May 10th, 1849
(New York: H. M. Ranney, 1849), p. 15.

54. See Frank Luther Mott, *American Journalism: A History of Newspapers in the United States through 250 years, 1690–1940* (New York: Macmillan & Co., 1941), esp. pp. 201–5 on old-style papers. An excellent brief history of change in publication practices is provided by James L. Crouthamel, "The Newspaper Revolution in New York, 1830–1860," *New York History* 45, 2 (April 1964): 91–113, who points out the enormous increases in personnel by 1860 (compared, e.g., to an *Evening Post* editorial staff of four in 1842) and the cost of presses that could, and did, break many of the older papers (pp. 104–6). A well-wrought account of the revolution in the press in the antebellum decades is also provided by Schudson, *Discovering the News*, pp. 12–60.

One example of political–newspaper ties is provided in Bank of the U.S. support to and from newspapers; an estimated two-thirds sided with the bank in its war with Andrew Jackson (see Paul J. Wellman, *The House Divides: The Age of Jackson and Lincoln, from the War of 1812 to the Civil War* [New York: Doubleday & Co., 1966], p. 129). A different view of "Father Andrew" and the "Mother Bank" is presented in Michael P. Rogin, *Fathers and Children: Andrew Jackson and the Subjugation of the American Indian* (New York: Alfred A. Knopf, 1975); and in Anne Norton, *Alternative Americas: A Reading of Antebellum Political Culture* (Chicago: U. of Chicago Press, 1986). On postal changes affecting newspapers and journals, see Denning, *Mechanic Accents*, p. 19, who points out that a publishing boom in storypapers between 1845 and 1857 was spurred by a drop in postal rates for books. (Jackson's manipulation of such rates vis-à-vis newspapers is widely referenced.) For theatrical magazines and magazines featuring theatrical commentary, see Mott, *History of American Magazines*. Of particular interest are the *New York Mirror*, *Spirit of the Times*, and the *Ladies Companion*.

To all of these considerations, the literacy level is crucial. The 1840 census set it at 97 percent of whites over 21 in the Northeast and 91 percent in the old Northwest; recent studies take these as too high for more than minimal literacy and reckon 89 percent among northern artisans and 76 percent of northern farmers by the Civil War (see Denning, *Mechanic Accents*, p. 31). All sources agree on lower literacy in the South, an article of faith among abolitionists (see Norton).

55. See Mott's *American Journalism*, p. 271, for the *Tribune* quote. Dissatisfaction with melodrama is summarized in Salvaggio's "American Dramatic Criticism, 1830–1860," pp. 121–31, and in Mott's *History of American Magazines*, pp. 169–88. As Mott points out, the inadequacies of melodrama were often tied to early arguments for a native drama (for these, see also Angotti, "American Dramatic Criticism, 1800–1830"; Meserve, *Heralds of Promise;* and Grimsted, *Melodrama Unveiled*). An example of the dog and pony repertory, a hard-times recourse, is provided by many entries in Durham, *American Theatre Companies,* including mine for the Bowery Theatre. For the variety of entertainments available in these decades, see Click, *Spirit of the Times,* and Davis, *Parades and Power.*

For audiences as middle class, masses, or common people, see the *New York Dramatic Mirror* of 25 April 1841 ("Philadelphia Theatricals," p. 54) and the *Bos-*

ton Herald for 31 July 1854 ("The New Theatre," p. 4). For foreign support of theatre's elite audience, see George Combe, *Notes on the United States of America*, 2 vols. (Edinburgh: Maclachlan, Stewart, & Co., 1841), vol. 1, pp. 28–9; and Louis F. Tasistro, *Random Shots and Southern Breezes* (New York: Harper & Bros., 1842), vol. 1, pp. 65–6. Caution in assessing these sources is appropriate. For example, Tocqueville observes (*Democracy in America*, vol. 2, p. 78) that, in democracies, "the literary canons of aristocracy will be gently, gradually, and, so to speak legally modified; at the theatre they will be riotously overthrown." As public places, the acting out of larger issues in theatres with a characteristic vigor is not a surprising assessment of 1831–2 America. What is missing from Tocqueville's picture is any sense of class as a relational manifestation produced by interactions, appropriation, and commodification, as well as by contest and resistance. Was class in France and Great Britain during these decades as fixed as foreign assessments (see, e.g., the Faron remark in n. 23, above) imposed it here?

56. Click, *Spirit of the Times*, pp. 35–6. Click's reading (p. 35 and n. 4) is that the South was no different than the North in audience behavior, types of theatre offerings, or theatre architecture. For Mrs. Trollope, see her *Domestic Manners of the Americans*, p. 74. Tyrone Power, *Impressions of America During the Years 1833, 1834 and 1835* (London: Bentley, 1836), pp. 72–3. Fanny Kemble says of a visit to the Park Theatre on a Wednesday night in 1832 (*Journal*, vol. 1, p. 56): "the audience was considerable, but all men; scarce, I should think, twenty women in the dress circle." (No other women watched Wallack in the popular melodrama *The Rent Day*, or none Kemble would see from her box seat?) The predominance of males and the reticence of females to attend the theatre in the 1820s and 1830s is Bruce A. McConachie's conclusion in *Melodramatic Formations: American Theatre and Society, 1820–1870* (Iowa City: U. of Iowa Press, 1992), p. 9. David Ewen extends the absence of women in theatre audiences past the Civil War in his *The Story of America's Musical Theatre* (Philadelphia: Clinton Book Co., 1968), re-marking of the 1866 *Black Crook*, "Women (who at that time rarely went to the theater) wore heavy veils to hide their identity as they made their way into the theater" (p. 5). Neither descriptor nor conclusion is warranted.

57. Bennet's goal, as he stated in a 27 July 1836 editorial, was to "proclaim each morning on 15,000 sheets of thought and intellect the deep guilt that is encrusting our society." His mission was to serve this perception as the people's voice, while, as Mott points out (*American Journalism*, pp. 232–3), making money. For Haswell, see his *Reminiscences*, p. 362. For theatre attendance as a performance by patrons, see McConachie, *Melodramatic Formation*, p. 14. The brilliance of the newly gas-lit Bowery is discussed in the 23 August 1828 *New York Mirror*.

58. For theatre criticism, see Salvaggio, "American Dramatic Criticism, 1830–1860," and the histories of Joseph N. Ireland, *Records of the New York Stage from 1750 to 1860*, 2 vols. (1866; rpt. New York: Benjamin Blom, 1966); T. Allston Brown, *A History of the New York Stage*, 2 vols. (New York: Dodd, Mead & Co., 1903); Odell, *Annals;* and the more recent volumes by Walter Meserve, *An Emerging Entertainment: The Drama of the American People to 1828* (Bloomington: Indiana

U.P., 1977), and *Heralds of Promise*. For the transcendental connection, see "The Town" in Chapter 1. For theatre riots, see David Grimsted, "Rioting in Its Jacksonian Setting," *American Historical Review* 77, 2 (April 1972): 361–97; Buckley, "To the Opera House," pp. 162–96, who extends the discourse to crowd history; and Bruce A. McConachie, "'The Theatre of the Mob': Apocalyptic Melodrama and Preindustrial Riots in Antebellum New York," in *Theatre for Working-Class Audiences in the United States, 1830–1980*, ed. McConachie and Daniel Friedman (Westport, Conn.: Greenwood Press, 1985), pp. 17–46.

59. Concerning the Park, see Haswell, *Reminiscences*, p. 496; Trollope, *Domestic Manners of the Americans*, p. 339; "Our Actors," *Ladies Companion*, July 1837, p. 149; Hewitt, "'King Stephen' of the Park and Drury Lane," pp. 88–9; and Buckley, "To the Opera House," pp. 85–101. The standard histories of the theatre, Frederic Litto's "Edmund Simpson of the Park Theatre, New York, 1809–1848," Ph.D. diss. (Indiana, 1969), and Durham, *American Theatre Companies*, are also relevant. Buckley deconstructs Searle's painting, concerning which see also "The City" in Chapter 1. On the Park and whorehouses, see Joe Cowell, *Thirty Years Passed*, and Chapters 1 and 3.

60. Concerning the Bowery, see Shank, "Bowery Theatre" (up to 1836), and my entry in Durham, *American Theatre Companies*, for an account and sources. Also see Trollope, *Domestic Manners of the Americans*. An interesting comparison of the regard in which the men and their theatres were held is provided in Ireland's *Records of the New York Stage*, vol. 2, pp. 489–91, concerning Simpson's retirement and death, and pp. 521–6, concerning Hamblin's accession to management of the Park and its burning.

61. For the Park's elite campaign, see Hewitt's "'King Stephen'"; for Hamblin's marketing the Bowery as "the nursery of native talent," see the *New York American*, 17–18 October 1831, and the *New York Gazette*, 24 September 1832; and see Odell, *Annals*, vol. 3, pp. 628–9. A comparison of the repertories of these theatres can be pursued via Litto, "Edmund Simpson of the Park," and Shank, "Bowery Theatre," or the information given for the Bowery and Park in Durham, *American Theatre Companies*. Mott notes of antebellum periodicals (*History of American Magazines*, p. 452) that "the violent political contests of the times . . . neighbor with poetry, art criticism, the familiar essay, and the short story," and were often as partisan. Trollope, *Domestic Manners of the Americans*, p. 340; the *Spirit of the Times*, 14 April 1832 and 3 January 1835; the *Mirror*, 15 March 1835. The *Mirror* again confirmed (20 August 1836) the Bowery's fashionable audience – a result, it speculated, of producing new plays.

62. For the *New York Mirror* on taste and the Park, see the 12 April 1828 number. "Puffing" played a role in the contradictory receptions of these theatres; see, for example, the 10 October 1833 *Mirror;* my entry in Durham, *American Theatre Companies*, for Gilfert's use of a press agent in the Bowery's early years; and Brown, *History of the New York Stage*, vol. 1, p. 105. On Fay's and Morris's novels, see my "Theatre and Narrative Fiction," and Mott, *History of American Magazines*, pp. 320–30. For Fay's profit, see the 5 March 1836 *Mirror* and the 27 February 1836 *Spirit of the Times*.

3. Spaces of Legitimation

1. The characterization of the disorder of the antebellum decades paraphrases the titles of some leading studies of it, chiefly: Theodore Hammett, "Two Mobs of Jacksonian Boston: Ideology and Interest," *Journal of American History* 62, 4 (March 1976): 845–68; Paul O. Weinbaum, *Mobs and Demagogues: The New York Response to Collective Violence in the Early Nineteenth Century* (Ann Arbor: UMI Press, 1977); Michael Feldberg, *The Turbulent Era: Riot and Disorder in Jacksonian America* (New York: Oxford U.P., 1980); Paul Gilje, "The Baltimore Riots of 1812 and the Breakdown of the Anglo-American Mob Tradition," *Journal of Social History* 13, 4 (Summer 1980): 547–64, and his *The Road to Mobocracy: Popular Disorder in New York City, 1763–1834* (Chapel Hill: U. of North Carolina Press, 1987). For theatre riots, see: David Grimsted, "Rioting in Its Jacksonian Setting," *American Historical Review* 77, 2 (April 1972): 361–97; and Bruce A. McConachie, "'The Theatre of the Mob': Apocalyptic Melodrama and Preindustrial Riots in Antebellum New York," in *Theatre for Working Class Audiences in the United States, 1830–1980*, eds. McConachie and Daniel Friedman (Westport, Conn.: Greenwood, 1985), pp. 17–46. The quote is from Eric H. Monkkonen, *Police in Urban America, 1860–1920* (Cambridge: Cambridge U.P., 1981), p. 10.

2. For symbolic order and social multiplicity, see Mary P. Ryan, *Women in Public: Between Banners and Ballots, 1825–1880* (Baltimore: Johns Hopkins U.P., 1990), pp. 74–5. Ryan speaks of the "mental maps" created by popular works such as those by Junius Brown, George Foster, and authors and journals referenced in Chapter 2. Philip Fisher discusses commanding myths in "American Literary and Cultural Studies Since the Civil War," in *Redrawing the Boundaries: The Transformation of English and American Literary Studies*, ed. Stephen Greenblatt and Giles Gunn (New York: MLAA, 1992), pp. 232–50. For "social control," see Lawrence F. Kohl, "The Concept of Social Control and the History of Jacksonian America," *Journal of the Early Republic* 5, 1 (Spring 1985): 21–34. Kohl points out that the motives of antebellum reformers are usually overdefined – seen as altruistic on one side and self-serving and repressive on the other (e.g., temperance and abolition) – whereas reformers and their targets often shared social and antielitist assumptions and aspirations (p. 29). Similarly, reform targets might accept, reject, or internalize reform goals, modifying them in the process (pp. 32–3). For recent discussions and presentations of paradigms in performance and history, see Thomas Postlewait, "History, Hermeneutics, and Narrativity," in *Critical Theory and Performance*, eds. Janelle G. Reinelt and Joseph R. Roach (Ann Arbor: U. of Michigan Press, 1992), pp. 356–68; and Marvin Carlson, *Theories of Theatre*, exp. ed. (Ithaca: Cornell U.P., 1993), pp. 505–40.

3. For the Athenaeum, see Ronald Story, "Class and Culture in Boston: The Athenaeum, 1807–1860," *American Quarterly* 27, 2 (May 1975): 178–99. For married women's property acts, see Norma Basch, *In the Eyes of the Law: Women, Marriage, and Property in Nineteenth-Century New York* (Ithaca: Cornell U.P., 1982), esp. pp. 27–8, 226–30. Basch points out that antebellum innovations such as life insurance, savings banks, and corporate stockholding among women added di-

mensions to the classic problem of women's property wasted or mortgaged by men. For marketplace analogies with associationalism, see Thomas L. Haskell, "Capitalism and the Origins of the Humanitarian Sensibility," *American Historical Review* 90, 2 (April 1985): 339–61, and 90, 3 (June 1985): 547–66.

4. For the antebellum shift in marketing, see Faye E. Dudden, *Serving Women: Household Service in Nineteenth Century America* (Middletown, Conn.: Wesleyan U.P., 1983), p. 138. Mrs. Trollope describes men marketing in her *Domestic Manners of the Americans*, ed. Donald Smalley (New York: Vintage Books, 1960), p. 85: "It is the custom for the gentlemen to go to market at Cincinnati; the smartest men in the place, and those of the 'highest standing' do not scruple to leave their beds with the sun, six days in the week, and, prepared with a mighty basket, to sally forth in search of meat, butter, eggs, and vegetables. I have continually seen them returning with their weighty basket on one arm and an enormous ham depending from the other" (see sketch by Hervieu, opposite p. 41 in this edition). Marketing was an important task and does not appear to have been delegated to servants or home delivery in these years. For the increase in activities pitched to female audiences, see Ryan, *Women in Public*, pp. 76–84. For dining habits, see Haswell, cited in George C. D. Odell, *Annals of the New York Stage* (New York: Columbia U.P., 1928), vol. 3, p. 474; and Richard B. Stott, *Workers in the Metropolis: Class, Ethnicity, and Youth in Antebellum New York City* (Ithaca: Cornell U.P., 1990), p. 202, linking boarding, transportation, and workers who returned home for lunch, the biggest meal of their day. For the equitable sharing of the streets, see Susan G. Davis, *Parades and Power: Street Theatre in Nineteenth-Century Philadelphia* (Philadelphia: Temple U.P., 1986), p. 33. For Lydia Maria Child, see her *Letters from New-York: Second Series* (New York: Charles S. Francis, 1845), p. 171.

5. Contraceptive information, practices, and devices, and abortion and sodomy prosecutions are discussed in John D'Emilio and Estelle Freedman, *Intimate Matters: A History of Sexuality in America* (New York: Harper & Row, 1988), pp. 59–66, 121–3. They point out that prosecutions for abortion were few (thirty-two trials in Massachusetts between 1849 and 1857), convictions fewer (none in the Massachusetts cases). Attitudes toward sexuality are discussed on pp. 70–1. The conceptualization of these in antebellum America is also a text in: Carroll Smith-Rosenberg, *Disorderly Conduct: Visions of Gender in Victorian America* (New York: Alfred A. Knopf, 1985), see pp. 53–164 for these decades; Mary Jacobus, Evelyn Fox Keller, and Sally Shuttlesworth, eds., *Body Politics: Women and the Discourses of Science* (New York: Routledge, 1990), see esp. pp. 11–68; John S. Haller and Robin M. Haller, *The Physician and Sexuality in Victorian America* (Urbana: U. of Illinois Press, 1974); Kathy Peiss and Christina Simmons, eds., *Passion and Power: Sexuality in History* (Philadelphia: Temple U.P., 1989), which skirts the antebellum decades, but see in that volume Marybeth H. Arnold, "'The Life of a Citizen in the Hands of a Woman': Sexual Assault in New York City, 1790–1820," pp. 35–56. Also relevant are *Meanings for Manhood: Constructions of Masculinity in Victorian America*, ed. Mark C. Carnes and Clyde Griffen, esp. the essays pp. 9–95; and Peter Gay's *The Bourgeois Experience: Victoria to*

Freud, 2 vols. (New York: Oxford U.P., 1984, 1986). A useful bibliography of studies (to the early 1980s) of both Britain and America in the nineteenth century is provided by John Maynard, "The Worlds of Victorian Sensuality: Work in Progress," in *Sexuality and Victorian Literature*, ed. Don R. Cox (Knoxville: U. of Tennessee Press, 1984), pp. 251–65.

6. Cautionary sex literature from the antebellum decades is cited below in nn. 7–8; n. 7 references antebellum assumptions about desire and health; on romance, see D'Emilio and Freedman, *Intimate Matters*, p. 84. Some of the historiographical stakes in the discourses of gender and sexuality are considered by William H. Sewell in his "Review of Joan Wallach Scott's *Gender and the Politics of History*," *History and Theory* 29, 1 (February 1990): 71–82. Gender and sexuality research concerning antebellum America reflects many of the conceptual changes that have swept historiography in the past twenty-five years (see, e.g., "Class" in Chapter 2); yet historical practice tends to read the antebellum years as prologue to the Victorian "repression" of the later nineteenth century, which helps keep the discourse tied to totalizing and evolutionary theory.

7. Heroic purges were still routine in the antebellum pharmacopoeia, surgeries were performed upon women to curb their sexual appetites, and the folk belief that sex with a virgin would cure syphillis remained current. For women and science, see n. 5 above, esp. Jacobus et al., *Body Politics*. For diet and medicine, see Stephen Nissenbaum, *Sex, Diet, and Debility in Jacksonian America: Sylvester Graham and Health Reform* (Westport, Conn.: Greenwood Press, 1980); and Jayme A. Sokolow, *Eros and Modernization: Sylvester Graham, Health Reform, and the Origins of Victorian Sexuality in America* (Cranberry, N.J.: Associated University Presses, 1983). For the folk belief concerning venereal disease – a belief still held by U.S. subcultures in the twentieth century – see Anthony E. Simpson, "Vulnerability and the Age of Female Consent: Legal Innovation and Its Effect on Prosecutions for Rape in Eighteenth Century London," in *Sexual Underworlds of the Enlightenment*, ed. G. S. Rousseau and Roy Porter (Chapel Hill: U. of North Carolina Press, 1988), pp. 192–6, and n. 54 on pp. 203–4 (see also, in this context, Arnold, "Life of a Citizen"); Simpson and Arnold connect this belief to child-rape cases in England between 1730 and 1830.

   The Graham diet did not produce a society of vegetarians, but it is cited as instrumental in the drop in alcohol and meat consumption (178 lbs. of the latter was an annual household average in 1830); moreover, Graham's regimen was cheap, though heavy eating persisted throughout the century (see Sokolow, *Eros and Modernization*, pp. 119–21; Dudden, *Serving Women*, p. 133). The quote is from Nissenboum, p. 142. Sokolow suggests control (probably abstinence) played a role in the drop in both premarital and marital U.S. birth rates in the nineteenth century (pp. 23–9). For Grahamite advocates, see Nissenbaum, *Sex, Diet, and Debility*, p. 28; and Sokolow, pp. 81–2.

8. For Graham on sex, see Nissenbaum, *Sex, Diet, and Debility*, p. 32, and Graham's *Lectures to Young Men on Chastity* (Providence, R.I.: Weeden & Cory, 1834). Cautionary sex literature prior to 1830 addressed masturbation (an address by Cotton Mather in 1723 and the anonymous *Onania* of 1724 offer two exam-

ples) and adultery (e.g., Parson Wadsworth's sermon of 1716). For the increase
in publications about sex on a number of fronts after 1830 (e.g., Robert Dale
Owen's *Moral Physiology* [1829] and Charles Knowlton's *Fruits of Philosophy*
[1832] on birth control) – an increase perhaps spurred by cheap printing and the
creation of a readership – see Nissenbaum, pp. 28–9, and Sokolow, *Eros and Modernization*, pp. 89–95. For prescriptions concerning how much intercourse het-
erosexuals should undertake, see Russell T. Troll, *Sexual Physiology: A Scientific
and Popular Exposition of the Fundamental Problems in Sociology* (New York: Miller, Wood, & Co., 1866), p. 295 for the quote. Mary Nichols, a Grahamite, lectured for the diet and against lacing, and considered sex for women "permiss-
able twelve times a year if all other indications were positive" (Sokolow, pp. 132–
3, also for a discussion of Noyes and other "free love" communities). Tappan's
connection to self-improvement generally is drawn in T. J. Jackson Lears, *No
Place of Grace: Antimodernism and the Transformation of American Culture, 1880–
1920* (New York: Pantheon Books, 1981), p. 72. Dudden argues (*Serving Women*,
p. 141) that water cures made bathing more popular in the 1840s and 1850s, although we do not know how that translated into the frequency of changing
clothes, or into cleanliness as a spur to sexual activity.

9. For epidemics, see Sokolow, *Eros and Modernization*, p. 168, and Robert Ernst,
Immigrant Life in New York City, 1825–1863 (New York: Columbia U. / King's
Crown Press, 1949), pp. 22–3, 52–5. Epidemics ravaged Amerindian populations,
particularly during removal; for accounts, see Rogin, *Fathers and Children;* and
Ronald N. Satz, *American Indian Policy in the Jacksonian Era* (Lincoln: U. of
Nebraska Press, 1975). Anita Levy in *Other Women: The Writing of Class, Race,
and Gender, 1832–1898* (Princeton: Princeton U.P., 1991), p. 37, argues the cholera
epidemic in Manchester in 1832 was considered a visitation upon the poor for
their bad habits (inebriety, uncleanliness, idleness, sexuality). So, too, poverty
and slums could be personalized at the expense of attending to the political or
economic factors causing them (p. 40). For the general state of knowledge about
disease in the nineteenth century, see George Rosen, "Disease, Debility, and
Death," in vol. 2 of *The Victorian City*, ed. H. J. Dyos and Michael Wolff (London: Routledge & Kegan Paul, 1973), pp. 625–67; statistics for epidemics in
London are on pp. 634–6. The health reform text posited self-improvement rather than social control as the key to well-being (Sokolow, pp. 177–8). Central contemporaneous texts in the sex–health debate are Henry Mayhew's 1861–2 *London
Labour and the London Poor* (rpt. New York: Dover, 1968); and William Sanger's
The History of Prostitution: Its Extent, Causes and Effects Throughout the World
(1859; New York: Medical Publishing Co., 1921). See also Edward Crapsey, *The
Nether Side of New York; or, The Vice, Crime, and Poverty of the Great Metropolis* (New York: Sheldon & Co., 1872). All of these proceed through the "scientific" accumulation of statistics. Outlawing single and working women as a "species
of sexual misconduct" in nineteenth-century England is a text in Levy's *Other
Women* (pp. 42–5, 47), where she also discusses the Contagious Disease Acts and
their legislating of prostitutes and poor women (pp. 45–6).

10. The quote is from Timothy J. Gilfoyle, "City of Eros: New York City, Prostitution, and the Commercialization of Sex, 1790–1920," Ph.D. diss. (Columbia,

1987), pp. 22–3 (although published under the same title by W. W. Norton in 1992, the dissertation is cited here).

11. Casual prostitution is discussed by both Gilfoyle ("City of Eros," p. 25) and Christine Stansell, *City of Women: Sex and Class in New York, 1789–1860* (New York: Alfred A. Knopf, 1986), p. 176. Gilfoyle discusses estimates of the number of prostitutes in New York on pp. 26–30, and see his Table 1 (p. 26) and n. 19 (p. 35). His figures are as follows:

Decade	Range
1830–9	1,850 – 3,700
1840–9	3,500 – 7,000
1850–9	6,100 – 12,200
1860–9	6,500 – 13,000

Ryan points out (*Women in Public*, p. 110) that, given Gilfoyle's data, Sanger's 1859 *History of Prostitution*, an accounting of six thousand prostitutes at work in New York City, is probably too conservative. For the geography of New York's brothels and a profile of their landlords, see Gilfoyle's dissertation chapter entitled "Sexual Geography of New York, 1790–1860," pp. 37–96. The West Wards had no theatres; the sixth ward, which had many brothels, had several theatres. Brothels in other antebellum cities may also have been scattered in these decades; at least historians note the jumble of functions and residences (see Ryan, *Women in Public*, e.g., pp. 60–1) in ways hostile to modern zoning sensibilities, though not untypical even today of American cities. Crapsey considered the high amount of crime and prostitution in Five Points to be due to the number of immigrants, only the worst of whom, he held, stayed in New York (*Nether Side of New York*, p. 7).

12. For Morse, see his "City Boarding Houses," *Young Men's Magazine* (September 1857): 199; for Arthur Tappan, see "Class" in Chapter 2 and the accompanying n. 48. For cautionary literature, see nn. 7, 8 above; for etiquette and advice books, see "Class" in Chapter 2, and Barbara Ehrenreich and Dierdre English, *For Her Own Good: 150 Years of the Experts' Advice to Women* (Garden City, N.Y.: Doubleday, 1978). For the age of consent, see Arnold, "Life of a Citizen," p. 42 (U.S.); Simpson, "Vulnerability," pp. 186–91 (England); and Stansell, *City of Women*, pp. 257–78, and Gilfoyle, "City of Eros," p. 181 (both New York City). Based upon a shift in language in indictments, Arnold assumes an 1813 rise in consent age to 14 for women but cannot confirm this from the New York legal code (see her n. 29, pp. 54–5). For the onset of menarche, see Peter Laslett, *The World We Have Lost Further Explored*, rev. ed. (New York: Charles Scribner's Sons, 1984), p. 84. In addition to the horror of virgins debauched as a cure for venereal disease, child prostitutes were recruited as not likely to become pregnant by the trade. On domestic service as an entree to rape, seduction, venereal disease, and prostitution, see Simpson for England, p. 198. Sanger's *History of Prostitution* implicates service, and for other U.S. sources making the link, see Dudden, *Serving Women*, and Stansell's *City of Women*. The ages of prostitutes are taken in Sanger's report, and see Gilfoyle, pp. 164–7. An interesting analysis

of Parent-Duchâtelet's harrowing views of prostitutes as sewers is provided in Charles Bernheimer, *Figures of Ill Repute: Representing Prostitution in Nineteenth-Century France,* chap. 1 (Cambridge: Harvard U.P., 1989).

13. The "prostitutier" is the discourse of Claudia D. Johnson, "That Guilty Third Tier: Prostitution in Nineteenth-Century American Theatre," *American Quarterly* 27, 5 (December 1975): 575–84. The article was reprinted in *Victorian America,* ed. Daniel W. Howe (Philadelphia: U. of Pennsylvania Press, 1976), pp. 111–20, and it and its thesis have been widely reprised by historians in, for example, Stuart M. Blumin, *The Emergence of the Middle Class: Social Experience in the American City, 1760–1900* (Cambridge: Cambridge U.P., 1989); in Ryan, *Women in Public;* Peter G. Buckley, "To the Opera House: Culture and Society in New York City, 1820–1860," Ph.D. diss. (State Univ. of New York–Stony Brook, 1984); Gilfoyle, "City of Eros"; Stansell's *City of Women;* Sean Wilentz, *Chants Democratic: New York City and the Rise of the American Working Class, 1788–1850* (Oxford: Oxford U.P., 1984); McConachie, "'The Theatre of the Mob'"; and others. A compact version of issues raised by "that guilty third tier" is offered in my "Hustlers in the House: The Bowery Theatre as a Mode of Historical Information," in *The American Stage,* eds. Tice Miller and Ron Engle (Cambridge: Cambridge U.P., 1993), pp. 47–64. William Dunlap, *History of the American Theatre* (1832; New York: Burt Franklin, 1963), vol. 1, pp. 407–12, for the whole regulation text; the quoted passages are, respectively, pp. 407, 408, 408, 410. Dunlap never describes women as "prostitutes," a word he reserves for other vices.

14. Dunlap, *History of the American Theatre,* vol. 1, pp. 409, 411, 412, respectively.

15. The quotes from Dunlap, *History of the American Theatre,* vol. 1, are on pp. 408, 409–10, and 409, respectively. Buckley, "To the Opera House," p. 113, describes "a separate entrance from the street" for prostitutes but does not identify the theatre, unless he means us to understand it to be the one (the Park in 1822) depicted by Searle.

16. Noah M. Ludlow, *Dramatic Life as I Found It* (1880; rpt. New York: Benjamin Blom, 1966), pp. 478–9. Olive Logan, *Before the Footlights and Behind the Scenes* (Philadelphia: Parmelee & Co., 1870), pp. 537–43. George G. Foster, *New York by Gas-Light* (New York: DeWitt & Davenport, 1850), p. 88. For the quote regarding areas of assignation, see Bruce A. McConachie, *Melodramatic Formations: American Theatre and Society, 1820–1870* (Iowa City: U. of Iowa Press, 1992), p. 173.

17. Linda Mahood, *The Magdalens: Prostitution in the Nineteenth Century* (London: Routledge, 1990), p. 72; Stansell, *City of Women,* pp. 93–4. For the dress and manner of the Bowery G'hal, see "Work" in Chapter 2. Dickens thought the dress of even "fashionable" American women gaudy (*American Notes* [1842; rpt. London: Mandarin, 1991], p. 85). Dunlap, *History of the American Theatre,* speaks of the Federal Street Theatre and borrowed finery (vol. 1, pp. 409–10). Charles Haswell, *Reminiscences of an Octogenarian of the City of New York, 1816–1860* (New York: Harper & Bros., 1897), p. 362. For Ludlow's separate entrance, see his *Dramatic Life,* p. 477. *The Diary of George Templeton Strong,* ed. Allan Nevins and Milton Halsey Thomas (New York: Macmillan, 1952), vol. 2, pp. 455–6. The

patrician Strong was not entirely elated by the democratization of culture. Ryan's *Women in Public* devotes a chapter to prostitutes in three nineteenth-century American cities and includes many references to the theatre. Histories of locales and specific theatres often speak of separate seating for women (see, e.g., Odell, *Annals*, or Patricia C. Click, *The Spirit of the Times: Amusements in Nineteenth-Century Baltimore, Norfolk, and Richmond* [Charlottesville: U.P. of Virginia, 1989]).

18. On the conflation of working women with prostitutes, see Levy, *Other Women*, p. 46, and Mahood, *Magdalens*, pp. 72–4. Stansell, *City of Women*, p. 180. Wilentz extends the classist and sexist texts in the cause of proletarianizing the "prostitutier" at the Bowery Theatre in the 1830s, saying its presence brought "workingmen patrons an amenity [prostitutes] long available at respectable theatres" (*Chants Democratic*, p. 258).

19. Moreau de Saint-Méry, *Moreau de Saint-Méry's American Journey* [1793–8], · trans. Kenneth and Anna M. Roberts (Garden City, N.Y.: Doubleday & Co., 1947), p. 347. Joseph N. Ireland, *Records of the New York Stage from 1750 to 1860* (1866; rpt. New York: Benjamin Blom, 1966), vol. I, p. 29, quotes a playbill of 1 January 1759 from Cruger's Wharf Theatre in New York, stating: "The Doors for the Gallery will be opened at Four O'Clock, but the Pit and the Boxes, that Ladies may be well accommodated with seats – not till Five – and the Play begins precisely at Six." It is Johnson's reading that women seated with blacks must have been prostitutes ("That Guilty Third Tier," p. 581). I evaluate these arguments in "Hustlers in the House." For the Camp Street Theatre, see John S. Kendall, *The Golden Age of the New Orleans Theatre* (1952; rpt. New York: Greenwood Press, 1968), pp. 38–9.

20. The "guilty third tier" is sometimes called a box (McConachie, *Melodramatic Formations*, p. 173), which may be what Dunlap had in mind when he indicted the "scandalous practice of setting apart a portion of the boxes for this most disgusting display of shameless vice" (*History of the American Theatre*, vol. I, p. 409). The 18 July 1846 *Spirit of the Times* identifies it as a "third row." On the other hand, Patricia C. Click, *Spirit of the Times*, p. 36, cites "a row or two of front seats" set aside for unescorted women that "were especially coveted" by the fashionable. Johnson allies the gallery with the theatre saloon ("That Guilty Third Tier," p. 113), citing (via Barnard Hewitt) Washington Irving's Jonathan Oldstyle letters, published November 1802–January 1803, "which note that the gallery is kept 'in *excellent* order by the constables,' but later recommend that the upper tier have 'less grog and better constables.' Again there is no clear mention of the gallery's being given over to prostitutes and their customers, but, obviously, it was sufficiently rowdy to demand policing, which suggests that Irving left unsaid what Dunlap knew to be true, that the third tier was the domain of prostitutes." The groggery and the "whoreacracy" were frequently united in criticism of antebellum theatre, the aggregate of "vice" (see, e.g., the 18 July 1846 *Spirit of the Times*). Managers were accused of promoting the connection because the resulting bar trade made the third tier the "most valuable part of the house" (*Commercial Advertiser*, 15 March 1833). Not all theatres had third-floor saloons; some

third floors gave access to saloons or salons elsewhere in the house, while house police patrolled (however ineffectually) the whole theatre, which seems to be Irving's satirical view. He does not, it should be noted, discuss prostitutes or place them in the third-tier gallery.

For parquette seating, see Click, *Spirit of the Times*, p. 45; and McConachie, *Melodramatic Formations*, p. 173. Lavishly illustrated with pictures of female performers at work and play, John J. Jennings's *Theatrical and Circus Life; or, Secrets of the Stage, Green Room, and Sawdust Arena* (St. Louis: Historical Pub. Co., 1882) invites the nineteenth-century (male) reader to a reminiscence that, despite its occasional high moral tone, serves well as a guide to misbehavior, though hardly equal to the sexual guidebooks cited in the text. For Jennings on St. Louis theatre, see pp. 66–7; for Haswell, *Reminiscences*, p. 362. For other sightings of prostitutes in theatres, see Anna Cora Mowatt's *Autobiography of an Actress* (Boston: Ticknor, Reed, & Fields, 1854), p. 445, and Logan, *Before the Footlights*, pp. 33–5.

21. The Empire Theatre is referenced in Eric Trudgill, "Prostitution and Paterfamilias," in *Victorian City*, vol. 2, ed. Dyos and Wolff, p. 695. Contemporaries in the 1890s found its halls full of cruising prostitutes and clients, who had free admission to the theatre once the play was well under way. See n. 20 concerning the theatre saloon. George G. Foster, *New York Naked* (New York: DeWitt & Davenport, 1854), p. 145.

22. Reports like the *Sun's* were sauce for ministers who conflated playhouses and whorehouses. For one example among very many, see C. B. Parson's *The Pulpit and the Stage* (Nashville: Southern Methodist Pub. House, 1860), pp. 60–74, one of an upwelling of religious publications of which Mary P. Ryan speaks in her *Cradle of the Middle Class: The Family in Oneida County, New York, 1790–1865* (Cambridge: Cambridge U.P., 1981). Ludlow, *Dramatic Life*, p. 478. For the reform society report, see Gilfoyle, "City of Eros," p. 103.

23. For unescorted women in theatres, see Click, *Spirit of the Times*, pp. 35–6, but she also notes "infrequent" ads requiring women be escorted (p. 45). Sanger, *History of Prostitution*, p. 557; he later notes (p. 558), "Others of them [prostitutes] visit the third tier of such theatres as will admit them, and there exert their charms to secure conquest."

24. "Lovyer" and "DeKock" are in the New-York Historical Society; "Butt Ender's" contribution to erotic topography is held by Prof. Leo Hershkowitz of Queens College, City University of New York, who with Prof. Gilfoyle made many helpful suggestions and lent moral support to this then-embryonic project. The brothel–theatre data are in Gilfoyle, "City of Eros," p. 84.

25. For brothels advertising, see Gilfoyle, "City of Eros," p. 82; for the National, p. 105. The quotation regarding the Park joins material on pp. 82 and 107 of Gilfoyle, who cites "Butt Ender." Buckley notes a "third tier" was still operating in the Park when it burned in 1848 ("To the Opera House," p. 415).

26. The association of prostitution with gambling is drawn by Click, *Spirit of the Times*, pp. 60–7, who notes that upper-class gaming houses had bedrooms as well as food and drink. In addition to *Harper's*, Grant Thorburn, in his *The Life and Writings of Grant Thorburn* (New York: Edward Walker, 1852), reproves a theat-

rical acquaintance with the reflection that wherever Thorburn "had seen a play-house erected, there sprung up immediately around it a porter-house, a gambling-house, an oyster-house, and a house that perhaps was worse than any of them, and that the frequenters of the former were generally the supporters of the lat-ter" (p. 183). Trudgill suggests prostitution in London after midcentury migrat-ed away from theatres (p. 695), a pattern some see in America. Child, *Letters from New-York: Second Series,* p. 175. More than tolerating prostitutes, theatre managers were accused of giving them free or cut-price tickets (Trudgill, p. 695; Buckley, p. 114).

27. Gilfoyle, "City of Eros," p. 244. In addition to the sources already cited in this chapter, the following take up "disturbances," reform, and regulation in a vari-ety of antebellum contexts: Leonard Richards, *"Gentlemen of Property and Stand-ing": Anti-Abolition Mobs in Jacksonian America* (New York: Oxford U.P., 1970); Ronald G. Walters, *American Reformers, 1815–1860* (New York: Hill & Wang, 1978); John B. Jentz, "Artisans, Evangelicals, and the City: A Social History of Abolition and Labor Reform in Jacksonian New York," Ph.D. diss. (City Univ. of New York, 1977); William Stanton, *The Leopard's Spots: Scientific Attitudes Toward Race in America, 1815–1859* (Chicago: U. of Chicago Press, 1960); David Brion Davis, *The Slave Power Conspiracy and the Paranoid Style* (Baton Rouge: Louisiana State U.P., 1969); W. J. Rorabaugh, *The Alcoholic Republic: An Ameri-can Tradition* (New York: Oxford U.P., 1979); Ian R. Tyrrell, *Sobering Up: From Temperance to Prohibition in Antebellum America, 1800–1860* (Westport, Conn.: Greenwood, 1979); Brian Harrison, "Pubs," in *Victorian City,* vol. 1, ed. Dyos and Wolff, pp. 161–90; Paul E. Johnson, *A Shopkeeper's Millennium: Society and Revivals in Rochester, New York, 1815–1837* (New York: Hill & Wang, 1978); Paul Boyer, *Urban Masses and Moral Order in America, 1820–1920* (Cambridge, Mass.: Harvard U.P., 1978); Benjamin J. Klebaner, "Poverty and Its Relief in American Thought, 1815–1861," *Social Science Review* 38, 4 (December 1964): 382–99; Jay P. Dolan, *The Immigrant Church: New York's Irish and German Catholics, 1815–1865* (Baltimore: Johns Hopkins U.P., 1975); Carol Groneman-Pernicone, "The 'Bloody Ould Sixth': A Social Analysis of a New York City Working-Class Community in the Mid-Nineteenth Century," Ph.D. diss. (Univ. of Rochester, 1973); Edward Pessen, *Riches, Class, and Power before the Civil War* (Lexington, Mass.: D. C. Heath & Co., 1973); and David J. Rothman, *The Discovery of the Asylum: Social Order and Disorder in the New Republic,* rev. ed. (Boston: Little, Brown & Co., 1990).

28. "Riot" data vary by date, locale, and type of disturbance; as a result, authorities' totals often disagree. Weinbaum takes the national figure of seventy-seven includ-ing New York City from *Niles' Weekly Register,* finding the New York newspa-pers' estimates of seventy-nine riots nationwide between 1833 and 1835 *excluding* New York City too high (*Mobs and Demagogues,* p. 69, n. 1). That fifty-two riots were logged for New York between 1833 and 1837 is Buckley's compilation ("To the Opera House," p. 181). Richards, also drawing from *Niles' Weekly Register,* logs sixty-four disturbances between 1830 and 1850, with the heaviest concentra-tion between 1834 and 1844 (*"Gentlemen,"* p. 12). He breaks abolition-related dis-

turbances down by decades, regions, and urban vs. rural. The figure of twenty-five theatre riots I take from both Gilje's meticulous list (*Road to Mobocracy*, Table 2, p. 249) of twenty-one disturbances of all types (tavern fights, the Anderson and Farren crowd actions, etc.) between November 1825 and July 1834, to which are added four actor incidents cited by Buckley between the Farren "riot" (July 1834) and the Astor Place riot (pp. 192–3). The total number of theatre disturbances of all kinds that came before a judge in New York City or nationwide between 1825 and 1860 is at present unknown. The kinds of disorders are logged by Gilje; for the judge's rebuke, see the 15 April 1822 *National Advocate*.

29. Press influence forms a wide text in Weinbaum, *Mobs and Demagogues*, see esp. pp. 27–38, and 41–8 for the quote concerning the *Gazette*. Sensationalism is the text of Thomas Boyle's study of the Victorian press and sensation novel, *Black Swine in the Sewers of Hampstead: Beneath the Surface of Victorian Sensationalism* (New York: Viking, 1989). The definition of sensation, quoted by Boyle (p. 187), is from the *Old English Dictionary* (1779).

30. Buckley says, "By 1838, the popular theatre of the Bowery was an adjunct to the political stage, not just in the content of the plays themselves, but in the act of performance" ("To the Opera House," p. 44). The performance mode is, to me, the telling thing; it is discussed in the context of power not contained by the political in Davis, *Parades and Power*, p. 13. The antebellum extension of causal sequences to varied movements and group actions is discussed in Haskell, "Capitalism," p. 566. Weinbaum argues contemporary histories overemphasize the eight 1833–5 riots pitting mobs against organizations or authorities in that antebellumites were more concerned about demogogues than riots (*Mobs and Demagogues*, p. 66). Ordinary life as news is taken up by Michael Schudson, *Discovering the News: A Social History of American Newspapers* (New York: Basic Books, 1978), pp. 27–30. The rapid growth of publications is suggested by his figures (p. 13): 1830 – 650 weeklies, 65 dailies nationwide, roughly seventy-eight thousand daily circulation; 1840 – 1,141 weeklies, 138 dailies nationwide, roughly three hundred thousand circulation. The loss of the power of presence on the part of officials is taken up in Weinbaum, p. 119. Gilje (*Road to Mobocracy*, pp. 273–4) considers the absence of an economic spur to good behavior, and elsewhere makes the point that riots ceased to represent the actions of a whole community in the early nineteenth century, becoming instead actions by factions against specific targets ("Baltimore Riots of 1812," p. 557).

31. For types of parading, see Ryan's *Women in Public*, chap. 1; and, of course, Davis, *Parades and Power* (parade types and the relationship between performers and audience are discussed on pp. 157–9). For types of "mob" action, see Weinbaum, *Mobs and Demagogues;* Feldberg, *Turbulent Era*, pp. 78–80; and Gilje's *Road to Mobocracy*.

32. For the police-control argument, see Feldberg, *Turbulent Era*, p. 114. The transition from a constable-watch system to uniformed police took from 1838 to 1859 in Boston, 1843 to 1853 in New York, and 1848 to 1859 in Cincinnati, and was not accomplished in Philadelphia until 1854. See Monkkonen, *Police in Urban Amer-*

ica, p. 42; and Wilentz, *Chants Democratic*, p. 322. New York and London are compared in Wilber R. Miller, *Cops and Bobbies: Police Authority in New York and London, 1830–1870* (Chicago: U. of Chicago Press, 1973). For consensus and voluntary compliance, see Gilje, *Road to Mobocracy*, p. 229; for Brownson and the transcendentalists, see "The Town" in Chapter 1. The texts of both *The Drunkard* and Aiken's *Uncle Tom's Cabin* are provided, with useful commentary, in *Dramas from the American Theatre, 1762–1909*, ed. Richard Moody (Boston: Houghton Mifflin, 1966); subsequent citations of the play texts refer to this edition.

33. For the nature of the tavern, see Harrison, "Pubs," p. 172; Kym S. Rice, *Early American Taverns: For the Entertainment of Friends and Strangers* (Chicago: Regnery Gateway & Fraunces Tavern Museum, 1983); and Jon M. Kingsdale, "The 'Poor Man's Club': Social Functions of the Urban Working-Class Saloon," *American Quarterly* 25, 4 (October 1973): 472–89. For drink in America generally, see Rorabaugh, *Alcoholic Republic;* for the antebellum decades particularly, see Tyrrell, *Sobering Up*. Temperance is also taken up by Wilentz, *Chants Democratic*, especially the Washingtonians, for which see also Paul Johnson, *Shopkeeper's Millennium*, p. 195 (wherein see pp. 5–6 for revivals). See Tyrrell, p. 9, for three-phase temperance, and pp. 20–6 for market changes.

34. For early drinking habits, see Tyrrell, *Sobering Up*, pp. 16–18; and Rorabaugh, *Alcoholic Republic*, pp. 5–21. For reduced consumption, see Tyrrell, p. 137, and charts 1.1 and 1.2 and text in Rorabaugh, pp. 8–10. For voluntary sobering, see Tyrrell, p. 12. Jeffrey D. Mason, *Melodrama and the Myth of America* (Bloomington: Indiana U.P., 1993) extends his consideration of alcohol consumption into the twentieth century and follows these sources in settling on two gallons per capita as the national norm for annual alcohol consumption (see his chap. 3, pp. 62–3, and nn. 4 and 10 to this material). Licensing laws were enacted in smaller antebellum cities to control where alcohol was sold, largely a move against neighborhood groceries and places of congregation selling liquor (see Johnson, *Shopkeeper's Millennium*, pp. 48–60). For print and women, see Tyrrell, pp. 67–8, and Ryan's discussion in *Women in Public*. For organizations for young men, see Horlick, *Country Boys and Merchant Princes*, pp. 243–63; for clubs see Click, *Spirit of the Times*, pp. 77–82. For the temperance advancement text, see Tyrrell, pp. 319–20; Johnson's *Shopkeeper's Millennium;* Ryan's *Cradle of the Middle Class;* and the advice books cited in Chapter 2.

35. See John W. Frick, "'He Drank from the Poisoned Cup': Theatre, Culture, and Temperance in Antebellum America," *Journal of American Drama and Theatre* 4, 2 (Spring 1992): 25, for entertainments; for entertainment and instruction linked, see Click, *Spirit of the Times*, pp. 22–9. For the national danger, see Johnson, *Shopkeeper's Millennium*, p. 140; for lifetime control agendas, see Ryan, *Cradle of the Middle Class*, and the discussion of class in Chapter 2.

36. For the performance history of the play, moral lectures, and sacred music, see Moody's introduction, *Dramas from the American Theatre*, pp. 277–80; and Walter J. Meserve, *Heralds of Promise: The Drama of the American People in the Age*

of Jackson, 1829–1849 (Westport, Conn.: Greenwood 1986), pp. 152–3. Meserve and Moody give different dates for the Boston Museum opening and different lengths for its run. For *The Drunkard*'s impact on the long run, see Barnard Hewitt, *Theatre U.S.A.* (New York: McGraw–Hill, 1959), p. 160. Meserve discusses Smith's history in the theatre. For the Boston Museum, see my entry in *American Theatre Companies, 1749–1887,* ed. Weldon B. Durham (Westport, Conn.: Greenwood, 1986).

37. For burlesques and temperance companies, see Moody, *Dramas from the American Theatre.* Tyrrell observes of antitemperance that the desire to preserve individual freedom was wedded to a concern for retaining traditional status (*Sobering Up,* p. 108). The connection between politics and drink makes this interplay particularly evident. For the "nothing to be done" response, see Tyrrell, pp. 129–30; it is a reaction similar to the one ignoring the socioeconomic conditions that affected working women and produced prostitution. Romance distances sex in *The Drunkard,* as in the novels read by the play's comic old maid, Miss Spindle (I.iii, p. 285). Steven Marcus observes in *The Other Victorians: A Study of Pornography in Mid-Nineteenth Century England* (New York: Basic Books / Bantam, 1966), p. 286, that "the growth of pornography was one of the results" of processes of isolation, distancing, and denial, "as, in another context, was the development of modern romantic love."

38. For drinking parsons, see II.ii, p. 291; this practice in the antebellum decades is discussed by Tyrrell, *Sobering Up,* p. 17. For the training of clerks, see Horlick, *Country Boys and Merchant Princes,* pp. 73–9. The system began to break down at midcentury, when "country boys" as well as "merchant princes" were put to clerking. That this is the field that took up the excess of artisanal labor is evident in Ryan's *Cradle of the Middle Class* and Johnson's *Shopkeeper's Millennium,* and see Chapter 2. For advice manuals, heavily referenced in that chapter as well, see Horlick, pp. 151–7. Horlick considers voluntary associations like the YMCA and Mercantile Library Association to be controlling but mediating (pp. 243–66). For the estimate of clerks in New York, see p. 257 in Horlick; for Charles Tracy, the YMCA official, p. 263.

39. Edward's rejection of forgery – remarkably coherent, given advanced alcoholism – is in III.i, p. 296. According to Johnson, *Shopkeeper's Millennium,* the citizens of Rochester inveighed endlessly against disturbances: against the theatre in 1828 for keeping residents awake (p. 54), against the circus and theatres being too near businesses or homes (pp. 114–15), against drinking on Sundays (pp. 103–6). Indeed, William says (III.v, p. 300), "Well, if this New York isn't the awfullest place for noise." For the washing wife, see II.ii, p. 297 (it is a sneer of Miss Spindle's: "Sank so far as to take in washing"); for poverty, II.v, pp. 298–9 – the fall is rapid. Rencelaw's rescue is IV.i, pp. 391–2. For the restoration of the Ophelia-like maiden Agnes, the Yankee William's sister, see V.i, pp. 305–6. The final tableau is detailed on p. 307.

40. For William's rescue of Mary from Cribbs (by chance, of course), III.v, pp. 299–300. For Rencelaw's detection, IV.iii, pp. 303–4 (the scene is Broadway, with a view of Barnum's Museum). Living and dying a villain is Cribbs's last line,

V.ii, p. 307. For the revival agenda, see Johnson, *Shopkeeper's Millennium*, pp. 138–41. *The Drunkard* achieves some of its effects with metaphoric associations: Arden = paradise; Cribbs = steals / thieves' houses; Spindle = distaff, spinster.

41. See V.i, p. 303, for the quote.

42. Considerable controversy is evident in *Uncle Tom's Cabin* scholarship. For several views and a market capital analysis of the Conway and Aiken dramatizations, see Bruce A. McConachie, "Out of the Kitchen and Into the Marketplace: Normalizing *Uncle Tom's Cabin* for the Antebellum Stage," *Journal of American Drama and Theatre* 3, 1 (Winter 1991): 5–28. For analysis of the play in the context of abolition, see Mason, *Melodrama and the Myth of America*, chap. 4; for a proletarian reading, see Eric Lott, *Love and Theft: Blackface Minstrelsy and the American Working Class* (New York: Oxford U.P., 1993), chap. 8.

43. Mrs. Stowe's letter to temperance singer Asa Hutchinson is reprinted in Moody's introduction to the play, *Dramas from the American Theatre*, p. 350. For Catherine Beecher, and for her and Stowe's book, see Chapter 2, n. 38, and the related text.

44. The production history of Aiken's *Uncle Tom's Cabin* is provided by Moody, *Dramas from the American Theatre* (whence come all subsequent citations of the play text); for *Tom* commodifications, see Daniel C. Gerould's introduction to his anthology *American Melodrama* (New York: PAJ Publications, 1983), p. 14.

45. McConachie, "Out of the Kitchen"; Stowe is quoted on p. 9. For the humanitarian sensibility, see Haskell, "Capitalism." George Harris's lines are from Aiken's play text, I.i, pp. 360–1. On work and class in the play, see Lott, *Love and Theft*, pp. 232–3. For the conflation of cause with cure, see Klebaner, "Poverty and Its Relief" (p. 396 for charity to the old, young, and ill). McConachie's article explores the vitiation of Stowe's women in both Aiken's and Conway's dramatizations of her novel.

46. For Phineas Fletcher, the Ohio roarer, see I.iv, p. 364. For Ophelia's racism, see II.ii, pp. 368–9, and III.i, p. 377. For Topsy on color, see II.iv, p. 373. The connection between slave catchers and drink is drawn through Loker, I.iv, p. 365, and in St. Clare's death as the result of a barroom brawl, IV.iii, p. 383.

47. Elizabeth Ammons's positioning of Uncle Tom as the heroine of Stowe's novel in "Heroines in *Uncle Tom's Cabin*," in her edition of *Critical Essays on Harriet Beecher Stowe* (Boston: G. K. Hall, 1980), p. 160, "feminizes" Tom as a compendium of womanly virtues. This stance is problematic when transferred from the novel to the stage, given the need for heroines in melodrama to uphold the right (see McConachie's "Out of the Kitchen" and my "The Second Face of the Idol: Women in Melodrama," in *Women in American Theatre*, ed. Helen Krich Chinoy and Linda Walsh Jenkins (New York: Crown, 1981), pp. 238–43. This they may do in words rather than fistfights, but they must *act* (not just suffer). On Legree and his mother, see VI.iii, pp. 393–4.

48. For Foucault on discourse, see *The History of Sexuality*, trans. Robert Hurley (New York: Vintage, 1980), vol. 1, pp. 102, 101, respectively, for the quotes. Sidney Kaplan observes in "The Portrayal of the Negro in American Art" (cited in Karen M. Adams, "The Black Image in the Paintings of William Sidney Mount,"

American Art Journal 7, 2 [November 1975]: 54) that "there is a way of killing a stereotype without rejuvenating the man." For George Harris on liberty and Indian kidnappers, see II.iii, p. 371.

49. Henry Louis Gates, in his essay "African American Criticism" (in *Redrawing the Boundaries*, ed. Greenblatt and Gunn, pp. 303–19), suggests the theoretical complexity of critical exchanges intersecting race. These complexities are evident in the analyses of *Uncle Tom's Cabin* in Lott's *Love and Theft* and Mason's *Melodrama and the Myth of America*, and particularly in McConachie's comparisons of dramatic texts and Stowe's novel in his "Out of the Kitchen."

50. For New York City departments, see Charles Burr Todd, "Telegraphs and Railroads, and Their Impulse to Commerce, 1847–1855," in *The Memorial History of the City of New-York from Its First Settlement to the Year 1892,* ed. James Grant Wilson (New York: New-York History Co., 1893), vol. 3, p. 430. For associations and "political" control by elites, see Pessen, *Riches, Class, and Power,* pp. 277–8, 284–7; for voluntary groups as church and state replacements, see Boyer, *Urban Masses,* pp. 8–15, and on aid versus asylums, p. 96. Asylums form the central text in Rothman's *Discovery of the Asylum,* which sees them as attempts to create ideal colonial communities using the methods of industrialism (p. 154). A useful chart of urban services is provided by Richard B. Calhoun, "From Community to Metropolis: Fire Protection in New York City, 1790–1875," Ph.D. diss. (Columbia U., 1973), table 1, p. 13:

City	Bd. of Health	Police	Fire	Water Supply
New York	1805	1845	1865	1836
Boston	1823	1838	1837	1848
Philadelphia	1806	1830	1870	1801
Baltimore	1797	1857	1858	1854
Chicago	1867	1861	1858	1861
Cincinnati	1865	1859	1853	1839
St. Louis	—	1846	1857	1835

51. For charity volunteers as neighbors of the poor, see Weinbaum, *Mobs and Demagogues,* pp. 134–45. For Rochester and Utica, respectively, see Johnson's *Shopkeeper's Millennium* and Ryan's *Cradle of the Middle Class.* For middle-class values imposed on working women, see Mahood, *Magdalens,* pp. 76–86. For fire companies, see Calhoun, "From Community to Metropolis"; Stephen F. Ginsberg, "The History of Fire Protection in New York City, 1800–1842," Ph.D. diss. (New York U., 1968); and Bruce Laurie, "Fire Companies and Gangs in Southwark: The 1840s," in *The Peoples of Philadelphia: A History of Ethnic Groups and Lower-Class Life, 1790–1940,* ed. Allen F. Davis and Mark H. Haller (Philadelphia: Temple U.P., 1973), pp. 71–87. Despite fire losses averaging $1,582,000 annually in New York City between 1841 and 1865, a professional fire force was not introduced until 1865 (Calhoun, p. 52). Both Ginsberg and Calhoun make clear, despite intimations to the contrary by Fanny Kemble (*Journal,* 2 vols. [London: John Murray, 1835], vol. 1, p. 76) and Charles H. Haswell (*Reminiscences,* pp.

145–6) that, from at least the 1830s, New York firemen were not the "sons of the gentlemen" of the city, a point Laurie affirms for Philadelphia (pp. 75–6). For an assessment of Five Points, see Groneman-Pernicone, "'Bloody Ould Sixth,'" pp. 200–7. On the city as a different kind of order, see Ryan, *Women in Public*, p. 175. See Ernst for ethnic fire and police (*Immigrant Life*, pp. 163–5), Calhoun for waiting lists to join fire companies (pp. 123–6, 148).

52. For assimilation in the fire department, for example – close to half of which was Irish by 1860 – see Calhoun, "From Community to Metropolis," tables on pp. 142, 144. Ryan, *Women in Public*, pp. 135–41; for Catholic volunteerism, see Dolan, *Immigrant Church*, pp. 121–39. On political parties, see Michael Wallace, "Changing Concepts of Party in the United States: New York, 1815–1828," *American Historical Review* 74, 2 (December 1968): 453–9. For issue orientations, see Michael F. Holt, "The Election of 1840, Voter Mobilization, and the Emergence of the Second American Party System: A Reappraisal of Jacksonian Voting Behavior," in *A Master's Due: Essays in Honor of David Herbert Donald*, ed. William J. Cooper, Jr., et al. (Baton Rouge: Louisiana State U.P., 1985): 16–58. Jerome Mushkat, *Tammany: The Evolution of a Political Machine, 1789–1865* (Syracuse: Syracuse U.P., 1971), see esp. pp. 364–5.

53. Ryan, *Women in Public*, p. 175. Lott, *Love and Theft*, pp. 131–5 for the Farren affair, which is also taken up in the following histories: Richards, *"Gentlemen"*; Weinbaum, *Mobs and Demagogues;* Gilje's *Road to Mobocracy*; Wilentz, *Chants Democratic;* McConachie's "'Theatre of the Mob'"; Buckley, "To the Opera House"; and Theodore Shank, "The Bowery Theatre, 1826–1836," Ph.D. diss. (Stanford Univ., 1956).

54. For abolitionists targeting opponents, see Walters, *American Reformers*, p. 85; for the antiabolition press targeting, see Richards, *"Gentlemen,"* p. 117. The four brief quotes that follow are from the *Commercial Advertiser* and *Courier and Enquirer*, respectively, both of 8 July 1834. For the transition from religious to secular modes in a wide range of reform groups, see Walters, pp. 75–83. For abolition petitions, see Jentz, "Artisans, Evangelicals, and the City," pp. 187–205; for mob/abolition compositions, see Richards, pp. 136–52. Lott, *Love and Theft*, also sees the riots as planned and purposive (p. 132) and effective in driving merchants and professionals out of abolitionism (p. 134). For colonization, see Richards, pp. 26–9; for race views, see Stanton, *Leopard's Spots*, pp. 192–3, and the discussion of monocreationism and racism, pp. 119–21.

55. Davis, *Slave Power Conspiracy*, p. 24. Richards discusses the "foreign plot" notion (*"Gentlemen,"* pp. 68–9) and connects Irish immigrant antiabolitionism to abolition's supposedly English origin. For Tappan's antiunionism, see Wilentz, *Chants Democratic*, p. 265. For actions by the city's postmaster, Samuel L. Gouverneur (secretary of the association that built the Bowery Theatre), and Postmaster General Amos Kendall, see Richards, p. 74. For Jackson's tendency to ignore the Constitution and the Supreme Court, see Rogin, *Fathers and Children*, and "The Frontier" section of Chapter 1.

56. An outline of the Farren affair is provided in Shank, "Bowery Theatre," pp. 378–84. McConachie ("'Theatre of the Mob'") and Buckley ("To the Opera House")

take up the Farren events in context with the Astor Place Riot. See also Grimsted's "Rioting."

57. Richards, *"Gentlemen,"* traces these disturbances on pp. 115–20. For Weinbaum's account, see *Mobs and Demagogues*, pp. 38–40; for Wilentz, *Chants Democratic*, pp. 264–6; for Buckley, "To the Opera House," pp. 184–90. There is disagreement both about the cohesion of the mob and whether it had labor motivations (see esp. Richards, p. 115, Gilje, *Road to Mobocracy*, pp. 164–6; and Wilentz). Shank's account of the benefit/riot is "Bowery Theatre," pp. 382–4. For the New York newspapers not cited in the text, see: the 9 July 1834 *Sun;* the 10 July 1834 *Evening Star, Courier and Enquirer, Journal of Commerce, Sun,* and *Mercantile Advertiser;* the 11 July 1834 *Sun, Evening Post,* and *Journal of Commerce;* and the 12 July 1834 *Sun, Daily Advertiser, Times,* and *Transcript and Wasp.* These provide various estimates of crowd size.

58. Weinbaum, *Mobs and Demagogues,* pp. 38–40, estimates the theatre crowd at five hundred and argues, against Richards, *"Gentlemen,"* and contemporaneous accounts, that the Bowery invaders and the antiabolition crowd at the Chatham were initially different groups. The importance of the one-or-two-crowd argument is the degree of uniformity of intent and of orchestration that informs these disturbances. The quote is the 10 July 1834 *American.* For Hone's account, see *The Diary of Philip Hone, 1828–1851,* ed. Allan Nevins (New York: Dodd, Mead & Co., 1927), vol. 1, p. 109; for Haswell, *Reminiscences,* pp. 289–90. For Shank on these events, "Bowery Theatre," pp. 382–5. See also Alvin F. Harlow, *Old Bowery Days* (New York: D. Appleton, 1931), p. 291; and Joel T. Headley, *The Great Riots of New York* (New York: E. B. Treat, 1873), pp. 84–7. Lott, *Love and Theft,* p. 133. The complexity of incidents is suggested by the essentially proabolition *Sun* encouraging mob action against Farren in its 8 July 1834 number as both a right and a duty, meanwhile condemning similar actions against abolitionists.

59. Buckley, "To the Opera House," p. 190; Richards, *"Gentlemen,"* p. 118. Lewis and Arthur Tappan were brothers. The McKinney claque's accusations and Hamblin's rejoinder are both in the *New York Evening Star,* 18 January 1834; and see Shank, "Bowery Theatre," pp. 380–2. The sex–race connection is drawn by Richards (p. 113), but it was a common refrain among antiabolitionists. An example of this connection can also be seen in the revocation of Lydia Maria Child's library privileges at the private Boston Athenaeum after she used the collection to produce an antislavery tract (Story, "Class and Culture in Boston," p. 195).

60. For Farren's fate, see Shank, "Bowery Theatre," pp. 386–7. For class issues in the incident, see Richards, *"Gentlemen,"* p. 116; Weinbaum, *Mobs and Demagogues,* p. 39; and Wilentz, *Chants Democratic,* pp. 265–6. It was earlier noted that the Chatham Theatre had become a Presbyterian chapel in 1832 (see "The City" in Chapter 1). According to Lott (*Love and Theft,* p. 131), Arthur Tappan converted the theatre into a chapel for Charles Grandison Finney.

61. See Odell, *Annals,* vol. 3, pp. 631–2, p. 637; and Shank, "Bowery Theatre," pp. 367–74, as well as his appendix of Rice's performances at the Bowery, pp. 629–30. "Patting Juba" is considered in Hans Nathan, *Dan Emmett and the Rise of*

Early Negro Minstrelsy (Norman: U. of Oklahoma Press, 1974), pp. 71–92. Other minstrel sources include Carl Wittke, *Tambo and Bones* (1930; rpt. Westport, Conn.: Greenwood Press, 1968); Robert Toll, *Blacking Up: The Minstrel Show in Nineteenth Century America* (New York: Oxford U.P., 1974); Alexander Saxton, "Blackface Minstrelsy and Jacksonian Ideology," *American Quarterly* 27, 1 (March 1975): 3–28, and his *Rise and Fall of the White Republic* (London: Verso, 1990). Festivals and parades on such holidays as Election Day and Pinkster are discussed by Shane White, "'It Was a Proud Day': African Americans, Festivals, and Parades in the North, 1741–1834," *Journal of American History* 81, 1 (June 1994): 13–50. (I am most grateful to George A. Thompson, Jr., for bringing this article to my attention.) "Jim Crow" clones appeared both at the Park and Richmond Hill theatres in the 1833–4 season (Odell, vol. 3, pp. 615, 646). Rice does not appear to have been playing at the Bowery 9 July, though he performed there in June 1834 and was frequently paired with Forrest.

62. Odell, *Annals*, vol. 3, pp. 684–5. It is worth recalling, regarding *Life in New York*, that Mrs. Trollope lived in Cincinnati between February 1828 and March 1830, when Rice was in the area, and that the Samuel Drakes were friends of hers and performed at Mrs. Trollope's Bazaar. Hamblin's ballyhoo for the "Entertainment" is contained in a 22 April 1834 preshow playbill in the Harvard Theatre Collection, portions of which are reproduced in Odell (pp. 684–5) and Shank ("Bowery Theatre," pp. 361–3). James H. Hackett, famous for his staged Yankees and frontiersmen, brought out a competing play, *Major Jack Downing; or, The Retired Politician* at the Park Theatre 10 May 1834. (Apropos staged types, this is also the season in which Rice played the City Marshall in the Bowery production *Black Hawk* [27 January 1834].) Wittke considers the extension of the staged Negro from song to play to be an essential step in the creation of the minstrel show, which he dates to the Bowery Amphitheatre early in 1843 (*Tambo and Bones*, p. 41).

63. Wittke, *Tambo and Bones*, p. 17, for "Zip Coon" and Natchez. For Dixon, see Odell, *Annals*, vol. 3, p. 354. For T. D. Rice in the West, see esp. Ludlow, *Dramatic Life;* and Sol Smith, *Theatrical Management in the West and South for Thirty Years* (1868; rpt. New York: Benjamin Blom, 1968). For Dixon's 1834 performance and the Bowery season, which in 1834 ended 16 July, see Odell, vol. 3, pp. 673, 687; for his popularity, pp. 421, 468. Lott, *Love and Theft,* analyzes *Oh! Hush!* on pp. 133–4.

64. Lott, *Love and Theft,* pp. 107, 207, 222, on sectionalism and conflict; pp. 178–9 for a reprint of the "Zip Coon" sheet music ("Baltimore. Published and sold by Geo. Willig, Jr.").

65. Hans Nathan reprints the cover of Atwell's version of "Zip Coon," published in New York, on p. 58, and sheet music and lyrics on p. 167. See Nathan, *Dan Emmett*, pp. 50–7, for "Jim Crow" lyrics. For Mrs. Trollope, see *Domestic Manners of the Americans*, chap. 2, pp. 350–1, and illustration XXIV opposite p. 361. For Kemble, see her *Journal*, vol. 1, pp. 74–5. For Emmeline Stuart-Wortley, see *Travels in the United States . . . during 1849–1850* (New York: Harper & Bros., 1851), chap. 12. Mrs. Trollope's account of the fashionable black male is favorable, Lady Emmeline's largely scornful.

66. For Lott on the dandy and the riots of July 1834, see *Love and Theft*, pp. 131–5. James Kennard, Jr., "Who Are Our National Poets?", *Knickerbocker Magazine* 26, 4 (April 1845): 333, 336. Margaret Fuller, "Entertainments of the Past Winter," *Dial* 3, 1 (July 1842): 52.

67. For slaves and minstrel songs, see Nathan, *Dan Emmett*, pp. 185–7; for Juba, see Chapter 2. For W. E. B. DuBois's valorization of Stephen Foster's compositions as African American, see Lott, *Love and Theft*, pp. 16–17. White use of black music (unacknowledged and acknowledged, rewarded and unrewarded) should require no rehearsal here, but see Toll, *Blacking Up*, pp. 44–51; and Saxton, "Blackface Minstrelsy," pp. 7–8. For a social reading of these forms in addition to Lott, see Wilentz, *Chants Democratic*, pp. 258–9; and Saxton, "Blackface Minstrelsy," pp. 8–15 – a text developed at length in his *White Republic*.

68. Nathan, *Dan Emmett*, describes the development of minstrelsy in Emmett's hands, a transition from Rice's pieces to the formalized minstrel shows of the Civil War era and after. The carnivalesque and some of the problems that devolve from trying to tidy its messiness are considered in Anthony Wall and Clive Thompson's review essay, "Cleaning Up Bakhtin's Carnival Act," *Diacritics* 23, 2 (Summer 1993): 47–70. See Lott, *Love and Theft*, p. 18, for white investments in black culture, and p. 8 and p. 17 concerning binary racial categories. Henry Louis Gates, "African American Criticism," p. 309.

Epilogue: Simultaneous Spaces

1. For the quoted material, see: Frederic Saunders, *Memories of the Great Metropolis; or, London, from the Tower to the Crystal Palace* (New York: G. P. Putnam Pubs., 1851), p. xi; Marcus Cunliffe, "America at the Great Exhibition of 1851," *American Quarterly* 3, 2 (Summer 1951): 118; Saunders, 43–4 (the London *Times* citation is on p. 44). Studies of the Crystal Palace exhibition informing this discussion include: Richard D. Altick, *The Shows of London* (Cambridge, Mass.: Harvard U.P., 1978); Christopher Hobhouse, *1851 and the Crystal Palace* (New York: E. P. Dutton Co., 1937); C. H. Gibbs-Smith, *The Great Exhibition of 1851: A Commemorative Album* (London: Victoria and Albert Museum, 1950); Yvonne Ffrench, *The Great Exhibition of 1851* (London: Harvill Press, 1950); Kenneth Luckhurst, *The Story of Exhibitions* (London: Studio, 1951); Merle Curti, "America at the World Fairs, 1851–1893," *American Historical Review* 55, 4 (July 1950): 833–56; C. R. Fay, *Palace of Industry, 1851: A Study of the Great Exhibition and Its Fruits* (Cambridge: Cambridge U.P., 1951); Patrick Beaver, *The Crystal Palace, 1851–1936: A Portrait of Victorian Enterprise* (London: Hugh Evelyn, 1970); John Allwood, *The Great Exhibitions* (London: Studio Vista, 1977); Paul Greenhalgh, *Ephemeral Vistas: The Expositions Universelles, Great Exhibitions and World's Fairs, 1851–1939* (Manchester: Manchester U.P., 1988); and William H. Truettner, *The Natural Man Observed: A Study of Catlin's Indian Gallery* (Washington: Smithsonian Inst. Press, 1979), for Catlin's contribution to the exhibition. In addition, a wealth of contemporaneous sources survive, among them: *The Official Catalogue*

of the Great Exhibition of the Works of Industry of All Nations, 1851, corrected ed. (London: W. Clowes & Sons, 1851); *Tallis's History and Description of the Crystal Palace and the Exhibition of the World's Industry in 1851* (London: John Tallis & Co., n.d.); *The Art-Journal Illustrated Catalogue* (London: George Virtue Pubs., 1851; rpt. as *The Crystal Palace Exhibition Illustrated Catalogue: London, 1851*, with an introduction by John Gloag [New York: Dover Pubs., 1970]); Horace Greeley, *Glances at Europe in a Series of Letters* (New York: DeWitt & Davenport, 1851); and Charles T. Rodgers, *American Superiority at the World's Fair* (Philadelphia: John J. Hawkins, 1852).

2. Robert W. Rydell, *All the World's a Fair: Visions of Empire at American Industrial Expositions, 1876–1916* (Chicago: U. of Chicago Press, 1984), p. 3. Prince Albert and Queen Victoria clearly had education in view in supporting the Great Exhibition, the Queen noting in her journal (3 May 1851) that it "ought to do wonders in enlightening young people, both high and low" (Fay, *Palace of Industry*, p. 50). The American Crystal Palace of 1853 remains an underresearched and undercontextualized phenomenon. It has gained some recent attention in two works by A. H. Saxon: his edition of *Selected Letters of P. T. Barnum* (New York: Columbia U.P., 1983) and his *P. T. Barnum: The Legend and the Man* (New York: Columbia U.P., 1989). Barnum himself references both Crystal Palaces in *Struggles and Triumphs; or, Forty Years' Recollections of P. T. Barnum (Written by Himself)*, author's ed. (New York: American News Co., 1871). The New York enterprise is given brief mention in T. Allston Brown, *A History of the New York Stage*, 2 vols. (New York: Dodd, Mead & Co., 1903), reprised in George C. D. Odell, *Annals of the New York Stage* (New York: Columbia U.P., 1931), vol. 6. An account of both expositions features in Edo McCullough's *World's Fair Midways* (New York: Exposition Press, 1966).

3. For a longer meditation on physics and cultural history, see my "Time, Space, Timespace, Spacetime: Theatre History in Simultaneous Universes," *Journal of Dramatic Theory and Criticism* 5, 2 (Spring 1991): 63–84. The article references several sources, influential among them Fred Alan Wolf's *Parallel Universes* (New York: Simon & Schuster, 1988); and John Wheeler and Wojciech H. Zurek, *Quantum Theory and Measurement* (Princeton: Princeton U.P., 1983). Wolf sketches the relationship between parallel universes and memory/time on pp. 59–60; for Wigner, see Wheeler and Zurek, p. 194.

4. Gibbs-Smith, *Great Exhibition: Commemorative Album*, pp. 5–11; Hobhouse, *1851 and the Crystal Palace*, pp. 1–23; Ffrench, *Great Exhibition of 1851*, pp. 71–85.

5. On Jerrold, see Hobhouse, *1851 and the Crystal Palace*, pp. 37–8; and see Gibbs-Smith, *Great Exhibition: Commemorative Album*, p. 32; for the *Times*, Ffrench, *Great Exhibition of 1851*, pp. 97–8; for general criticism of the building's design, see Gibbs-Smith, p. 10, and Beaver, *Crystal Palace, 1851–1936*, pp. 21–2. Fay states that Paxton's design was one of the first examples in London of standardized production, that is, that the material used in the building was interchangeable (*Palace of Industry*, p. 15).

6. For excellent illustrations of the building process and of its halls and opening ceremonies, see particularly Gibbs-Smith, *Great Exhibition: Commemorative Al-*

bum; but see also Beaver, *Crystal Palace, 1851–1936,* who follows the exhibition hall to its residence at Sydenham. Attendance figures are taken from Gibbs-Smith, p. 33, profits p. 34; see Fay, *Palace of Industry,* pp. 73–74 for proportional estimates. For entertainments, see Altick, *Shows of London,* pp. 467, 469. Queen Victoria linked exhibition and entertainment by attending two acts of the opera *The Hugenots* on the evening of opening day (see Fay, p. 49). For the excursion trains, which were kept on after the exhibition was over, see Luckhurst, *Story of Exhibitions,* p. 116. For Cook's, see Allwood, *Great Exhibitions,* p. 22; for the Queen's diary (entry for 14 June 1851), see Fay, p. 60. (Her Majesty confided that the parishioners had been advised to see the exhibition by their clergyman.) Saunders, *Memories of the Great Metropolis,* pp. 309–11. The cartoon in the *Illustrated London News* (Fig. 23) appeared in the 19 July 1851 issue.

7. Technological change in England is summarized in Ffrench, *Great Exhibition of 1851,* p. 3. Guarding the British Museum is discussed in Altick, *Shows of London,* pp. 456–7, in context with the other ills beside demonstrations it was feared the fair would bring in its wake. For entrance fees, see Gibbs-Smith, *Great Exhibition: Commemorative Album,* p. 33, and the inside cover of the *Official Catalogue.*

8. Sources disagree concerning how many prize categories there were. Greeley enumerates three classes of medals (*Glances at Europe,* p. 35); Gibbs-Smith (*Great Exhibition: Commemorative Album,* p. 150) speaks of the large Council Medal for originality of design application and a smaller Prize Medal for craftsmanship (170 of the former were given and 2,918 of the latter). Rodgers's account supports Gibbs-Smith and enumerates American prizewinners in each of thirty classes (*American Superiority,* pp. 142–3). The Crystal Palace was a major employer of workmen; an average of two thousand men were involved in its construction and decoration from November 1850 through March 1851 (Gibbs-Smith, p. 10). In addition to the *Times* article, the granting of holidays to clerks is mentioned in a letter to the *Morning Chronicle;* for extracts of it, see Gibbs-Smith, p. 31.

9. Mistresses sending maids to the exhibition is recorded by the *Illustrated London News* and cited by Luckhurst, *Story of Exhibitions,* p. 116. On charity excursions, see Fay, *Palace of Industry,* p. 132, citing the *Times,* and for Queen Victoria's 16 July observation to her journal of public interest in royal finery, p. 65. On the dignity of work, see Henry Mayhew and George Cruikshank, *1851; or, The Adventures of Mr. and Mrs. Sandboys and Family Who Came Up to London to "Enjoy Themselves," and to See the Great Exhibition* (London: George Newbold, 1851), pp. 129–32. For Cole on the security of exhibits, see Gibbs-Smith, *Great Exhibition: Commemorative Album,* p. 31.

10. *Official Catalogue,* and see Luckhurst, *Story of Exhibitions,* p. 116. *Punch* 20 (1851), p. 218, p. 243, p. 246. *Tallis's History and Description,* p. 67. Greeley, *Glances at Europe,* p. 34 and p. vi. Queen Victoria, who visited the exhibition often, notes that new items were frequently added (see, e.g., her journal entry for 8 August 1851). Greeley criticized British displays as often unremarkable advertisements for their manufacturers. For the New Jersey commissioners, see Curti, "America at the World Fairs," p. 838; for more optimistic American assessments, see Rodgers, *American Superiority,* p. 6.

11. Curti, "America at the World Fairs," pp. 837–8. Queen Victoria's journal entries concerning the Great Exhibition are given in detail in Fay, *Palace of Industry* (see p. 54 for the 19 May observation about the American section), and are abridged in Gibbs-Smith, *Great Exhibition: Commemorative Album;* the Bowie-knife entry is 10 May 1851 (p. 52 in Fay and p. 19 in Gibbs-Smith). Curti (p. 840) and Cunliffe ("America at the Great Exhibition," p. 122) cite different Council Medalists and offer different assessments of the prize's significance; Cunliffe says that the U.S. showing was poor (compared to France's 56 medals), Curti that "in proportion to the number of articles displayed, American exhibitors won more prizes than many of the Continental nations, and, indeed, more relatively than Britain herself." Rodgers (*American Superiority*, pp. 142–3) supplies the five winners listed in the text and identifies many American Prize Medalists. The Liverpool *Times* is cited in Curti, p. 841, and Rodgers, p. 89.

12. *Official Catalogue*, p. 15. Catlin's model of Niagara Falls, "representing in perfect relief, proportion, and colour, every house, tree, bridge, rocks," is described in Altick, *Shows of London*, p. 392. Powers's sculpture is illustrated in both Gibbs-Smith, *Great Exhibition: Commemorative Album*, and *Tallis's History and Description* (for the quote, see p. 42). Gibbs-Smith extracts contemporaneous reactions to the sculpture (p. 129), which is excoriated, along with Victorian art in general, by both Hobhouse, *1851 and the Crystal Palace*, and Beaver, *Crystal Palace, 1851–1936*.

13. For U.S. displays, see the *Official Catalogue*, pp. 184–92. The response to Canada's exhibit is quoted in Gibbs-Smith, *Great Exhibition: Commemorative Album*, p. 73. On Uncle Sam as an Indian, see Cunliffe, "America at the Great Exhibition," p. 122. Catlin's Indian Gallery is taken up in Altick, *Shows of London* (see esp. pp. 275–9, 281, 291, 455); and Truettner, *Natural Man Observed*, pp. 44–9. For Barnum's involvement with the Indian Gallery, see both Altick, p. 380, and Barnum's two letters to Moses Kimball in Barnum's *Selected Letters*, pp. 27–8. For the extended stay in Europe of the second party of Ojibway over Truettner's account, see Christopher Mulvey, "Among the Sag-a-noshes: Ojibwa and Iowa Indians with George Catlin in Europe, 1843–1848," pp. 253–75, in *Indians and Europe: An Interdisciplinary Collection of Essays*, ed. Christian F. Feest (Aachen: Rader Verlag, 1987), and the "Account . . ." of Maungwudaus in *The Elders Wrote: An Anthology of Early Prose by North American Indians, 1768–1931*, ed. Bernd Peyer (Berlin: Reimer Verlag, 1982), pp. 66–74.

14. Truettner, *Natural Man Observed*, p. 49 for his quote; and see *Official Catalogue*, p. 22 of the advertising section. For the Crystal Palace exhibit and Catlin's subsequent imprisonment for debt, see Truettner, p. 53.

15. Rydell, *All the World's a Fair*, pp. 6–7. For the museums built with Crystal Palace profits, see Gibbs-Smith, *Great Exhibition: Commemorative Album*, p. 37; but see also Fay, *Palace of Industry;* Hobhouse, *1851 and the Crystal Palace;* Ffrench, *Great Exhibition of 1851;* and others. For London entertainments, see Altick, *Shows of London*, pp. 260–7, 469; and Mayhew and Cruikshank, *1851; or, The Adventures of Mr. and Mrs. Sandboys*, pp. 132–3. For the play, the *Illustrated London News*, 31 May 1851, p. 483.

16. Gibbs-Smith, *Great Exhibition: Commemorative Album*, pp. 9, 39. Altick, *Shows of London*, pp. 483–5, 507. Hobhouse, *1851 and the Crystal Palace*, catalogues the following (p. 145): twelve pickpocket arrests on the grounds; eleven persons caught removing minor exhibits; £90 in counterfeit taken at the doors ("nearly all on the half crown and five shilling days," notes Rodgers [*American Superiority*, p. 143], "when the richer and more exclusive portion of the community visited"); "three women violently assaulted by a party of Welsh abstainers"; three petticoats, two bustles, three pincushions, and twelve monocles lost and never claimed; one baby born in the building; and one small fire. Omnibus drivers are complained of in the 14 July 1851 London *Daily News* (see Fay, *Palace of Industry*, p. 77). Even though the Crystal Palace was very well policed, the few incidents connected with the Great Exhibition, given its millions of visitors, seems remarkable. (Some contemporaries attributed this quietude to the prohibition of liquor sales in the building.) For the *Times* on Barnum, see Rodgers, *American Superiority*, p. 61. Barnum records (*Struggles and Triumphs*, p. 366) sending over a Chinese troupe and a panorama, with lecture, that did poor business.

17. For Cole's vision of expositions and progress, see Ffrench, *Great Exhibition of 1851*, pp. 278–9. The site and the New York building are discussed in: McCullough, *World's Fair Midways*, p. 27; Barnum, *Struggles and Triumphs*, p. 381; Saxon, *P. T. Barnum*, p. 189; and Brown, *History of the New York Stage*, p. 22.

18. For the cost of the building, see McCullough, *World's Fair Midways*, p. 28; and Luckhurst, *Story of Exhibitions*, p. 220 (their figures do not agree). The receipt figure for New York is taken from Luckhurst, but I have otherwise used Gibbs-Smith's figures for the London Exposition (*Great Exhibition: Commemorative Album*, p. 34). Luckhurst does not indicate how many days, months, or years are included in his calculation of New York receipts. Brown, *History of the New York Stage*, p. 22. President Pierce troped the then-recent conflict with Mexico by riding his war horse Black Prince in the parade.

19. Odell, *Annals*, vol. 6, p. 261. An analogy between the exhibitions and the design of department stores is drawn by Fay (*Palace of Industry*, p. 95), who sees the erection of the latter in London – along with other glass and iron constructions – as influenced by the Hyde Park structure. For the observatory, see McCullough, *World's Fair Midways*, p. 29. For the 15 April letter, see Barnum, *Selected Letters*, p. 67; for his responses about novelty, Barnum, *Struggles and Triumphs*, p. 381; for Barnum's letter to Greeley, *Selected Letters*, p. 73.

20. Brown, *History of the New York Stage*, p. 22; Saxon, *P. T. Barnum*, pp. 189–90, 245; *The Diary of George Templeton Strong*, ed. Allan Nevins and Milton Halsey Thomas (New York: Macmillan, 1952), vol. 2 (entry for 18 June 1854), pp. 176–7; McCullough, *World's Fair Midways*, p. 30.

21. Barnum, *Selected Letters*, pp. 77–8. Barnum, motivated by a desire to recoup his own investment in the building, also told Moses Kimball, "My Museum last year cleared $50,000, about double what it would have done had it not been for the Crystal Palace." Beaver, *Crystal Palace, 1851–1936*, p. 141; McCullough, *World's Fair Midways*, p. 30.

22. Robert Bogdan, *Freak Show: Presenting Human Oddities for Amusement and Profit* (Chicago: U. of Chicago Press, 1988), pp. 47–8. See also Rydell, *All the World's a Fair*, pp. 62–3, on the Midway Plaisance; and Luckhurst, *Story of Exhibitions*, p. 116, on the excursion habit.

23. John Pintard, *Letters from John Pintard to his Daughter Elizabeth Pintard Davidson* (New York: New-York Historical Society, 1940–1), pp. 25–6. *The Diary of Philip Hone, 1828–1851*, ed. Allen Nevins (New York: Dodd, Mead & Co., 1927), vol. 2, p. 98. For considerations of the decrease in elite support of theatre in the antebellum decades, see: Peter G. Buckley, "To the Opera House: Culture and Society in New York City, 1820–1860," Ph.D. diss. (State Univ. of New York–Stony Brook, 1984); Lawrence W. Levine, *Highbrow/Lowbrow: The Emergence of Cultural Hierarchy in America* (Cambridge: Harvard U.P., 1988); Bruce A. McConachie, *Melodramatic Formations: American Theatre and Society, 1820–1870* (Iowa City: U. of Iowa Press, 1992). For considerations of culture in antebellum Chicago, see: William Cronon, *Nature's Metropolis: Chicago and the Great West* (New York: W. W. Norton, 1991); on "simple living" there, Mary Drummond, "Long Ago," her memoir of the 1850s, cited in John Moses and Joseph Kirkland, *The History of Chicago, Illinois* (Chicago: Munsell, 1895), vol. 1, p. 140; on Chicago society, Harriet Martineau's 1838 *A Retrospect of Western Travel* (rpt. Westport, Conn.: Greenwood Press, 1970), vol. 3, p. 30; for Joseph T. Ryerson's recollection that a "small circle of business and professional men, and others of note, were generally well acquainted with or known to one another" in 1840s Chicago, see "Gleanings from a Family Memoir," in Moses and Kirkland, vol. 1, p. 71. For a view of elite culture in several antebellum cities, see Frederic Cople Jahrer, *The Urban Establishment: Upper Strata in Boston, New York, Charleston, Chicago, and Los Angeles* (Urbana: U. of Illinois Press, 1982): for Chicagoans on enterprise and egalitarianism, pp. 470–2; for Hone, Strong, and their set on the beau monde in New York in the 1820s to 1850s, pp. 246–8. Jahrer describes the plantocracy in these decades in Charleston and its political reach on pp. 359, 371; for Simms, see p. 377. Eugene D. Genovese and Elizabeth Fox-Genovese argue in "The Slave Economies in Political Perspective," their epilogue to Eugene Genovese's *The Political Economy of Slavery*, 2d ed. (Middletown, Conn.: Wesleyan U.P., 1989), p. 303, that "So long as slavery existed, no foundation for industrialization or economic diversification was laid" in the Old South – conditions conducive to cultural stagnation.

24. For nineteenth-century American views of leisure, see Melvin L. Adelman, *A Sporting Time: New York City and the Rise of Modern Athletics, 1820–1870* (Urbana: U. of Illinois Press, 1986); for its relationship to health, pp. 274–6. Ralph Nicholson Wornum, "The Exhibition as a Lesson in Taste," appended pp. i–xxii, in the *Illustrated Catalogue*. John Gloag notes in his introduction to this catalogue (p. xiii) that the excesses of ornamentation Wornum condemned came to characterize post-1851 applied arts, perhaps encouraged by the Great Exhibition's confusion of design with ornament and its validation of jumbled styles and revivals.

25. Donald M. Scott, "The Popular Lecture and the Creation of a Public in Mid-Nineteenth-Century America," *Journal of American History* 66, 4 (March 1980): 792–3; attendance figures are p. 800. A popular speaker could bring individual audiences of fifteen hundred to three thousand (a special train was put on in 1856 when Beecher lectured). For the needs such lectures fulfilled, see Scott, pp. 800–1, for the quote p. 806. Beaumont Newhall, *The Daguerreotype in America* (New York: New York Graphic Society, 1961), pp. 11, 79–80, 85–91. The daguerreotype was also used in science, especially astronomy, until its replacement (by 1860) by the photograph.

26. Herbert Blau, Association for Theatre in Higher Education Conference, panel entitled "Theory and Criticism Seminar: Herbert Blau," Chicago, 29 July 1994; but see Blau's many books about audiences, seeing, bodies, memory, and history.

Bibliography

Articles

Adams, Karen M. "The Black Image in the Paintings of William Sidney Mount." *American Art Journal* 7, 2 (November 1975): 42–59.

Allen, Paula Gunn. "'Border' Studies: The Intersection of Gender and Color." In *Introduction to Scholarship in Modern Languages and Literatures*. 2d Ed. Ed. Joseph Gibaldi. New York: Modern Language Association of America, 1992, pp. 303–19.

Amacher, Richard E. "Behind the Curtain with the Noble Savage: Stage Management of Indian Plays, 1825–1860." *Theatre Survey* 7, 2 (November 1966): 101–14.

Ammons, Elizabeth. "Heroines in Uncle Tom's Cabin." In *Critical Essays on Harriet Beecher Stowe*. Ed. Elizabeth Ammons. Boston: G. K. Hall, 1980, pp. 152–65.

Anderson, Marilyn J. "The Image of the Indian in American Drama during the Jacksonian Era, 1829–1845." *Journal of American Culture* 1, 4 (Winter 1978): 800–10.

Arnold, Marybeth H. "'The Life of a Citizen in the Hands of a Woman': Sexual Assault in New York City, 1790–1820." In *Passion and Power: Sexuality in History*. Ed. Kathy Peiss and Christina Simmons. Philadelphia: Temple University Press, 1989, pp. 35–56.

Baker, Charles E. "The American Art-Union." In *The American Academy of Fine Arts and The American Art-Union*. Ed. Mary B. Cowdery. New York: New-York Historical Society, 1953, pp. 95–240.

Bank, Rosemarie K. "Antedating the Long Run: A Prolegomenon." *Nineteenth Century Theatre Research* 13, 1 (Summer 1985): 33–6.

"Hustlers in the House: The Bowery Theatre as a Mode of Historical Information." In *The American Stage*. Ed. Ron Engle and Tice Miller. Cambridge: Cambridge University Press, 1993, pp. 47–64.

"Mrs. Trollope Visits the Theatre: Cultural Diplomacy and Historical Appropriation." *Journal of American Drama and Theatre* 5, 3 (Fall 1993): 16–27.

"The Second Face of the Idol: Women in Melodrama." In *Women in American Theatre*. Ed. Helen Krich Chinoy and Linda Walsh Jenkins. New York: Crown, 1981, pp. 238–43.

"Staging the 'Native': Making History in American Theatre Culture, 1828–1838." *Theatre Journal* 45, 4 (December 1993): 461–86.

"Theatre and Narrative Fiction in the Work of the Nineteenth-Century American Playwright Louisa Medina." *Theatre History Studies* 3 (1983): 54–67.

"Time, Space, Timespace, Spacetime: Theatre History in Simultaneous Universes." *Journal of Dramatic Theory and Criticism* 5, 2 (Spring 1991): 63–84.

Benjamin, Walter. "Theses on the Philosophy of History." Section IX, in *Illuminations*. Trans. Harry Zahn. Ed. Hannah Arendt. New York: Harcourt, Brace & World, 1968, pp. 259–60.

Bhabha, Homi K. "Postcolonial Criticism." In *Redrawing the Boundaries: The Transformation of English and American Literary Studies*. Ed. Stephen Greenblatt and Giles Gunn. New York: Modern Language Association of America, 1992, pp. 437–65.

Blumin, Stuart M. "Explaining the New Metropolis: Perception, Depiction, and Analysis in Mid-Nineteenth Century New York City." *Journal of Urban History* 11, 1 (November 1984): 9–38.

"The Hypothesis of Middle Class Formation in Nineteenth-Century America: A Critique and Some Proposals." *American Historical Review* 90, 2 (April 1985): 99–118.

"Mobility and Change in Ante-Bellum Philadelphia." In *Nineteenth Century Cities: Essays in the New Urban History*. Ed. Stephen Thernstrom and Richard Sennett. New Haven: Yale University Press, 1969, pp. 165–208.

Borges, Jorge Luis. "The Garden of Forking Paths." In *Ficciones*. Trans. Helen Temple and Ruthven Todd. Ed. Anthony Kerrigan. New York: Grove Press, 1962: 89–101.

"The Garden of Forking Paths." In *Labrynth*. Trans. Donald A Yates. Ed. Donald A. Yates and James E. Irby. New York: New Directions, 1962: 19–29.

Buckley, Peter G. "'The Place to Make an Artist Work': Micah Hawkins and William Sidney Mount in New York City." In *Catching the Tune: Music and William Sidney Mount*. Ed. Janice Gray Armstrong. New York: Museums at Stony Brook, 1984, pp. 22–39.

Buettinger, Craig. "Economic Inequity in Early Chicago, 1849–1850." *Journal of Social History* 11, 3 (Spring 1978): 413–18.

Camp, Charles. "American Indian Oratory in the White Image: An Analysis of Stereotypes." *Journal of American Culture* 1, 4 (Winter 1978): 811–17.

Caponigri, A. Robert. "Individual, Civil Society, and State in American Transcendentalism." In *Critical Essays on American Transcendentalism*. Ed. Philip F. Gura and Joel Myerson. Boston: G. K. Hall, 1982, pp. 541–60.

Clark, Clifford E. "The Vision of the Dining Room: Plan Books, Dreams and Middle Class Realities." In *Dining in America, 1850–1900*. Ed. Kathryn Grover. Amherst: University of Massachusetts Press, 1987, pp. 142–72.

Coleridge, Samuel Taylor. "Table Talk, 27 April 1823." In *Table Talk and Omniana*. Oxford: Oxford University Press, 1917, pp. 44–6.

Cott, Nancy. "On Man's History and Woman's History." In *Meanings for Manhood: Constructions of Masculinity in Victorian America.* Ed. Mark C. Carnes and Clyde Griffen. Chicago: University of Chicago Press, 1990, pp. 205–11.

Crouthamel, James L. "The Newspaper Revolution in New York, 1830–1860." *New York History* 45, 2 (April 1964): 91–113.

Cunliffe, Marcus. "America at the Great Exhibition of 1851." *American Quarterly* 3, 2 (Summer 1851): 115–26.

Curti, Merle. "America at the World Fairs, 1851–1893." *American Historical Review* 55, 4 (July 1950): 833–56.

Curtis, Julia. "Chatham Garden Theatre Salary Book: 1827–1828." *Theatre History Studies* 13 (1993): 1–16.

Davis, Jim, and Tracy C. Davis. "The People of the 'People's Theatre': The Social Demography of the Britannia Theatre (Hoxton)." *Theatre Survey* 32, 2 (November 1991): 139–70.

Dewberry, Jonathan. "The African Grove Theatre and Company." *Black American Literary Forum* 16, 4 (Winter 1982): 128–31.

Dorson, Richard. "Mose, the Far-Famed and World Renowned." *American Literature* 15, 3 (November 1943): 289–300.

Dougherty, J. Hampden. "Ten Years of Municipal Vigor, 1837–1847." In *The Memorial History of the City of New-York from Its First Settlement to the Year 1892.* Vol. 3. Ed. James Grant Wilson. New York: New-York History Co., 1893, pp. 364–412.

Fisher, Philip. "American Literary and Cultural Studies Since the Civil War." In *Redrawing the Boundaries: The Transformation of English and American Literary Studies.* Ed. Stephen Greenblatt and Giles Gunn. New York: Modern Language Association of America, 1992, pp. 232–50.

Flynn, Joyce. "Academics on the Trail of the Stage 'Indian': A Review Essay." *Studies in American Indian Literature* 2, 1 (Winter 1987): 1–16.

"A Complex Causality of Neglect." *American Quarterly* 41, 1 (March 1989): 123–7.

Foucault, Michel. "Of Other Spaces." *Diacritics* 16, 1 (Spring 1986): 22–7.

Francis, Richard. "The Ideology of Brook Farm." In *Studies in the American Renaissance.* Ed. Joel Myerson. Bloomington, Ind.: Twayne, 1978, pp. 561–95.

Frick, John W. "'He Drank from the Poisoned Cup': Theatre, Culture, and Temperance in Antebellum America." *Journal of American Drama and Theatre* 4, 2 (Spring 1992): 21–41.

Frith, Simon. "The Good, the Bad, and the Indifferent: Defending Popular Culture from the Populists." *Diacritics* 21, 4 (Winter 1991): 102–15.

Fuller, Margaret. "Entertainments of the Past Winter." *Dial* 3, 1 (July 1842): 46–72.

Gafford, Lucille. "Transcendentalist Attitudes Toward Drama and the Theatre." *New England Quarterly* 12, 3 (September 1940): 442–66.

Gates, Henry Louis. "African American Criticism." In *Redrawing the Boundaries: The Transformation of English and American Literary Studies.* Ed. Stephen Greenblatt and Giles Gunn. New York: Modern Language Association of America, 1992, pp. 303–19.

ilje, Paul. "The Baltimore Riots of 1812 and the Breakdown of the Anglo-American Mob Tradition." *Journal of Social History* 13, 4 (Summer 1980): 547–64.

Goodman, Dena. "Public Sphere and Private Life: Toward a Synthesis of Current Historiographical Approaches to the Old Regime." *History and Theory* 31, 1 (February 1992): 1–20.

Gorn, Elliot J. "'Good-Bye Boys, I Die a True American': Homicide, Nativism, and Working-Class Culture in Antebellum New York City." *Journal of American History* 74, 2 (September 1987): 388–410.

"'Gouge and Bite, Pull Hair and Scratch': The Social Significance of Fighting in the Southern Backcountry." *American Historical Review* 90, 1 (February 1985): 18–43.

Green, Rayna. "The Pocahontas Perplex: The Image of Indian Women in American Culture." In *Unequal Sisters: A Multicultural Reader in U.S. Women's History.* Ed. Ellen C. Dubois and Vicki L. Ruiz. New York: Routledge, 1990, pp. 15–21.

Griffen, Clyde. "Reconstructing Masculinity from the Evangelical Revival to the Waning of Progressivism: A Speculative Synthesis." In *Meanings for Manhood: Constructions of Masculinity in Victorian America.* Ed. Mark C. Carnes and Clyde Griffen. Chicago: University of Chicago Press, 1990, pp. 183–204.

"Workers Divided: The Effect of Craft and Ethnic Differences in Poughkeepsie, New York, 1850–1880." In *Nineteenth Century Cities: Essays in the New Urban History.* Ed. Stephen Thernstrom and Richard Sennett. New Haven: Yale University Press, 1969, pp. 49–97.

Grimsted, David. "Rioting in Its Jacksonian Setting." *American Historical Review* 77, 2 (April 1972): 361–97.

Gutman, Herbert G. "The Reality of the Rags-to-Riches 'Myth': the Case of the Patterson, New Jersey, Locomotive, Iron and Machinery Manufacturers, 1830–1880." In *Nineteenth Century Cities: Essays in the New Urban History.* Ed. Stephen Thernstrom and Richard Sennett. New Haven: Yale University Press, 1969, pp. 98–124.

Hammett, Theodore. "Two Mobs of Jacksonian Boston: Ideology and Interest." *Journal of American History* 62, 4 (March 1976): 845–68.

Harrison, Brian. "Pubs." In *The Victorian City.* Vol. 1. Ed. H. J. Dyos and Michael Wolff. London: Routledge & Kegan Paul, 1973, pp. 161–90.

Haskell, Thomas L. "Capitalism and the Origins of the Humanitarian Sensibility." *American Historical Review* 90, 2 (April 1985): 339–61; 90, 3 (June 1985): 547–66.

Hewitt, Barnard. "'King Stephen' of the Park and Drury Lane." In *The Theatrical Manager in England and America.* Ed. Joseph Donohue. Princeton: Princeton University Press, 1971, pp. 87–141.

Hills, Patricia. "Picturing Progress in the Era of Westward Expansion." In *The West as America: Reinterpreting Images of the Frontier, 1820–1920.* Ed. William Truettner. Washington: National Museum of American Art / Smithsonian Institution Press, 1991, pp. 97–147.

Holt, Michael F. "The Election of 1840, Voter Mobilization, and the Emergence of the Second American Party System: A Reappraisal of Jacksonian Voting Behavior." In *A Master's Due: Essays in Honor of David Herbert Donald.* Ed. William J. Cooper, Jr., Michael F. Holt, and John McCardell. Baton Rouge: Louisiana State University Press, 1985, pp. 16–58.

Horsman, Reginald. "Scientific Racism and the American Indian in the Mid-Nineteenth Century." *American Quarterly* 27, 2 (May 1975): 152–68.

Jensen, Joan M. "Native American Women and Agriculture: A Seneca Case Study." In *Unequal Sisters: A Multicultural Reader in U.S. Women's History*. Ed. Ellen C. Dubois and Vicki L. Ruiz. New York: Routledge, 1990, pp. 51–65.

Johns, Elizabeth. "Settlement and Development." In *The West as America: Reinterpreting Images of the Frontier, 1820–1920*. Ed. William Truettner. Washington: National Museum of American Art / Smithsonian Institution Press, 1991, pp. 191–235.

Johnson, Claudia D. "That Guilty Third Tier: Prostitution in Nineteenth-Century American Theatre." *American Quarterly* 27, 5 (December 1975): 575–84.

Joyaux, Georges J. "Victor Cousin and American Transcendentalism." *French Review* 24, 2 (December 1955): 117–30.

Kasson, John F. "Rituals of Dining: Table Manners in Victorian America." In *Dining in America, 1850–1900*. Ed. Kathryn Grover. Amherst: University of Massachusetts Press, 1987, pp. 114–41.

Katz, Michael B. "Social Class in North American Urban History." *Journal of Interdisciplinary History* 11, 4 (Spring 1981): 579–605.

Kennard, James, Jr. "Who Are Our National Poets?" *Knickerbocker Magazine* 26, 4 (April 1845): 331–41.

Kern, Alexander. "The Rise of Transcendentalism, 1815–1860." In *Transitions in American Literary History*. Ed. Harry H. Clark. Durham: Duke University Press, 1954, pp. 247–314.

Kingsdale, Jon M. "The 'Poor Man's Club': Social Functions of the Urban Working-Class Saloon." *American Quarterly* 25, 4 (October 1973): 472–89.

Klebaner, Benjamin J. "Poverty and Its Relief in American Thought, 1815–1861." *Social Science Review* 38, 4 (December 1964): 382–99.

Knights, Peter R. "Population Turnover, Persistence, and Residential Mobility in Boston." In *Nineteenth Century Cities: Essays in the New Urban History*. Ed. Stephen Thernstrom and Richard Sennett. New Haven: Yale University Press, 1969, pp. 258–74.

Kohl, Lawrence F. "The Concept of Social Control and the History of Jacksonian America." *Journal of the Early Republic* 5, 1 (Spring 1985): 21–34.

Lampard, Eric. "The Urbanizing World." In *The Victorian City*. Vol. 1. Ed. H. J. Dyos and Michael Wolff. London: Routledge & Kegan Paul, 1973, pp. 3–57.

Laurie, Bruce. "Fire Companies and Gangs in Southwark: The 1840s." In *The Peoples of Philadelphia: A History of Ethnic Groups and Lower-Class Life, 1790–1940*. Ed. Allen F. Davis and Mark H. Haller. Philadelphia: Temple University Press, 1973, pp. 71–87.

"'Nothing on Compulsion': Life Styles of Philadelphia Artisans, 1820–1850." *Labor History* 15, 3 (Summer 1974): 337–66.

Lerner, Gerda. "The Lady and the Mill Girl: Changes in the Status of Women in the Age of Jackson." In *Our American Sisters*. Ed. Jean E. Friedman and William G. Shade. Boston: Allyn & Bacon, 1973, pp. 82–95.

Logan, Olive. "The Leg Business." *Galaxy* 4 (August 1867): 440–4.

Mammen, Edward W. "The Old Stock Company: The Boston Museum." *More Books* 19 (January 1944): 3–18; (February 1944): 49–63; (March 1944): 100–7; (April 1944): 132–49; (May 1944): 176–95.

Margo, Robert A., and Georgia C. Villaflor. "The Growth of Wages in Antebellum America: New Evidence." *Journal of Economic History* 42, 4 (December 1987): 873–95.

Mason, Jeffrey. "The Politics of *Metamora*." In *The Performance of Power*. Ed. Sue-Ellen Case and Janelle Reinelt. Iowa City: University of Iowa Press, 1991, pp. 92–110.

Matthews, Brander. "Americans on the Stage." *Scribner's Monthly* 18, 3 (July 1879): 321–33.

Maungwudaus. "An Account of the Chippewa Indians, Who Have Been Traveling among the Whites, in the United States, England, Ireland, Scotland, France and Belgium." In *The Elders Wrote: An Anthology of Early Prose by North American Indians, 1768–1931*. Ed. Bernd Peyer (Berlin: Reimer Verlag, 1982).

Mayer, Arno J. "The Lower Middle Class as Historical Problem." *Journal of Modern History* 47, 3 (Fall 1975): 409–36.

Maynard, John. "The Worlds of Victorian Sensuality: Work in Progress." In *Sexuality and Victorian Literature*. Ed. Don R. Cox. Knoxville: University of Tennessee Press, 1984: 251–65.

McClymer, John F. "The Historian and the Poverty Line." *Historical Methods* 18, 3 (Summer 1985): 105–10.

McConachie, Bruce A. "Out of the Kitchen and Into the Marketplace: Normalizing *Uncle Tom's Cabin* for the Antebellum Stage." *Journal of American Drama and Theatre* 3, 1 (Winter 1991): 5–28.

"Towards a Postpositivist Theatre History." *Theatre Journal* 37, 4 (December 1985): 465–86.

"'The Theatre of the Mob': Apocalyptic Melodrama and Preindustrial Riots in Antebellum New York." In *Theatre for Working-Class Audiences in the United States, 1830–1980*. Ed. Bruce A. McConachie and Daniel Friedman. Westport, Conn.: Greenwood Press, 1985, pp. 17–46.

Morse, Verranus. "City Boarding Houses." *Young Men's Magazine* (September 1857): 199.

Mouffe, Chantal. "Hegemony and New Political Subjects: Toward a New Concept of Democracy." In *Marxism and the Interpretation of Culture*. Ed. Cary Nelson and Lawrence Grossberg. Urbana: University of Illinois Press, 1988, pp. 89–101.

Mulvey, Christopher. "Among the Sag-a-noshes: Ojibwa and Iowa Indians with George Catlin in Europe, 1843–1848." In *Indians and Europe: An Interdisciplinary Collection of Essays*. Ed. Christian F. Feest (Aachen: Rader Verlag, 1987), pp. 253–75.

Nelligan, Murray H. "American Nationalism on the Stage: The Plays of George Washington Parke Custis (1781–1857)." *Virginia Magazine of History and Biography* 58, 3 (July 1950): 299–324.

"The New Theatre." *Boston Herald* (31 July 1854), p. 4.

Nichols, Harold J. "The Prejudice against Native American Drama from 1778 to 1830." *Quarterly Journal of Speech* 60, 3 (October 1974): 279–88.

"Our Actors." *Ladies Companion* (July 1837), p. 149.

Paulding, James Kirke. "The American Drama." *American Quarterly Review* 2 (June 1827): 331–57.

"Philadelphia Theatricals." *New York Dramatic Mirror* (25 April 1841), p. 54.

Postlewait, Thomas. "History, Hermeneutics, and Narrativity." In *Critical Theory and Performance.* Ed. Janelle G. Reinelt and Joseph R. Roach. Ann Arbor: University of Michigan Press, 1992, pp. 356–68.

Quinn, Michael L. "*Theatrewissenschaft* in the History of Theatre Study." *Theatre Survey* 32, 2 (November 1991): 123–36.

Rinear, David L. "F. S. Chanfrau's Mose: The Rise and Fall of an Urban Folk Hero." *Theatre Journal* 33, 2 (May 1981): 199–212.

Rosen, George. "Disease, Debility, and Death." In *The Victorian City.* Vol. 1. Ed. H. J. Dyos and Michael Wolff. London: Routledge & Kegan Paul, 1973, pp. 625–67.

Saxton, Alexander. "Blackface Minstrelsy and Jacksonian Ideology." *American Quarterly* 27, 1 (March 1975): 3–28.

Schimmel, Julie. "Inventing 'the Indian.'" In *The West As America: Reinterpreting Images of the Frontier, 1820–1920.* Ed. William Truettner. Washington: National Museum of American Art / Smithsonian Institution Press, 1991: 149–89.

Scott, Donald M. "The Popular Lecture and the Creation of a Public in Mid-Nineteenth-Century America." *Journal of American History* 66, 4 (March 1980): 791–809.

Sewell, William H. "Review of Joan Wallach Scott's *Gender and the Politics of History.*" *History and Theory* 29, 1 (February 1990): 71–82.

Simpson, Anthony E. "Vulnerability and the Age of Female Consent: Legal Innovation and Its Effect on Prosecutions for Rape in Eighteenth Century London." In *Sexual Underworlds of the Enlightenment.* Ed. G. S. Rousseau and Roy Porter. Chapel Hill: University of North Carolina Press, 1988, pp. 181–205.

Smith, Duane E. "Romanticism in America: The Transcendentalists." *Review of Politics* 35, 3 (July 1973): 302–25.

Stansell, Christine. "The Origins of the Sweatshop: Women and Early Industrialization in New York City." In *Working-Class America.* Ed. Michael H. Frisch and Daniel J. Walkowitz. Urbana, Ill.: University of Illinois Press, 1983, pp. 78–103.

"Women, Children, and the Uses of the Streets: Class and Gender Conflict in New York City, 1850–1860." In *Unequal Sisters: A Multicultural Reader in U.S. Women's History.* Ed. Ellen C. Dubois and Vicki L. Ruiz. New York: Routledge, 1990, pp. 92–108.

Stearns, Bertha M. "Nineteenth-Century Writers in the World of Art." *Art in America* 40, 1 (Winter 1952): 29–41.

Stearns, Peter N. "The Middle Class: Toward a Precise Definition." *Comparative Studies in Society and History* 21, 3 (July 1979): 377–96.

Stevens, John Austin. "The Beginning of New York's Commercial Greatness, 1825–1837." In *The Memorial History of the City of New-York from Its First Settlement to the Year 1892.* Vol. 3. Ed. James Grant Wilson. New York: New-York History Co., 1893, pp. 334–63.

Story, Ronald. "Class and Culture in Boston: The Athenaeum, 1807–1860." *American Quarterly* 27, 2 (May 1975): 178–99.

Stull, A. Frank. "Where Famous Actors Learned Their Art." *Lippincott's Monthly Magazine* 75, 3 (March 1905): 374–5.

Taylor, George Rogers. "The Beginnings of Mass Transportation in Urban America." *Smithsonian Journal of History* 1, 2 (Summer 1966): 35–50; 1, 3 (Fall 1966): 31–54.

"Gaslight Foster: A New York 'Journeyman Journalist' at Mid-Century." *New York History* 58 (July 1977): 297–312.

Thompson, Cameron. "John Locke and New England Transcendentalism." *New England Quarterly* 35, 4 (December 1962): 435–57.

Tichi, Cecelia. "American Literary Studies to the Civil War." In *Redrawing the Boundaries: The Transformation of English and American Literary Studies.* Ed. Stephen Greenblatt and Giles Gunn. New York: Modern Language Association of America, 1992, pp. 209–31.

Todd, Charles Burr. "Telegraphs and Railroads, and Their Impulse to Commerce, 1847–1855." In *The Memorial History of the City of New-York from Its First Settlement to the Year 1892.* Vol. 3. Ed. James Grant Wilson. New York: New-York History Co., 1893, pp. 413–17.

Trudgill, Eric. "Prostitution and Paterfamilias." In *The Victorian City.* Vol. 1. Ed. H. J. Dyos and Michael Wolff. London: Routledge & Kegan Paul, 1973, pp. 693–705.

Truettner, William. "The West and the Heroic Ideal: Using Images to Interpret History." *Chronicle of Higher Education* (20 November 1991): B1–B2.

Wall, Anthony, and Clive Thompson. "Cleaning Up Bakhtin's Carnival Act." *Diacritics* 23, 2 (Summer 1993): 47–70.

Wallace, Michael. "Changing Concepts of Party in the United States: New York, 1815–1828." *American Historical Review* 74, 2 (December 1968): 453–91.

Webster, Daniel. "Opening of the Northern Railroad to Lebanon, N.H." In *The Philosophy of Manufactures.* Ed. Michael B. Folsom and Steven D. Lubar. Cambridge: MIT Press, 1982, pp. 443–6.

White, Richard Grant. "Opera in New York." Parts I and II. *Century Magazine* 23, 5 (March 1882): 686–703; 23, 6 (April 1882): 865–82.

White, Shane. "'It Was a Proud Day': African Americans, Festivals, and Parades in the North, 1741–1834." *Journal of American History* 81, 1 (June 1994): 13–50.

Wilmeth, Don B. "Noble or Ruthless Savage? The American Indian Onstage in the Drama." *Journal of American Drama and Theatre* 1, 2 (Spring 1989): 39–78.

"Tentative Checklist of Indian Plays (1606–1987)." *Journal of American Drama and Theatre* 1, 3 (Fall 1989): 34–54.

Winter, Marian Hannah. "Juba and American Minstrelsy." *Dance Index* 6, 2 (February 1947): 28–48.

Wolff, Michael, and Fox, Celina. "Pictures from the Magazines." In *The Victorian City.* Vol. 1. Ed. H. J. Dyos and Michael Wolff. London: Routledge & Kegan Paul, 1973, pp. 559–82.

Wornum, Ralph Nicholson. "The Exhibition as a Lesson in Taste." In *The Art-Journal Illustrated Catalogue.* London: George Virtue Pubs., 1851. Rpt. as *The Crystal Palace Exhibition Illustrated Catalogue: London, 1851.* With an introduction by John Gloag. New York: Dover Pubs., 1970, pp. i–xxii.

Yacavone, Donald. "Abolitionists and the 'Language of Fraternal Love.'" *Meanings for*

Manhood: Constructions of Masculinity in Victorian America. Ed. Mark C. Carnes and Clyde Griffen. Chicago: University of Chicago Press, 1990, pp. 85–95.

Yoder, R. A. "The Equilibrist Perspective: Toward a Theory of American Romanticism." *Studies in Romanticism* 12, 4 (Fall 1973): 705–40.

Books

Adelman, Melvin L. *A Sporting Time: New York City and the Rise of Modern Athletics, 1820–1870.* Urbana: University of Illinois Press, 1986.

Allwood, John. *The Great Exhibitions.* London: Studio Vista, 1977.

Altick, Richard D. *The Shows of London.* Cambridge, Mass.: Harvard University Press, 1978.

Aronowitz, Stanley. *Science as Power: Discourse and Ideology in Modern Society.* Minneapolis: University of Minnesota Press, 1988.

The Art-Journal Illustrated Catalogue. London: George Virtue Pubs., 1851. Rpt. as *The Crystal Palace Exhibition Illustrated Catalogue: London, 1851.* With an introduction by John Gloag. New York: Dover Pubs., 1970.

Asbury, Herbert. *The Gangs of New York.* New York: Alfred A. Knopf, 1927.

Austin, Gayle. *Feminist Theories for Dramatic Criticism.* Ann Arbor: University of Michigan Press, 1990.

Baker, Benjamin A. *A Glance at New York.* New York: Samuel French, n.d.

Baltzell, E. Digby. *Puritan Boston and Quaker Philadelphia.* New York: Free Press, 1979.

Barnes, Eric. *The Lady of Fashion: The Life and Theatre of Anna Cora Mowatt.* New York: Charles Scribner's Sons, 1954.

Barnum, P. T. *Selected Letters of P. T. Barnum.* Ed. A. H. Saxon. New York: Columbia University Press, 1983.

Struggles and Triumphs; or, Forty Years' Recollections of P. T. Barnum (Written by Himself). Author's Ed. New York: American News Co., 1871.

Basch, Norma. *In the Eyes of the Law: Women, Marriage, and Property in Nineteenth-Century New York.* Ithaca: Cornell University Press, 1982.

Bauer, John I. H. *John Quidor: 1801–1881.* New York: Brooklyn Museum, 1942.

Baym, Nina. *Novels, Readers, and Reviewers: Responses to Fiction in Antebellum America.* Ithaca: Cornell University Press, 1984.

Beaver, Patrick. *The Crystal Palace, 1851–1936: A Portrait of Victorian Enterprise.* London: Hugh Evelyn, 1970.

Beecher, Catherine. *Treatise on Domestic Economy.* New York: Marsh, Capen, Lyon, & Webb, 1841; rpt. New York: Schoken, 1977.

Beecher, Catherine, and Harriet Beecher Stowe. *The American Woman's Home.* 1869; rpt. Salem, N.H.: Ayer Co. Pubs., 1972.

Bernheimer, Charles. *Figures of Ill Repute: Representing Prostitution in Nineteenth-Century France.* Cambridge, Mass.: Harvard University Press, 1989.

Black Hawk. *Black Hawk: An Autobiography.* Ed. Donald Jackson. 1883; rpt. Champaign: University of Illinois Press, 1964.

Blackmar, Elizabeth. *Manhattan for Rent, 1785–1850*. Ithaca: Cornell University Press, 1989.

Blair, Walter. *Native Humor*. New York: American Book Co., 1937; rpt. San Francisco: Chandler Pub. Co., 1960.

Bledstein, Burton J. *The Culture of Professionalism: The Middle Class and the Development of Higher Education in America*. New York: W. W. Norton, 1976.

Blumin, Stuart M. *The Emergence of the Middle Class: Social Experience in the American City, 1760–1900*. Cambridge: Cambridge University Press, 1989.

Bogdan, Robert. *Freak Show: Presenting Human Oddities for Amusement and Profit*. Chicago: University of Chicago Press, 1988.

Boller, Paul F. *American Transcendentalism, 1830–1860: An Intellectual Inquiry*. New York: G. P. Putnam's Sons, 1974.

Boyer, Paul. *Urban Masses and Moral Order in America, 1820–1920*. Cambridge, Mass.: Harvard University Press, 1978.

Boyle, Thomas. *Black Swine in the Sewers of Hampstead: Beneath the Surface of Victorian Sensationalism*. New York: Viking, 1989.

Brandon, Edgar E., comp. and ed. *A Pilgrimage of Liberty: A Contemporary Account of the Triumphal Tour of General Lafayette Through the Southern and Western States in 1825, as Reported by the Local Newspapers*. Athens, Ohio: Lawhead Press, 1944.

Brooks, Peter. *The Melodramatic Imagination*. New Haven: Yale University Press, 1976.

Brown, T. Allston. *A History of the New York Stage*. 2 vols. New York: Dodd, Mead & Co., 1903.

Burge, James C. *Lines of Business: Casting Practice and Policy in the American Theatre, 1752–1899*. New York: Peter Lang, 1986.

Callow, James T. *Kindred Spirits: Knickerbocker Writers and American Artists, 1807–1855*. Chapel Hill: University of North Carolina Press, 1967.

Carlson, Marvin. *Theories of Theatre*. Exp. Ed. Ithaca: Cornell University Press, 1993.

Carnes, Mark C., and Clyde Griffen, eds. *Meanings for Manhood: Constructions of Masculinity in Victorian America*. Chicago: University of Chicago Press, 1990.

Case, Sue-Ellen. *Feminism and Theatre*. London: Macmillan, 1988.

   ed. *Performing Feminisms: Feminist Critical Theory and Theatre*. Baltimore: Johns Hopkins University Press, 1990.

Case, Sue-Ellen, and Janelle Reinelt, eds. *The Performance of Power: Theatrical Discourse and Politics*. Iowa City: University of Iowa Press, 1991.

Child, Lydia Maria. *Letters from New-York*. New York: Charles S. Francis, 1843.

   Letters from New-York: Second Series. New York: Charles S. Francis, 1845.

Clapp, William. *A Record of the Boston Stage*. Boston: J. Munroe, 1853; rpt. New York: Benjamin Blom, 1968.

Clark, T. J. *The Painting of Modern Life*. New York: Alfred A. Knopf, 1985.

Click, Patricia C. *The Spirit of the Times: Amusements in Nineteenth-Century Baltimore, Norfolk, and Richmond*. Charlottesville: University Press of Virginia, 1989.

Cogan, Frances B. *All American Girl: The Ideal of Real Womanhood in Mid-Nineteenth Century America*. Athens: University of Georgia Press, 1989.

Cohen, Hennig, and William Dillingham. *Humor of the Old Southwest.* Boston: Houghton Mifflin, 1964.

Cole, Doris. *From Tipi to Skyscraper: A History of Women in Architecture.* New York: George Braziller, 1973.

Combe, George. *Notes on the United States of America.* 3 vols. Edinburgh: Maclachlan, Stewart & Co., 1841.

Condon, George E. *Stars in the Water.* New York: Doubleday, 1974.

Cowell, Joe. *Thirty Years Passed among the Players in England and America.* 2 vols. New York: Harper & Bros., 1844.

Crapsey, Edward. *The Nether Side of New York; or, The Vice, Crime, and Poverty of the Great Metropolis.* New York: Sheldon & Co., 1872.

Cromley, Elizabeth Collins. *Alone Together: A History of New York's Early Apartments.* Ithaca: Cornell University Press, 1990.

Cronon, William. *Nature's Metropolis: Chicago and the Great West.* New York: W. W. Norton, 1991.

The Crystal Palace Exhibition Illustrated Catalogue, see The Art-Journal Illustrated Catalogue.

Curry, Leonard P. *The Free Black in Urban America, 1800–1850.* Chicago: University of Chicago Press, 1981.

Davis, David Brion. *The Slave Power Conspiracy and the Paranoid Style.* Baton Rouge: Louisiana State University Press, 1969.

Davis, Susan G. *Parades and Power: Street Theatre in Nineteenth-Century Philadelphia.* Philadelphia: Temple University Press, 1986.

Dayton, Abram. *Last Days of Knickerbocker Life.* New York: G. P. Putnam's Sons, 1897.

Degler, Carl N. *At Odds: Women and the Family in America from the Revolution to the Present Day.* New York: Oxford University Press, 1980.

D'Emilio, John, and Estelle Freedman. *Intimate Matters: A History of Sexuality in America.* New York: Harper & Row, 1988.

Denning, Michael. *Mechanic Accents: Dime Novels and Working-Class Cultures in America.* New York: Verso, 1987.

Derrida, Jacques. *Writing and Difference.* Trans. Alan Bass. Chicago: University of Chicago Press, 1978.

DeVoe, Thomas F. *The Market Book.* 1862; rpt. New York: Burt Franklin, 1969.

Dickens, Charles. *American Notes.* 1842; rpt. London: Mandarin, 1991.

Dolan, Jay P. *The Immigrant Church: New York's Irish and German Catholics, 1815–1865.* Baltimore: Johns Hopkins University Press, 1975.

Dolan, Jill. *The Feminist Spectator as Critic.* Ann Arbor: UMI Research Press, 1988.

Dorson, Richard M. *American Folklore.* Chicago: University of Chicago Press, 1959.

Downs, Robert B. *Images of America: Travelers from Abroad in the New World.* Champaign: University of Illinois Press, 1987.

Drake, Benjamin. *The Life and Adventures of Black Hawk; with Sketches of Keokuk, the Sac and Fox Indians, and the Late Black Hawk War.* Cincinnati: George Conclin, 1838.

Drew, Louisa Lane. *Autobiography*. New York: Charles Scribner's Sons, 1899.

Dudden, Faye E. *Serving Women: Household Service in Nineteenth Century America*. Middletown, Conn.: Wesleyan University Press, 1983.

Dunlap, William. *History of the American Theatre*. 2 vols. 1832; rpt. New York: Burt Franklin, 1963.

Durand, John. *The Life and Times of A. B. Durand*. New York: Charles Scribner's Sons, 1894.

Durham, Weldon B., ed. *American Theatre Companies, 1749–1887*. Westport, Conn.: Greenwood Press, 1986.

Dyos, H. J., and Michael Wolff, eds. *The Victorian City*. 2 vols. London: Routledge & Kegan Paul, 1973.

Eby, Cecil. *"That Disgraceful Affair," the Black Hawk War*. New York: W. W. Norton & Co., 1973.

Edmunds, R. David, and Joseph L. Peyser. *The Fox Wars: The Mesquakie Challenge to New France*. Norman: University of Oklahoma Press, 1993.

Eggleston, Edward, and Lillie Eggleston Seelye. *Brant and Red Jacket*. New York: Dodd, Mead & Co., 1879.

Ehrenreich, Barbara, and Deidre English. *For Her Own Good: 150 Years of The Experts' Advice to Women*. New York: Doubleday, 1978.

Elias, Norbert. *The Civilizing Process: The History of Manners*. Trans. Edmund Jephcott. New York: Urizen Books, 1978.

Emerson, Ralph Waldo. *Selected Writings*. New York: Signet/NAL, 1983.

Ernst, Robert. *Immigrant Life in New York City, 1825–1863*. New York: Columbia University / King's Crown Press, 1949.

Ewen, David. *The Story of America's Musical Theatre*. Philadelphia: Clinton Book Co., 1968.

Fairfield, Francis G. *The Clubs of New York*. New York: Henry L. Hinton, 1873.

Faron, Henry B. *Sketches of America*. London: Longman, Hurst, Rees, Orme, & Brown, 1818.

Fay, C. R. *Palace of Industry, 1851: A Study of the Great Exhibition and Its Fruits*. Cambridge: Cambridge University Press, 1951.

Feldberg, Michael. *The Turbulent Era: Riot and Disorder in Jacksonian America*. New York: Oxford University Press, 1980.

Flexner, Stuart Berg. *Listening to America*. New York: Simon & Schuster, 1982.

Flint, Timothy. *Recollections of the Last Ten Years Passed in Occasional Residences and Journeyings in the Valley of the Mississippi*. 1826; rpt. New York: DaCapo Press, 1968.

Foreman, Grant. *Indian Removal: The Emigration of the Five Civilized Tribes of Indians*. Norman: University of Oklahoma Press, 1953.

Foster, George G. *New York by Gas-Light*. New York: Dewitt & Davenport, 1850.
New York in Slices. New York: William Graham, 1849.
New York Naked. New York: Dewitt & Davenport, 1854.

Foucault, Michel. *The Foucault Reader*. Ed. Paul Rabinow. New York: Pantheon Books, 1984.
The History of Sexuality. 3 vols. Trans. Robert Hurley. New York: Vintage, 1978, 1985, and 1986.

Language, Counter-Memory, Practice. Ed. Donald F. Bouchard. Ithaca: Cornell University Press, 1977.

Michel Foucault: Politics, Philosophy, and Culture. Ed. Lawrence D. Kritzman. New York: Routledge, 1988.

Power/Knowledge. Ed. Colin Gordon. New York: Pantheon Books, 1980.

Fox-Genovese, Elizabeth, and Eugene D. Genovese. *The Fruits of Merchant Capital.* New York: Oxford University Press, 1983.

Ffrench, Yvonne. *The Great Exhibition of 1851.* London: Harvill Press, 1950.

Gay, Peter. *The Bourgeois Experience: Victoria to Freud.* 2 vols. New York: Oxford University Press, 1984, 1986.

Genovese, Eugene. *The Political Economy of Slavery.* 2d Ed. Middletown, Conn.: Wesleyan University Press, 1989.

Gerould, Daniel C. *American Melodrama.* New York: PAJ Publications, 1983.

Gibbs-Smith, C. H. *The Great Exhibition of 1851: A Commemorative Album.* London: Victoria and Albert Museum, 1850.

Giddens, Anthony. *The Class Structure of the Advanced Societies.* London: Hutchinson, 1975.

Gilfoyle, Timothy J. *City of Eros: New York City, Prostitution, and the Commercialization of Sex, 1790–1920.* New York: W. W. Norton, 1992.

Gilje, Paul A. *The Road to Mobocracy: Popular Disorder in New York City, 1763–1834.* Chapel Hill: University of North Carolina Press, 1987.

Gilpin, William. *The Central Gold Region.* 1860. Rev. Ed. (as *The Mission of the North American People*), 1873; rpt. New York: DaCapo Press, 1974.

Glanz, Dawn. *How the West Was Drawn: American Art and the Settling of the Frontier.* Ann Arbor: UMI Press, 1982.

Graham, Sylvester. *Lectures to Young Men on Chastity.* Providence, R.I.: Weeden & Cory, 1834.

Greeley, Horace. *Glances at Europe in a Series of Letters.* New York: Dewitt & Davenport Pubs., 1851.

Greenhalgh, Paul. *Ephemeral Vistas: The Expositions Universelles, Great Exhibitions and World's Fairs, 1851–1939.* Manchester: Manchester University Press, 1988.

Grimsted, David. *Melodrama Unveiled: American Theatre and Culture, 1800–1850.* Chicago: University of Chicago Press, 1968.

Hagan, William T. *The Sac and Fox Indians.* Norman: University of Oklahoma Press, 1958.

Hall, Basil. *Travels in North America, 1827–1828.* 3 vols. London: Simpkin & Marshal, 1829.

Haller, John S., and Robin M. Haller. *The Physician and Sexuality in Victorian America.* Champaign: University of Illinois Press, 1974.

Halttunen, Karen. *Confidence Men and Painted Women: A Study of Middle-Class Culture in America, 1830–1870.* New Haven: Yale University Press, 1982.

Hardie, James. *The Description of the City of New York.* New York: Samuel Marks, 1827.

Harlow, Alvin F. *Old Bowery Days.* New York: D. Appleton, 1931.

Hart, Linda, ed. *Making a Spectacle: Feminist Essays on Contemporary Women's Theatre.* Ann Arbor: University of Michigan Press, 1989.

Hartley, L. P. *The Go-Between*. London: Hamish Hamilton, 1953.

Haswell, Charles. *Reminiscences of an Octogenarian of the City of New York, 1816–1860*. New York: Harper & Bros., 1897.

Headley, Joel T. *The Great Riots of New York*. New York: E. B. Treat, 1873.

Helsinger, Elizabeth K., Robin Lauterbach Sheets, and William Veeder. *The Woman Question: Society and Literature in Britain and America, 1837–1883*. 3 vols. New York: Garland, 1983; rpt. Chicago: University of Chicago Press, 1989.

Hewitt, Barnard. *Theatre U.S.A.* New York: McGraw–Hill, 1959.

Higham, John, and Paul K. Conkin, eds. *New Directions in American Intellectual History*. Baltimore: Johns Hopkins University Press, 1979.

Hill, Stephen P. *Theatrical Amusements*. Philadelphia: Baptist General Tract Society, 1830.

Hobhouse, Christopher. *1851 and the Crystal Palace*. New York: E. P. Dutton Co., 1937.

Hodge, Francis. *Yankee Theatre: The Image of America on the Stage, 1825–1850*. Austin: University of Texas Press, 1964.

Hone, Philip. *The Diary of Philip Hone, 1828–1851*. 2 vols. Ed. Allan Nevins. New York: Dodd, Mead & Co., 1927.

Horlick, Allan S. *Country Boys and Merchant Princes: The Social Control of Young Men in New York*. Lewisburg, Pa.: Bucknell University Press, 1975.

Horton, James O., and Lois E. Horton. *Black Bostonians: Family Life and Community Struggle in the Antebellum North*. New York: Holmes & Meier, 1979.

Howe, Daniel W., ed. *Victorian America*. Philadelphia: University of Pennsylvania Press, 1976.

Hubbard, J. Niles. *An Account of Sa-Go-Ye-Wat-Ha; or, Red Jacket and His People (1750–1830)*. 1885; rpt. New York: Burt Franklin, 1971.

Hutchinson, William R. *Transcendentalist Ministers*. New Haven: Yale University Press, 1959.

Ireland, Joseph N. *Records of the New York Stage from 1750 to 1860*. 2 vols. 1866; rpt. New York: Benjamin Blom, 1966.

Jacobus, Mary, Evelyn Fox Keller, and Sally Shuttlesworth, eds. *Body Politics: Women and the Discourses of Science*. New York: Routledge, 1990.

Jahrer, Frederic Cople. *The Urban Establishment: Upper Strata in Boston, New York, Charleston, Chicago, and Los Angeles*. Champaign: University of Illinois Press, 1982.

Jennings, John J. *Theatrical and Circus Life; or, Secrets of the Stage, Green Room, and Sawdust Arena*. St. Louis: Historical Pub. Co., 1882.

Johnson, Paul E. *A Shopkeeper's Millennium: Society and Revivals in Rochester, New York, 1815–1837*. New York: Hill & Wang, 1978.

Jones, J(oseph). S. *The Carpenter of Rouen*. New York: Samuel French, 1840.

Kasson, John F. *Rudeness and Civility: Manners in Nineteenth-Century Urban America*. New York: Hill & Wang, 1990.

Kaye, Harvey J. *The British Marxist Historians*. Cambridge: Polity Press, 1984.

Kemble, Fanny [Frances Anne]. *Journal*. 2 vols. London: John Murray, 1835.

Kendall, John S. *The Golden Age of the New Orleans Theatre*. 1952; rpt. New York: Greenwood Press, 1968.

Klamkin, Marian. *The Return of Lafayette, 1824–1825.* New York: Charles Scribner's Sons, 1975.

Knowlton, Charles. *The Fruits of Philosophy.* 1832; rpt. in *Birth Control and Morality in Nineteenth Century America.* New York: Arno Press, 1972.

Koster, Donald N. *Transcendentalism in America.* Boston: Twayne Publishers, 1975.

Kroker, Arthur, and David Cook. *The Postmodern Scene: Excremental Culture and Hyper-Aesthetics.* New York: St. Martin's Press, 1986.

Laslett, Peter. *The World We Have Lost Further Explored.* Rev. Ed. New York: Charles Scribner's Sons, 1984.

Laurie, Bruce. *Working People of Philadelphia, 1800–1850.* Philadelphia: Temple University Press, 1980.

Lears, T. J. Jackson. *No Place of Grace: Antimodernism and the Transformation of American Culture, 1880–1920.* New York: Pantheon Books, 1981.

Levasseur, Auguste. *Lafayette in America in 1824 and 1825; or, Journal of a Voyage to the United States.* Trans. John D. Goodman. 2 vols. Philadelphia: Carey & Lea, 1829.

Levine, Lawrence W.. *Highbrow/Lowbrow: The Emergence of Cultural Hierarchy in America.* Cambridge, Mass.: Harvard University Press, 1988.

Levy, Anita. *Other Women: The Writing of Class, Race, and Gender, 1832–1898.* Princeton: Princeton University Press, 1991.

Lofland, Lyn H. *A World of Strangers: Order and Action in Urban Public Space.* New York: Basic Books, 1973.

Logan, Olive. *Before the Footlights and Behind the Scenes.* Philadelphia: Parmelee & Co., 1870.

Long, Clarence D. *Wages and Earnings in the United States, 1860–1890.* Princeton: Princeton University Press, 1960.

Lott, Eric. *Love and Theft: Blackface Minstrelsy and the American Working Class.* New York: Oxford University Press, 1993.

Luckhurst, Kenneth. *The Story of Exhibitions.* London: Studio, 1951.

Ludlow, Noah M. *Dramatic Life as I Found It.* 1880; rpt. New York: Benjamin Blom, 1966.

McConachie, Bruce A. *Melodramatic Formations: American Theatre and Society, 1820–1870.* Iowa City: University of Iowa Press, 1992.

McCullough, Edo. *World's Fair Midways.* New York: Exposition Press, 1966.

McKenney, Thomas L., and James Hall. *The Indian Tribes of North America.* 2 vols. 1844; rpt. Edinburgh: John Grant, 1933–4.

Mahood, Linda. *The Magdalens: Prostitution in the Nineteenth Century.* London: Routledge, 1990.

Marcus, Steven. *The Other Victorians: A Study of Pornography in Mid-Nineteenth Century England.* New York: Basic Books / Bantam, 1966.

Marryat, Frederick. *Diary in America.* 3 vols. London: Longman, Orme, Brown, Green & Longmans, 1839.

Martineau, Harriet. *A Retrospect of Western Travel.* 3 vols. 1838; rpt. Westport, Conn.: Greenwood Press, 1970.

Society in America. New York: Saunders & Otley, 1837.

Mason, Jeffrey D. *Melodrama and the Myth of America.* Bloomington: Indiana University Press, 1993.

Mathews, Cornelius. *Pen and Ink Panorama of New York City.* New York: John S. Taylor, 1853.

Matthiessen, F. O. *American Renaissance: Art and Expression in the Age of Emerson and Whitman.* New York: Oxford University Press, 1941.

Mayhew, Henry. *London Labour and the London Poor.* 1861–2; rpt. New York: Dover 1968.

Mayhew, Henry, and George Cruikshank. *1851; or, The Adventures of Mr. and Mrs. Sandboys and Family Who Came Up to London to "Enjoy Themselves," and to See the Great Exhibition.* London: George Newbold, 1851.

Medina, Louisa. *Nick of the Woods.* Boston: Spenser's Boston Theatre, n.d.

Meserve, Walter J. *An Emerging Entertainment: The Drama of the American People to 1828.* Bloomington: Indiana University Press, 1977.

—— *Heralds of Promise: The Drama of the American People in the Age of Jackson, 1829–1849.* Westport, Conn.: Greenwood Press, 1986.

Miller, Wilber R. *Cops and Bobbies: Police Authority in New York and London, 1830–1870.* Chicago: University of Chicago Press, 1973.

Monkkonen, Eric H. *Police in Urban America, 1860–1920.* Cambridge: Cambridge University Press, 1980.

Moody, Richard, ed. *Dramas from the American Theatre.* Boston: Houghton Mifflin, 1966.

Morris, Clara. *Life on the Stage.* New York: McClure, Phillips & Co., 1901.

Moses, John, and Joseph Kirkland. *The History of Chicago, Illinois.* 2 vols. Chicago: Munsell, 1895.

Moses, Montrose J. *Representative Plays by American Dramatists.* 3 vols. 1925; rpt. New York: Arno Press, 1978.

Mott, Frank Luther. *American Journalism: A History of Newspapers in the United States through 250 years, 1690–1940.* New York: Macmillan & Co., 1941.

—— *A History of American Magazines, 1741–1850.* Cambridge, Mass.: Harvard University Press, 1939.

Mowatt, Anna Cora. *Autobiography of an Actress.* Boston: Ticknor, Reed, & Fields, 1854.

Mulvey, Christopher. *Anglo-American Landscapes: A Study of Nineteenth-Century Anglo-American Travel Literature.* Cambridge: Cambridge University Press, 1983.

Mushkat, Jerome. *Tammany: The Evolution of a Political Machine, 1789–1865.* Syracuse: Syracuse University Press, 1971.

Nathan, Hans. *Dan Emmett and the Rise of Early Negro Minstrelsy.* Norman: University of Oklahoma Press, 1974.

Nevins, Allan. *American Social History as Recorded by British Travellers.* New York: Henry Holt & Co., 1923.

Newhall, Beaumont. *The Daguerreotype in America.* New York: New York Graphic Society, 1961.

Nissenbaum, Stephen. *Sex, Diet, and Debility in Jacksonian America: Sylvester Graham and Health Reform.* Westport, Conn.: Greenwood Press, 1980.

Nolan, J. Bennett. *Lafayette in America Day by Day.* Baltimore: Johns Hopkins University Press, 1934.

Norton, Anne. *Alternative Americas: A Reading of Antebellum Political Culture.* Chicago: University of Chicago Press, 1986.

Novak, Barbara. *American Painting of the Nineteenth Century: Realism, Idealism and the American Experience.* 2d ed. New York: Harper & Row, 1979.

Novick, Peter. *That Noble Dream: The 'Objectivity Question' and the American Historical Profession.* Cambridge: Cambridge University Press, 1988.

Odell, George C. D. *Annals of the New York Stage.* 15 vols. New York: Columbia University Press, 1927–48.

The Official Catalogue of the Great Exhibition of the Works of Industry of All Nations, 1851. Corrected Ed. London: W. Clowes & Sons, 1851.

Owen, Robert Dale. *Moral Physiology.* 1829; rpt. in *Birth Control and Morality in Nineteenth Century America.* New York: Arno Press, 1972.

Parker, A. C. *Red Jacket: Last of the Seneca.* New York: McGraw–Hill, 1952.

Parry, Ellwood C. *The Image of the Indian and the Black Man in American Art, 1590–1900.* New York: George Braziller, 1974.

Parson, C. B. *The Pulpit and the Stage.* Nashville: Southern Methodist Pub. House, 1860.

Paulding, James Kirke, John Augustus Stone, and William Bayle Bernard. *The Lion of the West.* Ed. James N. Tidwell. Stanford: Stanford University Press, 1954.

Pearce, Roy Harvey. *The Savages of America: A Study of the Indian and the Idea of Civilization.* Rev. Ed. Baltimore: Johns Hopkins University Press, 1965.

Peiss, Kathy, and Christina Simmons, eds. *Passion and Power: Sexuality in History.* Philadelphia: Temple University Press, 1989.

Persons, Stow. *The Decline of Gentility.* New York: Columbia University Press, 1973.

Pessen, Edward. *Riches, Class and Power before the Civil War.* Lexington, Mass.: D. C. Heath & Co., 1973.

Peters, Virginia B. *The Florida Wars.* Hamden, Conn.: Archon Books, 1979.

Phillips, Jonas B. The Carpenter of Rouen. New York: Samuel French, 1840.

Pintard, John. *Letters from John Pintard to his Daughter Elizabeth Pintard Davidson.* New York: New-York Historical Society, 1940–1.

Postlewait, Thomas, and Bruce A. McConachie, eds. *Interpreting the Theatrical Past: Essays in Historiography of Performance.* Iowa City: University of Iowa Press, 1989.

Power, Tyrone. *Impressions of America During the Years 1833, 1834 and 1835.* London: Bentley, 1836.

Pritchard, John Paul. *Literary Wise Men of Gotham: Criticism in New York, 1815–1860.* Baton Rouge: Louisiana State University Press, 1963.

Pugh, David G. *Sons of Liberty: The Masculine Mind in Nineteenth-Century America.* Westport, Conn.: Greenwood Press, 1983.

Quinn, Arthur Hobson. *A History of the American Drama from the Beginning to the Civil War.* New York: Appleton–Century–Crofts, 1923.

Ranney, H. M. *Account of the Terrific and Fatal Riot at the New-York Opera House, on the Night of May 10th, 1849.* New York: H. M. Ranney, 1849.

Reinelt, Janelle G., and Joseph R. Roach, eds. *Critical Theory and Performance.* Ann Arbor: University of Michigan Press, 1992.

Reynolds, Larry J. *James Kirke Paulding.* Boston: Twayne Publishing, 1984.

Rice, Kym S. *Early American Taverns: For the Entertainment of Friends and Strangers.* Chicago: Regnery Gateway & Fraunces Tavern Museum, 1983.

Richards, Leonard. *"Gentlemen of Property and Standing": Anti-Abolition Mobs in Jacksonian America.* New York: Oxford University Press, 1970.

Rinear, David L. *The Temple of Momus: Mitchell's Olympic Theatre.* Metuchen, N.J.: Scarecrow Press, 1987.

Rock, Howard B. *Artisans of the New Republic.* New York: New York University Press, 1979.

Rodgers, Charles T. *American Superiority at the World's Fair.* Philadelphia: John J. Hawkins, 1852.

Rogin, Michael P. *Fathers and Children: Andrew Jackson and the Subjugation of the American Indian.* New York: Alfred A. Knopf, 1975.

Rorabaugh, W. J. *The Alcoholic Republic: An American Tradition.* New York: Oxford University Press, 1979.

Rothman, David J. *The Discovery of the Asylum: Social Order and Disorder in the New Republic.* Rev. Ed. Boston: Little, Brown & Co., 1990.

Rourke, Constance. *American Humor.* 1931; rpt. New York: Anchor Books, 1953.

Ryan, Kate. *Old Boston Museum Days.* Boston: Little, Brown, 1915.

Ryan, Mary P. *Cradle of the Middle Class: The Family in Oneida County, New York, 1790–1865.* Cambridge: Cambridge University Press, 1981.

Women in Public: Between Banners and Ballots, 1825–1880. Baltimore: Johns Hopkins University Press, 1990.

Rydell, Robert W. *All the World's a Fair: Visions of Empire at American Industrial Expositions, 1876–1916.* Chicago: University of Chicago Press, 1984.

Saint-Méry, Moreau de. *Moreau de Saint-Méry's American Journey* [1793–8]. Trans. Kenneth and Anna M. Roberts. Garden City, N.Y.: Doubleday & Co., 1947.

Sanger, William. *The History of Prostitution: Its Extent, Causes and Effects Throughout the World.* 1859; rpt. New York: Medical Publishing Co., 1921.

Satz, Ronald N. *American Indian Policy in the Jacksonian Era.* Lincoln: University of Nebraska Press, 1975.

Saunders, Frederic. *Memories of the Great Metropolis; or, London, from the Tower to the Crystal Palace.* New York: G. P. Putnam Pubs., 1851.

Saxon, A. H. *P. T. Barnum: The Legend and the Man.* New York: Columbia University Press, 1989.

Saxton, Alexander. *The Rise and Fall of the White Republic: Class Politics and Mass Culture in Nineteenth-Century America.* London: Verso, 1990.

Schudson, Michael. *Discovering the News: A Social History of American Newspapers.* New York: Basic Books, 1978.

Schlueter, June, ed. *Feminist Rereadings of Modern American Drama.* Rutherford, N.J.: Fairleigh Dickinson University Press, 1989.

Senelick, Laurence. *The Age and Stage of George L. Fox, 1825–1877.* Hanover, N.H.: University Press of New England, 1988.

Shaw, Ronald E. *Erie Water West.* Lexington: University of Kentucky Press, 1966.

Siegel, Adrienne. *The Image of the American City in Popular Literature, 1820–1870.* Port Washington, N.Y.: Kennikat Press, 1981.

Silko, Leslie Marmon. *Ceremony.* New York: Penguin Books, 1979.

Skinner, Otis. *Footlights and Spotlights.* Indianapolis: Bobbs Merrill, 1924.

Smith, James L., ed. *Victorian Melodramas.* London: J. M. Dent, 1976.

Smith, Seba. *May-Day in New-York; or, House-Hunting and Moving.* New York: Burgess, Stringer, 1845.

Smith, Sol. *Theatrical Management in the West and South for Thirty Years.* 1868; rpt. New York: Benjamin Blom, 1968.

Smith-Rosenberg, Carroll. *Disorderly Conduct: Visions of Gender in Victorian America.* New York: Alfred A. Knopf, 1985.

Sokolow, Jayme A. *Eros and Modernization: Sylvester Graham, Health Reform, and the Origins of Victorian Sexuality in America.* Cranberry, N.J.: Associated University Presses, 1983.

Sollers, Werner. *Beyond Ethnicity: Consent and Descent in American Culture.* Oxford: Oxford University Press, 1986.

Stansell, Christine. *City of Women: Sex and Class in New York, 1789–1860.* New York: Alfred A. Knopf, 1986.

Stanton, William. *The Leopard's Spots: Scientific Attitudes Toward Race in America, 1815–1859.* Chicago: University of Chicago Press, 1960.

Stott, Richard B. *Workers in the Metropolis: Class, Ethnicity, and Youth in Antebellum New York City.* Ithaca: Cornell University Press, 1990.

Strasser, Susan. *Never Done: A History of American Housework.* New York: Pantheon Books, 1982.

Strong, George Templeton. *The Diary of George Templeton Strong.* 4 vols. Ed. Allan Nevins and Milton Halsey Thomas. New York: Macmillan, 1952.

Stuart-Wortley, Emmeline. *Travels in the United States . . . during 1849–1850.* New York: Harper & Bros., 1851.

Sweeney, J. Gray. *The Columbus of the Woods: Daniel Boone and the Typology of Manifest Destiny.* St. Louis: Washington University Gallery of Art, 1992.

Tallis's History and Description of the Crystal Palace and the Exhibition of the World's Industry in 1851. London: John Tallis & Co., n.d.

Tasistro, Louis F. *Random Shots and Southern Breezes.* New York: Harper & Bros., 1842.

Thayer, Stuart. *Annals of the American Circus, 1793–1829.* Manchester, Mich.: Rymack Press, 1976.

Thorburn, Grant. *The Life and Writings of Grant Thorburn.* New York: Edward Walker, 1852.

Thoreau, Henry David. *Walden and On the Duty of Civil Disobedience.* New York: Harper & Row, 1965.

Tocqueville, Alexis de. *Democracy in America.* Ed. Phillips Bradley. 2 vols. New York: Random House / Vintage Books, 1990.

Todd, Charles Burr. *The Story of The City of New York.* New York: G. P. Putnam's Sons, 1888.

Todorov, Tzvetan. *The Conquest of America*. Trans. Richard Howard. New York: Harper & Row, 1984.

Toll, Robert. *Blacking Up: The Minstrel Show in Nineteenth Century America*. New York: Oxford University Press, 1974.

Transactions of the Buffalo Historical Society, vol. 3: Red Jacket. Buffalo: Buffalo Historical Society, 1885.

Troll, Russell T. *Sexual Physiology: A Scientific and Popular Exposition of the Fundamental Problems in Sociology*. New York: Miller, Wood, & Co., 1866.

Trollope, Frances. *Domestic Manners of the Americans*. Ed. Donald Smalley. New York: Vintage Books, 1960.

Truettner, William. *The Natural Man Observed: A Study of Catlin's Indian Gallery*. Washington: Smithsonian Institution Press, 1979.

   ed. *The West as America: Reinterpreting Images of the Frontier, 1820–1920*. Washington: National Museum of American Art / Smithsonian Institution Press, 1991.

Turnbull, Robert. *The Theatre*. Hartford, Conn.: Caulfield & Robins, 1837.

   The Theatre in Its Influence upon Literature, Morals, and Religion. Boston: Gould, Kendall, & Lincoln, 1839.

Tyrrell, Ian R. *Sobering Up: From Temperance to Prohibition in Antebellum America, 1800–1860*. Westport, Conn.: Greenwood Press, 1979.

Viola, Herman J. *The Indian Legacy of Charles Bird King*. New York: Doubleday & Co. / Smithsonian Institution Press, 1976.

Walters, Ronald G. *American Reformers, 1815–1860*. New York: Hill & Wang, 1978.

Wellman, Paul J. *The House Divides: The Age of Jackson and Lincoln, from the War of 1812 to the Civil War*. New York: Doubleday & Co., 1966.

Weinbaum, Paul O. *Mobs and Demagogues: The New York Response to Collective Violence in the Early Nineteenth Century*. Ann Arbor: UMI Press, 1977.

Wheeler, John, and Wojciech H. Zurek, eds. *Quantum Theory and Measurement*. Princeton: Princeton University Press, 1983.

Wilentz, Sean. *Chants Democratic: New York City and the Rise of the American Working Class, 1788–1850*. Oxford: Oxford University Press, 1984.

Wilmerding, John, ed. *American Light: The Luminist Movement, 1850–1875*. Princeton: Princeton University Press, 1989.

   ed. *The Genius of American Painting*. New York: William Morrow, 1973.

Wilson, James Grant, ed. *The Memorial History of the City of New-York from Its First Settlement to the Year 1892*. 3 vols. New York: New-York History Co., 1893.

Wittke, Carl. *Tambo and Bones*. 1930; rpt. Westport, Conn.: Greenwood Press, 1968.

Wolf, Fred Alan. *Parallel Universes*. New York: Simon & Schuster, 1988.

Wood, William B. *Personal Recollections of the Stage*. Philadelphia: H. C. Baird, 1853.

Wyllie, Irvin G. *The Self-Made Man in America: The Myth of Rags to Riches*. New York: Free Press, 1954.

Young, William C. *Documents of American Theatre History*. 2 vols. Chicago: American Library Association, 1973.

Dissertations

Angotti, Vincent L. "American Dramatic Criticism, 1800–1830." Ph.D. diss. University of Kansas, 1967.

Buckley, Peter G. "To the Opera House: Culture and Society in New York City, 1820–1860." Ph.D. diss. State University of New York–Stony Brook, 1984.

Calhoun, Richard B. "From Community to Metropolis: Fire Protection in New York City, 1790–1875." Ph.D. diss. Columbia University, 1973.

Gilfoyle, Timothy J. "City of Eros: New York City, Prostitution, and the Commercialization of Sex, 1790–1920." Ph.D. diss. Columbia University, 1987.

Ginsberg, Stephen F. "The History of Fire Protection in New York City, 1800–1842." Ph.D. diss. New York University, 1968.

Groneman-Pernicone, Carol. "The 'Bloody Ould Sixth': A Social Analysis of a New York City Working-Class Community in the Mid-Nineteenth Century." Ph.D. diss. University of Rochester, 1973.

Grose, Burl D. "'Here Come the Indians': An Historical Study of the Representations of the Native American upon the North American Stage, 1808–1969." Ph.D. diss. University of Missouri, 1979.

Jentz, John B. "Artisans, Evangelicals, and the City: A Social History of Abolition and Labor Reform in Jacksonian New York." Ph.D. diss. City University of New York, 1977.

LaBudde, Kenneth J. "The Mind of Thomas Cole." Ph.D. diss. University of Minnesota, 1954.

Litto, Frederic. "Edmund Simpson of the Park Theatre, New York, 1809–1848." Ph.D. diss. Indiana University, 1969.

Moehring, Eugene P. "Public Works and the Patterns of Urban Real Estate Growth in Manhattan, 1847–1855." Ph.D. diss. City University of New York, 1976.

Mulvey, Kathleen A. "The Growth, Development, and Decline of the Popularity of American Indian Plays before the Civil War." Ph.D. diss. New York University, 1978.

Salvaggio, Odette C. "American Dramatic Criticism, 1830–1860." Ph.D. diss. Florida State University, 1979.

Shank, Theodore. "The Bowery Theatre, 1826–1836." Ph.D. diss. Stanford University, 1956.

Nineteenth-Century Periodicals

American Quarterly Review. June 1827: 331–57; September 1830: 134–61; December 1832: 509–31.

Art-Union Journal. 4 (1842): 282–3.

Boston Herald. 31 July 1854

Commercial Advertiser. 15 March 1833; 8 July 1834.

Courier and Enquirer. 8 July 1834; 10 July 1834.

Daily Advertiser. 10 July 1834; 12 July 1834.

Daily News (London). 14 July 1851.

Frankfort (Kentucky) Commonwealth. 30 July 1833.

Illustrated London News. 31 May 1851.

Journal of Commerce. 10–11 July 1834.

Ladies Companion. July 1837.

Mercantile Advertiser. 10 July 1834.

National Intelligencer. 6–11 February 1836.

New York American, for the Country. 17–18 October 1831.

New York Argus. 3 August 1844.

New York Aurora. 7 October 1843.

New York Clarion. 13 October 1839; 19 November 1849.

New York Dramatic Mirror. 25 April 1841.

New York Evening Post. 11 July 1834; 5 November 1825.

New York Evening Star. 18 January 1834; 10 July 1834.

New York Gazette. 24 September 1832.

New York Herald. 23 September 1836; 26 April 1848.

New York Mirror. 15 May 1824; 4 December 1824; 15 April 1826; 12 April 1828; 23 August 1828; 10 October 1833; 15 March 1835; 5 March 1836; 20 August 1836.

New York Morning News. 17 December 1845.

New York Sun. 2 April 1834; 9–12 July 1834.

New York Times. 12 July 1834; 9 October 1866.

Niles' Weekly Register. 15 June 1833.

Spirit of the Times. 14 April 1832; 21 December 1833; 3 January 1835; 27 February 1836; 18 July 1846.

Transcript and Wasp. 12 July 1834.

Washington Globe. 8 February 1836; 11 February 1836; 15 February 1836; 19 February 1836.

Unpublished Materials

Blau, Herbert. "Theory and Criticism Seminar: Herbert Blau." Association for Theatre in Higher Education Conference, Chicago, 29 July 1994.

Index

abolition, *see* slavery, abolitionism
abortion, 229n46
achievement, urban creed for, 55, 56
actors, 38, 39, 93–4, 95–6, 116
  and audience participation, 84
  club membership, 203n21
  and criticism, 115
  lines of work, 94
  salaries of, 94–5
Adams, John Quincy, 17–18, 60
advice books, 80, 107, 109, 114, 122, 127, 141,
  145
African Americans, 93, 154, 156
  employment, 81, 93
  free blacks, 17; in cities, 46; in competition
    for housing and jobs, 81; Lafayette and,
    21–2; segregation of, 50–1; and theatres,
    96–7, 113
  market, street, and tavern performers, 16,
    97–9, 159
  mob assaults on, 158
  Revolutionary War veterans, 21–2
  segregation, 50–1, 96–7, 133, 148, 152
  women equated with prostitutes, 133
  see also character types, Negro; minstrelsy;
    slavery
African (Grove) Theatre (New York), 96–7
Aiken, George L., 147, 148, 149, 150
Albert of Saxe-Coburg-Gotha (prince consort
  of Queen Victoria), 167, 172, 182, 253n2
Alcott, Bronson, 33
Alcott, William, 145
Aldridge, Ira, 97

Allston, Washington, 35
Almanacs (Crockett), 63
Altick, Richard D., 182
America, *see* United States
America (yacht), 177
American Art-Union, 69
American (Caldwell's) Theatre (New Orleans),
  21
American Museum (New York), 11, 48
*American Scenery. Time: Afternoon with a
  Southwest Haze* (artwork), 35
"American School" of ethnology, 154
American Theatre, Bowery, *see* Bowery
  Theatre
American Woman's Home, The (Beecher and
  Stowe), 147
Anderson, Joshua, 116, 156
  "riot" pertaining to (1831), 115, 116, 158
Apartments to Let (play), 182
art, American, 31, 187
  frontier in, 69
  literature referenced, 36, 69
  and ornamentation, 188–9
  town in, 35–6
artisan tradition, 82, 88, 100
  and manliness, 81–9
  as myth, 14, 80, 81, 90, 142
Association for the Exhibition of the Industry
  of All Nations, *see* New York Crystal
  Palace
Astor, Henry, 48, 51
Astor, John Jacob, 46, 127
Astor Place Theatre riot, 111–12, 115

281

audiences
　behavior, 54, 82–4, 117, 141, 157; control of,
　　128–38, 139, 158
　and class, 48–50, 84–5, 93, 111–13, 115–18, 132,
　　232n55
　free blacks in, 96–7, 113
　morality, 128, 129, 131–2
　self-performances of, 112, 153
　women in, 113–14, 122
　see also prostitutes, in theatres
Austin, Mrs., 48
authenticity, 7–8, 9, 59–60
　in cultural performance, 164
　in Indian drama, 67
　of staged Yankee, 42
　in transcendent town, 41
　in urban space, 56, 57

Babbling Brook, The (artwork), 37
Baker, Benjamin A., 86
Bank of the United States, 232n54
Barnum, P. T., 62, 180, 182, 183, 184–6, 188
Barnum's American Museum (New York), 48,
　143
Bateman, H. L., 103
Bateman, Sidney F., 103–7
Battle of Lake Erie, 24
Battle of New Orleans, 20
Beecher, Catherine, 102, 147, 149
Beecher, Henry Ward, 35
Beekman, John, 46
Bells, The (play), 103
Benjamin, Walter, 8
Bennett, James Gordon, 112, 114, 120
Benton, Thomas Hart, 216n74
Bernard, William Bayle, 70
Bhabha, Homi, 4
Bingham, George Caleb, 36, 69
Bird, Robert Montgomery, 36, 72, 117
Black Hawk, 64–6, 68, 139
Black Hawk (play), 251n62
Black Hawk War (1832), 22, 65
blacks, *see* African Americans
Blau, Herbert, 189
boarders, 100, 102
Bogdan, Robert, 186
Bohr, Niels, 169
Booth, Junius Brutus, 84
Borges, Jorge Luis, 1–2, 3
Boston, 41, 44, 46
　Lafayette in, 11, 14, 22
　population turnover, 43
Boston Athenaeum, 121, 250n59
Boston Museum, 94, 143
Boucicault, Dion, 55–9, 210n44

Bowery Amphitheatre, 251n62
Bowery B'hoy, 6, 74, 82, 85–90, 99, 107, 123,
　164, *Figs. 14–17*
Bowery G'hal, 3, 6, 88, 90–3, 119, 131–2, 162,
　Figs. 17, 19
Bowery Theatre (New York), 13, 46–8, 50,
　51–2, 59, 72, 94, 98, 135
　audience behavior, 84
　class and gentility in, 115–18, 119,
　　209n41
　destruction of, 152, 155–7, 158
　gas lighting, 103
　local color at, 159–60
　nativism, 90, 116
　and prostitution, 136
　staged Negro at, 161
　street connection, 87
　ticket prices, 51
Brace Rock, Brace's Cove (artwork), 70
Brecht, Bertolt, 8, 189
Briar Cliff (novel, play), 118
Broglie, Louis de, 169
Brook Farm, 32, 33–5
　theatre at, 34–5
brothels, *see* prostitution
Brougham, John, 143–4
Brown, Junius, 235n2
Brown, T. Allston, 183, 185
Brownson, Orestes, 33, 41, 42, 141
Bryant, William Cullen, 36
Buchanan, James, 60
Buckley, Peter, 157
Bunker Hill monument, 14, 22
Bunker Hill Monument (play), 12

Caldwell's Camp Street Theatre (New
　Orleans), 133
California News (artwork), 69
Caliph of Bagdad, The (opera), 34
Carpenter of Rouen, The (play), 90
Carstensen, Georg J. B., 183
Castle Garden (New York), 11, 12–13, 14, 25,
　48, 132, 184
Cataract of the Ganges, The (play), 117
Catharine Street Market (New York), 97,
　98
Catlin, George, 24, 62, 63, 65, 66, 177, 178,
　188, 189
　Indian Gallery, 177, 178–81, 190, *Fig. 26*
celebration, 5, 9
　of Erie Canal opening, 24–5, *Fig. 3*
　of Lafayette, 9–23
Centennial Exposition (Philadelphia), 186
Chambers Street Theatre (New York), 103
Chanfrau, Frank, 86–8, 90, *Figs. 15–17*

character types, 31–2, 38–42, 76, 88, 90, 97–9
  frontiersman, 71–2, *Figs. 8–9*
  Indian, 64, 66, 68
  Negro, 97, 159, 160–4 (*see also* minstrelsy)
  urban, 54, 82–4 (*see also* Bowery B'hoy;
    Bowery G'hal)
  Yankee, 29, 31, 37–42, 68, 90, 103–4, 149,
    159, 160, 251n62; female, 38, 42, 204n28
  see also local color
charity, 148–9
Charleston, 50, 78, 96, 187
Chartists, 73
Chatham Garden Theatre (New York), 11, 12,
  13, 16, 46, *Fig. 7; see also* Chatham Theatre
Chatham Museum (New York), 48
Chatham Street Chapel (New York), 155–6, 158
Chatham Theatre (New York), 48, 50, 51–4,
  86, 98, 136; *see also* Chatham Garden
  Theatre
Chestnut Street Theatre (Philadelphia), 14
Chicago, 187
Child, Lydia Maria, 31, 123, 137, 250n59
child labor, 100
child rearing, 101–2, 103–7, 111
Cincinnati, 11, 50, 54, 96, 113, 130, 159
Cinderella (opera), 48–9, 51
circuses, 48, 62
cities, 5, 6, 14, 29, 42–59, 60, 75, 190
  "city books," 43
  control of, 59
  heroes and heroines in, 110
  as historical sites, 72–3
  neighborhoods, 152, 153
  in popular literature, 210n44
  population growth, 42–3
  social organization of, 43–4
  as spaces of representation, 76
  and theatre culture, 153–4
  women in, 122–3
  see also urban planning; urban space
civic disorder/disturbance, 120, 141
  containment, 151–2
  regulation of, 111, 129–40
  theatres and, 115, 139–40, 156–8
civil disobedience, 32, 33–4, 42
Civil War, 68
Clark, T. J., 5
class, 99–119
  in American plays, 41, 54, 56–7, 88
  Brook Farm and, 33
  Crystal Palace exhibition and, 168, 173–4,
    188, *Figs. 21–22*
  Farren "riot" and, 157
  as liminal, 109–10
  middle class, 58, 76, 99, 110; desire to be, 82;

and family planning, 229n46; gentility
    scenario, 107–8, 113, 119; home, 101–3,
    206n33 (*see also* housing); survival
    strategies, 107–8
  performance of, 8, 107, 119
  race and, 99, 160–4
  theatre audience and, 48–50, 84–5, 93, 111–13,
    115–18, 132, 232n55
  tripartite structuring of, 76–7, 133, 115–18
  and upward mobility, 77, 88–9
  working class, 92, 131
clerks, 78, 80, 82, 104, 246n38
  rules for, 108
  and temperance, 144
Click, Patricia C., 113
Clinton, De Witt, 23, 24
club membership, 30, 108, 203n21
"Coal Black Rose" (song), 160
Cole, Henry, 175, 182
Cole, Thomas, 35–6, 69
Coleridge, Samuel Taylor, 30, 31
comedy, 111
commodification, 7, 13–14, 23, 109, 186, 188–9,
  190, 233n55
communal (the), individual and, 30, 33, 72–3,
  141, 147, 148
Comstock, Anthony, 126
conspiracy theories, 140, 154–5, 157
Contrast, The (play), 39
Cook, Thomas, 172
Cooper, James Fenimore, 36
Coowescoowe, *see* Ross, John
Corps of Men of Colour, 21
Corsair, The (play), 34
country manners, 109, 110
Courier and Enquirer, 154, 156
Cousin, Victor, 30, 31
Cowell, Joe, 52, 82, 103, 136
Cramer, John, 169
Crockett, Davy, 63, 70, 71, 162, 231n51
Cruger's Wharf Theatre (New York), 133
Crystal Palace exhibition (London), 7, 167–82,
  186, 187, 188, 189, 190, *Figs. 22–25*
  American Committee for, 168
  American display at, 176–82, *Fig. 25*
  Building Committee for, 170–1
  craftsmen and craft at, 174–5
  cultural benefits, 181
  as staging of culture, 177, 178, 181
  in Sydenham, 182
cult of domesticity, 102, 121
culture, 2, 6, 9
  and control, 5–6, 7, 118, 119, 187
  and elites, 26, 73, 187
  exhibits of, 62, 186

culture *(cont.)*
  hierarchies of, 50, 170
  and nationalism, 12–13, 90
  and race, 97, 159–64
  as simultaneous, 186
  and tourism, 173–4
  see also theatre culture
Curry, Leonard P., 46, 50, 80–1, 96
Cushman, Charlotte, 95
Custis, George Washington Parke, 64, 66–7, 68

daguerreotype, 189
Daniel Boone and His Cabin at Great Osage Lake (artwork), 36
Daniel Boone Escorting Settlers (artwork), 69
Daniel Boone's First View of Kentucky (artwork), 63
Davis, David Brion, 154, 229n47, 230n49
Davis, Jefferson, 184
Davis, Susan G., 14, 92
democracy, 28, 73
  in *Fashion*, 54–5
  transcendental, 33
De Voe, Thomas, 97
Dickens, Charles, 31, 98, 109
Dictionary (Webster), 76
Dixon, George Washington, 160, 163
Dolan, Jay, 153
domestic architecture, 108, 230n49
Domestic Manners of the Americans (Trollope), 48–9, 109
Dream of Arcadia (artwork), 69
Drew, Glover, 34
Drew, Louisa Lane, 94, 95
Drunkard, The; or, the Fallen Saved (play), 38, 41, 141, 143–7, 148, 149
  and the temperance movement, 2
Drury Lane Theatre, 115
Dunlap, William, 36, 128–30, 132, 133, 138, 241n20
Durand, Asher, 36, 37
Dwight, John S., 34

École des Vieillards, L' (play), 21
education, 109
Ellsler, Fanny, 34
Emerson, Ralph Waldo, 201n9, 204n28
  and Brook Farm, 33
  and the Over-Soul, 31, 39, 216n72
  and social theory, 32–3, 41, 109
  and theatre, 35
  and transcendentalism, 30–2, 43, 70, 147
employment, *see* labor
Engels, Friedrich, 6

entertainment
  "edifying," 188–9
  honoring Lafayette, 11–12, 21, 21, 19–21, 22
  London, 172
  places of, in U.S., 114
  and temperance movement, 143
  variety type, 113
Erie Canal, 22, 28, 78
  opening of, 5, 9, 10, 23–5, 26, 81
etiquette books, 3, 107, 110, 122
Everett, Hugh, 169
"Exhibition as a Lesson in Taste, The" (Wornum), 188
Exhibition Herald and Excursion Organizer, 172
exhibitions/expositions, 186
  fairs, contents and ideologies of, 168–9, 181
  see also Crystal Palace exhibition; New York Crystal Palace
expansionism (U.S.), 60, 68–9, 73

Farmers Nooning (artwork), 36
Farren, George, 155–6, 157, 158
  "riot" pertaining to (1834), 115, 154, 155–8, 159, 161, 162
Fashion (play), 54–6, 57, 70, 99, 104
Fay, Theodore S., 118
Federal Street Theatre (Boston), 129–30, 132
Fichte, Johann, 30
fire companies, 82, 87, 152, 153
Fisher, Philip, 165
Five Points (New York), 52, 56, 98, 127, 152, 158, *Figs. 4, 13*
Flynn, Joyce, 3
Flynn, Thomas, 158
Forest Rose, The; or, American Farmers (play), 36–7, 38, 41, 42, 54, 144
Forrest, Edwin, 70, 73, 90, 155, 156, *Fig. 10*
Foster, George G., 107, 130, 132, 135, 136, 235n2
Foucault, Michel, 5–6, 150
Fourier, François, 34
Fourierism, 33, 34
Fredericksburg, Va., 17
free blacks, *see* African Americans
Frémont, John Charles, 181
Frith, Simon, 6
Front Street Theatre (Baltimore), 65
frontier (the), 5, 6, 14, 29, 59–72, 75, 216n72
  in history, 60, 72–3
  ideological content of depictions of, 69
  as space of representation, 76
frontiersman (type), *see* character types, frontiersman
Fuller, Margaret, 35, 41, 163

Garrick, David, 117
Gates, Henry Louis, 164
Gazette and General Advertiser, 140
gender, 2–3, 4–5, 110, 164
    constructs of, 109–10
    Crystal Palace exhibition and, 168
    Farren "riot" and, 158
    staged Negro and, 162
    Stowe and, 147
gentility, 6
    class location via, 113
    in melodramas, 106, 109, 117, 118
    performance of, 107–8, 109
    rebellion against, 107
    in theatres, 114–18
gentrification campaign, 109, 113, 114–15, 138
Georgia Champion Minstrels, 98
Gildemeister, Charles, 183
Gilfoyle, Timothy J., 126, 136, 138
Gilpin, William, 68
Gladiator, The (play), 96
Glance at New York, A (play), 86–8, 90–2
Gorn, Elliot, 82
Gouverneur, Samuel, 51, 249n55
Graham, Sylvester, 124–5
"Grand Aquatic Display," 25
Great Exhibition of the Works of Industry of
    All Nations, *see* Crystal Palace exhibition
Greek Slave, The (artwork), 177, 190
Greeley, Horace, 112, 115, 176, 183, 184
Green Mountain Boy, The (play), 37
"guilty third tier," *see* prostitutes, in theatres

Hackett, James H., 39, 41, 63, 70, 71, 90,
    203n22, 251n62, *Fig. 8*
Hamblin, Thomas, 52, 89–90, 94, 95, 116–17,
    135, 143, 157, 158, 160, 209n41
    club membership, 203n21
    and Farren "riot," 155, 156–7
    repertory, 209n42
"Hamblin Guards" militia, 87
Harper's Weekly, 137
Hartley, L. P., 8
Haswell, Charles H., 84, 86, 92, 109, 114, 132,
    134, 156, 158
Hawkins, Micah, *Fig. 2*
Hawthorne, Nathaniel, 70
health movement, 141, 238n9
    and epidemics, 125
Heisenberg, Werner, 169
heroes/heroines, 7, 40, 42, 110, 118, 164
    in *The Drunkard*, 146–7
    manly hero, 90
    in *Uncle Tom's Cabin*, 149
    in urban spaces, 54

Hervieu, Auguste, 11, *Fig. 6*
Hill, George Handel "Yankee," 39, 41, 90,
    103–4
Hill, Harry, *Fig. 20*
historiography, *see* theatre culture, and histori-
    ography
history, 59, 99, 190
    as construct, 7–8, 189
    myths in, 121; totalizing, 165
    revisionist, 59–60
    as spatial, 2
    see also theatre culture
History of the American Theatre (Dunlap), 128–
    30
Holt, Michael, 153
home, 101–3, 206n33; *see also* housing
Home in the Woods (artwork), 36
Hone, Philip, 43, 65, 109, 127, 156, 157, 158, 187
Honeymoon, The (play), 12
housing, 206nn33–4, 211n51
    New York City, 44, 102–3
    size and cost, 102–3
Howard, George C., 148
Hudson River school of landscape painting, 28,
    69
Hyde Park, 170, 171, 182

ideology, town/city/frontier, 69, 72–3
"Illuminations," 11
immigrants, 43, 81
Importance of Being Earnest, The (play), 135
Indians, 6, 18, 28, 73, 74, 76, 216n75
    ceremonies, 61–2
    cultural control and assimilation attempts,
        61–8, 70, 73–4
    and Erie Canal, 26
    exhibitions concerning, 178–81, 186, *Fig. 26*
    and Lafayette, 17–19, 21–2
    and "manifest destiny," 68–9
    "natural" (unassimilated), 62, 64–5, 66
    as noble/doomed savages, 6, 61
    portrayed: paintings, 62–3; plays, *see specific
        play title*
    race theories about, 154
    removal, 17–18, 22, 32, 60–1, 63, 64, 66, 68,
        70, 212–13n59
    stereotypes, 64
    tribes, 17, 18, 19, 61, 62, 67, 180; Cherokee,
        63, 66, 67–8; confederations, 22, 62,
        197n32; Sauk, 64–5; Seneca, 25, 62
    U.S. government and, 60–1, 63, 64, 68
    view of history, 1–2
    women, 101, 216n75
    see also specific individual
Indian Prophesy (play), 66

individualism, 5, 41
  and the communal, 30, 33, 72–3, 141, 147,
    148
  and society, 41, 42
  and the state, 32, 33, 42
Ingraham, Daniel, 51–2
Irving, Henry, 103
Irving, Washington, 36, 64–5, 82, 116

Jackson, Andrew, 20, 60–1, 63, 65, 67, 155, 162
Jacksonianism, 38, 42
Jarvis, John Wesley, 65
Jefferson, Joseph, Jr., 203n21
Jefferson, Joseph, Sr., 14
Jefferson, Thomas, 52, 196n23
Jerrold, Douglas, 34, 171
Jewett, Ellen, 138
Jewett, William S., 69
"Jim Crow" (character), 159, 160, 161, 162–3;
  see also African Americans, market, street,
  and tavern performers; slavery
Johnson, Francis, 97
Johnson, Samuel, 28
Jolly Flat Boat Men, The (artwork), 69
Jonathan in England (play), 203n22
Jones, Joseph Stevens, 39–41, 90, 103, 117
Judd, Sylvester, 202n15
Jullien, Monsieur Louis, 184–5
justice, 9, 16, 22–3

Kant, Immanuel, 30
Kasson, John F., 85, 230n49
Kean, Edmund, 31, 156
  riot pertaining to (1825), 115
Keene, Laura, 95
Kemble, Fanny, 209n42
Kendall, Amos, 249n55
Kendall, John S., 133
Kennard, James, Jr., 162–3
Kensett, John Frederick, 69
*Kentuckian; or, A Trip to New York, see Lion
  of the West*
Keokuk, 65
Kimball, Moses, 95, 143, 186
Kindred Spirits (artwork), 36
King, Charles Bird, 62, 65, 66
Kotzebue, August von, 34

labor, 16, 32, 80
  craftsmen and factory work, 77, 78, *Fig. 11*
  divisions: along racial/ethnic/gender lines,
    80–1; in theatres, 93–4, 95–6
  income and class, 99–118, 205n31
  nature and perception of, 77
  outworking, 78, 100, 101
  and riots, 157, 250n57

staged, 90 (*see also* Bowery B'hoy; Bowery
  G'hal)
"sweating," 78, 81, 100
value reduced, 46
wages, 77, 80, 92–3, 102, 206n33, 219n7; for
  theatre work, 93–5; and ticket prices, 51, 93
  and women, 90–2, 100–1, 103–7, 122, 138,
    206n33; as domestics, 92–3
  workplace, 78–9, *Figs. 11–12*; separated from
    home, 100–1
Lafayette, George Washington, 10
Lafayette, Marquis de (Marie-Joseph-Paul-
  Yves-Roch-Gilbert du Motier), 25, 139
  entertainments honoring, 11–12, 19–21, 22;
  parades, 11, 14–16, 20
  as icon, 14–15, 16, 22–3
  and patriotism, 13, 19
  triumphal return to U.S., 5, 9–23, 28, 65,
    189; souvenirs of, 10–11, *Fig. 1*
Lafayette Amphitheatre (New York), 12, 25
Lafayette Circus (New York), 48, 52, 59
Lafayette in New Orleans (vaudeville), 21
Lafayette Museum (New York), 11
La Fayette; or, the Castle of Olmutz (play), 12,
  21
Lafayette Theatre (New York), 136, 159, 160,
  Fig. 21
Landing of Lafayette, The (artwork), 11
Lane, Fitz Hugh, 35, 69–70
Lane, William Henry ("Juba"), 98
Last of the Mohicans, The (novel), 69
Lattig Observatory, 183, 185
Leaves of Grass (poetry), 30
lectures, 189
Lectures to Young Men on Chastity (Graham),
  124–5
legitimation, 6–7, 121, 164–5
  delegitimation, 163–4
  discourses of control, 121–2, 138
  see also spaces of legitimation
leisure, 188
Levasseur, Auguste, 10, 12, 13, 16, 18–19, 20,
  21, 22, 196n23
Liberal Advocate, 142–3
Life in New York; or, The Major's Come (play),
  159–60
Lights and Shadows of New York Life
  (McCabe), 43
liminal spaces, 6, 75–119, 164–5
  of heroes and heroines, 118
Lion of the West, The; or, the Kentuckian (play),
  70–2, 99, *Fig. 8*
Livingston, John R., 127
local color, 56, 89, 104, 159–60, 210n47; *see also*
  character types
Locke, John, 27, 29, 31, 60

Logan, Olive, 95, 130, 132
Long Island Juba; or, Love by the Bushel (play), 98, 159
Lott, Eric, 148, 150, 153, 156, 162, 164
Lowe, "Uncle" Jim, 98
Ludlow, Noah, 130, 132, 135, 158, 159, 203n4
luminist painting, 35, 69, 215n71
Lyceum (London), 103

McAdam, John Loudon, 173
McCabe, James Dabney, 43
McConachie, Bruce, 51
McGindy, Sarah, 137
McIntosh, Chilly, 18, 19
McKinney, D. D., 155, 157, 158
Magdalene Societies, 125
Makataimeshekiakiah, *see* Black Hawk
Major Jack Downing; or, The Retired Politician (play), 251n62
manifest destiny, 5, 23, 68–9, 75
  transcendentalism and, 216n72
"manly mechanic," *see* artisan tradition
manners, 109, 230n49
"Manners" (Emerson), 109
manufacturing, 117
  as class leveler, 168–9
  as indication of prosperity, 11, 13, 23
  small-shop, 77–8
Marble, Danforth, 39, 41, 90
Margaret (play), 202n15
Market Book, The (De Voe), 97
Martineau, Harriet, 101, 187
Marx, Karl, 6
Mason, Jeffrey D., 4, 165
"Massa Georgee Washington and General Lafayette" (song), 16–17, *Fig. 2*
materialism, 32, 109
Mathews, Charles, Sr., 52, 97, 203n22
Mayhew, Henry, 125–6, 175
Medina, Louisa, 36, 70, 72, 117
melodrama, 38, 110, 111, 112–13, 117, 133, 188, 203n20
  in antislavery movement, 154–5
  appeal of, 110
  character values in, 110, 118
  class in, 118, 119
  genteel, 113, 114
  social/cultural, 107
  temperance, 143, 145–6
  villains in, 40–1
  see also specific title; gentility, in melodramas; plays
Memories of the Great Metropolis; or, London, from the Tower to the Crystal Palace, 167, 168, 172–3

Merchants' Exchange (New York), 44
Meserve, Walter, 38
Metamora; or, The Last of the Pollywogs (burlesque), 144
Metamora; or, The Last of the Wampanoags (play), 64, 66, 70, 155, 156, *Fig. 10*
middle class, *see* class
Midland Railway Excursions, 172
Midsummer Night's Dream, A (play), 34
minstrelsy, 16, 98, 99, 153, 159, 162–3, 251n62, 252n68
Mitchell, William, 86, 95
Mitford, Miss (Mary Russell), 48, 51
mob (the)/mobocracy, 7, 121; *see also* civic disorder/disturbance; "riots"
Moncrieff, William Thomas, 160
Monroe, James, 60, 61
Monroe Doctrine, *see* manifest destiny
Monsieur Tonson (play), 52
morality/morals, 164
  audience, 128, 129
  and authenticity, 56, 57
  home and, 101, 102
  race and, 133
Morris, Clara, 94
Morris, George Pope, 117–18
Morse, Verranus, 127–8
Mouffe, Chantal, 4
Mount, William Sidney, 36, 69
"Mount Washington" (illustration), 69
Mowatt, Anna, 54–6, 57, 104, 117
multiculturality, 214n61
Mushkat, Jerome, 153
myths
  in American history, 59, 60
  colonization of scholarship by, 5, 193n7
  historical, 121
  of origin and mission, 29
  Pocahontas, 60, 66
  totalizing, 165
  see also artisan tradition, as myth

National Institute, 168, 181
National Theatre (New York), 86
  brothels near, 136
National Theatre (Washington, D.C.), 66–7, 68
nationalism, 55, 157
Native Americans, *see* Indians
nativism, 81, 158, 220n9
nature, *see* transcendentalism
Nature (Emerson), 30
Negro songs/characters, *see* character types, Negro
New York American, 156–7
New York as It Is (play), 86, 88

New York City, 3, *Fig. 5*
  black wards, 158
  departments and voluntary associations,
    151–2; fire department, 210n47
  housing, 44, 102–3
  Lafayette in, 10, 11, 12
  manumission laws, 16
  moving day, 43
  percent of foreign born in, 81
  prostitutes in, 126, 127
  theatres as local and national, 115–17
  urban development, 44–6, 58–9
  work in, 77, 78, 80
  working-community mores in, 92
  young single males in, 82
  see also Five Points
New York Clipper, 188
New York Commercial Advertiser, 152, 154, 156
New York Crystal Palace, 7, 169, 182–6, 187,
    253n2, *Fig. 27*
New York Herald, 86, 98, 112, 114, 120, 134, 188
New York Mirror, 53, 82, 84, 98, 116, 117, 118
New York Naked (Foster), 135
New York State, 23, 24
New York Sun, 135, 156, 157
New York Times, 80, 92, 188
New York Tribune, 80, 92, 112, 115, 152
newspapers, 7, 112, 113, 139–40
  editors, 111, 112
Niagara of Black Rock (ship), 24–5
Niblo's Theatre (New York), 130
Nick of the Woods (novel, play), 36, 70, 72,
    Fig. 9
Nissenbaum, Stephen, 124
Noah, Mordecai M., 117
Noah's Ark (ship), 24, 25
Norma (opera), 34
Norman Leslie (novel, play), 118
Norton, Anne, 68
Noyes, John Humphrey, 125
Nutt, George Washington, 184

Odell, George C. D., 160, 184, 186
Oh! Hush! or, The Virginny Cupids (play), 159,
    160
Old American Company, 115
Olympic Theatre (New York), 86
Oregon City on the Willamette River (artwork),
    35
Orleans Theatre (New Orleans), 21
O'Sullivan, John L., 68
Othello (play), 96
Our American Cousin (play), 39
outworking, *see* labor, outworking
Owens, John E., 41, 103–4, 203n24

Panharmonicom, 11
Panisciowa, 22
Papyrotomia, 11
parades, 140–1
  honoring Lafayette, 11, 14–16, 20
  opening of Erie Canal, 25
  workers in, 16
paradise America, 5, 27–9, 30, 36–7, 60, 76,
    120, 211n54
  in art, 69
  conflicts in, 41
  narcissism devolving from, 198n1
  village as, 38
parallel universes (theory), 1, 169
Park Theatre (New York), 12, 46, 48, 49, 50,
    51, 52, 54, 70, 114, 155, 159
  class and gentility in, 115–18, 119
  as dive, 136–7
  ticket prices, 51
Paulding, James Kirke, 70–2
Paxton, Joseph, 171–2, 182, 183
Peabody, George, 176
Peale, Rubens, 62
Peale's Museum (New York), 48, 62, 63
Pelby, Miss (Ophelia), 114
People's Lawyer, The (play), 37, 39–41, 54, 56,
    90, 103
Perry, Robert, 24
Pessen, Edward, 151
Philadelphia, 44, 46, 54, 100
  Lafayette in, 14, 15–17, *Fig. 1*
  work in, 77, 78, 80
Phillips, Jonas B., 159
Phyfe, Duncan, 10
Pierce, Franklin, 183–4
Pintard, John, 187
Pizarro in Peru; or, the Death of Rolla (play), 34
playhouses, *see* theatres, organization/operation
plays, 38
  aesthetic criticism of, 115
  call for American, 232n55
  conventions, 89, 104
  genres in repertory, 111
  painterly vocabulary applied, 31, 36
  run length, 95, 96
  see also melodrama
Po-ca-hon-tas; or, The Gentle Savage (bur-
    lesque), 143
Pocahontas; or, The Settlers of Virginia (play),
    64, 66–7, 68
Pocahontas myth, 60, 66
political parties, 80, 86, 153
Poor of Liverpool, The (play), 55
Poor of New York, The (play), 54, 55–9, 80,
    103, 149, 210n44

poverty, 7, 58, 81, 152
families in, 227n36
and health/disease, 125, 238n9
liminal space of, 80
poor as cause of, 152, 154
and prostitution, 126
Power, Tyrone, 113–14
Powers, Hiram, 177, 178, 190
Price, Stephen, 115–16
Proctor, Joseph, 72
Promised Land, The (artwork), 69
prostitutes
equated with: African Americans, 133;
working women, 92, 131–3
in theatres, 3, 128–9, 130–1, 132, 133–6,
241nn18,20
prostitution, 152, *Fig. 18*
and brothels, 126, 127, 137; proximity of
theatres, 52, 136
control of, 127–8
as health issue, 125–6
as legitimating discourse, 136–7
as social concern, 125–31
public gardens (New York), 48; *see also* Castle
Garden; Chatham Garden Theatre
public spaces, 46
publishing, 109, 112–13, 117, 229n48
and riots, 140, 157
see also newspapers
Punch, 173, 176

quantum measurement theories, 169
Quidor, John, 36

race, 4–5, 46, 110, 164
and character types, 90, 160–2
Crystal Palace exhibition and, 168
and Indian removal, 60–1, 212–13n59
relationship with work and class, 99
racism, 38, 154, 216n74
in American theatre history, 132, 133
in American village play, 41, 42
and character types, 31–2, 64, 164
in *Fashion*, 55
and white supremacy, 73, 181
Raftsman Playing Cards (artwork), 36
Rankin, Arthur, 180
Ranney, William T., 63
Red Jacket, 22, 24, 62–3, 66, 68
Reed, Matthew, 51
Reinagle, T., 13
Reinelt, Janelle, 4
religious revivals, 141
Rent Day, The (play), 34
rentiers, 44, 52

repertory company system, *see* theatres, organ-
ization/operation
Revolutionary War, 8, 20, 22, 26, 140
Indians in, 62
stagings of, 14
veterans of, 10, 14, 20; black, 21–2
Rice, Thomas Dartmouth ("Daddy," "Jim
Crow"), 97–8, 159, 160, 163
Richards, Leonard, 157
Rienzi (play), 48, 51
"riots," 117, 139, 140, 141, 153, 244n30
re Anderson (1831), 115, 116, 158
at Astor Place Theatre, 111–12, 115
re Farren (1834), 115, 154, 155–8, 159, 161, 162
re Kean (1825), 115
labor and, 157, 250n57
see also civic disorder/disturbance
Ripley, George, 30, 31, 35
Roach, Joseph, 3, 4–5, 7
Roanoke, tale of, 60
Roberts, James, 16
Robinson, Richard P., 138
Romanticism, 30, 31, 32, 33, 201n11
Ross, John, 66, 67–8
Rousseau, Jean-Jacques, 27
Ryan, Kate, 94
Ryan, Mary P., 6, 107, 152, 153, 229n46
Rydell, Robert W., 168, 181

Sabbatarians, 10, 197n31
Sagoyewatha, *see* Red Jacket
St. Louis, 134, 135
St. Louis Theatre (Ludlow's and Smith's), 132
Saint-Méry, Moreau de, 133
Sanger, William, 126, 136
Saxton, Alexander, 30, 37, 38, 41, 99
Scarlet Letter, The (novel), 70
Schelling, Friederich Wilhelm Joseph von, 30,
201n11
School for Scandal, The (play), 12
Schrödinger, Erwin, 169
Scott, Sir Walter, 34
Searle, John, 52, 116
Sedgewick, Theodore, 109, 184
Self (play), 103–7, 108, 109
self-made man, 80
self-performance, 92, 104, 110, 111, 118, 122
texts of, 143
in theatres, 12, 50, 52, 114, 153
self-reliance, 32, 142, 148, 149
promoted in plays, 55, 56
Seneca Chief (ship), 24, 25
sensation, 122, 138–51, 165
crossing socioeconomic lines, 154
in Farren "riot," 157

sensation *(cont.)*
  regulation of, 7
  and temperance, 144, 146
sex
  control and regulation of, 7, 123–6, 127–8
  guidebooks, 136
  and health, 124–5, 229n46, 237nn7,8
  homosexuality, 123
  and theatre, 128–38
  see also prostitution
sexism, 92, 132, 164
Shakespeare, William, 34, 97, 117, 129, 164
Shank, Theodore, 160
Shaw, Ronald, 24
She Stoops to Conquer (play), 12
Sheridan, Richard Brinsley, 12, 34, 117
Ships in Ice off Ten Pound Island, Gloucester
  (artwork), 35
Siege of Yorktown, The (play), 12
Silsbee, Joshua, 39, 90
Simms, William Gilmore, 187
Simpson, Edmund, 52, 54, 115, 116, 117, 209n41
simultaneous spaces, 7, 167–90
slavery, 13, 21, 26, 32, 73, 141, 147, 148–9, 150–1,
  152, 164
  abolitionism, 16, 17, 147, 149–58, 163, 196n23
  antiabolitionism, 154, 155, 156, 162, 249n55
  and Indians, 18
  performances by slaves, 97
  see also Uncle Tom's Cabin
Smith, Matthew Hale, 43
Smith, Seba, 159
Smith, Solomon Frankin, 158, 203n21
Smith, W. H., 143–7
Smithsonian Institution, 168, 181
social control, 6–7, 74, 121–2, 165, 206n34
  of audience behavior, 128–38
  elite involvement, 187
  of employees, 108
  by exclusion, 122
  of sexuality, 123–4
  of theatres, 111
social experiments, 33–5
Society for the Reformation of Juvenile Delinquents, 135
Soldier's Daughter, The (play), 12
spaces of legitimation, 6–7, 120–66
  prostitution as, 127–8
  uniformity/multiplicity in, 164–5
spaces of representation, 27–74, 76
  cultural tensions in, 6
  universal American in, 5
Spectaculum, 11
Spirit of the Times, 82–4, 117, 163
Spy, The (novel), 36

staged types, *see* character types
Stanley, John Mix, 35, 215n65
Stansell, Christine, 92, 124, 126, 132
stars, 93, 95, 96, 116; *see also* actors
Stephenson, Peter, 177
Stevenson, Robert Louis, 8
Stone, John Augustus, 64, 66, 70
Stone, William L., 154
storypapers, 112
Stowe, Harriet Beecher, 102, 147, 148, 149
Streets of Dublin, The (play), 55
Streets of London, The (play), 55
Streets of Philadelphia, The (play), 55
Strickland, William, 14
Strong, George Templeton, 109, 132, 185
Stuart-Wortley, Lady Emmeline, 162
Stull, Frank A., 95–6
Sully, Robert, 65
Sunshine and Shadow in New York (Smith), 43,
  Fig. 4
Superior (ship), 24

tableaux vivants, 34, *Fig. 26*
*Tallis's History and Description of the Crystal
  Palace*, 176, 177
Tammany Hall, 153, 155, 157
Tappan, Arthur, 108, 127–8, 154–5, 157, 158, 162
Tappan, Lewis, 157, 162
Taylor, Mary, *Fig. 17*
technology, 157, 173
temperance movement, 141–7, 153
  dramas reflecting, 2, 39, 143
Ten Nights in a Bar-Room (play), 39
theatre, social aspects
  exclusivity, 52, 233n55
  fashion, 46–59, 109
  mechanic culture, 89, 90
  morality of audiences, 128, 129, 131–2
  politics, 244n30
  religious objections to, 35, 111
  riots, 115, 117, 139
  views of theatre workers, 115
theatre culture, 5–6, 7–8, 188, 190
  concept explained, 2–4
  enacted in cities, 98–9, 153–4; frontier staged,
    59–60, 72
  and historiography, 169–70, 192n4
  melodrama as, 110
  and a national theatre, 117–18
  and totalizing myths, 165–6
  and transcendental philosophy, 31–2, 35
theatres, organization/operation
  architecture, 50, 53; and audience behavior,
    134, 135
  genres of plays performed, 111

managers, 46, 54, 93, 95, 96, 138; and
audience behavior, 130, 132; club membership, 203n21; and criticism, 115; and public
issues, 139
repertory company, 93–4, 95–6, 208n40,
209n42
ticket prices, 51, 90, 92–3, 117, 135
wardrobe (costumes), 94
workers, 93–4, 95–6, 103, 115
see also actors; plays
Thorburn, Grant, 242–3n26
Thoreau, Henry David, 30, 42, 70, 201n9
Tichi, Cecelia, 5
Times (London), 168, 170, 171–2, 174, 176, 182
Timm–Taylor affair (1844), 115
Timour the Tartar (play), 117
Tocqueville, Alexis de, 28, 30, 99, 227n37,
233n55
Tom and Jerry (play), 160
Tom Thumb, 184, 188
Tontine Coffee House (New York), 44
towns, 14, 29–42, 43, 60, 75, 122, 190
as historical sites, 72, 73
as idyllic villages, 29
as models of civil order, 38
social problems, 38
as space of representation, 76
villains in, 40–1
see also transcendentalism, and towns
Tracy, Charles, 145
Transcendental Club, 30–1
transcendentalism, 30–5, 36–7, 38–9, 40, 41, 42,
43, 72, 141, 201n9
and human nature, 31
and intuition, 200n8
and manifest destiny, 216n72
and politics, 32, 38
and progress, 32
and theatre, 34–5, 111, 201n15
and towns, 38–9, 40, 41, 42, 110, 147
Universal Spirit, 31
Treatise on Domestic Economy (Beecher), 102,
147
Tremont Street Theatre (Boston), 113
Trip to America, A (play), 97, 203n22
triumphal arches, 14, 20
Trollope, Anthony, 28
Trollope, Frances (Mrs. Trollope), 51, 52, 53,
114
on America(ns), 28, 92, 109, 113; theatre,
48–50, 54, 77, 82, 116, 117
her Bazaar, 11, 103, 177
on Negroes, 97, 98–9, 162
satirized, 71, 160
Truettner, William H., 180

Turner, Frederick Jackson, 60
Twelfth Night, 11
Tyler, Royall, 39

uncertainty principle, 169
Uncle Tom's Cabin (play), 38, 39, 141, 147–51;
see also slavery
Unitarian theology, 31
United States
"America" defined, 29
aristocracy in, 14, 20, 52
cultural performance of, 8–9, 58, 74, 187–90,
194n10
depictions of, 69–70
displays at Crystal Palace exhibition, 176–82,
Fig. 25
drama in, 38
federal government and Indians, 60–1, 63,
64, 68
population, 42–4; during Jackson presidency,
60–1; during Lafayette's visit, 9–10
see also paradise America
universal spaces, 1–26, 169
in American history, 59
universes
multiple, coexistent, 169–70
simultaneous, 1–2, 188, 190
symbolic, 168–9
urban planning, 46, 52
grid system, 44
urban space, 54
authenticity of, 56, 57
property ownership, 43–4
social problems in, 153
utopian communities, 32

Vampire, The (play), 117
Vauxhall Gardens (New York), 48
Vermont Wool Dealer, The (play), 38
Victoria (queen of Great Britain), 172, 174–5,
177, 180, 182, 253n2, 254n10
villains, 40–1, 155, 164
voluntary associations, 108, 109, 127, 145, 151,
246n38
as agency of control and socialization, 121,
151–3
goals of, 138–9, 148
and temperance, 142
of women, 3

wages, *see* labor, wages
Walden (Thoreau), 30
Wallack, J. W., 59, 95
Wallack's Theatre (New York), 59, 95, 118
Walsh, Mike, 86

War News from Mexico (artwork), 69
War of 1812, 22, 24, 26, 60
Warren, William, Sr., 14
Washington, D.C., 12, 17, 54
Washington, George, 12, 16–17, 20, 24, 52, 66
  as icon, 14–15
  statue of, 13
Webb, James Watson, 154
Webster, Daniel, 75–6
Weinbaum, Paul O., 139
Weir, Robert, 62–3
Westervelt, Jacob A., 183–4
Wetmore, Prosper, 52
Wheeler, John, 169
Whitman, Walt, 30, 216n72
Wigner, Eugene, 169
Wilde, Oscar, 135
Wilkie, Sir David, 34
Winter, Marion, 98
Wise, Daniel, 145
women, 165
  African-American, 93, 133, 134
  in audience, 113–14, 122
  in cities, 122–3
  cultural constructions of, 122–38
  female staged Yankee, 38, 42, 204n28
  legislation affecting, 122
  literacy rate (white), 101–2

  Native American, 101, 216n75
  regulated, in theatres, 122, 130, 134–6
  volunteerism, 3, 151, 153
  in work force, 90–2, 100–1, 122, 138, 206n33;
    as domestics, 92–3; equated with prosti-
    tutes, 92, 131–3; wages, 95; work and
    behavior expected, 103–7
  see also Bowery G'hal; prostitutes; prostitu-
    tion
Woodville, Richard Caton, 69
Woodworth, Samuel, 12, 25, 36–7
work, *see* labor
working class, 92, 131; *see also* class
World's Columbian Exposition (Chicago),
  186
Wornum, Ralph Nicholson, 188
Wounded Indian, The (artwork), 177
Wyld, James, 181

Yankee character, *see* character types, Yankee
Young Lion of the West (ship), 25
Young Man's Counsellor, The (Wise), 145
Young Man's Guide (Alcott), 145

Zampa (opera), 34
"Zip Coon" (character), 99, 156, 159, 160–3; *see
  also* African Americans, market, street,
  and tavern performers; slavery